CIMA

How to access your on-line resources

Kaplan Financial students will have a MyKaplan account and these extra resources will be available to you online. You do not need to register again, as this process was completed when you enrolled. If you are having problems accessing online materials, please ask your course administrator.

If you are not studying with Kaplan and did not purchase your book via a Kaplan website, to unlock your extra online resources please go to www.en-gage.co.uk (even if you have set up an account and registered books previously). You will then need to enter the ISBN number (on the title page and back cover) and the unique pass key number contained in the scratch panel below to gain access.

You will also be required to enter additional information during this process to set up or confirm your account details.

If you purchased via the Kaplan Publishing website you will automatically receive an e-mail invitation to register your details and gain access to your content. If you do not receive the e-mail or book content, please contact Kaplan Publishing.

Your code and information

This code can only be used once for the registration of one book online. This registration and your online content will expire when the final sittings for the examinations covered by this book have taken place. Please allow one hour from the time you submit your book details for us to process your request.

Please scratch the film to access your unique code.

Please be aware that this code is case-sensitive and you will need to include the dashes within the passcode, but not when entering the ISBN.

KAPLAN

PUBLISHING

CIMA

Subject BA2

Fundamentals of Management Accounting

Study Text

Published by: Kaplan Publishing UK

Unit 2 The Business Centre, Molly Millars Lane, Wokingham, Berkshire RG41 2QZ

Acknowledgements

We are grateful to the CIMA for permission to reproduce past examination questions. The answers to CIMA Exams have been prepared by Kaplan Publishing, except in the case of the CIMA November 2010 and subsequent CIMA Exam answers where the official CIMA answers have been reproduced. Questions from past live assessments have been included by kind permission of CIMA,

Notice

British Library Cataloguing in Publication Data

A catalogue record for this book is available from the British Library.

ISBN: 978-1-78740-487-8

Printed and bound in Great Britain

Contents

Introduction

How to Use the Materials

These Kaplan Publishing learning materials have been carefully designed to make your learning experience as easy as possible and to give you the best chances of success in your CIMA Cert BA Objective Test Examination.

The product range contains a number of features to help you in the study process. They include:

- a detailed explanation of all syllabus areas

- extensive 'practical' materials

- generous question practice, together with full solutions.

This Study Text has been designed with the needs of home-study and distance-learning candidates in mind. Such students require very full coverage of the syllabus topics, and also the facility to undertake extensive question practice. However, the Study Text is also ideal for fully taught courses.

The main body of the text is divided into a number of chapters, each of which is organised on the following pattern:

- **Detailed learning outcomes.** These describe the knowledge expected after your studies of the chapter are complete. You should assimilate these before beginning detailed work on the chapter, so that you can appreciate where your studies are leading.

- **Step-by-step topic coverage.** This is the heart of each chapter, containing detailed explanatory text supported where appropriate by worked examples and exercises. You should work carefully through this section, ensuring that you understand the material being explained and can tackle the examples and exercises successfully. Remember that in many cases knowledge is cumulative: if you fail to digest earlier material thoroughly, you may struggle to understand later chapters.

- **Activities.** Some chapters are illustrated by more practical elements, such as comments and questions designed to stimulate discussion.

- **Question practice.** The text contains exam-style objective test questions (OTQs).

- **Solutions.** Avoid the temptation merely to 'audit' the solutions provided. It is an illusion to think that this provides the same benefits as you would gain from a serious attempt of your own. However, if you are struggling to get started on a question you should read the introductory guidance provided at the beginning of the solution, where provided, and then make your own attempt before referring back to the full solution.

If you work conscientiously through this Official CIMA Study Text according to the guidelines above you will be giving yourself an excellent chance of success in your Objective Text Examination. Good luck with your studies!

Quality and accuracy are of the utmost importance to us so if you spot an error in any of our products, please send an email to mykaplanreporting@kaplan.com with full details, or follow the link to the feedback form in MyKaplan.

Our Quality Coordinator will work with our technical team to verify the error and take action to ensure it is corrected in future editions.

Icon explanations

 Definition – These sections explain important areas of knowledge which must be understood and reproduced in an assessment environment.

 Key point – Identifies topics which are key to success and are often examined.

 Supplementary reading – These sections will help to provide a deeper understanding of core areas. The supplementary reading is **NOT** optional reading. It is vital to provide you with the breadth of knowledge you will need to address the wide range of topics within your syllabus that could feature in an assessment question. **Reference to this text is vital when self-studying.**

 Test your understanding – Following key points and definitions are exercises which give the opportunity to assess the understanding of these core areas.

 Illustration – To help develop an understanding of particular topics. The illustrative examples are useful in preparing for the Test your understanding exercises.

 Exclamation mark – This symbol signifies a topic which can be more difficult to understand. When reviewing these areas, care should be taken.

Study technique

In this section we briefly outline some tips for effective study during the earlier stages of your approach to the Objective Test Examination. We also mention some techniques that you will find useful at the revision stage. Use of effective study and revision techniques can improve your chances of success in the CIMA Cert BA and CIMA Professional Qualification examinations.

Planning

To begin with, formal planning is essential to get the best return from the time you spend studying. Estimate how much time in total you are going to need for each subject you are studying. Remember that you need to allow time for revision as well as for initial study of the material.

With your study material before you, decide which chapters you are going to study in each week, and which weeks you will devote to revision and final question practice.

Prepare a written schedule summarising the above and stick to it!

It is essential to know your syllabus. As your studies progress you will become more familiar with how long it takes to cover topics in sufficient depth. Your timetable may need to be adapted to allocate enough time for the whole syllabus.

Students are advised to refer to the CIMA website, www.cimaglobal.com, to ensure they are up-to-date.

Students are advised to consult the syllabus when allocating their study time. The percentage weighting shown against each syllabus topic is intended as a guide to the proportion of study time each topic requires.

Tips for effective studying

(1) Aim to find a quiet and undisturbed location for your study and plan as far as possible to use the same period of time each day. Getting into a routine helps to avoid wasting time. Make sure that you have all the materials you need before you begin so as to minimise interruptions.

(2) Store all your materials in one place, so that you do not waste time searching for items every time you want to begin studying. If you have to pack everything away after each study period, keep your study materials in a box, or even a suitcase, which will not be disturbed until the next time.

(3) Limit distractions. To make the most effective use of your study periods you should be able to apply total concentration, so turn off all entertainment equipment, set your phones to silent mode, and put up your 'do not disturb' sign.

(4) Your timetable will tell you which topic to study. However, before diving in and becoming engrossed in the finer points, make sure you have an overall picture of all the areas that need to be covered by the end of that session. After an hour, allow yourself a short break and move away from your Study Text. With experience, you will learn to assess the pace you need to work at. Each study session should focus on component learning outcomes – the basis for all questions.

(5) Work carefully through a chapter, making notes as you go. When you have covered a suitable amount of material, vary the pattern by attempting a practice question. When you have finished your attempt, make notes of any mistakes you made, or any areas that you failed to cover or covered more briefly. Be aware that all component learning outcomes are examinable.

(6) Make notes as you study, and discover the techniques that work best for you. Your notes may be in the form of lists, bullet points, diagrams, summaries, 'mind maps' or the written word, but remember that you will need to refer back to them at a later date, so they must be intelligible. If you are on a taught course, make sure you highlight any issues you would like to follow up with your lecturer.

(7) Organise your notes. Make sure that all your notes, calculations etc. can be effectively filed and easily retrieved later.

Progression

There are two elements of progression that we can measure: how quickly students move through individual topics within a subject; and how quickly they move from one course to the next. We know that there is an optimum for both, but it can vary from subject to subject and from student to student. However, using data and our experience of student performance over many years, we can make some generalisations.

A fixed period of study set out at the start of a course with key milestones is important. This can be within a subject, for example 'I will finish this topic by 30 June', or for overall achievement, such as 'I want to be qualified by the end of next year'.

Your qualification is cumulative, as earlier papers provide a foundation for your subsequent studies, so do not allow there to be too big a gap between one subject and another. For example, E1 *Managing finance in a digital world* builds on your knowledge of the finance function from certificate level and lays the foundations for E2 *Managing performance* and all strategic papers particularly E3 *Strategic management* and P3 *Risk management*.

We know that exams encourage techniques that lead to some degree of short term retention, the result being that you will simply forget much of what you have already learned unless it is refreshed (look up Ebbinghaus Forgetting Curve for more details on this). This makes it more difficult as you move from one subject to another: not only will you have to learn the new subject, you will also have to relearn all the underpinning knowledge as well. This is very inefficient and slows down your overall progression which makes it more likely you may not succeed at all.

In addition, delaying your studies slows your path to qualification which can have negative impacts on your career, postponing the opportunity to apply for higher level positions and therefore higher pay.

You can use the following diagram showing the whole structure of your qualification to help you keep track of your progress. Make sure you carefully review the 2019 CIMA syllabus transition rules and seek appropriate advice if you are unsure about your progression through the qualification.

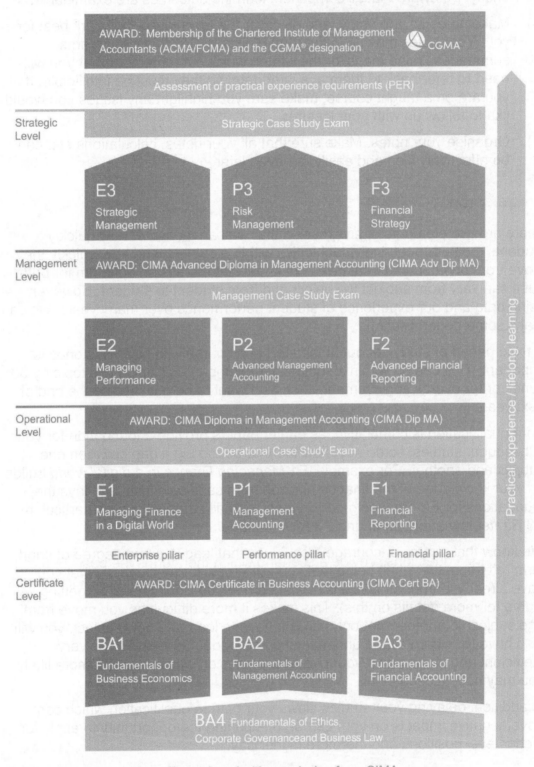

Reproduced with permission from CIMA

Objective Test

Objective Test questions require you to choose or provide a response to a question whose correct answer is predetermined.

The most common types of Objective Test question you will see are:

- multiple choice, where you have to choose the correct answer(s) from a list of possible answers – this could either be numbers or text

- multiple response with more choices and answers, for example, choosing two correct answers from a list of five available answers – this could be either numbers or text

- number entry, where you give your numeric answer to one or more parts of a question, for example, gross profit is $25,000 and the accrual for heat and light charges is $750.

- drag and drop, where you match one or more items with others from the list available, for example, matching several accounting terms with the appropriate definition

- drop down, where you choose the correct answer from those available in a drop down menu, for example, choosing the correct calculation of an accounting ratio, or stating whether an individual statement is true or false

- hot spot, where, for example, you use your computer cursor or mouse to identify the point of profit maximisation on a graph

- other types could be matching text with graphs and labelling/indicating areas on graphs or diagrams.

CIMA has provided the following guidance relating to the format of questions and their marking:

- questions which require narrative responses to be typed will not be used

- for number entry questions, a small range of answers will be accepted. Clear guidance will usually be given about the format in which the answer is required e.g. 'to the nearest $' or 'to two decimal places'

- item set questions provide a scenario which then forms the basis of more than one question (usually 2–4 questions). These sets of questions would appear together in the test and are most likely to appear in BA2 and BA3

- all questions are independent so that, where questions are based on a common item set scenario, each question will be distinct and the answer to a later question will not be dependent upon answering an earlier question correctly

- all items are equally weighted and, where a question consists of more than one element, all elements must be answered correctly for the question to be marked correct.

Throughout this Study Text we have introduced these types of questions, but obviously we have had to label answers A, B, C etc. rather than using click boxes. For convenience we have retained quite a few questions where an initial scenario leads to a number of sub-questions. There will be questions of this type in the Objective Test Examination but they will rarely have more than three sub-questions.

Guidance re CIMA on-screen calculator

As part of the CIMA Objective Test software, candidates are provided with a calculator. This calculator is on-screen and is available for the duration of the assessment. The calculator is available in Objective Test Examinations for BA1, BA2 and BA3 (it is not required for BA4).

Guidance regarding calculator use in the Objective Test Examinations is available online at: https://connect.cimaglobal.com/

CIMA Cert BA Objective Tests

The Objective Tests are a two-hour assessment comprising compulsory questions, each with one or more parts. There will be no choice and all questions should be attempted. The numbers of questions in each assessment are as follows:

BA1 Fundamentals of Business Economics – 60 questions

BA2 Fundamentals of Management Accounting – 60 questions

BA3 Fundamentals of Financial Accounting – 60 questions

BA4 Fundamentals of Ethics, Corporate Governance and Business Law
– 85 questions

All questions are equally weighted. All parts of a question must be answered correctly for the question to be marked correct. Where questions are based upon a common scenario, each question will be independent, and answers to later questions will not be dependent upon answering earlier questions correctly.

Structure of subjects and learning outcomes

Each subject within the syllabus is divided into a number of broad syllabus topics. The topics contain one or more lead learning outcomes, related component learning outcomes and indicative syllabus content.

A learning outcome has two main purposes:

(a)   to define the skill or ability that a well prepared candidate should be able to exhibit in the examination

(b)   to demonstrate the approach likely to be taken in examination questions.

The learning outcomes are part of a hierarchy of learning objectives. The verbs used at the beginning of each learning outcome relate to a specific learning objective e.g.

Calculate the break-even point, profit target, margin of safety and profit/volume ratio for a single product or service.

The verb **'calculate'** indicates a level three learning objective. The following table lists the learning objectives and the verbs that appear in the CIMA Cert BA syllabus learning outcomes.

CIMA VERB HIERARCHY

CIMA place great importance on the definition of verbs in structuring objective tests. It is therefore crucial that you understand the verbs in order to appreciate the depth and breadth of a topic and the level of skill required. The objective tests will focus on levels one, two and three of the CIMA hierarchy of verbs. However, they will also test levels four and five, especially at the management and strategic levels.

Skill level	Verbs used	Definition
Level 3 Application How you are expected to apply your knowledge	Apply	Put to practical use
	Calculate	Ascertain or reckon mathematically
	Conduct	Organise and carry out
	Demonstrate	Prove with certainty or exhibit by practical means
	Prepare	Make or get ready for use
	Reconcile	Make or prove consistent/compatible
Level 2 Comprehension What you are expected to understand	Describe	Communicate the key features of
	Distinguish	Highlight the differences between
	Explain	Make clear or intelligible/state the meaning or purpose of
	Identify	Recognise, establish or select after consideration
	Illustrate	Use an example to describe or explain something
Level 1 Knowledge What you are expected to know	List	Make a list of
	State	Express, fully or clearly, the details/facts of
	Define	Give the exact meaning of
	Outline	Give a summary of

CIMA Cert BA resources

Access to CIMA Cert BA resources including syllabus information is available online at www.cimaglobal.com.

Additional resources

This Study Text is designed to be comprehensive and therefore sufficient to meet the needs of students studying this subject. However, CIMA recognises that many students also want to read around particular topic(s), either to extend their knowledge and understanding, or because it is particularly relevant to their work environment.

CIMA has therefore produced a related reading list for those students who wish to extend their knowledge and understanding, whether for personal interest or to help support work activities as follows:

BA1 – Fundamentals of Business Economics

Principles of Economics 3rd ed.	McDowell & Thom
Applied Economics 12th ed.	Griffiths & Wall
Mathematics for Economists: An Introductory Textbook 4th ed.	Pemberton & Rau

BA2 – Fundamentals of Management Accounting

Management and Cost Accounting	Colin Drury
Management Accounting	Catherine Gowthorpe

BA3 – Fundamentals of Financial Accounting

Financial Accounting – An Introduction	Pauline Weetman
Frank Wood's Business Accounting 1 & 2	Frank Wood & Alan Sangster

BA4 – Fundamentals of Ethics, Corporate Governance and Business Law

Students can find out about the specific law and regulation in their jurisdiction by referring to appropriate texts and publications for their country.

Managing Responsible Business	CGMA Report 2015
Global Management Accounting Principles	CIMA 2015
Embedded Ethical Values: A guide for CIMA Partners	CIMA Report 2014
Business Ethics for SMEs: A Guide for CIMA Partners	CIMA Report 2014
Ethics: Ethical Checklist	CIMA 2014
Ethics Support Guide	CIMA 2014
Acting under Pressure: How management accountants manage ethical issues	CIMA 2012

Information concerning formulae and tables will be provided via the CIMA website, www.cimaglobal.com.

SYLLABUS GRIDS

BA2: Fundamentals of Management Accounting

Syllabus overview

This subject deals with the fundamental knowledge and techniques that underpin management accounting. It identifies the position of the management accountant within organisations and the role of CIMA. The subject portrays the role of management accounting in the contexts of commercial and public sector bodies and its wider role in society.

The identification and classification of costs and their behaviour provides the basis for understanding and applying the tools and techniques needed to plan, control and make decisions. Budgetary control requires the setting of targets and standards which then allow the performance of organisations to be reported and analysed by the calculation of variances. Investment appraisal, break-even analysis and profit maximisation are used to inform both long and short-term decision making.

Assessment strategy

There will be a two hour computer based assessment, comprising 60 compulsory objective test questions. Short scenarios may be given to which one or more objective test questions relate.

Syllabus structure

The syllabus comprises the following topics and weightings:

Content area	Weighting
A The context of management accounting	10%
B Costing	25%
C Planning and control	30%
D Decision making	35%
	100%

BA2A: The context of management accounting (10%)

Learning outcomes

On completion of their studies, students should be able to:

Lead	Component	Level	Indicative syllabus content
1. Explain the purpose of management accounting and the role of the Management Accountant.	a. Explain the need for management accounting.	2	• The Global Management Accounting Principles.
	b. Explain the characteristics of financial information for operational, managerial and strategic levels within organisation.	2	• Characteristics of financial information. • The CIMA definition of the role of the management accountant.
	c. Explain the role of the management accountant.	2	• The IFAC definition of the domain of the professional accountant in business.
	d. Explain the relationships between the management accountant and the organisation's managers.	2	• The positioning of management accounting within the organisation.
2. Explain the role of CIMA as a professional body for Management Accountants.	a. Explain the role of CIMA in developing the practice of management accounting.	2	• The need for a professional body in management accounting. • CIMA's role in relation to its members, students, the profession of management accounting and society.

BA2B: Costing (25%)

Learning outcomes

On completion of their studies, students should be able to:

Lead	Component	Level	Indicative syllabus content
1. Demonstrate cost identification and classification.	a. Explain the classification of costs in relation to output.	2	• Direct and indirect costs.
	b. Explain the classification of costs in relation to activity level.	2	• Variable, semi-variable, stepped and fixed costs.
	c. Calculate appropriate costs having identified cost behaviour.	3	• The use of 'high-low', graphical and regression analysis methods to establish and predict total cost.
	d. Explain the classification of costs in relation to decisions.	2	• Relevant and irrelevant costs.
2. Apply absorption costing and marginal costing.	a. Prepare overhead cost statements.	3	• Overhead cost statements: allocation, apportionment and reciprocal servicing.
	b. Calculate the full cost of products, services and activities.	3	**Note:** The repeated distribution and simultaneous equations methods will be used for reciprocal servicing.
	c. Calculate the marginal cost of products, services and activities.	3	• The treatment of direct and indirect costs in ascertaining the full cost of a 'cost object' e.g. a product, service, activity, customer.
	d. Reconcile the differences between profits calculated using absorption costing and those calculated using marginal costing.	3	• Overhead absorption rates. • Under or over absorbed overheads.
	e. Apply cost information in pricing decisions.	3	• The treatment of direct and indirect costs in ascertaining the marginal cost of a 'cost object' e.g. a product, service, activity, customer.
			• The difference between marginal and absorption profits.
			• Marginal cost pricing and full-cost pricing to achieve specified targets (return on sales, return on investment, mark-up and margins).
			Note: Students are not expected to have a detailed knowledge of activity-based costing (ABC).

BA2C: Planning and control (30%)

Learning outcomes

On completion of their studies, students should be able to:

Lead	Component	Level	Indicative syllabus content
1. Prepare budgets for planning and control.	a. Explain why organisations prepare forecasts and plans	2	• Budgeting for planning and control. • Functional budgets. • Master budget, including statements of profit and loss, financial position and cash flow. • The importance of cash budgets. • Fixed and flexible budgeting. • Budget variances.
	b. Prepare functional budgets	3	
	c. Explain budget statements	2	
	d. Identify the impact of budgeted cash surpluses and shortfalls on business operations	2	
	e. Prepare a flexible budget	3	
	f. Calculate budget variances.	3	
2. Apply variance analysis to reconcile budgeted and actual profits in a marginal format.	a. Explain why planned standard costs, prices and volumes are useful.	2	• Principles of standard costing. • Standards for the selling price and variable costs of a product or service. • Variances: materials (total, price and usage); labour (total, rate and efficiency); variable overhead (total, expenditure and efficiency); sales (sales price and sales volume contribution). • The use of variances to reconcile the budgeted and actual profits that have been calculated using marginal costing. • Interpretation of variances.
	b. Calculate variances for materials, labour, variable overheads, sales prices and sales volumes.	3	
	c. Prepare a statement that reconciles budgeted profit with actual profit calculated using marginal costing.	3	
	d. Explain why variances could have arisen and the inter-relationships between variances.	2	
3. Calculate appropriate financial and non-financial performance measures.	a. Explain the need for appropriate performance measures.	2	• Characteristics of service industries. • Responsibility accounting (authority, responsibility and controllability). • The use of appropriate financial and non-financial performance measures in a variety of contexts (e.g. manufacturing and service sectors). **Note:** Detailed knowledge of the balanced scorecard is not required.
	b. Calculate appropriate financial and non- financial performance measures in a variety of contexts.	3	
4. Prepare accounts and reports for managers.	a. Explain the integration of the cost accounts with the financial accounting system.	2	• Manufacturing accounts including raw material, work-in-progress, finished goods and manufacturing overhead control accounts. • Integrated ledgers including accounting for over and under absorption of production overhead. • The treatment of variances in integrated ledger systems. • Job and batch costing. • Cost accounting statements for management information in manufacturing, service and not-for-profit organisations.
	b. Prepare a set of integrated accounts, showing standard cost variances.	3	
	c. Prepare appropriate accounts for job and batch costing.	3	
	d. Prepare reports in a range of organisations.	3	

BA2D: Decision making (35%)

Learning outcomes

On completion of their studies, students should be able to:

Lead	Component	Level	Indicative syllabus content
1. Demonstrate the impact of risk.	a. Explain the concepts of risk and uncertainty.	2	• Risk and uncertainty.
	b. Demonstrate the use of expected values and joint probabilities in decision making.	3	• Probability and its relationship with proportions and percentages.
			• Expected values and expected values tables.
	c. Calculate summary measures of central tendency and dispersion for both grouped and ungrouped data.	3	• Limitations of expected values.
			• Arithmetic mean, median, mode, range, variance, standard deviation and coefficient of variation for both ungrouped and grouped data.
	d. Demonstrate the use of the normal distribution.	3	
			• Graphs/diagrams and use of normal distribution tables.
			Note: Students will not be asked to apply techniques to deal with uncertainty.
2. Demonstrate the use of appropriate techniques for short-term decision making.	a. Apply breakeven analysis.	3	• Breakeven charts, profit volume graphs, breakeven point, target profit, margin of safety.
	b. Demonstrate make or buy decisions.	3	
	c. Calculate the profit maximising sales mix after using limiting factor analysis.	3	• Make or buy decisions.
			• Limiting factor analysis for a multi-product company that has one scarce resource.
3. Demonstrate the use of appropriate techniques for long-term decision making.	a. Explain the time value of money.	2	• The time value of money.
	b. Apply financial mathematics.	3	• Discounting, compounding, annuities and perpetuities.
	c. Calculate the net present value, internal rate of return and payback for an investment or project.	3	• Net present value, internal rate of return and payback.

The context of management accounting

Chapter learning objectives

After completing this chapter, you should be able to

- explain the need for management accounting

- explain the characteristics of financial information for operational, managerial and strategic levels within organisations

- explain the role of the management accountant

- explain the relationships between the management accountant and the organisation's managers

- explain the role of CIMA in developing the practice of management accounting.

1 Session content diagram

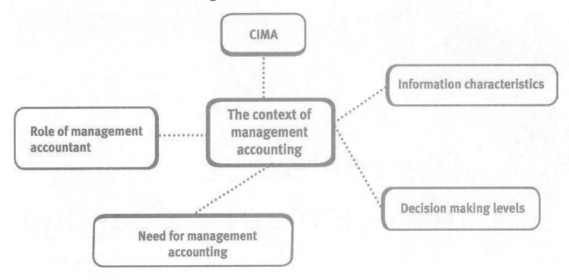

2 Management accounting

Accountancy involves the measurement, analysing and reporting of financial and non-financial information to help managers, shareholders and other interested parties make decisions about organisations.

As a student of CIMA, you have decided to focus on management accounting and this subject, *Fundamentals of Management Accounting*, will introduce you to all the main aspects of management accounting. We will start with defining what management accounting is.

 The *CIMA Terminology* defines **management accounting** as 'the application of the principles of accounting and financial management to create, protect, preserve and increase value for the stakeholders of for-profit and not-for-profit enterprises in the public and private sectors.'

The key phrase in this definition is the focus on **value**. Management accounting aims to 'create… and increase' the value of an organisation. It achieves this by providing **relevant information** to the management of these organisations, who use this information to make decisions regarding the organisation. These decisions are what will create and increase the value of the organisation.

An important skill of the management accountant is to **communicate** effectively with management in order to influence the decision making process and that management must **trust** the information provided by the management accountant as they will act on it.

3   The Global Management Accounting Principles

Business environments are constantly changing, at a faster rate than ever before and organisations must be able to respond quickly in order to ensure that they maintain and improve their competitive position and stay successful. A feature of organisations today is that they have vast amounts of data available to them, from a variety of sources. The challenge they face is how to turn that data into useful information which can enhance their decision making.

Good information and quality decision making is crucial within organisations today. CIMA believe that management accounting is at the heart of good decision making and that effective management accounting is about '**improving decisions and building successful organisations**'.

CIMA, together with the American Institute of CPAs (AICPA) have developed the Global Management Accounting Principles which should be used to guide best practice in management accounting.

The four Global Management Accounting Principles are:

Influence	Relevance
Trust	Value

We will now expand on the Global Management Accounting Principles to give us a better insight about how CIMA view the role of management accounting within today's organisations.

Influence	Relevance
Communication provides insight that is influential. Management accounting begins and ends with conversations. The Principles have been designed to help organisations encourage integrated thinking, leading to better decision making.	Information is relevant. Management accounting makes relevant information available to decision makers when they need it. The Principles provide guidance on identifying past, present and future information, including financial and non-financial data from internal and external sources. This includes social, environmental and economic data.
Trust	**Value**
Stewardship builds trust. Accountability and scrutiny make the decision-making process more objective. Balancing short-term commercial interests against long run value for stakeholders enhances credibility and trust.	Impact on value is analysed. Management accounting connects the organisation's strategy to its business model. This Principle helps organisations to simulate different scenarios to understand their impact on generating and preserving value.

Throughout your management accounting studies you should focus on these Principles and remember that the focus is on creating, protecting, preserving and increasing value.

In *Fundamentals of Management Accounting* you will learn many techniques which will help you provide relevant information to management within all types of organisations.

4 Management information

From the above we can see that the key to successful business is good decision making and the key to good decision making is good, relevant information. So we need to consider what information actually is, what types of information different managers need and what makes information good.

Thanks to technological advances, the operations of organisations generate a huge quantity of **data**. Data consist of raw facts and statistics before they have been processed. Once data have been processed into a useful form, it can be called **information**.

Data vs information

An organisation must record every sale of every product each day. At the end of a period this could equate to a long list of sales transactions. This list would be classified as data, and in itself would not be very useful for decision making.

It would be more helpful to group the data in meaningful ways, such as the sales for a particular product or the sales for a particular day. Using these groupings turns the data into information which is much more useful. It is useful to see which product has the highest level of sales, or on which day of the month the sales are highest. Knowing these things can affect decisions such as the amount of each product which should be available for sale each month, or the number of members of staff required each day.

Characteristics of good information

From the example above you can see that the sales data could be analysed in a variety of ways and a lot of information could be provided to management. However, not all information is worthwhile.

A useful way to remember the characteristics of good information is

ACCURATE

This stands for:

A. Accurate: The degree of accuracy depends on the reason the information is needed.

For example, reports may show figures to the nearest $1,000, or to the nearest $100,000 for a report on the performance of different divisions. Alternatively, when calculating the cost of a unit of output, managers may want the cost to be accurate to the nearest dollar or even cent.

C. Complete: Managers should be given all the information they need, but information should not be excessive, for example a complete control report on variances should include all standard and actual costs necessary to understand the variance calculations.

C. Cost beneficial: The cost of producing information should not exceed its value. Management information is valuable, because it assists decision making. If a decision backed by information is different from what it would have been without the information, the value of information equates the amount of money saved or generated as a result.

U. Understandable: Use of technical language or jargon must be limited. Accountants must always be careful about the way in which they present financial information to non-financial managers.

R. Relevant: The information contained within a report should be relevant to its purpose. Redundant parts should be removed as this can make it harder for the user to get a clear picture of what is important.

A. Authoritative: Information should be trusted and provided from reliable sources so that the users can have confidence in their decision making.

T. Timely: Information should be provided to a manager in good time to allow them to make decisions based on that information. Using out of date information can result in poor decisions being made.

E. Easy to use: We must always think about the person using the information we provide and make sure the information meets their needs.

Test your understanding 1

M is a management accountant. One of her roles is to provide each functional manager with a monthly report. The production manager has complained to M about his report, stating the following:

- The report for month 2 was not received until month 5 making the information too out of date to be useful.

- The report contained terminology which he did not understand.

- The report was too long which made it difficult for him to find the parts he really needed and some of the important information he required was missing.

Which elements of ACCURATE has M NOT managed to address in her report for the production manager?

Information for different levels of management

Now that we know what good information is, we can consider the different information needs of different levels of management.

Organisations are generally split into three levels; strategic, managerial/tactical and operational/functional.

Information needs differ at each of these levels.

Strategic level: Top-level management need to know about developments in the markets in which they operate and in the general economic situation. They also need to know about any new technology that emerges, and about the activities of competitors. Decisions made at this level:

- will have a large impact on the whole organisation
- will be long term
- tend to be unstructured.

Tactical level: Management at this level might want to know about issues such as product or service quality, speed of handling customer complaints, customer satisfaction levels, employee skills levels and employee morale. Decisions made at this level:

- will have a medium impact on the whole organisation
- will be medium-term
- will act as a bridge between the strategic and operational levels.

Operational level: Lower-level management may want to know about the number of rejects per machine, the lead time for delivering materials and the number of labour and machine hours available. Decisions made at this level:

- will have a small impact on the whole organisation; they will normally only affect one business unit or department
- will be short-term
- tend to be highly structured.

You can see from the above that the information requirements change at the different levels within the organisation. The nature of the information also changes.

Illustration 1

XYZ is a successful pizza restaurant which currently operates a chain of four restaurants, all of which offer the same standard menu.

Consider the following decisions which XYZ may have to make and suggest at what levels these decisions would be made.

- Start producing frozen pizzas and selling these through supermarkets.

- Hire a new waiter in one of the restaurants.

- Decide on the pricing of the dishes on the standard menu.

- Open a new restaurant.

Solution:

- Starting production and sales of frozen pizzas is a fundamental change to what the company currently do and involves entering a new market. This would therefore be a **strategic** decision.

- Hiring a new waiter would be an **operational** decision as it involves a day to day decision which should be able to be made at a lower level.

- Deciding on the pricing is likely to be a **tactical** decision. In general the strategic level will decide on which markets in which to operate and the managerial level will decide on how to operate within these markets. Pricing would come under this remit.

- Opening a new restaurant is a more difficult one. In this case a decision to expand the number of restaurants would likely be a **strategic** decision. In some much larger organisations this type of decision would be made at the tactical level, however given that XYZ only has four restaurants, then the decision to open a fifth would likely be made by the senior managers.

Test your understanding 2

LMN is an international clothing manufacturer specialising in producing waterproof jackets.

Consider the following decisions and match each to the level of the organisation where these decisions would be made.

Decision	Level
A decision to take over a rival company in order to expand its production into different markets	Strategic
A decision on the ordering of material for production	Tactical
A decision about the pricing of the products	Operational

Now we have looked at the levels of decision, we can return to our pizza restaurant, XYZ, example and consider some of the different types of information which could be required for each decision.

Note: These lists give some suggestions for types of information required but they are not exhaustive.

Start producing frozen pizzas and selling these through supermarkets.

- The cost to produce frozen pizzas.
- The cost of packaging equipment.
- The selling prices of competitors' frozen pizzas.
- The estimated demand for their frozen pizzas.

Hire a new waiter in one of the restaurants.

- The hours required to be worked by the new waiter.
- The average rate of pay for trained waiters in the local area.
- The rates of pay of existing members of staff.
- The availability of trained labour in the area.

Decide on the pricing of the dishes on the standard menu.

- The cost of the ingredients for each dish.
- The prices charged by competitors.
- The profit required by each restaurant.

Open a new restaurant.

- The cost of available premises.
- The cost of fitting out the restaurant.
- The estimated number of potential customers.
- The number and types of existing local restaurants.
- The average prices at existing restaurants.

You can see from this that the type of information required changes with each decision.

Information required for lower level decisions tends to be more **accurate** and **detailed** (e.g. the new waiter is required for 20 hours per week and will be paid $10 per hour) and is usually needed within a **shorter timescale**. It also tends to be information which is **more readily available** (e.g. the average rate of pay trained waiters in the local area is $9.50).

Strategic level information tends to be more **summarised** (e.g. the average price of a frozen pizza is $2) and will contain **more subjective** estimates (e.g. the estimated number of potential customers is 1,000 per week).

Strategic information also tends to require more **external** information whereas operational information tends to be mainly from **internal** sources.

For the tactical level, just as tactical decision making forms a link between strategic and operational management, the information it requires has some of the characteristics of each.

The table below provides a useful summary:

Information	Strategic level	Operational level
Source	Historical and forecasts.	Historical.
Timeliness	The timeliness is less crucial at this level as decisions tend to be taken over a period of months or years.	Information must be available immediately as decisions are taken daily.
Accuracy	Information will contain many subjective estimates.	Information will be objective and accurate.
Breadth	Wide variety of information in different forms, covering many aspects of the organisation's operations.	Focused on the decision to be made.
Detail	Highly summarised.	Detailed.

Test your understanding 3

Use the following words to complete the sentences regarding levels of information.

- Strategic
- Tactical
- Operational
- Higher
- Lower
- More
- Less

A decision to diversify into a new market would be taken at the _____ level.

Information for operational level decisions will have a _____ level of detail than information for strategic level decisions.

Strategic level information will be _____ subjective than operational level information.

5   Non-financial information

In the example of a pizza business, some of the information was financial, such as the cost of ingredients, but some was not, such as the number of expected customers.

Information which is not given in $ terms is called non-financial information and it is very important that management accountants provide both types to management.

Financial information is important for management because many objectives of an organisation are financial in nature, such as making profits. While profit cannot be ignored as it is usually the main objective of commercial organisations, performance measures should not focus on profit alone. Managers also need information of a non-financial nature such as customer numbers, number of complaints or the number of orders processed.

This distinction will be looked at in more detail in the performance measurement chapter.

Requirements of different users

We have seen that management information is required by a variety of different users, each with different needs. Below we briefly consider the needs of different types of organisations.

Commercial organisations

The main objective of commercial organisations is usually to maximise the wealth of its shareholders (owners). Key financial information required by this type of business would focus on the profit made by each area or each product/service.

There are different types of commercial organisations. For example manufacturing companies produce goods, retail companies sell goods and service companies sell services. Each of these types of organisations could require different types of information relevant to their type of operation.

Not-for-profit organisations

Not-for-profit organisations are organisations whose main objective is not to make profit. These include public bodies, such as state run schools and hospitals, and charities. The objective of not-for-profit organisations is often value for money.

The main objective of public bodies is to provide services to the public in line with government requirements. The information requirement of public bodies will differ from commercial organisations. There will be no profit measurements but there will still be a requirement for financial information which will focus more on cost management and efficiency. As these bodies must be run in the public interest, the level of information must be detailed and accurate and allow assessment of the efficiency and effectiveness of the organisation to be assessed by central government and by the public.

Charities are also not-for-profit organisations with objectives such as helping feed the poor, or raising funds to research illnesses. Again different information will be required by charities such as funds raised and amounts donated to their causes. The objective of a school could be 'to educate children' or the objective of a charity could be 'to improve the lives of the poor'. These are difficult objectives to measure and it is therefore difficult to determine what information needs to be provided.

Reporting for different types of organisations will be looked at in more detail in the preparing accounts and reports for management chapter.

Society

In addition to the organisations discussed above, society also has a need for information relating to the organisations it deals with. Members of the public may be shareholders, employees or customers of these organisations and they will have an interest in how these organisations are run and are performing. Society will also be interested in the impact organisations have on the local and wider community. For example, environmental reporting, where organisations measure and report on their impact on the environment, can be of great use to the public.

6 The purpose of management accounting

We have now looked at the importance of providing relevant information and the types of information we may need to provide to management so that they can make good decisions.

While providing information for decision making is clearly key to what management accountants do, their role is usually expanded to include **three** main elements:

- **Planning**
- **Control**
- **Decision making**.

Planning

Planning involves establishing the objectives and goals of an organisation, i.e. what they are trying to achieve, and formulating relevant strategies (long-term plans) that can be used to achieve those objectives and goals.

In order to make plans, it helps to know what has happened in the past so that decisions about what is achievable in the future can be made. For example, if a manager is planning future sales volumes, it would help to know what sales volumes have been achieved in the past.

We looked at the levels of the organisation earlier. Planning can also be done at different levels in an organisation:

- **Strategic** – long-term planning carried out by the highest level of the organisation.

- **Tactical** – short- to medium-term planning, carried out by middle level management.

- **Operational** – short-term planning for day-to-day operations.

The main types of plans that management accountants get involved in are **budgets** where an estimation of the revenue and expenses over a specified future period of time is made.

Planning is looked at in more detail in the budgeting chapter.

Control

Once planning has been carried out, and budgets prepared, targets can be set. This allows for evaluation of performance. Without targets it is difficult to judge how good the performance has been.

Information relating to the actual results of an organisation must be gathered and compared to the targets. The differences between the actual and the planned results can be calculated and reported to management. These are known as **variances**. This type of information facilitates managers to control their operations.

Many measures can be used to measure performance within an organisation; it is largely dependent on the type of organisation. Some common performance measurements are:

- **Variances** – comparison of actual results against budgeted results.

- **Financial/profitability measures**.

- **Non-financial measures**.

This type of control and the production of performance measures allow management to focus on areas that require attention and helps them to drive the business forward and 'add value'.

These measures will be covered in more detail in the performance measurement chapter.

Decision making

We have seen already that decision making involves considering information that has been provided and making informed decisions. In most situations, decision making involves making a choice between two or more alternatives. Managers need reliable information to compare the different courses of action available and understand what the consequences might be of choosing each of them.

These three purposes of management accounting (planning, control and decision making) form the basis of your *Fundamentals of Management Accounting subject.* Each of these areas will be looked at in detail throughout this text book.

7   Financial accounting

Now that we are very clear about the purpose of management accounting we can compare it with another branch of accounting, financial accounting, which you will study as part of your CIMA qualification.

 The *CIMA Terminology* defines **financial accounting** as 'classification and recording of the monetary transactions of an entity in accordance with established concepts, principles, accounting standards and legal requirements and their presentation, by means of statements of profit or loss, statements of financial position and cash flow statements, during and at the end of an accounting period'.

Look back at the definition of management accounting and you will see that these two are very different.

You can see from this that the role of the financial accountant is much more clearly defined and narrower than that of the management accountant. There is also a legal aspect to financial accounting. It is a legal requirement for organisations to produce financial statements which show a true and fair view of their financial position for each accounting period. There is no legal requirement to have management accounting.

Financial accounting is also governed by many rules and regulations whereas there are no rules covering how the management accountant provides information. They will provide whatever is required by their managers in whatever format suits.

Financial accountants deal with historical (past) financial information, while management accountants deal with all types of information (financial and non-financial) both historical and future.

The main role of financial accounting is to produce the statutory financial statements, whereas management accountants provide any information needed by management.

It is important from this to see that the audiences using management and financial accounting information are different. Management accountants provide information internally to managers. The statutory financial reports produced by the financial accountants are available to the public and to anyone who has an interest in the organisation.

The differences can be summarised as follows:

Financial accounting	Management accounting
For external use	For internal use
Statutory requirement	At the discretion of management
Concerned with the production of statutory accounts for an organisation	Concerned with the provision of information to management to aid decision making
Governed by many rules and regulations	Not governed by rules or regulations, can be provided in any format

Test your understanding 4

Consider the following statements relating to financial accounting:

(i)   The main purpose of financial accounting statements is to provide a true and fair view of the financial position of an organisation at the end of an accounting period.

(ii)   Financial information may be presented in any format deemed suitable by management.

Which of the above statements is/are true?

A   (i) and (ii)

B   (i) only

C   (ii) only

D   neither

8   The management accountant

At this point it is worth looking in more detail at the various roles management accountants play in organisations and how this has changed over the years.

The whole of the accountancy profession is changing, and this is especially true for the management accountant.

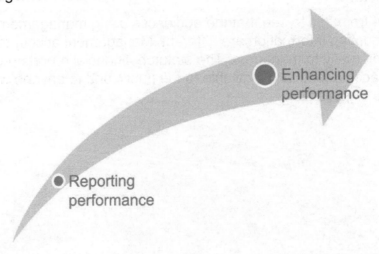

Enhancing performance

Reporting performance

The traditional management accountant was largely involved in reporting business results to management, but this is no longer the case. Management accountants today are seen as **value-adding business partners** and are expected to not only forecast the future of the business, but to assist in delivering this future by identifying opportunities for enhancing organisational performance. Management accountants now work alongside business managers as mentors, advisors and drivers of performance.

Management accountants are an integral part of any business, providing a variety of information to management for the purposes of planning, control and decision making. Management accountants often hold senior positions in the organisation.

 CIMA's definition of the role of the management accountant

The work of the Chartered Management Accountant (produced by CIMA):

Chartered management accountants help organisations establish viable strategies and convert them into profit (in a commercial context) or into value for money (in a not-for-profit context). To achieve this they work as an integral part of multi-skilled management teams in carrying out the:

- formulation of policy and setting of corporate objectives

- formulation of strategic plans derived from corporate objectives

- formulation of shorter-term operational plans

- acquisition and use of finance

- design of systems, recording of events and transactions and management of information systems

- generation, communication and interpretation of financial and operating information for management and other stakeholders

- provision of specific information and analysis on which decisions are based

- monitoring of outcomes against plans and other benchmarks and the initiation of responsive action for performance improvement

- derivation of performance measures and benchmarks, financial and non-financial, quantitative and qualitative, for monitoring and control; and

- improvement of business systems and processes through risk management and internal audit review.

Through these forward-looking roles and by application of their expert skills management accountants help organisations improve their performance, security, growth and competitiveness in an ever more demanding environment.

We will start to look at some of these functions in the *Fundamentals of Management Accounting* syllabus, and others will be studied in later subjects.

It can be seen from this that there is no one clear definition of the role of the management accountant. Their work, experience and responsibilities are extraordinarily varied and continue to change to reflect the changing needs of stakeholders.

The domain of the professional accountant in business

The **IFAC (International Federation of Accountants)** is the worldwide organisation for the accounting profession. Its members include the professional accounting bodies across the world, including **CIMA**. It represents more than 2.5 million accountants.

Of the 2.5 million professional accountants who are members of the IFAC, over half of these work in business. This includes those who work in commerce, industry, the public sector, education and the not-for-profit sector.

According to the IFAC, the roles of the professional accountant in business include:

- implementing and maintaining operational and fiduciary controls

- providing analytical support for strategic planning and decision making

- ensuring that effective risk management processes are in place, and

- assisting management in setting the tone for ethical practices.'

The domain of the professional accountant in business:

The IFAC have analysed the main activities of the professional accountant in business as:

- The generation or creation of value through the effective use of resources (financial and otherwise) through the understanding of the drivers of stakeholder value (which may include shareholders, customers, employees, suppliers, communities, and government) and organisational innovation.

- The provision, analysis and interpretation of information to management for formulation of strategy, planning, decision making and control.

- Performance measurement and communication to stakeholders, including the financial recording of transactions and subsequent reporting to stakeholders typically under national or international Generally Accepted Accounting Principles (GAAP).

- Cost determination and financial control, through the use of cost accounting techniques, budgeting and forecasting.

- The reduction of waste in resources used in business processes through the use of process analysis and cost management.

- Risk management and business assurance.

Again, this demonstrates the extraordinarily varied nature of the roles undertaken by the accountant.

IFAC list of the typical mainstream job titles held by accountants in business

These include:

- finance director

- financial controller

- financial analyst

- treasurer

- planning manager

- strategy analyst

- internal auditor

- compliance officer

- project manager

- programme manager.

Many professional accountants also move on to have more general management responsibilities such as operations director, chief executive officer (CEO), chairman and non-executive director.

9 The positioning of management accounting within the organisation

It is clear that the breadth of the work carried out by management accountants, and their remit continues to grow. Accountants within business can be part of an internal finance function, or may be part of a business partnering role. When deciding on their structure, it is important for organisations to consider where best to position the management accountant within the organisation.

There are three options available:

- Dedicated business partners

- Shared services centres (SSC)

- Business Process Outsourcing (BPO).

Dedicated business partners

With this approach, the management accountant is an integral part of the business area that they support. This brings many benefits to both the accountants and the management of the area.

The relationship between the management accountant and the managers of the business area is an important business relationship. To work in the best interests of the company, they must work as business partners and the relationship must be based on trust, honesty and respect.

From the accountant's point of view, they must:

- **act professionally at all times** – as representatives of the accounting profession, they are expected to show professional care and attention in the way they conduct themselves

- **demonstrate technical awareness** – this can be demonstrated by being a qualified member of CIMA and maintaining their technical knowledge through continued professional development (CPD)

- **demonstrate business awareness** – they must be aware of the nature of the business and the needs of the managers

- **act with integrity** – the work of the management accountant should be done in the best interests of the company and society and they should never put themselves in a position where their personal interests conflict with these interests.

From the manager's point of view, they must:

- **trust** the accountant and the information being provided

- **respect** the accountant's knowledge, experience and professionalism

- be able to discuss all aspects of work **confidentially** with the accountant

- be able to **state clearly what their requirements are**.

It is important to remember that both the management accountant and the managers of the business want the business to succeed and they have to work together to achieve this.

The management accountant as an adviser

The management accountant plays a range of roles within the organisation from their more traditional score-keeping role to a full-fledged, value-adding, business partner. An advisory role falls in between these extremes. As a technical expert, the management accountant is expected to advise management on a range of topics, including financial and non-financial analysis, costing, pricing, Business Process Reengineering and performance management.

As advisers, management accountants no longer simply need financial skills, but increasingly, communication and presentation skills.

The advantages of this approach are:

- The management accounting function is part of the business it serves.

- Increased knowledge of the business area and its needs.

- Strong relationships can be built up between the accountant and the business.

The disadvantages of this approach are:

- Duplication of effort across the organisation.

- Lack of knowledge sharing. There is no sharing of knowledge which can happen within a larger, more diverse team.

- The accountants can feel isolated within the business and may develop their own ways of working which may not constitute best practice.

- The accountant can lose sight of the overall goals of the organisation.

Shared services centre (SSC)

An alternative to having the management accountant as a dedicated business partner is to set up a shared services centre (SSC). This is where the whole finance function is brought together as one centre and this centre provides all the accounting needs of the whole organisation.

The advantages of this approach are:

- Cost reduction. This comes from reduced headcount, premises and associated costs. The SSC, for example, may be located in a geographic area with favourable labour or property rates.

- Increased quality of service. The central team can become very experienced and adopt best practice.

- Consistency of management information throughout the organisation.

The disadvantages of this approach are:

- Loss of strong relationships between the accountant and the business.

- Less knowledge of the business areas and their needs.

- Standard reporting may not provide for all of the needs of each business area.

Business Process Outsourcing (BPO)

While setting up a SSC is often thought of as 'internal outsourcing', some organisations decide to outsource the finance function completely. BPO is contracting with a third party (external supplier) to provide all or part of a business process or function. Typically the functions which are outsourced include procurement, ordering, invoicing and reporting functions, although decision support and other corporate functions may also be outsourced.

The advantages of this approach are:

- Cost reduction. As with SSCs, there will be headcount reduction and reduction in property and associated costs.

- Access to specialist providers. This can bring new expertise into the organisation.

- Release of capacity. If only the more routine functions are outsourced, the retained finance function can concentrate on their role of providing the best information for management decision making.

The disadvantages of this approach are:

- Loss of control. The work is being carried out remotely so management are unable to supervise the function on a day-to-day basis.

- Over-reliance on external providers. Often the systems containing the information are not accessible to the organisation, meaning that they are only able to get the information the outsourcers provide. It can also become very difficult to bring the function back in-house.

- Confidentiality risk. Important information could end up getting into the wrong hands.

- Loss of quality. Quality requirements must be specified when the contract is set up and quality control must be put in place to monitor the work of the outsourced function.

Test your understanding 5

Which of the following is NOT an advantage of setting up a shared services centre?

A   Closer to the business needs

B   Cost savings

C   Consistency of information across the organisation

D   Adoption of best practice

10 The Chartered Institute of Management Accountants (CIMA)

CIMA was formed in 1919 (originally as the Institute of Cost and Works Accountants (ICWA)). It was granted its Royal Charter in 1975 and became known as the Chartered Institute of Management Accountants in 1986.

CIMA is the world's largest and leading professional body of management accountants, with over 200,000 members. Members and students are located in over 170 countries. CIMA supports organisations in both the private and public sector. It focuses on the needs of businesses, no matter what type of business.

The CIMA qualification

The CIMA qualification is very highly regarded across the world and CIMA members hold many high profile finance positions.

The CIMA qualification is constantly updated to ensure that it continues to meet the needs of business. Full details of the qualification, study resources and detailed guidance can be found on the cimaglobal website.

Before admission to membership, students must demonstrate their experience by completing their professional experience records. This ensures that CIMA members do not just have the technical knowledge, but also practical knowledge of business.

Members are required to undertake continuing professional development (CPD) to ensure that they maintain and develop their knowledge. Details about CPD requirements can be found on the cimaglobal website. The website also contains a range of CPD resources to support members in maintaining and developing their knowledge throughout their careers.

All of this ensures that CIMA members and students will enhance any business they join and it gives assurances to potential employers that they are recruiting well-trained and knowledgeable individuals.

The cimaglobal website also contains a full recruitment site where CIMA members and students can find career advice and employment opportunities.

Professional standards

In addition to the technical requirements for members, CIMA are committed to upholding the highest **ethical and professional standards**. This ensures that employers and members of the public can have confidence in CIMA and CIMA members and students.

CIMA has a **code of ethics** which all members and students are required to comply with.

The code of ethics is made up of five fundamental principles:

- **Integrity**: Being straightforward, honest and truthful in all professional and business relationships.

- **Objectivity**: Not allowing bias, conflict of interest or the influence of other people to override your professional judgement.

- **Professional competence and due care**: An ongoing commitment to your level of professional knowledge and skill.

- **Confidentiality**: You should not disclose professional information unless you have specific permission, or a legal or professional duty, to do so.

- **Professional behaviour**: Compliance with relevant laws and regulations. You must also avoid any action that could negatively affect the reputation of the profession.

Ethical support for members and students

CIMA provides students and members with guidance on how to handle situations where their ethics may be compromised. Such situations may arise from:

- Pressure from management or shareholders to achieve unrealistic deadlines or produce certain results

- Pressure to cut costs or operate with fewer resources

- Intimidation or threats from management

- Desire to act in one's own self-interest or in the interest of the organisation.

Members or students facing an ethical dilemma, concerned about threats to their professionalism or seeking advice on how to handle situations arising in their professional duties can contact CIMA for help and guidance. CIMA provide a free, confidential helpline for members and students offering support and advice.

Other member benefits

In addition to the above CIMA provides members with much more in terms of resources and support to help all members develop and reach their potential. CIMA and CGMA provide members with regular updates about what is happening in the profession and in business in general. Members receive regular magazines and newsletters to keep them up to date with recent developments.

Members can also network with other like-minded members at numerous events which are run from many locations, and on line throughout the year. CIMA use social media to keep in touch with members so that they are always aware of events which may be of interest to them and as a way of introducing members to each other. Networking is a valuable way to progress your career.

In addition CIMA provides research and insights to challenge members' thinking in order to keep CIMA members at the forefront of the profession.

CIMA is keen to support members throughout their career and offers advice and support to help with career development. It also provides a comprehensive job site which advertises suitable jobs from across the world.

Details of all of the above, including the CIMA jobs website can be found on the cimaglobal website.

Maintaining public confidence in management accounting

As part of its commitment to upholding the highest ethical and professional standards, and to maintaining public confidence in management accounting, CIMA will also deal with complaints against members or students. Any member of the public with a complaint about a student or member of CIMA can contact CIMA directly and it will investigate the complaint through its conduct process.

This process will aim to determine if the complaint is valid and if CIMA's standards of professional behaviour have been met. The conduct committee will determine what action, if any, should be taken.

The work of CIMA ensures that the public and businesses are protected and that members are trained to the highest levels and adhere to the highest ethical and professional standards.

Chartered Global Management Accountants (CGMA)

In 2012, CIMA undertook a joint venture with the AICPA (American institute of Certified Public Accountants). Together they have created a new designation for management accountants known as CGMA.

When you become a qualified CIMA member you will be entitled to use the CGMA designation.

The purpose of the new designation is to elevate the profession of management accounting around the world. Businesses around the world will recognise the CGMA designation and will be confident that members of CGMA will be able to assist them in making critical business decisions and will contribute to driving strong business performance.

Test your understanding 6

Mr H is a CIMA student, working in the finance department of a publishing company. He has recently undertaken a review of business expenses and has discovered that one of his colleagues, also a CIMA student, has been claiming for non-work related expenses.

This is against the expenses policy of the company.

Mr H is friendly with the colleague and does not want to get him into trouble but feels that he should report his findings.

If Mr H fails to report his findings to protect his friend, which of the fundamental principles would he be failing to comply with?

- Objectivity

- Confidentiality

- Professional behaviour

- Integrity

- Professional competence and due care

11 Chapter summary

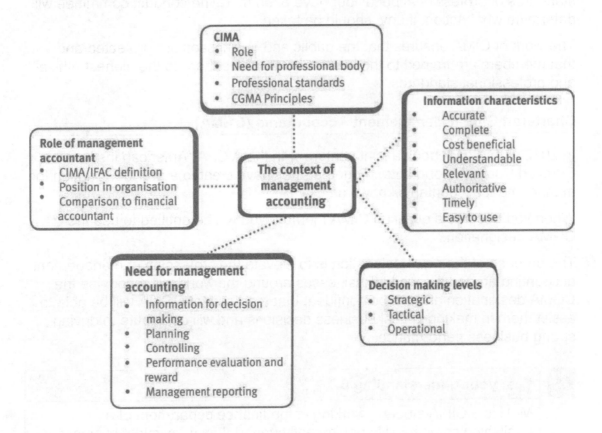

CIMA
- Role
- Need for professional body
- Professional standards
- CGMA Principles

Information characteristics
- Accurate
- Complete
- Cost beneficial
- Understandable
- Relevant
- Authoritative
- Timely
- Easy to use

Role of management accountant
- CIMA/IFAC definition
- Position in organisation
- Comparison to financial accountant

The context of management accounting

Need for management accounting
- Information for decision making
- Planning
- Controlling
- Performance evaluation and reward
- Management reporting

Decision making levels
- Strategic
- Tactical
- Operational

12 End of chapter questions

Question 1

What, if any, is the difference between data and information?

A   They are the same

B   Data can only be figures, whereas information can be facts or figures

C   Information results from sorting and analysing data

D   Data results from obtaining many individual pieces of information

Question 2

Which three of the following are possible disadvantages of business process outsourcing?

A   Loss of control

B   Reduction in quality

C   Duplication of effort

D   Increased cost

E   Confidentiality risk

Question 3

Which three of the following statements about CIMA are true?

A   CIMA's main focus is financial accounting

B   CIMA was established over 90 years ago

C   Members of CIMA are known as Chartered Global Management Accountants

D   CIMA only covers organisations based in the UK

E   CIMA has a code of ethics which all students and members must adhere to

Question 4

Which of the following is NOT one of the roles of management accounting as defined by CIMA?

A   Plan long, medium and short-run operations.

B   Design reward strategies for executives and shareholders.

C   Prepare statutory accounts consisting of statement of profit or loss, statement of financial position and cash flow statements.

D   Control operations and ensure the efficient use of resources.

E   Measure and report financial and non-financial performance to management and other stakeholders.

Question 5

Consider the following information characteristics.

For each, decide which characteristic is most appropriate at the strategic level and which would be more appropriate at the operational level.

	Strategic	Operational
Subjective/Objective		
Detailed/Summarised		
Historical/Future		
Focused/Wide ranging		
Frequent/Infrequent		

Question 6

The Global Management Accounting Principles have been developed to support organisations in benchmarking and improving their management accounting systems. The Principles help the public and private sectors make better decisions, respond appropriately to the risks they face and protect the value they generate.

From the list below, identify the four Global Management Accounting Principles:

- Influence
- Confidentiality
- Relevance
- Professional behaviour
- Integrity
- Trust
- Value

Question 7

State which three of the following characteristics relate to financial accounting:

A   For internal use

B   Governed by rules and regulations

C   Required by law

D   Output is mainly used by external parties

E   One of its main purposes is planning

Question 8

Which of the following are characteristics of good information? Mark all that apply.

- Cost beneficial
- Detailed
- Understandable
- Accurate
- Complete
- Regular
- Timely
- Accountable

Question 9

Which three of the following are fundamental principles from the CIMA code of ethics?

A   Confidentiality

B   Responsibility

C   Integrity

D   Accountability

E   Objectivity

Question 10

Decide whether the following statements are true or false.

	True	False
Financial accounting information is historical		
Financial accounting is concerned with the production of statutory accounts		
Management accounting information is used for internal decision making		
Management accounting information is used by company shareholders		

Test your understanding and end of chapter answers

Test your understanding 1

The report has failed in a number of respects:

The report is not **complete** as some important information is missing.

The report is not **understandable** as it uses terminology which the recipient does not understand.

The report is not **relevant** as it contains too much information, much of which is not required by the manager.

The report is not **timely** as it was received late, making the information less useful.

The report is not **easy to use** as M has not considered the user when producing it and as a result it does not meet the needs of the manager.

Test your understanding 2

The correct matching is:

Decision		Level
A decision to take over a rival company in order to expand its production into different markets		Strategic
A decision on the ordering of material for production		Operational
A decision about the pricing of the products		Tactical

Test your understanding 3

The completed sentences are:

A decision to diversify into a new market would be taken at the **strategic** level.

Information for operational level decisions will have a **higher** level of detail than information for strategic level decisions.

Strategic level information will be **more** subjective than operational level information.

Test your understanding 4

B

Statement (ii) is incorrect as statements for external use must be presented in the prescribed formats.

Test your understanding 5

A

Being closer to the business needs is an advantage of having the management accountant as a dedicated business partner.

B, C and D are advantages of a SSC.

Test your understanding 6

In this example if Mr H fails to report his findings to protect his friend, he would be breaching a number of principles:

Professional behaviour has been breached. By ignoring his colleague's action, Mr H is condoning dishonest behaviour which could discredit the profession.

Professional competence and due care is breached since Mr H is expected to deliver a competent behaviour towards his employer and act with due care in accordance with applicable technical and professional standards.

Objectivity has also been breached as this requires a professional accountant not to allow bias, conflict of interest or undue influence of others to override professional or business judgement. His friendship is compromising his objectivity.

Integrity is the requirement to act honestly. Covering up an illegal act is not acting honestly towards the company.

Confidentiality could also be seen as being breached. Mr H would have a duty to disclose this information to his superiors as part of his professional duty.

Question 1

C

The two terms are frequently used synonymously but strictly speaking they mean different things. Data consists of raw facts and statistics and is turned into information by sorting and analysis. Both data and information can comprise either facts or figures.

Question 2

A, B and E

C and D are disadvantages of business partnering.

Question 3

B, C and E

A is false. CIMA's main focus is management accounting.

D is false. CIMA is a worldwide organisation.

Question 4

C

Preparing statutory accounts is NOT a role of management accounting. It is a financial accounting role.

Question 5

Strategic	Operational
Subjective	Objective
Summarised	Detailed
Future	Historical
Wide ranging	Focused
Infrequent	Frequent

Question 6

The four Global Management Accounting Principles are:

- Influence

- Relevance

- Trust

- Value

Confidentiality, professional behaviour and integrity are three of the five fundamental principles of the CIMA code of ethics.

Question 7

B, C and D

A and E relate to management accounting.

Management accounting is internally focused and one of its main purposes is planning.

Financial accounting is governed by rules and regulations, required by law and its output is mainly used by external parties.

Question 8

- Cost beneficial
- Understandable
- Accurate
- Complete
- Timely

The characteristics of good information can be remembered using ACCURATE which stands for Accurate, Complete, Cost beneficial, Understandable, Relevant, Authoritative, Timely and Easy to use.

Question 9

A, C and E

Confidentiality, integrity and objectivity are all fundamental principles from the CIMA code of ethics. The other two principles are professional competence and due care and professional behaviour.

Question 10

	True	False
Financial accounting information is historical	✓	
Financial accounting is concerned with the production of statutory accounts	✓	
Management accounting information is used for internal decision making	✓	
Management accounting information is used by company shareholders		✓

Cost identification and classification

Chapter learning objectives

After completing this chapter, you should be able to

- explain the classification of costs in relation to output
- explain the classification of costs in relation to activity level
- explain the classification of costs in relation to decisions.

1 Session content diagram

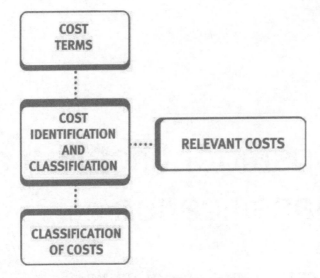

2 The importance of understanding costs

 The word **'cost'** can be used in two contexts. It can be used as a noun, for example when we are referring to the cost of an item. Alternatively, it can be used as a verb, for example we can say that we are attempting to cost an activity, when we are undertaking the tasks necessary to determine the costs of carrying out the activity.

The understanding of costs is fundamental to your accounting studies.

In financial accounting all costs must be recorded so that profit can be calculated and the true and fair value of assets can be presented in the financial statements.

In management accounting an understanding of costs is required in order to carry out the three main functions of planning, control and decision making. If we understand costs, we can produce information regarding:

- the cost to manufacture a product or provide a service
- the selling price we should charge for our products or services
- the products and services we should supply
- the cost to run a particular department or function, and much more.

Some terms that you will need to understand when studying cost:

- Historical cost
- Cost unit
- Composite cost unit
- Cost centre
- Cost object.

In this chapter the various terms relating to costs and the different ways in which costs can be classified will be covered. These terms and classifications will be used throughout your *Fundamentals of Management Accounting* studies and in subsequent higher level subjects.

3 Cost terms

Historical cost

The term historical cost is normally used when we consider the purchase of an asset. This applies to both non-current assets, such as buildings or vehicles, or current assets such as inventory. Historical cost is the **original cost** paid for the asset at the time of acquisition.

By their nature, historical costs are out of date and might not reflect the current value of the asset to the organisation.

The **economic value** of an asset is the value the organisation derives from owning and using the asset. This value can be higher or lower than the historical cost, depending on current circumstances. It can be affected by how the asset is currently being used, the alternative uses for the asset or the current inflation rate.

Cost units

 The *CIMA Terminology* defines a **cost unit** as 'a unit of product or service in relation to which costs are ascertained'.

This means that a cost unit can be **anything for which it is possible to ascertain the cost**. The cost unit selected in each situation will depend on a number of factors, including the amount of information available and the purpose for which the cost unit will be used.

Cost units can be developed for all kinds of organisations, whether manufacturing, service or not-for-profit. Some examples from the *CIMA Terminology* are as follows:

Industry sector	Cost unit
Brick-making	1,000 bricks
Electricity	Megawatt-hour (MwH)
Professional services	Chargeable hour
Education	Enrolled student

Activity	Cost unit
Credit control	Account maintained
Selling	Customer call

The above list is not exhaustive. A cost unit can be anything which is measurable and useful for cost control purposes. For example, with brick-making, 1,000 bricks is suggested as a cost unit. It would be possible to determine the cost per brick but perhaps in this case the larger measure of cost per 1,000 bricks is considered more useful for control purposes.

Notice that this list of cost units contains both tangible and intangible items. Tangible items are those which can be seen and touched, for example the 1,000 bricks. Intangible items cannot be seen and touched and do not have physical substance but they can be measured, for example a chargeable hour of accounting service.

Composite cost units

In service industries cost units are usually intangible and they are often made up of two or more parts. These are known as **composite cost units**. For example, a courier service could measure 'tonnes delivered' or 'miles travelled' for cost control. Neither of these is particularly useful on their own, so they could be combined as a composite cost unit 'tonne-mile'. The cost per tonne-mile would be a comparable measure whatever the length of journey and however large the load. This is therefore a valid and useful cost unit for control purposes.

Other examples of composite cost units might be as follows:

Business	Cost unit
Hotel	Bed-night
Bus company	Passenger-mile
Hospital	Patient-day

Cost centres

 A cost centre is a **production** or **service location**, a **function**, an **activity** or an **item of equipment** for which costs are accumulated.

A cost centre is one type of responsibility centre. Responsibility centres will be covered in the budgeting chapter.

A cost centre is used as a 'collecting place' for costs.

The cost of operating the cost centre is determined for the period, and then this total cost is related to the cost units which have passed through the cost centre.

An example of a production cost centre could be the machine shop in a factory. The production cost for the machine shop might be $100,000 for the period. If 1,000 cost units have passed through this cost centre we might say that the production cost relating to the machine shop was $100 for each unit.

Other examples of cost centres

A cost centre could also be a service location, a function, an activity or an item of equipment. Examples of these might be as follows but you should try to think of some others:

Type of cost centre	Examples
Service location	Stores, canteen
Function	Sales representative
Activity	Quality control
Item of equipment	Packing machine

If you are finding it difficult to see how a sales representative could be used as a cost centre, then work carefully through the following points:

- What are the costs which might be incurred in 'operating' a sales representative for one period?

  Examples might be the representative's salary cost, the cost of running a company car, the cost of any samples given away by the representative and so on. Say these amount to $80,000.

- Once we have determined this cost, the next thing we need to know is the number of cost units that can be related to the sales representative.

  The cost unit selected might be $100 of sales achieved. If the representative has achieved $800,000 of sales, then we could say that the representative's costs amounted to $10 per $100 of sales. The representative has thus been used as a cost centre or collecting place for the costs, which have then been related to the cost units.

Cost objects

> **A cost object is anything for which costs can be ascertained.**

The *CIMA Terminology* contains the following for **cost objects**: 'For example a product, service, centre, activity, customer or distribution channel in relation to which costs are ascertained.'

All of the cost units and cost centres we have described earlier in this chapter are therefore types of cost object.

Test your understanding 1

In a hotel, which of the following would be suitable cost units and cost centres?

	Suitable as cost centre	Suitable as cost unit
Restaurant	❏	❏
Guest-night	❏	❏
Meal served	❏	❏
Fitness suite	❏	❏
Bar	❏	❏

---

4 Classification of costs

Now that we have covered the main cost terms, we have to consider the different classifications of costs.

Costs can be classified in many different ways. It is necessary to be able to classify all costs, that is, to be able to arrange them into logical groups, in order to devise an efficient system to collect and analyse the costs. The classifications selected and the level of detail used in the classification groupings will depend on the purpose of the classification exercise.

 The *CIMA Terminology* defines **classification** as the 'arrangement of items in logical groups by nature, purpose or responsibility'.

We are going to look at four cost classifications:

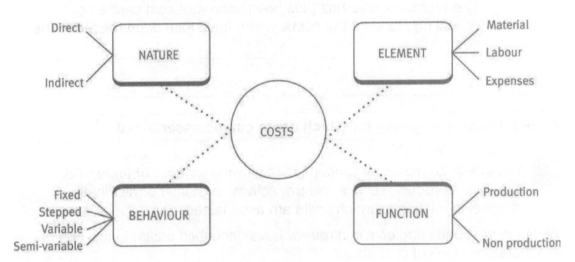

These classifications will be used throughout your study of management accounting. **It is essential that you are familiar with these classifications.**

Classification of costs according to their element

Classifying costs according to their element means grouping costs according to whether they are **material, labour** or **expense** cost. These are the three main cost elements.

Materials are the components bought in by the company which are used in manufacturing the product. For example, the materials used by a food producer could be meat or vegetables. Material costs include the cost of obtaining the materials and receiving them within the organisation. The cost of having the materials brought to the organisation is known as carriage inwards.

Labour costs are the costs of the people working for the organisation. These costs include wages and salaries, together with related employment costs.

Expense costs are external costs such as rent, business rates, electricity, gas, postage, telephones and similar items which will be documented by invoices from suppliers.

Subdivision of cost classifications

Note: Within the cost classifications there can be subdivisions; for example, within the materials classification the subdivisions might include the following:

- Raw materials, that is, the basic raw material used in the manufacturing process.

- Components, that is, complete parts that are used in the manufacturing process.

- Consumables, that is, cleaning materials, etc.

- Maintenance materials, that is, spare parts for machines, lubricating oils, etc.

This list of subdivisions is not exhaustive, and there may even be further subdivisions of each of these groups. For example, the raw materials may be further divided according to the type of raw material, for example steel, plastic, glass, etc.

Classification of costs according to their nature

When costs are classified having regard to their nature, the broadest classification of this type is to divide costs into **direct** costs and **indirect** costs.

Direct costs can be clearly identified with the cost object we are trying to cost. For example, suppose that a furniture maker is determining the cost of a wooden table. The manufacture of the table has involved the use of timber, screws and metal drawer handles. These items are classified as **direct materials**. The wages paid to the machine operator, assembler and finisher in actually making the table would be classified as **direct labour**. The designer of the table may be entitled to a royalty payment for each table made, and this would be classified as a **direct expense**.

The total of all direct costs is known as **PRIME COST**.

Indirect costs cannot be directly attributed to a particular cost unit, although it is clear that they have been incurred in the production of the table. These indirect costs are often referred to **as overheads**. Examples of indirect production costs are as follows:

Cost incurred	Cost classification
Lubricating oils and cleaning materials	Indirect material
Salaries of factory supervisors	Indirect labour
Factory rent and power	Indirect expense

Classification of costs according to their function

Another important classification of costs is by function. In manufacturing companies, which much of your studies will cover, the important classification is between production and non-production costs. Production costs would be incurred in the manufacture of the product. Non-production costs, while not directly involved in the manufacture of the product, are required to support the overall activity of the company. Examples of non-production costs would be sales, distribution and administration.

Test your understanding 2

QRS is an office cleaning business which employs a team of part-time cleaners who are paid an hourly wage. The business provides cleaning services for a number of clients, ranging from small offices to high-street shops and large open-plan offices.

In determining the cost of providing a cleaning service to a particular client, which of the following costs would be a direct cost of cleaning that client's office and which would be an indirect cost?

		Direct cost	Indirect cost
(a)	The wages paid to the cleaner who is sent to the client's premises.	❑	❑
(b)	The cost of carpet shampoo used by the cleaner.	❑	❑
(c)	The salaries of QRS's accounts clerks.	❑	❑
(d)	Rent of the premises where QRS stores its cleaning materials and equipment.	❑	❑
(e)	Travelling expenses paid to the cleaner to reach the client's premises.	❑	❑
(f)	Advertising expenses incurred in attracting more clients to QRS business.	❑	❑

Costing a cost object

Now we have looked at some of the basic cost classifications, we can use these to produce the total cost for a cost object.

Illustration 1 – Determining the total cost per unit

The outline cost statement for a single cost unit shows how the total or full cost for a unit might be built up and how this can be used to ascertain the selling price.

Notice in particular that a number of subtotals can be highlighted before the total cost figure is determined.

	$	$
Direct material		15
Direct labour		5
Direct expenses		2
		—
Prime cost or total direct cost		22
Production overhead:		
Indirect material	4	
Indirect labour	6	
Indirect expenses	6	
	—	
		16
		—
Total production/factory cost		38
Selling, distribution and administration overhead		2
		—
Total (full) cost		40
Profit		10
		—
Selling price		50
		—

Note that the costs are split by both element, nature and function. The direct costs are shown first, split by element.

Indirect costs (or overheads) are shown next, again split by element.

This now gives the **total production (or factory) cost**.

Once the non-production costs are added, **the total (or full) cost** can be ascertained.

The usefulness of each of these subtotals depends on the management action that is to be taken based on each of the totals.

Detailed cost analysis

Suppose that the cost analysis in Illustration 1 has been provided by the management accountant to help us to decide on the selling price to be charged for a hairdryer.

Let us look at the sort of costs that might be incurred in manufacturing and selling a hairdryer, and how each cost would be classified in terms of the above analysis of the elements of cost.

- **Direct materials**. This is the material that actually becomes part of the finished hairdryer. It would include the plastic for the case and the packaging materials. If we make another batch of hairdryers then we will need to purchase another batch of these and other direct materials.

- **Direct labour**. This is the labour cost incurred directly as a result of making one hairdryer. If we make another batch of hairdryers then we will need to pay more direct labour cost.

- **Direct expenses**. These are expenses caused directly as a result of making one more batch of hairdryers. For example, the company might be required to pay the designer of the hairdryer a royalty of $2 for each hairdryer produced.

The three direct costs are summed to derive the **prime cost** of $22. This is one measure of cost but we still have to add production overheads.

Production overheads are basically the same three costs as for direct cost, but they are identified as **indirect** costs because they cannot be specifically identified with any particular hairdryer or batch of hairdryers. Indirect costs must be shared out over all the cost objects using a fair and equitable basis.

- **Indirect materials**. These are those production materials that do not actually become part of the finished product. This might include the cleaning materials and lubricating oils for the machinery. It will probably not be necessary to spend more on these materials in order to manufacture a further batch. This cost is therefore only indirectly related to the production of this batch.

- **Indirect labour**. This is the production labour cost which cannot be directly associated with the production of any particular batch. It would include the salaries of supervisors who are overseeing the production of hairdryers as well as all the other products manufactured in the factory.

- **Indirect expenses**. These are all the other production overheads associated with running the factory, including factory rent and rates, heating and lighting, etc. These indirect costs must be shared out over all of the batches produced in a period.

The share of indirect production costs is added to the prime cost to derive the **total production cost** of $38. This is another measure of cost but we still have to add a share of the other non-production overheads.

- **Selling and distribution overhead**. These include the sales force salaries and commission, the cost of operating delivery vehicles and renting a storage warehouse, etc. These are indirect costs which are not specifically attributable to a particular cost unit.

- **Administration overhead**. These include the rent on the administrative office building, the depreciation of office equipment, postage and stationery costs, etc. These are also indirect costs which are not specifically attributable to a particular cost unit.

In this example, the non-production overheads amount to $2 per unit, this is added to the total production cost to give a **total (or full) cost** of $40.

Now that you understand the nature of each of the cost items which make up the full cost we can think a bit more about the price to be charged for the hairdryer.

In this example a profit of $10 has been added, suggesting a selling price of $50.

Incremental cost

From Illustration 1, we can also consider which costs would be incurred as a result of making one additional hairdryer.

The direct cost of $22 would definitely be incurred if another hairdryer was produced. This is the extra material that would have to be bought, the extra labour costs that would have to be paid and the extra expenses for royalties that would be incurred.

The $16 production overhead cost would not be incurred additionally if another hairdryer was produced. This is the share of costs that would be incurred anyway, such as the cleaning materials, the factory rent and the supervisors' salaries.

The $2 share of selling, distribution and administration overhead would probably not be incurred if another hairdryer was produced. This includes the office costs, the depreciation on the delivery vehicles and the rent of warehousing facilities. This sort of cost would not increase as a result of producing another hairdryer or batch of hairdryers. However, there may be some incremental or extra selling and distribution costs, for example we would probably need to pay a sales commission to the sales team for all their hard work in winning the sale, and there would be some costs involved in delivering the goods to the hotel chain. For the sake of our analysis let us suppose that this incremental cost amounts to $1 per hairdryer, rather than the full amount of $2 shown in the cost analysis.

You can see from the discussion in this exercise that in fact the only extra or **incremental cost** to be incurred in producing another hairdryer is $23 ($22 direct cost plus assumed $1 incremental selling and distribution costs).

Therefore if we were to sell the hairdryer for any price above $23 we would still be better off than if the sale had not been made.

Any sale achieved for more than $23 would at least contribute towards the costs which are being incurred anyway – the production overheads, administration overheads, etc.

This discussion has illustrated that the concept of cost needs to be qualified if it is to be meaningful. We need to know to which cost we are referring when we state something like 'The cost is $40'.

The $40 cost quoted is the full cost, which includes a fair share of all costs incurred on behalf of the cost object. In our discussion we derived the **incremental (or marginal) cost** of $23 which would be incurred as a direct result of making and selling another hairdryer.

Therefore, we have seen that different costs are useful in different circumstances and we must always qualify what we mean by 'cost'. Do we mean direct cost, incremental cost, full cost or some other measure of cost?

Note: This example introduces an important concept in management accounting known as **relevant cost**. This will be covered in more detail later in the chapter.

Test your understanding 3

BCD is a car manufacturer.

Write the correct classification for each of the costs below into the box provided, using the following classifications (each cost is intended to belong to only one classification):

- direct materials
- direct labour
- production overhead
- administration costs
- selling and distribution costs.

cost of advertising the car on television	
wages of workers moving raw materials from stores	
cost of metal used for the bodywork of the car	
cost of materials used to clean production equipment	
assembly worker's wages	
wages of office workers	
wages of storekeepers in material store	

5 Cost behaviour

The final cost classification we will look at is classifying costs depending on their behaviour.

In management accounting, when we talk about cost behaviour we are referring to the way in which costs are affected by **fluctuations in the level of activity**.

The level of activity can be measured in many different ways, including:

- the number of units produced
- miles travelled
- hours worked
- meals served
- percentage of capacity utilised.

An understanding of cost behaviour patterns is essential for many management tasks, particularly in the areas of planning, decision making and control. It would be impossible for managers to forecast and control costs without at least a basic knowledge of the way in which costs behave in relation to the level of activity.

The main cost behaviours are:

*   **Fixed**

*   **Variable**

*   **Semi-variable**

It is important to be able to identify the cost behaviour and also to be able to represent the cost graphically.

Fixed cost

 The *CIMA Terminology* defines a **fixed cost** as a 'cost incurred for an accounting period, that, within certain output or turnover limits, tends to be unaffected by fluctuations in the levels of activity (output or turnover)'.

Another term that can be used to refer to a fixed cost is a **period cost**. This highlights the fact that a fixed cost is incurred according to the time elapsed, rather than according to the level of activity.

Examples of fixed costs are:

*   rental of premises

*   insurance of premises

*   executive salaries.

A fixed cost can be depicted graphically as shown:

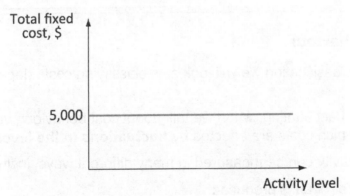

The graph shows that the cost is constant (in this case at $5,000) for all levels of activity. However, it is important to note that this is only true for the **relevant range** of activity. Consider, for example, the behaviour of the rent cost. Within the relevant range it is possible to expand activity without needing extra premises and therefore the rent cost remains constant.

Stepped fixed cost

If activity is expanded beyond the relevant range to the point where further premises are needed, then the rent cost will increase to a new, higher level.

This cost behaviour pattern can be described as a stepped fixed cost, as shown below:

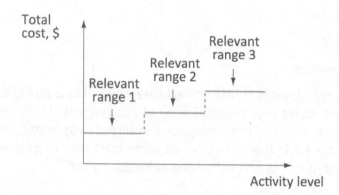

The cost is constant within the relevant range for each activity level but when a critical level of activity is reached, the total cost incurred increases to the next step.

When you are drawing or interpreting graphs of cost behaviour patterns, it is important that you pay great attention to the label on the vertical axis. In the previous examples for fixed cost and stepped fixed cost, the graphs depicted the **total cost** incurred. If the vertical axis had been used to represent the fixed cost **per unit**, then it would look as shown below:

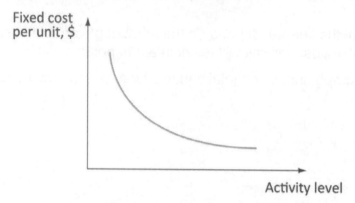

The fixed cost per unit reduces as the activity level is increased. This is because the same amount of fixed cost is being spread over an increasing number of units.

Variable cost

 The *CIMA Terminology* defines a **variable cost** as a 'cost that varies with a measure of activity'.

Examples of variable costs are:

*   direct material
*   direct labour
*   variable overheads.

The following graph depicts a **linear variable cost**. It is a straight line through the origin, which means that the cost is nil at zero activity level. When activity increases, the total variable cost increases in direct proportion. For example, if activity goes up by 10%, then the total variable cost also increases by 10%, as long as the activity level is still within the relevant range.

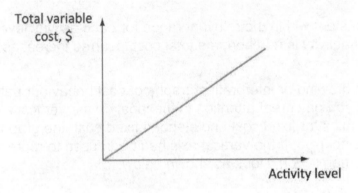

The gradient of the line will depend on the amount of variable cost per unit. A higher variable cost per unit will result in a steeper line.

The previous graph shows the total variable cost, we can also show the variable cost per unit:

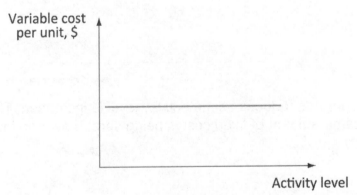

You will notice that this shows a horizontal line as it suggests that the variable cost **per unit** will not change over the relevant range.

Note: The graph showing the variable cost per unit looks exactly the same as the total fixed cost graph. It is always important to check the vertical axis on the graph as these two are easily confused.

Non-linear variable costs

In most assessment situations, and very often in practice, variable costs are assumed to be linear (as shown above, the total variable cost line is shown as a straight line). Although many variable costs do approximate to a linear function, this assumption may not always be realistic. A variable cost may be non-linear as depicted in the diagrams shown below:

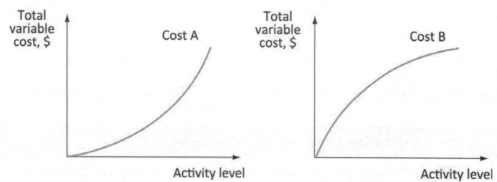

These costs are sometimes called **curvilinear variable costs**.

The graph of cost A becomes steeper as the activity level increases. This indicates that each successive unit of activity is adding more to the total variable cost than the previous unit. An example of a variable cost which follows this pattern could be the cost of direct labour where employees are paid an accelerating bonus for achieving higher levels of output. The graph of cost B becomes less steep as the activity level increases. Each successive unit of activity adds less to total variable cost than the previous unit. An example of a variable cost which follows this pattern could be the cost of direct material where quantity discounts are available.

Semi-variable cost

The *CIMA Terminology* defines a **semi-variable cost** as a 'cost containing both fixed and variable components and thus partly affected by a change in the level of activity'.

A semi-variable cost can also be referred to as a semi-fixed or mixed cost.

Examples of semi-variable costs are:

*   gas

*   electricity

*   telephone.

These expenditures consist of a fixed amount payable for the period regardless of the level of use, with a further variable amount which is related to the consumption of gas or electricity, or the number of telephone calls.

A graph of a semi-variable cost might look like the following:

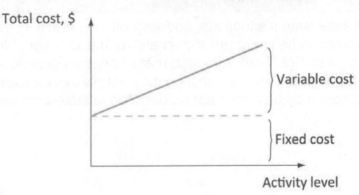

We will look at how to analyse semi-variable costs in the next chapter.

Alternative semi-variable cost behaviour

Alternatively a semi-variable cost behaviour pattern might look like this:

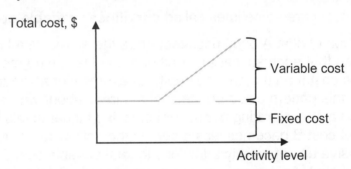

This cost remains constant up to a certain level of activity and then increases as the variable cost element is incurred. An example of such a cost might be the rental cost of a photocopier where a fixed rental is paid and no extra charge is made for copies up to a certain number. Once this number of copies is exceeded, a constant charge is levied for each copy taken.

Test your understanding 4

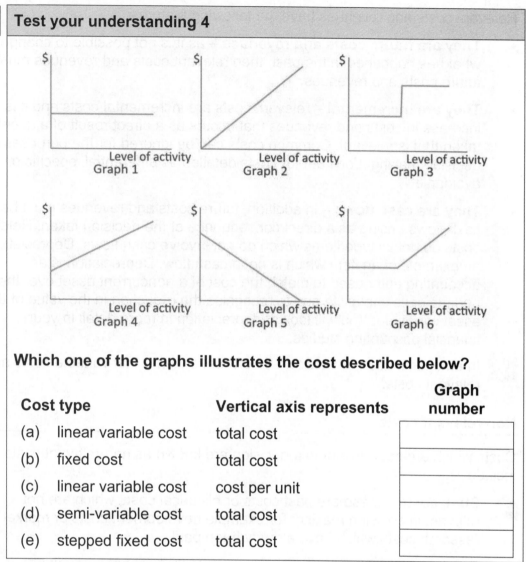

Which one of the graphs illustrates the cost described below?

Cost type		Vertical axis represents	Graph number
(a)	linear variable cost	total cost	
(b)	fixed cost	total cost	
(c)	linear variable cost	cost per unit	
(d)	semi-variable cost	total cost	
(e)	stepped fixed cost	total cost	

6 Relevant costs

We have looked at the various classifications of costs and how the different classifications are used depending on the information required and the decision to be made.

Organisations face many decisions, and they often must choose between two or more alternatives. Decisions will generally be based on taking the decision that maximises shareholder value. In all decision making, only **relevant costs and revenues** should be used.

Relevant costs and revenues are those costs and revenues that change as a direct result of a decision being taken.

Relevant costs and revenues have the following features:

- **They are future costs and revenues** – as it is not possible to change what has happened in the past, then relevant costs and revenues must be future costs and revenues.

- **They are incremental** – relevant costs are incremental costs and it is the increase in costs and revenues that occurs as a direct result of a decision taken that is relevant. Common costs can be ignored for the purposes of decision making. Look out for costs detailed as differential, specific or avoidable.

- **They are cash flows** – in addition, future costs and revenues must be cash flows arising as a direct consequence of the decision taken. Relevant costs do not include items which do not involve cash flows. Depreciation is an example of an item which is not a cash flow. Depreciation is an accounting entry used to match the cost of a noncurrent asset over the periods of its useful life and to recognise the reduction in the value of the asset over time. You will look at depreciation in more detail in your financial accounting studies.

 In an examination, unless told otherwise, assume that variable costs are relevant costs.

Non-relevant costs

Costs which are not relevant to a decision are known as non-relevant costs and include:

- **Sunk costs** – these are past costs or historical costs which are not relevant in decision making, for example development costs or market research costs which have already been paid.

- **Committed costs** – these are future costs that cannot be avoided, whatever decision is taken.

- **Non-cash flows** – these are costs which do not involve the flow of cash.

- **Notional costs** – these are costs that will not result in an outflow of cash either now or in the future, for example sometimes the head office of an organisation may charge a 'notional' rent to its branches. This cost will only appear in the accounts of the organisation but will not result in a 'real' cash expenditure. Another example would be notional interest which could be charged to departments for the use of internally generated funds.

- **General fixed overheads** – these are usually not relevant to a decision. However, some fixed overheads may be relevant to a decision, for example stepped fixed costs may be relevant if fixed costs increase as a direct result of a decision being taken.

- **Net book values** – these are not relevant costs because like depreciation, they are determined by accounting conventions rather than by future cash flows.

Test your understanding 5

In a short-term decision making context, which of the following would be a relevant cost?

A   Specific development costs already incurred

B   The cost of special material which will be purchased

C   Depreciation on existing equipment

D   The original cost of raw materials currently in inventory that will be used on the project

Opportunity costs

The *CIMA Terminology* defines **opportunity cost** as 'the value of the benefit sacrificed when one course of action is chosen in preference to an alternative. The opportunity cost is represented by the forgone potential benefit from the best rejected course of action'.

Opportunity cost is an important concept in decision making. The opportunity cost emphasises that decision making is concerned with alternatives and that the cost of taking one decision is the profit forgone by not taking the next best alternative.

If resources to be used on projects are scarce (e.g. labour, materials, machines), then consideration must be given to profits which could have been earned from alternative uses of these resources.

For example, the skilled labour which may be needed on a new project might have to be withdrawn from normal production. This withdrawal would cause a loss in profit which is obviously relevant to the project decision.

When considering relevant costs, the cash flows of a single department or division cannot be looked at in isolation. The effects on cash flows of the whole organisation must be considered.

Test your understanding 6

EFG currently produces two products, K and R. Details of the two products for last year are given below:

	K	R
Selling price	$40	$25
Variable cost per unit	$31	$17
Sales units	4,000	2,000

Fixed costs for the year were $35,000.

EFG is now considering expanding production of K. If the expansion goes ahead, the fixed costs will increase by $22,000 per annum. The selling prices of the two products will remain the same, but it is anticipated that the variable cost of product K will fall to $28 per unit. The sales of K are budgeted to increase to 5,500, but the additional sales of K will result in a fall in sales of R by 300 units.

The factory space which will be used to house the expansion is currently rented out to a local business at a rent of $500 per month.

Advise EFG if the expansion is worthwhile. Calculate the resulting increase or decrease in profit.

The concept of relevant cost will be used in all decision making. Short- and long-term decision making will be looked at in later chapters and relevant costs will be considered in more detail.

7 Chapter summary

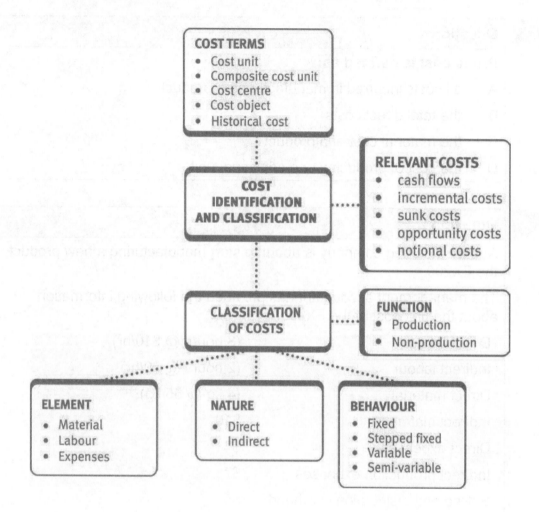

COST TERMS
- Cost unit
- Composite cost unit
- Cost centre
- Cost object
- Historical cost

COST IDENTIFICATION AND CLASSIFICATION

RELEVANT COSTS
- cash flows
- incremental costs
- sunk costs
- opportunity costs
- notional costs

CLASSIFICATION OF COSTS

FUNCTION
- Production
- Non-production

ELEMENT
- Material
- Labour
- Expenses

NATURE
- Direct
- Indirect

BEHAVIOUR
- Fixed
- Stepped fixed
- Variable
- Semi-variable

8   End of chapter questions

Question 1

Prime cost is defined as:

A   all costs incurred in manufacturing a product

B   the total direct costs

C   the material cost of a product

D   the cost of producing one additional unit

Question 2

A manufacturing company is about to start manufacturing a new product, the FX200.

The management accountant has provided the following information about the unit cost of the FX200:

Direct labour	(3 hours @ $10/hr)
Indirect labour	(2 hours @ $9/hr)
Direct material	(4 kg @ $5/kg)
Indirect material	$10
Direct expenses	$4
Indirect production expenses	$7
Selling and distribution overhead	$5

For one unit of FX200, calculate the following:

(i)   The prime cost.

(ii)   The total production cost.

(iii) The full cost.

Question 3

Fixed costs are conventionally deemed to be:

A   constant per unit of output

B   constant in total when production volume changes

C   outside the control of management

D   those unaffected by inflation

Question 4

DEF is a successful manufacturing company. Its success has meant that it needs to increase its factory capacity. It currently owns four buildings in an industrial estate. It uses buildings 1, 2 and 3 at present and rents building 4 to a local printing company for use as storage. The suggestion is to expand production into building 4. Additional machinery will be required to be purchased and fitted. Plans for the fitting have been produced. No additional staff will be required.

The management of DEF is meeting to decide whether or not to go ahead with the expansion.

Which TWO of the following would be relevant costs in the decision?

A   The purchase price of the new machinery.

B   The cost of drawing up the plans for the new building.

C   The salary cost of the factory manager.

D   The current rental income from building 4.

E   The depreciation charge for the existing factory machinery.

F   The depreciation charge for the new machinery.

Question 5

Consider the following costs. Which TWO would be classified as stepped costs?

A   The cost of materials is $3 per kg for purchases up to 10,000 kg. From 10,001 kg to 15,000 kg the cost is $2.80 per kg. Thereafter the cost is $2.60 per kg.

B   The cost of supervisory labour is $18,000 per period for output up to 10,000 units. From 10,001 units to 15,000 units the cost is $37,000 per period. Thereafter the cost is $58,000 per period.

C   The cost of machine rental is $4,500 per period for output up to 3,000 units. From 3,001 units to 6,000 units the cost is $8,700 per period. Thereafter the cost is $12,200 per period.

D   The mileage charge for a rental car is $0.05 per mile up to 400 miles. From 401 miles to 700 miles the charge is $0.07 per mile. Thereafter the cost is $0.08 per mile.

Question 6

Drag each of the following costs under the correct heading depending on whether they would be a direct cost or an indirect cost of the quality control activity which is undertaken in a company's factory.

Direct cost	Indirect cost

- The salary of the quality control supervisor.
- The rent of the factory.
- The depreciation of the quality testing machine.
- The cost of the samples destroyed during testing.
- The insurance of the factory.

Question 7

The following is a graph of cost against volume of output:

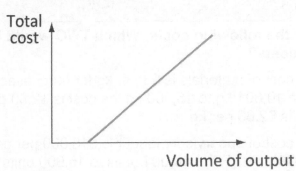

To which of the following costs does the graph correspond?

A   Electricity bills made up of a standing charge and a variable charge.

B   Bonus payments to employees when production reaches a certain level.

C   Sales commission payable per unit up to a maximum amount of commission.

D   Bulk discounts on purchases, the discount being given on all units purchased.

Question 8

The unit costs for product XX5 are given below.

	$
Direct labour	25
Indirect labour	12
Direct material	32
Indirect material	5
Direct expenses	6
Administration overhead	12

For one unit of XX5, calculate the following:

(i) The marginal cost.

(ii) The total production cost.

(iii) The full cost.

Question 9

A company carries out repairs on customers' electrical items, e.g. televisions, video recorders, etc.

Consider the following costs. For each cost, decide if it is a direct or indirect cost and if it is fixed or variable.

Cost	Direct/Indirect	Fixed/Variable
Business rates for repair shop		
Salary of repair shop supervisor		
Repair person paid per repair carried out		
Electricity for recharging repair tools		

Question 10

A company is making a business decision and is considering which costs would be relevant to the decision.

Consider the following statements regarding costs and state if each statement is true or false.

- The annual depreciation cost of a machine is a relevant cost if the decision involves replacing the machine.

- Fixed costs can be relevant if the decision causes a change to total fixed costs.

- The original purchase cost of an asset would be a sunk cost.

- Notional costs would not be relevant in decision making.

Test your understanding and end of chapter answers

Test your understanding 1

	Suitable as cost centre	Suitable as cost unit
Restaurant	☑	❑
Guest-night	❑	☑
Meal served	❑	☑
Fitness suite	☑	❑
Bar	☑	❑

Test your understanding 2

		Direct cost	Indirect cost
(a)	The wages paid to the cleaner who is sent to the client's premises.	☑	❑
(b)	The cost of carpet shampoo used by the cleaner.	☑	❑
(c)	The salaries of QRS's accounts clerks.	❑	☑
(d)	Rent of the premises where QRS stores its cleaning materials and equipment.	❑	☑
(e)	Travelling expenses paid to the cleaner to reach the client's premises.	☑	❑
(f)	Advertising expenses incurred in attracting more clients to QRS business.	❑	☑

The direct costs are (a), (b) and (e) because they can be directly identified with the cost object under consideration (this particular client). The other costs are indirect because they would have to be shared among all of the clients serviced by QRS.

Test your understanding 3

cost of advertising the car on television	selling and distribution costs
wages of workers moving raw materials from stores	production overhead
cost of metal used for the bodywork of the car	direct materials
cost of materials used to clean production equipment	production overhead
assembly worker's wages	direct labour
wages of office workers	administration costs
wages of storekeepers in material store	production overhead

Test your understanding 4

Cost type		Vertical axis represents	Graph number
(a)	linear variable cost	total cost	2
(b)	fixed cost	total cost	1
(c)	linear variable cost	cost per unit	1
(d)	semi-variable cost	total cost	4
(e)	stepped fixed cost	total cost	3

Test your understanding 5

B

This material will be purchased solely for use in this project, making it relevant. If the decision is not taken then the material will not be purchased.

Specific development costs have already been incurred and are therefore sunk costs.

Depreciation on existing equipment is a non-cash item.

The original cost of raw materials currently in inventory is a sunk cost.

Test your understanding 6

EFG should not to go ahead with the expansion as it will result in a loss of $400.

It is possible to calculate this type of question by looking at the profit before any expansion and then comparing it to the profit after the expansion, but this is time consuming. The quickest way to tackle this sort of question is to use an incremental approach:

	$
Product K:	
Reduction in variable cost (31 – 28) × 4,000	12,000
Profit from additional sales (5,500 – 4,000) × (40 – 28)	18,000
Product R:	
Lost profit from sales (25 – 17) × 300	(2,400)
Increase in fixed costs	(22,000)
Opportunity cost – loss of rental income ($500 × 12)[1]	(6,000)
Incremental profit (loss)	**(400)**

[1] The loss of rental income is an opportunity cost and must be included in the calculation. If EFG go ahead with the expansion, they can no longer obtain the rental income.

Question 1

B

Answer (A) describes total production cost. Answer (C) is only a part of prime cost. Answer (D) describes incremental or marginal cost.

Question 2

(i)   **Prime cost = $54**

(ii)   **Total production cost = $89**

(iii) **Full cost = $94**

	$
Direct labour (3 hours @ $10/hr)	30
Direct material (4 kg @ $5/kg)	20
Direct expenses	4
Prime cost	54
Indirect labour (2 hours @ $9/hr)	18
Indirect material	10
Indirect production expenses	7
Total production cost	89
Selling and distribution overhead	5
Total (full) cost	94

Question 3

B

The total amount of fixed costs remains unchanged when production volume changes, therefore the unit rate fluctuates. Fixed costs must still be controlled by management, although they may be controlled by senior management. Fixed costs would still be affected by inflation.

Question 4

The relevant costs are **A and D**.

The purchase price of the new machinery would only be incurred if the decision is made to expand the factory. It is therefore a relevant cost.

The current rental income from building 4 would be lost if the decision is made to expand the factory. It is therefore an opportunity cost and is therefore relevant.

The cost of drawing up the plans for the new building is not relevant as this has already taken place and is therefore a sunk cost.

The salary cost of the factory manager is not relevant as the manager is currently employed and is being paid already.

Depreciation is a non-cash flow and is therefore not relevant.

Question 5

Costs **(b) and (c)** are stepped costs.

The total expenditure on these costs remains constant for a range of activity levels until a critical activity level is reached. At this point, the cost increases to a new level and then remains constant for a further range of activity levels.

Costs (a) and (d) are non-linear variable costs. The gradient of a graph of cost (a) will become less steep as activity increases. The gradient of a graph of cost (d) will become steeper as activity increases.

It might help to actually draw a rough sketch graph of each cost described.

Question 6

Direct cost	Indirect cost
• The salary of the quality control supervisor. • The depreciation of the quality testing machine. • The cost of the samples destroyed during testing.	• The rent of the factory. • The insurance of the factory.

- The salary of the quality control supervisor is a **direct cost** of the quality control activity because it can be specifically attributed to this cost object.

- The rent of the factory is an **indirect cost** of the quality control activity because it cannot be specifically attributed to this cost object but must also be attributed to other activities undertaken in the factory.

- The depreciation of the quality testing machine is a **direct cost** of the quality control activity because it can be specifically attributed to this cost object.

- The cost of the samples destroyed during testing is a **direct cost** of the quality control activity because it can be specifically attributed to this cost object.

- The insurance of the factory is an **indirect cost** of the quality control activity because it cannot be specifically attributed to this cost object but must also be attributed to other activities undertaken in the factory.

Question 7

B

The graph shows a variable cost which starts to be incurred only beyond a certain volume of output. Only B fits this description of cost behaviour.

Question 8

(i) **Marginal cost = $63**

(ii) **Total production cost = $80**

(iii) **Full cost = $92**

	$
Direct labour	25
Direct material	32
Direct expenses	6
Marginal (Prime) cost	63
Indirect labour	12
Indirect material	5
Total production cost	80
Administration overhead	12
Full cost	92

Question 9

Cost	Direct/Indirect	Fixed/Variable
Business rates for repair shop	Indirect	Fixed
Salary of repair shop supervisor	Indirect	Fixed
Repair person paid per repair carried out	Direct	Variable
Electricity for recharging repair tools	Indirect	Variable

Direct costs are costs which can be clearly identified with the cost object we are trying to cost. Indirect costs cannot be directly attributed to a particular cost unit.

Question 10

- Depreciation is not a relevant cost as it is not a cash flow. This is **false**.

- Relevant costs are costs which change as a result of a decision being made. This is **true**.

- The original cost of an asset is a past cost and will not be changed as a result of any decision. This is **true**.

- Notional costs are not cash flows and would therefore not be relevant. This is **true**.

Analysing and predicting costs

Chapter learning objectives

After completing this chapter, you should be able to:

- Calculate appropriate costs having identified cost behaviour.

1   Session content diagram

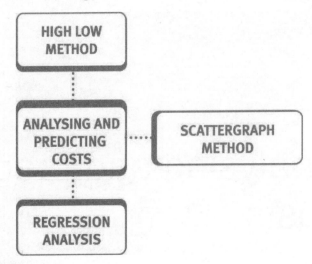

2   Cost behaviour

In the previous chapter we saw that understanding costs and cost behaviour is important. Managers must be able to identify if costs are fixed, variable, stepped or semi-variable.

 When managers understand how costs will behave under different levels of activity they can use this to predict cost values, both individually and in total, for different levels of activity.

We will use the following example to show how managers can identify the cost behaviour.

 Illustration 1 – Identifying cost behaviour

Consider the following costs for a manufacturing company at two different activity levels.

	100 units	**200 units**
Material	$500	$1,000
Labour	$1,000	$2,000
Rent	$2,000	$2,000
Electricity	$700	$900

Required:

Determine the behaviour of each type of cost provided.

Solution:

A useful way to do this is to calculate the unit cost at different levels of activity.

Material: Material would normally be a variable cost – the total cost is increasing as the number of units increases. To check if it is a linear variable cost, divide the total cost by the number of units and the unit cost should be the same for each level:

Material is $500 for 100 units, therefore $5 per unit, and $1,000 for 200 units, therefore $5 per unit. This suggests that **material is a variable cost.**

Labour: If you look at labour, you can see that **labour is also variable cost**. The unit cost for 100 units is ($1,000 ÷ 100 = $10) and the unit cost for 200 units is ($2,000 ÷ 200 = $10).

Rent: Rent is normally a fixed cost and in the example the total rent cost is $2,000 for each level of activity. This suggests that **rent is a fixed cost**.

Electricity: For electricity the total cost is increasing as the number of units increase, but if we work out the unit cost we can see that it varies at each level. Electricity is $700 for 100 units, therefore $7 per unit and $900 for 200 units, therefore $4.50 per unit. This suggests that **electricity is a semi-variable cost**.

Test your understanding 1

The following data have been collected for four costs, W, X, Y and Z, at two activity levels:

Cost	Total cost 100 units $	Total cost 140 units $
W	8,000	10,560
X	5,000	5,000
Y	6,500	9,100
Z	6,700	8,580

Where V = variable, SV = semi-variable and F = fixed, assuming linearity, the four costs W, X, Y and Z are:

	W	X	Y	Z
A	V	F	SV	V
B	SV	F	V	SV
C	V	F	V	V
D	SV	F	SV	SV

Analysing semi-variable costs

A semi-variable cost is made up of a fixed and a variable element.

Semi-variable costs, such as electricity, contain both a fixed and a variable element. We know that the fixed element will remain the same and the variable element will vary directly with the activity level but first we will have to split the cost into these two components.

Note: Total cost = Total fixed cost + Total variable cost

(Total variable cost = Variable cost per unit × Number of units)

Past records of costs and their associated activity levels are usually used to carry out the analysis. Your *Fundamentals of Management Accounting* syllabus requires you to know how to use three common methods for separating the fixed and variable elements and predicting total costs:

(1) **The high–low method**

(2) **The scatter graph (line of best fit) method**

(3) **Regression analysis**

 All three methods are used on semi-variable costs by analysing past data. The aim is to split the cost between its fixed and variable elements in order to better understand how the total cost changes as activity levels change. Once these relationships are known, predictions can be made about costs going forward.

3 The high–low method

This method picks out the highest and lowest **activity levels** from the available data and investigates the change in cost which has occurred between them. The highest and lowest points are selected to try to use the greatest possible range of data.

From this, the variable cost per unit and the fixed cost element can be calculated.

 Illustration 2 – The high-low method

An entity has recorded the following data for a semi-variable cost:

Month	Activity level (units)	Cost incurred ($)
January	1,800	36,600
February	**2,450**	41,150
March	2,100	38,700
April	2,000	38,000
May	**1,750**	36,250
June	1,950	37,650

The highest activity level occurred in February and the lowest in May.

Always select the highest and lowest **activity level**.

Since the amount of fixed cost incurred in each month is constant, the extra cost resulting from the activity increase must be the variable cost.

	Activity level (units)	$
February	2,450	41,150
May	1,750	36,250
Increase	700	4,900

The extra variable cost for 700 units is $4,900. We can now calculate the variable cost per unit:

$$\text{Variable cost per unit} = \frac{\text{Change in cost}}{\text{Change in units}}$$

Variable cost per unit = $4,900/700 = **$7 per unit**

Substituting this back in to the data for February, we can determine the amount of fixed cost:

February	$
Total cost	41,150
Variable cost (2,450 units × $7)	17,150
Therefore, fixed cost per month	**$24,000**

Note: The calculation for fixed costs could also have used the data for May.

We now know that the semi-variable cost has a fixed monthly amount of $24,000 and a variable cost per unit of $7.

Advantages and disadvantages of high-low method

Advantages

- It is easy to understand and easy to use.

Disadvantages

- It relies on historical cost data and assumes this data can reliably predict future costs.

- It assumes that the activity level is the only factor affecting costs.

- It uses only two values (highest and lowest) to predict future costs and these results may be distorted because of random variations which may have occurred.

- It assumes a linear relationship between the two variables.

4 The scatter graph (line of best fit) method

With the high-low method only two pairs of data are used and a linear relationship is assumed. However these two extreme points may hide the true relationship between the variables.

The second method for analysing and predicting costs is the scatter graph (line of best fit) method. This method takes account of all available historical data. It is a graphical method which uses the equation of a straight line.

First we should consider the equation of a straight line.

The equation of a straight line is:

$$y = a + bx$$

Where   y = dependent variable

a = intercept on y axis

b = gradient

x = independent variable

When drawing a graph it is good practice to set the variables so that the x-axis always shows the independent variable, i.e. that variable which is not affected by the other variable. The y-axis should always represent the dependent variable, i.e. that variable which depends on the other. A change in the value of the independent variable will cause the dependent variable to change.

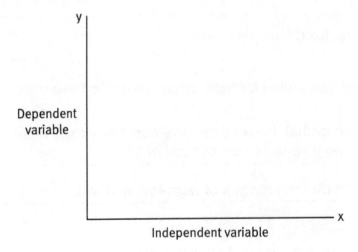

To use the scatter graph method:

(1) First a graph is drawn which plots all available pairs of data.

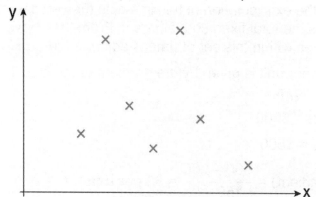

(2) The result is known as a scatter diagram, scatter graph or sometimes a scatter plot and is a visual way of determining if there might be a (linear) relationship between the variables x and y. If it looks as though there is such a relationship, we can then go on to calculate the correlation coefficient which measures the strength of the relationship between the two variables. This will be looked at later in the chapter.

(3) Where a clear relationship can be seen, a **line of best fit** can be drawn by eye. This is the line which, in the judgement of the user, appears to be the best representation of the gradient of the sets of points on the graph.

This is demonstrated below:

In this example, 12 pairs of data have been plotted on the graph. From these observations, a **line of best fit** has been drawn to represent the relationship between the two variables. This is shown as a solid line. The line has then been extrapolated out towards the y axis and intersects the y axis at $200.

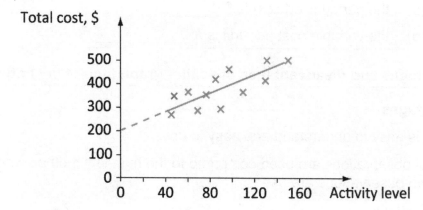

 The inaccuracies involved in drawing the line of best fit should be obvious to you. If you had been presented with this set of data, your own line of best fit might have been slightly different from the one shown.

(4) This line can be used to predict the outcome at different levels of activity.

In our example we are looking at the relationship between costs and activity levels.

The point where the extrapolation of this line cuts the vertical axis (the intercept) can be read off as the total fixed cost element. From the above diagram the fixed cost contained within this set of data is adjudged to be **$200**.

The variable cost per unit is given by the gradient of the line. The variable cost is calculated as follows:

Cost for zero units = $200

Cost for 150 units = $500

Variable cost (gradient) = $\dfrac{500 - 200}{150 - 0}$ = **$2 per unit**

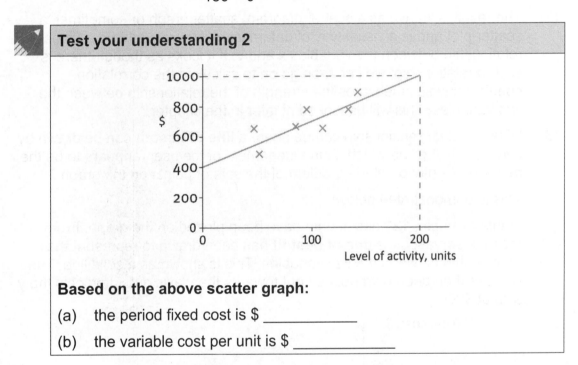

Test your understanding 2

Based on the above scatter graph:

(a) the period fixed cost is $ _____

(b) the variable cost per unit is $ _____

Advantages and disadvantages of scatter graph (line of best fit) method

Advantages

- It is easy to understand and easy to use.

- All observations are used compared to the high-low method where only two observations are used.

Disadvantages

- It relies on historical cost data and assumes this data can reliably predict future costs.

- It assumes that the activity level is the only factor affecting costs.

- The accuracy of the line of best fit is questionable. Faced with the same set of data, different lines may be drawn.

5   Regression analysis

The third method which can be used to analyse and predict costs is regression analysis.

The weakness of drawing a line of best fit 'by eye' should be obvious.

Regression analysis finds the line of best fit computationally rather than by estimating the line on a scatter diagram. It seeks to minimise the distance between each point and the regression line.

We know the equation of a straight line is $y = a + bx$. In regression analysis, a and b are calculated as:

$$b = \frac{n\Sigma xy - \Sigma x\Sigma y}{n\Sigma x^2 - (\Sigma x)^2}$$

where n = number of pairs of data

And $a = \bar{y} - b\bar{x}$

$\bar{x}$ is the arithmetic mean (or average) of x and is calculated as:

$$\bar{x} = \frac{\Sigma x}{n}$$

$\bar{y}$ is the arithmetic mean (or average) of y and is calculated as:

$$\bar{y} = \frac{\Sigma y}{n}$$

If we are looking at analysing costs in relation to activity, the equation of the line, **y = a + bx** would be made up of:

y = total cost

a = fixed cost

b = variable cost per unit

x = activity level

Suppose a cost has a cost equation of y = $5,000 + 10x, this can be shown graphically as follows:

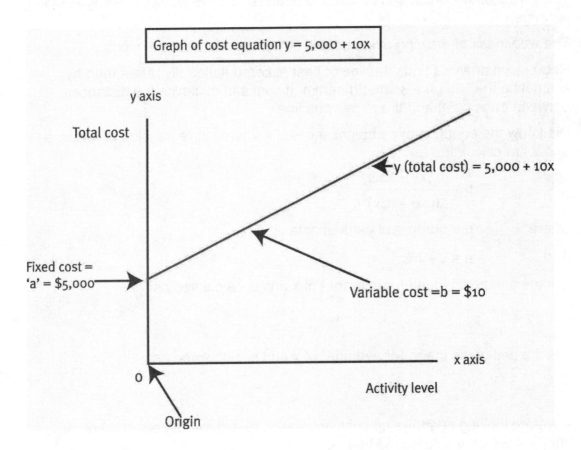

| Graph of cost equation y = 5,000 + 10x |

The gradient out of the line will be the variable cost per unit. This means that for every extra x (in this case units) there will be 10 extra y (in this case total costs).

The high-low method effectively uses the same approach but only considers the highest and lowest instances, which can lead to poor estimations. The scatter graph method uses all past observations but there is judgement used in drawing the line of best fit. Regression analysis is seen as a quicker and more accurate method. The method used in the *Fundamentals of Management Accounting* is **least squares regression**.

Illustration 3 – Regression analysis

An entity has the following data on its costs during the last year in each of its regions and the corresponding number of units sold during this time:

Region	Cost ($000)	Sales units (000)
A	236	11
B	234	12
C	298	18
D	250	15
E	246	13
F	202	10

Using least squares regression, calculate the fixed and variable cost elements and present your answer in the form y = a + bx.

Solution:

As we wish to forecast costs, we shall make this the dependent variable, y, and the number of sales units the independent variable, x.

The next step is to evaluate the parameters **a** (fixed cost) and **b** (variable cost per unit). It is best to use columns to calculate the figures required by the formulae:

x	y	x^2	xy
11	236	121	2,596
12	234	144	2,808
18	298	324	5,364
15	250	225	3,750
13	246	169	3,198
10	202	100	2,020
79	1,466	1,083	19,736

Thus

$$b = \frac{n\Sigma xy - (\Sigma x)(\Sigma y)}{n\Sigma x^2 - (\Sigma x)^2}$$

$$b = \frac{(6 \times 19{,}736) - (79 \times 1{,}466)}{6 \times 1{,}083 - 79^2} = \frac{2{,}602}{257} = 10.12$$

$$\bar{x} = \frac{79}{6} = 13.17$$

$$\bar{y} = \frac{1{,}466}{6} = 244.33$$

and so

$$a = 244.33 - (10.12 \times 13.17) = 111.05$$

Interpreting a and b

In this case, there is a fixed cost of $111,050 and a variable cost of $10.12 per unit of sales.

If this was drawn on a graph, the fixed cost (a) would be the point of intercept of the y axis and the variable cost per unit (b) would be the gradient of the line.

We can use this data to formulate the equation of the regression line in the form y= a + bx:

y = 111.05 + 10.12x

Comparing least squares regression and scatter graph

From Illustration 3 above, let's compare the lines created by these two methods.

In the top diagram below the scatter graph 'line of best fit' has been drawn 'by eye'. In the bottom diagram the line has been drawn, for the same data, using least squares regression.

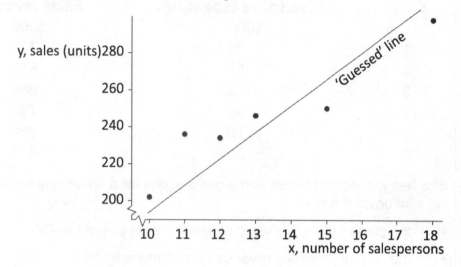

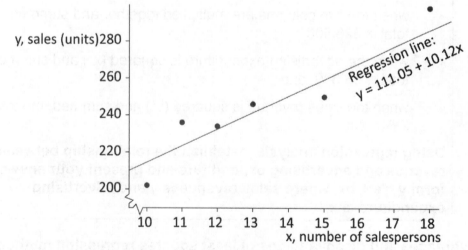

You should be able to see that the two lines are quite different and will give different results.

This demonstrates that the scatter graph gives an approximation but least squares regression gives a better, more accurate representation.

Note, for convenience, the scales on the axes do not start from zero.

Test your understanding 3

A small supermarket chain has 6 shops. Each shop advertises in their local newspapers and the marketing director is interested in the relationship between the amount that they spend on advertising and the sales revenue that they achieve. She has collated the following information for the 6 shops for the previous year:

Shop	Advertising expenditure $000	Sales revenue $000
1	80	730
2	60	610
3	120	880
4	90	750
5	70	650
6	30	430

She has further performed some calculations for a linear regression calculation as follows:

- the sum of the advertising expenditure (x) column is 450

- the sum of the sales revenue (y) column is 4,050

- when the two columns are multiplied together and summed (xy) the total is 326,500

- when the advertising expenditure is squared (x^2) and summed, the total is 38,300, and

- when the sales revenue is squared (y^2) and summed, the total is 2,849,300

Using regression analysis, establish the relationship between sales revenue and advertising expenditure and present your answer in the form y = a + bx, where sales revenue is y and advertising expenditure is x.

Advantages and disadvantages of least squares regression method

Advantages

- Provides a more accurate estimation of the relationship between two sets of data than other methods.

- Information required to complete the linear regression calculations should be readily available.

- Computer spreadsheet programmes often have a function that will calculate the relationship between two sets of data.

Disadvantages

- It relies on historical cost data and assumes that the historical behaviour of the data continues into the foreseeable future.

- Assumes a linear relationship between the variables.

- Only measures the relationship between two variables. In reality the dependent variable is affected by many independent variables.

- Only interpolated forecasts tend to be reliable. The equation should not be used for extrapolation.

6 Correlation

The reliability of the analysis we have carried out depends on the strength of the relationship between the two variables. In our line of best fit and least squares regression examples we have assumed a strong linear relationship but this may not always be the case. The strength of the relationship between variables is known as **correlation**.

Two variables are said to be **correlated** if they are related to one another, or, more precisely, if changes in the value of one tend to accompany changes in the other.

A scatter diagram can reveal a range of different types and degrees of correlation:

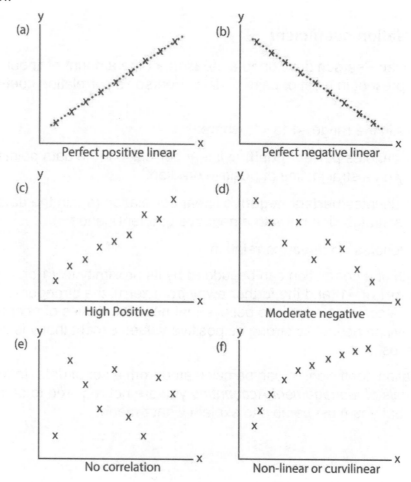

Graphs (a) and (b) show perfect correlation, i.e. there is a perfect linear relationship between the variables. In (a) the relationship is positive suggesting that as x increases, y also increases. In (b) the relationship is negative suggesting that as x increases, y falls.

Graph (c) suggests a strong but not perfect positive correlation as not all points on the graph would sit directly on the line of best fit.

Graph (d) shows a negative correlation. The relationship shown in (d) is less strong than that shown in (c) as the points would be further from the line of best fit.

Graph (e) shows no correlation suggesting that variable y has no relation to variable x. In this case it would be impossible to draw a meaningful line of best fit.

Graph (f) shows a clear positive correlation which is not linear. This is known as a curvilinear relationship.

The above shows that care must be taken in making predictions based on historical data. The methods we have used in this chapter have assumed perfect linear relationships. Where this is not the case, the predictions may not be able to be relied on.

It is therefore important to measure the strength of the correlation between the variables when using these methods. This can be done by calculating the correlation coefficient.

7 Correlation coefficient

The statistician Pearson developed a measure of the amount of linear correlation present in a set of pairs of data. Pearson's correlation coefficient, denoted as r.

r always lies in the range −1 to +1, where:

- r = +1 denotes **perfect positive** linear correlation (the data points lie exactly on a straight line of positive gradient)

- r = −1 denotes **perfect negative** linear correlation (again the data points lie on a straight line but with a negative gradient); and

- r = 0 denotes **no linear** correlation.

The strength of a correlation can be judged by its proximity to +1 or −1: the nearer it is to 1 or −1 (and the further away from zero), the stronger is the linear correlation. A common error is to believe that negative values of r cannot be strong. They can be just as strong as positive values except that y is decreasing as x increases.

The correlation coefficient, r, can be calculated from a set of data. In the *Fundamentals of Management Accounting* you are not required to carry out this calculation but you must be able to explain what r means.

Illustration 4 – Pearson's correlation coefficient

ABC is a retail company. It has been looking at the relationship between marketing expenditure and sales in the last six months for its three stores. The correlation coefficient for each store has been calculated:

Store	r
A	0.993
B	0.1
C	0.5

Comment on the strength of the relationship between marketing expenditure and sales in each of the three stores and recommend which store would benefit most from the marketing expenditure.

Solution:

Store A has a correlation coefficient of 0.993. This is close to 1 which suggests a strong positive relationship between marketing expenditure and sales.

Store B has a correlation coefficient of 0.1. This is close to zero suggesting little correlation between marketing expenditure and sales.

Store C has a correlation coefficient of 0.5. This suggests a moderate positive relationship between marketing expenditure and sales.

Store A shows the highest positive correlation which suggests that this store would benefit most from the marketing expenditure.

Test your understanding 4

A company owns six sales outlets in a certain city. For each it has calculated the correlation coefficient of sales of product L against the size of the outlet.

Outlet	r
A	0.5
B	0.95
C	−0.4
D	−0.1
E	−0.8
F	0.09

> **Match each outlet with the best description of the correlation coefficient calculated.**
>
> - Strong positive
> - Strong negative
> - Moderate positive
> - Moderate negative
> - Weak positive
> - Weak negative

8 The coefficient of determination

We have already seen how Pearson's correlation coefficient allows us to discuss the strength of the relationship between two sets of figures. However, the interpretation of the figure is made slightly easier if we square the correlation coefficient, r, to give the coefficient of determination, r^2.

The coefficient of determination, r^2, gives the proportion of changes in y that can be explained by changes in x, assuming a **linear** relationship between x and y.

For example:

If a correlation coefficient r = +0.7, then r^2 = 0.49 and we could state that 49% of the observed changes in y can be explained by the changes in x but that 51 % of the changes must be due to other factors.

Test your understanding 5

If the correlation coefficient is 0.8, what is the coefficient of determination?

A   0.64

B   89

C   20.8

D   0.4

9 Predicting costs

We have now looked in detail at the three methods we can use to analyse semi variable costs between the fixed and variable elements. Once the semi-variable cost has been split between fixed and variable elements, this information can be used to forecast the total cost for another activity level within the relevant range.

Extrapolating outside the relevant range

In many examples you are told that the cost structures will remain unaltered despite the increase in activity. In practice, you may need to do an extrapolation **outside** the range for which you have available data.

The possibility of changes occurring in cost behaviour patterns means that it is unreliable to predict costs for activity levels which are outside the relevant range. For example, our records might show the cost incurred at various activity levels between 100 units and 5,000 units. We should therefore try to avoid using this information as the basis for forecasting the level of cost which would be incurred at an activity of, say, 6,000 units, which is outside the relevant range.

Illustration 5 – Predicting future costs

Look back at the example from Illustration 1:

	100 units	200 units
Material	$500	$1,000
Labour	$1,000	$2,000
Rent	$2,000	$2,000
Electricity	$700	$900

We worked out that material and labour were variable costs, rent was a fixed cost and electricity was a semi-variable cost.

We can now use this information to predict the costs for a different level of activity.

Estimate the total cost of producing 180 units.

Solution:

Material is a variable cost of $5 per unit. So the cost for 180 units will be 180 × $5 = **$900**.

Labour is a variable cost of $10 per unit. So the cost for 180 units will be 180 × $10 = **$1,800**.

Rent is a fixed cost of **$2,000**. This will be the same for 180 units.

Electricity is a semi-variable cost so to predict the cost for another level of activity we first have to split it into its fixed and variable components using the high–low method.

$$\text{Variable cost per unit} = \frac{\text{Change in costs}}{\text{Change in units}}$$

$$\text{Variable cost} = \frac{900 - 700}{200 - 100} = \textbf{\$2.00 per unit}$$

Fixed cost = Total cost – Variable cost

Using 100 units: Fixed cost = $700 – (100 × 2) = **$500**

Total cost = Total fixed cost + (Variable cost per unit × Number of units)

So the estimated cost of producing 180 units = $500 + ($2 × 180) = **$860**.

The predicted total cost of producing 180 units will be:

	$
Material	900
Labour	1,800
Rent	2,000
Electricity	860
	___
Total	**5,560**

Test your understanding 6

The variable production cost per unit of product B is $2 and the fixed production overhead for a period is $4,000.

Calculate the total cost of producing 3,000 units of B in a period.

Test your understanding 7

A company has the following data on its profits and advertising expenditure over the last 6 years:

Profits $m	Advertising expenditure $m
11.3	0.52
12.1	0.61
14.1	0.63
14.6	0.70
15.1	0.70
15.2	0.75

Using regression analysis, forecast the profits for next year if an advertising budget of $800,000 is allocated.

10 Problems with using historical data to predict the future

In each of the methods considered in this chapter we have used historical data to predict the future.

The main problem which arises in the determination of cost behaviour is that the estimates are usually based on data collected in the past. **Events in the past may not be representative of the future** and managers should be aware of this if they are using the information for planning and decision making purposes.

11   Chapter summary

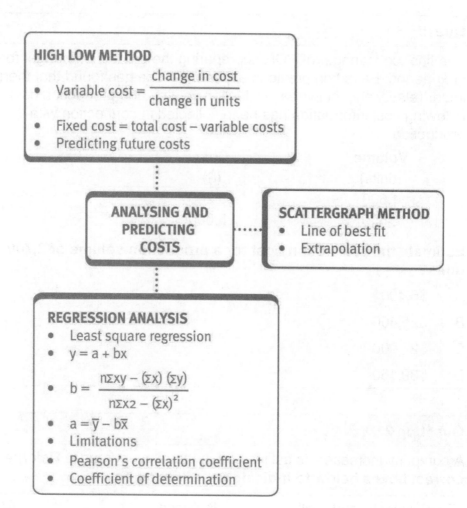

HIGH LOW METHOD

- Variable cost = $\dfrac{\text{change in cost}}{\text{change in units}}$

- Fixed cost = total cost − variable costs
- Predicting future costs

ANALYSING AND PREDICTING COSTS

SCATTERGRAPH METHOD
- Line of best fit
- Extrapolation

REGRESSION ANALYSIS
- Least square regression
- $y = a + bx$
- $b = \dfrac{n\Sigma xy - (\Sigma x)(\Sigma y)}{n\Sigma x2 - (\Sigma x)^2}$
- $a = \bar{y} - b\bar{x}$
- Limitations
- Pearson's correlation coefficient
- Coefficient of determination

12 End of chapter questions

Question 1

The finance manager of PQR is preparing the production budget for the next period. Based on previous experience, she has found that there is a linear relationship between production volume and production cost. The following cost information has been collected in connection with production:

Volume (units)	Cost ($)
1,600	23,200
2,500	25,000

Estimate the production cost for a production volume of 2,700 units?

A $5,400

B $25,400

C $27,000

D $39,150

Question 2

A company increases its activity within the relevant range. **Tick the correct boxes below to indicate the effect on costs.**

Total variable costs will:	increase	❏
	decrease	❏
	remain the same	❏
Total fixed cost will:	increase	❏
	decrease	❏
	remain the same	❏
The variable cost per unit will:	increase	❏
	decrease	❏
	remain the same	❏
The fixed cost per unit will:	increase	❏
	decrease	❏
	remain the same	❏

Question 3

The following data relate to two activity levels of an out-patient department in a hospital:

Number of consultations per period	4,500	5,750
Overheads	$269,750	$289,125

Fixed overheads are not affected by the number of consultations per period.

Required:

The variable overhead cost per consultation (to 2 dp) would be:

$ _____

Question 4

The following data relate to the overhead costs of a commercial laundry for the latest two periods.

Overhead cost $	Number of items laundered
5,140	2,950
5,034	2,420

A formula that could be used to estimate the overhead costs for a forthcoming period is:

Overhead cost = $ __a__ + ($ __b__ × number of items laundered)

Determine the value of a and b.

Question 5

ABC is trying to understand the relationship between sales and advertising expenditure. The management accountant has carried out some analysis and has found that the coefficient of determination is 0.49.

Which of the following is correct?

A   For every $0.49 spent on advertising, $1.00 of sales will be generated.

B   For every $1.00 spent on advertising, $0.49 of sales will be generated.

C   49% of the variation in sales can be explained by the corresponding variation in advertising.

D   49% of the variation in advertising can be explained by the corresponding variation in sales.

Question 6

The following data relate to the cost of contract cleaners at two activity levels:

Square metres cleaned	12,750	15,100
Cost	$73,950	$83,585

Using the high-low method, what is the estimated cost if 16,200 square metres are to be cleaned?

A $88,095

B $89,674

C $93,960

D $98,095

Question 7

Mr G has just opened 2 new stores in his local area. He knows if no money is spent on advertising then sales will be $300,000, but for every $1 spent on advertising sales revenue increases by $5. The predicted advertising expenditure is expected to be $150,000 for one store and $50,000 for the other.

Calculate the predicted total sales revenue for both stores.

$ _____

Question 8

XYZ is investigating its current cost structure. An analysis of production levels and costs over the first six months of the year has revealed the following:

Month	Production level (units) (000s)	Production cost ($000)
January	9.0	240
February	10.0	278
March	9.7	256
April	10.5	258
May	11.0	290
June	11.5	300

Further analysis has produced the following data:

$\sum x = 61.7$; $\sum y = 1,622$; $\sum xy = 16,772$; $\sum x^2 = 638.6$

Using regression analysis, which of the following statements are correct? Select all that apply.

A   The variable cost per unit is $22.44

B   The variable cost per unit is $39.57

C   The monthly fixed cost is $22.44k

D   The monthly fixed cost is $39.57k

E   If 12,000 units were produced, the estimated total cost would be $308,850

F   If 12,000 units were produced, the estimated total cost would be $474,862

Question 9

Which THREE of the following will adversely affect the reliability of a regression forecast?

A   Small sample

B   Low correlation

C   Extrapolation

D   Negative correlation

E   Large sample

Question 10

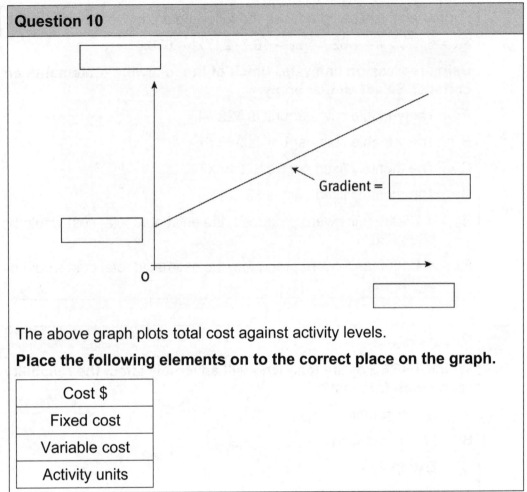

The above graph plots total cost against activity levels.

Place the following elements on to the correct place on the graph.

Cost $
Fixed cost
Variable cost
Activity units

Test your understanding and end of chapter answers

Test your understanding 1

B

X is clearly a fixed cost as it does not change over the different activity levels. For W, Y and Z it is not so clear, so calculate the cost per unit at each activity level:

Cost type	Cost per unit for 100 units	Cost per unit for 140 units
	$	$
W	80.00 (8,000/100)	75.43 (10,560/140)
Y	65.00 (6,500/100)	65.00 (9,100/140)
Z	67.00 (6,700/100)	61.29 (8,580/140)

The unit cost of Y is constant which suggests that Y is a variable cost.

The total cost and the cost per unit of W and Z vary at the different levels which suggests that W and Z are semi-variable costs.

Test your understanding 2

The period fixed cost is **$400**.

The variable cost per unit is **$3**.

$$\textbf{Variable cost per unit} = \frac{\textbf{Change in costs}}{\textbf{Change in units}}$$

$$\text{Variable cost} = \frac{1{,}000 - 400}{200 - 0} = \textbf{\$3 per unit}$$

Fixed cost = the intercept on the vertical axis = **$400**

Test your understanding 3

$$b = \frac{n\Sigma xy - \Sigma x\Sigma y}{n\Sigma x^2 - (\Sigma x)^2}$$

where   n = number of pairs of data

and $a = \bar{y} - b\bar{x}$

$$b = \frac{(6 \times 326{,}500) - (450 \times 4{,}050)}{(6 \times 38{,}300) - 202{,}500}$$

$$= \frac{136{,}500}{27{,}300} = \$5$$

$$a = \frac{4{,}050}{6} - 5 \times \frac{450}{6}$$

$$= 675 - 375$$

$$= \$300$$

The relationship between sales revenue (y) and advertising expenditure (x) is:

y = 300 + 5x

Test your understanding 4

Outlet	r	
A	0.5	Moderate positive
B	0.95	Strong positive
C	−0.4	Moderate negative
D	−0.1	Weak negative
E	−0.8	Strong negative
F	0.09	Weak positive

Test your understanding 5

A

The coefficient of determination is given by squaring the correlation coefficient.

Therefore $r^2 = 0.8^2 = 0.64$. This suggests that 64% of the changes in y can be explained by the changes in x.

Test your understanding 6

Total cost for 3,000 units = $4,000 + ($2 × 3,000) = **$10,000**.

Test your understanding 7

As we wish to forecast profits, we shall make this the dependent variable, y, and advertising expenditure the independent variable, x.

The next step is to evaluate the parameters a and b:

x	y	x^2	xy
0.52	11.3	0.2704	5.876
0.61	12.1	0.3721	7.381
0.63	14.1	0.3969	8.883
0.70	14.6	0.4900	10.220
0.70	15.1	0.4900	10.570
0.75	15.2	0.5625	11.400
———	———	———	———
3.91	82.4	2.5819	54.330

Thus

$$b = \frac{(6 \times 54.33) - (3.91 \times 82.4)}{(6 \times 2.5819) - 3.91^2} = \frac{3.796}{0.2033} = 18.67$$

$$\bar{x} = \frac{3.91}{6} = 0.652$$

$$\bar{y} = \frac{82.4}{6} = 13.73$$

and so:

a = 13.73 – (18.67 × 0.652) = 1.56

The least-squares regression line relating profits to advertising expenditure therefore has equation

$y = 1.56 + 18.67x$

Hence each extra million dollars of advertising generates an extra $18.67 million profits. Also, profits would be $1.56 million without any advertising.

If advertising expenditure is to be $800,000 (x = 0.8), then:

y = 1.56 + (18.67 × 0.8) = 16.496

Rounding this value off to a sensible level of apparent accuracy, we are forecasting profits of $16.5 million next year, if advertising expenditure is $800,000.

Question 1

B

Units	$
2,500	25,000
1,600	23,200
900	1,800

Variable cost per unit = $\dfrac{\$1,800}{900}$ = $2

Substitute in high activity:

	$
Total cost	25,000
Variable cost = 2,500 units × $2	5,000
Therefore fixed cost	20,000

Forecast for 2,700 units:

	$
Fixed cost	20,000
Variable cost 2,700 × $2	5,400
Total cost	**25,400**

Question 2

Total variable costs will **increase**

Total fixed cost will **remain the same**

The variable cost per unit will **remain the same**

The fixed cost per unit will **decrease**

Question 3

The variable cost per consultation would be **$15.50**.

With the same amount of fixed overheads at both activity levels, the change in overheads must be due to extra variable cost.

	Overheads $	Consultations
High	289,125	5,750
Low	269,750	4,500
Change	19,375	1,250

Variable overhead cost per consultation = $\dfrac{\$19{,}375}{1{,}250}$ = **$15.50**

Question 4

a (fixed cost) = **$4,550**

b (variable cost per unit) = **$0.20**

Variable cost per unit = $\dfrac{\text{Change in costs}}{\text{Change in units}}$

Variable cost = $\dfrac{5{,}140 - 5{,}034}{2{,}950 - 2{,}420}$ = **$0.20 per unit**

Fixed cost = Total cost – Variable cost

Using 2,950 units: Fixed cost = $5,140 – (2,950 × 0.20) = **$4,550**

A formula that could be used to estimate the overhead costs for a forthcoming period is:

Overhead cost = $4,550 + ($0.20 × Number of items laundered)

Question 5

C

The coefficient of determination gives the percentage of the variation in y (in this case, sales) which can be explained by the regression relationship with x (in this case, advertising).

Question 6

A

$$\text{Variable cost per square metre} = \frac{\text{Change in cost}}{\text{Change in square metres}}$$

Variable cost per square metre = ($83,585 – $73,950) ÷ (15,100 – 12,750) = **$4.10 per square metre**

Substituting this back in to the data for 12,750 square metres we can determine the amount of fixed cost:

Fixed cost = $73,950 – ($4.10 × 12,750) = **$21,675**

	$
So for 16,200 square metres:	
Fixed cost	21,675
Variable cost (16,200 units × $4.10)	66,420
Total cost	**$88,095**

Question 7

The predicted total sales revenue for both stores is **$1,600,000**

The equation of a straight line is y = a + bx. The information provided shows that the sales revenue is dependent on the level of advertising. The sales revenue is y and the money spent on advertising is x.

So the predicted total sales for the two stores is:

		$
Store 1	300,000 + (5 × 150,000)	1,050,000
Store 2	300,000 + (5 × 50,000)	550,000
Total		1,600,000

Question 8

A, D and E

$$b = \frac{n\Sigma xy - \Sigma x \Sigma y}{n\Sigma x^2 - (\Sigma x)^2}$$

where $\quad$ n = number of pairs of data

and $\quad$ $a = \bar{y} - b\bar{x}$

Variable cost (b) $= \dfrac{(6 \times 16{,}772) - (61.7 \times 1{,}622)}{(6 \times 638.6) - 61.7^2}$

$= \dfrac{554.6}{24.71} = \$22.44$

Fixed cost (a) $= \dfrac{1{,}622}{6} - (22.44 \times \dfrac{61.7}{6})$

$= 270.33 - 230.76$

$= \$39.57$

The estimated cost of 12,000 units will be given by the linear cost equation:

$y = a + bx$

$y = \$39.57 + \$22.44x$

$y = 39.57 + (22.44 \times 12) = 308.85 = \$308{,}850$

Question 9

A, B and C

It is the strength of the correlation but not its sign that influences the reliability of regression forecasts. Small samples, low correlation and extrapolation all tend to give unreliable forecasts. Correlation can be negative but still very strong so (D) is incorrect. The larger the sample, the better the forecast, so (E) is incorrect.

Question 10

The completed diagram is:

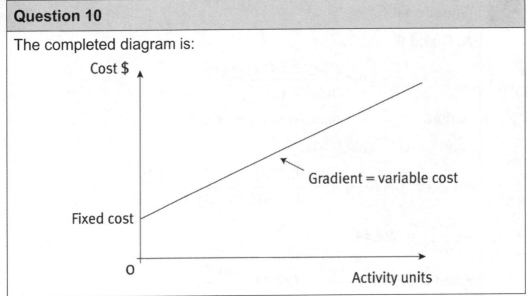

Overhead analysis

Chapter learning objectives

After completing this chapter, you should be able to

- prepare overhead cost statements
- calculate the full cost of products, services and activities
- calculate the marginal cost of products, services and activities.

1 Session content diagram

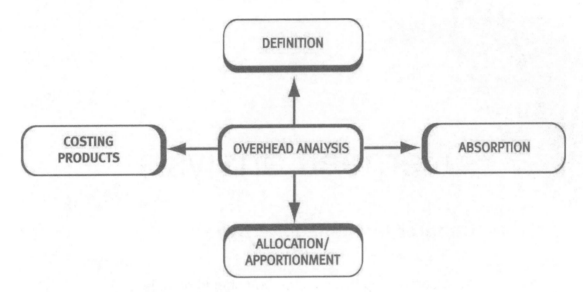

2 Introduction to overheads

Overheads (also referred to as **indirect costs**) were introduced in the cost identification and classification chapter. Overheads comprise indirect material, indirect labour and indirect expenses.

 An **overhead cost** is defined in the *CIMA Terminology* as 'expenditure on labour, materials or services that cannot be economically identified with a specific saleable cost unit'.

In the cost identification and classification chapter we learned that direct costs can be identified clearly with a cost unit, but that indirect costs cannot. This causes difficulty when we try to ascertain the total cost of a cost unit.

Remember the main objective is to find the **total cost per unit of product produced or service provided**.

Total cost per unit = Direct costs (prime costs) + Overheads

It is easy to determine the direct costs per unit, but how do we find the cost per unit including overheads/indirect costs? We cannot ignore these costs or we would not get the full cost of the item but we know that an overhead cost is a cost that cannot be economically identified with a cost unit therefore these costs need to be 'shared out' among the cost units as fairly and as accurately as possible.

3 Types of overheads

Firstly we must be familiar with the different types of overheads.

Overhead costs may be classified according to the function within the organisation responsible for incurring the cost. Examples of overhead cost classifications include:

- **production overhead**

- **selling and distribution overhead**

- **administration overhead.**

It is usually possible to classify the majority of overhead costs in this way, but some overhead costs relate to the organisation generally and may be referred to as **general overhead**.

Production overhead

In this chapter we shall focus mainly on production overhead. That is the indirect costs incurred by the production function. Organisations are often organised by function. If we consider a very straightforward manufacturing organisation which manufactures one product, it may have the following functions:

- **Production**. Concerned with the physical production of the product.

- **Sales**. Concerned with the selling and distribution of the finished product.

- **Administration**. Concerned with the general administration of the organisation for example dealing with customer accounts or orders.

- **Finance**. Concerned with all aspects of finance within the organisation.

These functions may not necessarily be located in the same geographical area.

The production function is usually divided into a number of departments or cost centres. Some of these cost centres are directly involved with the production process. These are called **production cost centres** and might include, for example, the cutting department and the finishing department.

Other cost centres which are part of the production department are not directly involved with the production process but provide support services for the production cost centres. These are called **service cost centres**, and examples include the maintenance department and material stores.

In this chapter you will learn how the 'sharing out' of production overheads is accomplished, using a costing method known as **absorption costing**.

4 Absorption costing

Focusing on production overheads, we can look at how the overheads can be 'shared out' to the individual cost units. A three step process is used:

- **Step 1: Allocation and apportionment** of production overhead to production and service cost centres

- **Step 2: Reapportionment** of overhead collected in service cost centres (from step 1) to production cost centres

- **Step 3: Absorption** of overheads from production cost centres into cost units using a predetermined overhead absorption rate (OAR)

Note: The terminology is important, i.e. **allocation, apportionment** and **absorption**

 You will need a thorough understanding of the contents of this chapter for your studies of the *Fundamentals of Management Accounting* syllabus and for subjects at later stages in the CIMA examinations.

5 Overhead allocation and apportionment

The first stage in the analysis of production overheads is the selection of appropriate cost centres. It was mentioned earlier in the chapter that the production function is usually broken down into cost centres. Some of these will be production cost centres and some will be service cost centres.

Having selected suitable cost centres, the next stage in the analysis is to determine the overhead cost for each cost centre. This is achieved through the process of allocation and apportionment.

Cost allocation is possible if we can identify a cost as specifically attributable to a particular cost centre. For example, the salary of the manager of the packing department can be allocated to the packing department cost centre. It is not necessary to share this salary cost over several different cost centres.

Cost apportionment is necessary when it is not possible to allocate a cost straight to a specific cost centre. In this case, the cost is shared out over two or more cost centres according to the estimated benefit received by each cost centre. As far as possible the basis of apportionment is selected to reflect this benefit received. For example, the cost of rent and rates might be apportioned according to the floor space occupied by each cost centre.

Illustration 1 – Overhead allocation and apportionment

The information given below relates to a four-week accounting period of WHW. WHW has three production cost centres (Machining, Assembly and Finishing) and one service cost centre (Stores).

	Machining	Assembly	Finishing	Stores
Area occupied (square metres)	24,000	36,000	16,000	4,000
Plant and equipment at cost ($000)	1,400	200	60	10
Number of employees	400	800	200	20
Direct labour hours	16,000	32,000	4,000	
Direct wages ($)	32,600	67,200	7,200	
Machine hours	32,000	4,000	200	
Store requisitions	310	1,112	100	
Allocated costs	$	$	$	$
Indirect wages	9,000	15,000	4,000	6,000
Indirect materials	394	1,400	600	
Maintenance	1,400	600	100	
Power	1,600	400	200	

Other costs (in total)	$
Rent	2,000
Business rates	600
Buildings insurance	200
Lighting and heating	400
Depreciation on plant and equipment	16,700
Wage-related costs	28,200
Administration and HR	7,100
Insurance on plant and equipment	1,670
Factory cleaning	800
	———
	57,670
	———

The data above distinguish between those costs which can be allocated to a cost centre and those which cannot. The first step is to construct an **overhead analysis sheet** having separate columns for each cost centre, together with a column for the total costs, a description of the cost item and the basis upon which the cost has been apportioned between the cost centres if applicable.

An explanation of the apportionment method is given beneath the analysis.

Item	Basis of apportionment	Machining $	Assembly $	Finishing $	Stores $	Total $
Indirect wages	Allocation	9,000	15,000	4,000	6,000	34,000
Indirect materials	Allocation	394	1,400	600	–	2,394
Maintenance	Allocation	1,400	600	100	–	2,100
Power	Allocation	1,600	400	200	–	2,200
Rent	Area occupied	600	900	400	100	2,000
Business rates	Area occupied	180	270	120	30	600
Buildings insurance	Area occupied	60	90	40	10	200
Lighting/heating	Area occupied	120	180	80	20	400
Depreciation on plant/equipment	Plant/equipment at cost	*14,000	2,000	600	100	16,700
Wage-related costs	Total wages	8,320	16,440	2,240	1,200	28,200
Administration and HR	No. of employees	2,000	4,000	1,000	100	7,100
Insurance on plant/equipment	Plant/equipment at cost	1,400	200	60	10	1,670
Factory cleaning	Area occupied	240	360	160	40	800
		39,314	41,840	9,600	7,610	98,364

You should note that the direct wages costs are not included in the analysis because they are not overhead costs. Also notice that the apportionment of wage-related costs is based on total wages. That is, the sum of the direct and indirect wages for each cost centre.

The apportioned costs are all calculated using the general formula:

$$\frac{\text{Total overhead cost}}{\text{Total value of apportionment base}} \times \text{Value of apportionment base of the cost centre being calculated}$$

* For example, in the case of depreciation on plant and equipment apportioned to the Machining cost centre. The basis is plant and equipment at cost. The total plant and equipment at cost = ($1,400,000 + $200,000 + $60,000 + $10,000) = $1,670,000, so:

$$\frac{\$16,700}{\$1,670,000} \times \$1,400,000 = \mathbf{\$14,000}$$

The result of the initial allocation and apportionment is that the organisation's production overhead costs have been identified with cost centres associated with production. However, the service cost centre (Stores) is not directly involved in the manufacture of the saleable cost units. Nevertheless, it is part of the production function and the total cost of operating the stores should be attributed to the saleable cost units.

Reapportionment

Now we have the overhead split between the four cost centres. We now need to share or reapportion the cost of the service cost centre to the production cost centres, as follows:

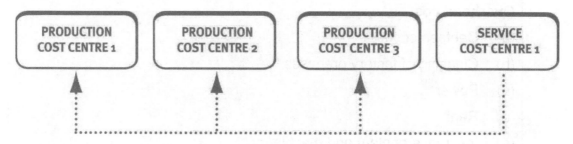

We will then be left with just the costs in the three production cost centres.

Again the problem is what basis to use to reapportion the costs. This should be done to reflect the benefit derived from the service area by the production areas, but this will be subjective.

Illustration 2 – Overhead reapportionment

If we now return to our WHW example, the next step is to reapportion the cost of Stores to the production cost centres.

Item	Basis of apportionment	Machining $	Assembly $	Finishing $	Stores $	Total $
B/fwd	(from Illustration 1)	39,314	41,840	9,600	7,610	98,364
Stores	Store requisitions	1,550	5,560	500	(7,610)	–
		40,864	47,400	10,100	–	98,364

We have now achieved the objective of allocating and apportioning all of the production overhead costs to the departments directly involved in the manufacture of the saleable cost units.

Note that the total overhead does not change.

Test your understanding 1

Match the overhead costs to the most appropriate basis of cost apportionment. An apportionment basis may be selected more than once.

Overhead cost

(a) Canteen costs

(b) Cleaning of factory premises

(c) Power

(d) Rent

(e) Insurance of plant and machinery

Apportionment bases

- Floor area
- Plant and equipment at cost
- Number of employees
- Machine running hours
- Direct labour hours

Test your understanding 2

Maintenance costs are to be apportioned to production cost centres on the basis of the number of maintenance hours worked in each cost centre.

	Machining	Assembly	Finishing
Maintenance hours worked	1,000	700	300

Complete the following extract from the overhead analysis sheet.

Overhead cost item	Total	Machining	Assembly	Finishing
	$	$	$	$
Maintenance cost	38,000			

6 Absorption of overheads into saleable cost units

The last stage in the analysis of overheads is their **absorption** into the cost units produced in the production cost centres. This is sometimes referred to as **overhead recovery**.

This can be shown as follows:

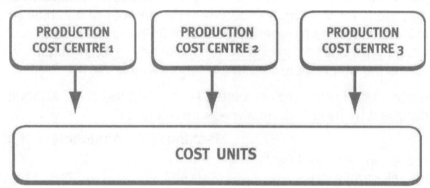

To begin with, we need to measure the level of production achieved. There are many measures which may be used, but the most common are:

- physical units produced

- labour hours worked

- machine hours operated.

It is quite likely that different production departments will measure their production in different ways. The objective is to use a measure which reflects the nature of the work involved. The physical unit measure is in theory the simplest but it is only valid if all of the items produced require the same amount of resources.

The total overhead costs of each production cost centre are then divided by the quantity of production achieved to calculate the amount of overhead cost to be attributed to each unit.

This is known as the overhead absorption rate (OAR):

> **Overhead absorption rate (OAR) =** $\dfrac{\textbf{Production cost centre overhead}}{\substack{\textbf{Quantity of absorption base} \\ \textbf{(units/labour hours/machine hours)}}}$

Illustration 3 – Overhead absorption

Continuing with our WHW example:

The output of the Machining department is to be measured using the number of machine hours, while the output of the Assembly and Finishing departments is to be measured using the number of direct labour hours. The reasons for this can be seen from the number of machine and direct labour hours for each department shown in the original data for the example. The Machining department is clearly machine-intensive, whereas the other departments are labour-intensive.

The absorption rates are calculated by dividing the costs attributed to the department by its appropriate measure of output.

	Machining	Assembly	Finishing
Production overhead costs (from Illustration 2)	$40,864	$47,400	$10,100
Number of:			
machine hours	32,000		
direct labour hours		32,000	4,000
Absorption rates:			
per machine hour	$1.277		
per labour hour		$1.481	$2.525

The overhead absorption rates (OARs) have been calculated as follows:

Machining (using machine hours):

OAR = $40,864/32,000 = **$1.277 per machine hour**

Assembly (using labour hours):

OAR = $47,400/32,000 = **$1.481 per labour hour**

Finishing (using labour hours):

OAR = $10,100/4,000 = **$2.525 per labour hour**

Applying the overhead absorption rate

When using an absorption method based either on direct labour hours or on machine hours the cost attributed to each unit is obtained by multiplying the time taken per unit by the absorption rate per hour.

For example, if a particular cost unit took three machine hours in the Machining department, and five direct labour hours in each of the Assembly and Finishing departments, the overhead cost absorbed by the cost unit would be as follows:

	$
Machining: 3 hours × $1.277	3.83
Assembly: 5 hours × $1.481	7.41
Finishing: 5 hours × $2.525	12.63
	─────
Overhead absorbed by cost unit	23.87

Overhead absorption methods

In addition to the three bases of absorption mentioned above (physical units produced, labour hours worked, machine hours operated), a percentage rate based on any of the following may be used:

- direct material cost

- direct labour cost

- prime cost.

In our WHW example, if a direct labour cost percentage is used the absorption rates would be as follows:

	Machining	Assembly	Finishing
	$	$	$
Production overhead costs	40,864	47,400	10,100
Direct wages cost	32,600	67,200	7,200
Direct labour cost percentage	125%	71%	140%

If our cost unit had a labour cost of $12 in the Machining department, and $20 in each of the Assembly and Finishing departments, the overhead cost absorbed by the cost unit using this method would be as follows:

	$
Machining: 125% × $12	15.00
Assembly: 71% × $20	14.20
Finishing: 140% × $20	28.00
Overhead absorbed by cost unit	57.20

The direct material cost and the prime cost methods work in a similar way.

The WHW example demonstrates how the calculated total production cost of a particular cost unit can be dramatically different, depending on the overhead absorption method selected. In Illustration 3 the cost unit absorbed $23.87 whereas in this example it has absorbed $57.20. The product manufactured has not changed, the total overhead has not changed, we have simply changed the basis of overhead absorption. It is important that the selected method results in the most **realistic** charge for overheads.

Do not make the common mistake of thinking that the best absorption method in this example would be the one which results in the lowest overhead charge to the cost unit. Remember that the same total cost centre overhead is being shared out over the cost units produced, whichever absorption method is selected. If one cost unit is given a lower charge for overhead, then other cost units will be charged with a higher amount so that the total overhead is absorbed overall.

A major factor in selecting the absorption rate to be used is a consideration of the practical applicability of the rate. This will depend on the ease of collecting the data required to use the selected rate.

It is generally accepted that a time-based method should be used wherever possible, that is, the machine hour rate or the labour hour rate. This is because many overhead costs increase with time, for example indirect wages, rent and rates. Therefore, it makes sense to attempt to absorb overheads according to how long a cost unit takes to produce. The longer it takes, the more overhead will have been incurred in the cost centre during that time.

In addition to these general considerations, each absorption method has its own advantages and disadvantages:

Rate per unit. This is the easiest method to apply but it is only suitable when all cost units produced in the period are identical. Since this does not often happen in practice this method is rarely used.

Direct labour hour rate. This is a favoured method because it is time-based. It is most appropriate in labour-intensive cost centres, which are becoming rarer nowadays and so the method is less widely used than it has been in the past.

Machine hour rate. This is also a favoured method because it is time-based. It is most appropriate in cost centres where machine activity predominates and is therefore more widely used than the direct labour hour rate. As well as absorbing the time-based overheads mentioned earlier, it is more appropriate for absorbing the overheads relating to machine activity, such as power, maintenance, repairs and depreciation.

Direct wages cost percentage. This method may be acceptable because it is to some extent time-based. A higher direct wages cost may indicate a longer time taken and therefore a greater incidence of overheads during this time. However, the method will not produce equitable overhead charges if different wage rates are paid to individual employees in the cost centre. If this is the case, then there may not be a direct relationship between the wages paid and the time taken to complete a cost unit.

Direct materials cost percentage. This is not a very logical method because there is no reason why a higher material cost should lead to a cost unit apparently incurring more production overhead cost. The method can be used if it would be too costly and inconvenient to use a more suitable method.

Prime cost percentage. This method is not recommended because it combines the direct wages cost percentage and direct materials cost percentage methods and therefore suffers from the combined disadvantages of both.

7 Determining the cost of products

Now we have looked at how to absorb overhead costs into individual products, we can look at how to determine the full cost of a product.

Illustration 4 – Determining the cost of products

RST manufactures two products, the AC12 and the B52. Both products pass through two processes during production, Assembly and Finishing.

The following data are available for one unit of each of the products:

	AC12	B52
Selling price	$80	$100
Direct material	$10	$12
Direct expenses	$5	$3
Direct labour hours:		
Assembly	1	0.5
Finishing	2	3
Machine hours:		
Assembly	3	4
Finishing	1	2

Direct labour is paid at $10 per hour.

Total production overheads are $10,500 for Assembly and $15,000 for Finishing. Further details of the two production departments are given:

	Assembly	Finishing
Machine hours	5,000	5,000
Direct labour hours	2,000	6,000

Each unit of AC12 and B52 also absorbs a selling and distribution overhead of 10% of selling price.

Calculate the following for AC12 and B52:

(a) The prime cost per unit

(b) The total production overhead cost per unit

(c) The total production cost per unit

(d) The full cost per unit

(e) The profit per unit

Solution:

(a)   The prime cost per unit is **$45.00 for AC12** and **$50.00 for B52**

(b)   The total production overhead cost per unit is **$11.30 for AC12** and **$15.90 for B52**

(c)   The total production cost per unit is **$56.30 for AC12** and **$65.90 for B52**

(d)   The full cost per unit is **$64.30 for AC12** and **$75.90 for B52**

(e)   The profit per unit is **$15.70 for AC12** and **$24.10 for B52**

Workings:

	AC12		B52
	$		$
Direct material	10.00		12.00
Direct labour (3 × $10)	30.00	(3.5 × $10)	35.00
Direct expenses	5.00		3.00
PRIME COST	45.00		50.00
Production overhead (W1)	11.30		15.90
TOTAL PRODUCTION COST	56.30		65.90
Selling and distribution overhead (10% × 80)	8.00	(10% × 100)	10.00
FULL COST	64.30		75.90
Selling price	80.00		100.00
PROFIT	15.70		24.10

(W1) **Production overhead**

Overhead absorption rate for Assembly = $10,500 ÷ 5,000 = $2.10 per machine hour

Overhead absorption rate for Finishing = $15,000 ÷ 6,000 = $2.50 per labour hour

	AC12		B52
	$		$
Assembly ($2.10 × 3)	6.30	($2.10 × 4)	8.40
Finishing ($2.50 × 2)	5.00	($2.50 × 3)	7.50
Production overhead	11.30		15.90

Test your understanding 3

A manufacturing company produces a range of products.

Details for one unit of product M15 are as follows:

	M15
Prime cost	$25
Direct labour hours	4
Machine hours	3.5

The following budgeted information is available:

Production overheads	$184,875
Machine hours	15,700
Labour hours	25,500

Production overheads are absorbed on the basis of labour hours.

Calculate the total production cost per unit of product M15.

$ _____

Test your understanding 4

A company produces a range of products, all of which pass through three production departments, A, B and C.

The following details have been provided for one unit of product 7Y:

	7Y
Direct material	6 kg at $4.50 per kg
Direct labour hours:	
A	1
B	2
C	1.5
Machine hours:	
A	2
B	3.2
C	4

Direct labour is paid at $12 per hour. Each unit of 7Y absorbs a selling and distribution overhead of $2.50.

118

> The OARs of the production departments have been calculated as follows:
>
> A: $2.59 per machine hour
>
> B: $3.05 per machine hour
>
> C: $1.40 per labour hour
>
> **Which THREE of the following statements relating to one unit of product 7Y are correct?**
>
> A   The prime cost is $27.00
>
> B   The prime cost is $81.00
>
> C   The total production cost is $91.79
>
> D   The total production cost is $98.04
>
> E   The full cost is $100.54
>
> F   The full cost is $104.04

8   Reciprocal servicing

In our WHW example of apportionment and reapportionment, there was only one service cost centre. In many examples there will be more than one and this can create a complication when it comes to reapportionment of overheads from the service cost centres to the production cost centres. The complication arises when the service cost centres use each other's services.

For example, if two services cost centres were canteen and maintenance, it is possible that the maintenance staff could use the services of the canteen and should therefore pick up a share of the canteen's costs. It is also possible that the canteen uses the services of the maintenance department and should therefore also pick up a share of the maintenance department costs. This is known as **reciprocal servicing**.

This can lead to a complicated situation because we do not know the total of the maintenance costs until a proportion of the canteen costs has been charged to it. Similarly, we do not know the total of the canteen costs until the total of the maintenance costs has been apportioned.

There are two methods which can be used to solve this problem:

*   the repeated distribution method

*   the equation method.

Illustration 5 – The repeated distribution method

ABC reapportions the costs incurred by two service cost centres (Stores and Inspection) to three production cost centres (Machining, Finishing and Assembly).

The following are the overhead costs which have been allocated and apportioned to the five cost centres:

	$000
Machining	400
Finishing	200
Assembly	100
Stores	100
Inspection	50

Estimates of the benefits received by each cost centre are as follows:

	Machining %	Finishing %	Assembly %	Stores %	Inspection %
Stores	30	25	35	–	10
Inspection	20	30	45	5	–

These percentages indicate the use which each of the cost centres makes of Stores and Inspection facilities.

Calculate the charge for overhead to each of the three production cost centres, including the amounts reapportioned from the two service centres.

Solution:

Using the repeated distribution method the service cost centre costs are apportioned backwards and forwards between the cost centres until the figures become very small. At this stage it might be necessary to round the last apportionments.

In the workings that follow we have chosen to begin the reapportionment with the Inspection costs. The $50,000 inspection cost is reapportioned according to the percentages provided, then the total of Stores department is reapportioned and so on. The final result would have been the same if we had chosen instead to reapportion Stores costs first.

	Machining $	Finishing $	Assembly $	Stores $	Inspection $
Initial allocation	400,000	200,000	100,000	100,000	50,000
Apportion Inspection	10,000	15,000	22,500	2,500	(50,000)
Apportion Stores	30,750	25,625	35,875	(102,500)	10,250
Apportion Inspection	2,050	3,075	4,612	513	(10,250)
Apportion Stores	154	128	180	(513)	51
Apportion Inspection*	11	16	24	–	(51)
Total charge for overhead	442,965	243,844	163,191	0	0

* When the service department cost reduces to a small amount, the final apportionment is adjusted for roundings.

The objective has been achieved and all of the overheads have been apportioned to the production cost centres, using the percentages given.

Test your understanding 5

CDE has commenced the preparation of its fixed production overhead cost budget for year 2 and has identified the following costs:

	$000
Machining	600
Assembly	250
Finishing	150
Stores	100
Maintenance	80
	1,180

The Stores and Maintenance departments are production service departments. An analysis of the services they provide indicates that their costs should be apportioned as follows:

	Machining	Assembly	Finishing	Stores	Maintenance
Stores	40%	30%	20%	–	10%
Maintenance	55%	20%	20%	5%	–

Required:

After the apportionment of the service department costs, the total overheads of the production departments will be (to the nearest $500):

Machining $ _____

Assembly $ _____

Finishing $ _____

9 The equation method

The other option for calculating the total overhead in each production department is the equation method which involves using algebraic equations. Some people will find it a quicker option but others prefer to reapportion using the repeated distribution method as in the previous solution. Whichever you choose you should arrive at the same answer.

Note: For this section some basic algebra is required. Many students will have studied this previously, but may want to recap the basics. See the section at the end of this chapter for some practice in dealing with algebraic equations.

In the ABC example in Illustration 5 we used the repeated distribution method to reapportion the service cost centres. We can now attempt the same reapportionment using the equation method.

 Illustration 6 – The equation method

A reminder of the data from Illustration 5:

ABC reapportions the costs incurred by two service cost centres (Stores and Inspection) to three production cost centres (Machining, Finishing and Assembly).

The following are the overhead costs which have been allocated and apportioned to the five cost centres:

	$000
Machining	400
Finishing	200
Assembly	100
Stores	100
Inspection	50

Estimates of the benefits received by each cost centre are as follows:

	Machining %	Finishing %	Assembly %	Stores %	Inspection %
Stores	30	25	35	–	10
Inspection	20	30	45	5	–

We can produce equations to show the total overheads of the two service departments:

Stores total overhead = overhead already allocated and apportioned + a proportion of the Inspection overhead:

Stores = $100,000 + 5% × Inspection overhead

We can do the same for Inspection:

Inspection = $50,000 + 10% × Stores overhead

We can shorten these to:

S = 100,000 + 0.05I

I = 50,000 + 0.1S

In this case, there are two unknowns in both equations (S and I). We can substitute one formula into the other to calculate the unknowns. (Either formula can be used).

S = 100,000 + 0.05(50,000 + 0.1S)

Now there is only one unknown (S) which can be solved.

Remove the brackets:

S = 100,000 + (0.05 × 50,000) + (0.05 × 0.1S)

S = 100,000 + 2,500 + 0.005S

This can be rearranged and solved for S:

S – 0.005S = 100,000 + 2,500

0.995S = 102,500

S = 103,015

We can now substitute this value into the other equation and solve for I.

I = 50,000 + (0.1 × 103,015)

I = 60,301

Now the total overhead for each production centre can be calculated:

Machining = 400,000 + 0.3S + 0.2I

= 400,000 + (0.3 × 103,015) + (0.2 × 60,301) = **442,965**

Finishing = 200,000 + 0.25S + 0.3I

= 200,000 + (0.25 × 103,015) + (0.3 × 60,301) = **243,844**

Assembly = 100,000 + 0.35S + 0.45I

= 100,000 + (0.35 × 103,015) + (0.45 × 60,301) = **163,191**

You can see that this is the same as the answer we got using the repeated distribution method.

Test your understanding 6

The total overheads allocated and apportioned to the production and service departments of LMN are as follows.

	$
Assembly	17,350
Finishing	23,970
Maintenance	18,600
Canteen	6,600

An analysis of the costs of the Maintenance department and the Canteen has been carried out and it has been agreed that a suitable basis for apportioning their costs would be:

	Assembly	Finishing	Maintenance	Canteen
	%	%	%	%
Maintenance	50	40	–	10
Canteen	30	50	20	–

Required:

Reapportion the service departments' overheads to the production departments using the equation method and calculate the total overhead for the Assembly and Finishing departments.

Total overhead for Assembly department $ _____

Total overhead for Finishing department $ _____

The difficulty with reciprocal servicing

The task of accounting for reciprocal servicing can be fairly laborious, particularly if it must be performed manually. Managers must therefore ensure that the effort is worthwhile.

Generally, if the service centre costs are significant and they make considerable use of each other's services, then accounting for reciprocal servicing is probably worthwhile. In other cases the reciprocal servicing could be ignored, or alternatively the service centre which does the most work for the other service centres could be apportioned first. The other service centres could then be apportioned directly to the production cost centres.

The overriding consideration must be the usefulness to managers of the resulting information. If the improved accuracy of the overhead absorption rates is deemed to be worthwhile, then reciprocal servicing should be taken into account in service cost reapportionment.

A spreadsheet or similar software package would obviously be helpful here!

 In the assessment, you must never ignore the existence of reciprocal servicing unless you are specifically instructed to do so.

The question may specify which method to use, but this will not always be the case. The equation method is recommended as it is quicker and, with a bit of practice, easier.

10 Predetermined overhead absorption rates

Overhead absorption rates are usually predetermined, that is, they are calculated in advance of the period over which they will be used, **using budgeted or expected costs and activity levels**.

The main reason for this is that overhead costs are not incurred evenly throughout the period. In some months the actual expenditure may be very high and in others it may be relatively low. The actual overhead rate per hour or per unit will therefore be subject to wide fluctuations. If the actual rate was used in product costing, then product costs would also fluctuate wildly. Such product costs would be very difficult to use for planning and control purposes.

Fluctuations in the actual level of production would also cause the same problem of fluctuating product costs. It is often impractical for a company to change its selling price regularly in line with the changes in production costs.

A further advantage of using predetermined rates is that managers have an overhead rate permanently available which they can use in product costing, price quotations and so on. The actual overhead costs and activity levels are not known until the end of the period. It would not be desirable for managers to have to wait until after the end of the period before they had a rate of overhead that they could use on a day-to-day basis.

Under- or over-absorption of overheads

The problem with using predetermined overhead absorption rates is that the actual figures for overhead and for the absorption base are likely to be different from the estimates used in calculating the absorption rate.

At the end of the period, the company must determine if it has absorbed too much or too little overhead into the products. Two things could have changed during the period:

- The amount of the overhead could be more or less than was budgeted.

- The quantity of the absorption base (units/labour hours/machine hours) could have been more or less than budgeted.

It is these differences which cause an under- or over-absorption of production overheads.

Illustration 7 – Overhead under-/over-absorption

We will now return to our WHW example to see how this is calculated, assuming that machine/labour hour rates have been used to absorb the overheads.

We will assume that all of the values used in the calculations in our example so far are estimates based on WHW's **budgets**.

The **actual** costs for the same four-week period have now been allocated and apportioned using the same techniques and bases as shown in our earlier example, with the following total actual costs being attributed to each cost centre:

	Machining	Assembly	Finishing
	$	$	$
Actual costs	43,528	49,575	9,240

Actual labour and machine hours recorded against each cost centre were:

	Machining	Assembly	Finishing
Machine hours	32,650		
Labour hours		31,040	3,925

The amount of **overhead cost absorbed** into each department's total number of saleable cost units will be calculated as follows:

> **Overhead absorbed = budgeted OAR × actual hours**

The budgeted OARs were calculated in Illustration 3.

Amount absorbed:	Machining	Assembly	Finishing
	$	$	$
32,650 hours × $1.277	41,694		
31,040 hours × $1.481		45,970	
3,925 hours × $2.525			9,911

This is compared to the **actual cost incurred** and the difference is the under-/over-absorption of production overhead:

	Machining	Assembly	Finishing
	$	$	$
Amount absorbed	41,694	45,970	9,911
Actual cost incurred	43,528	49,575	9,240
Over-/(Under-) absorption	(1,834)	(3,605)	671

If the amount absorbed exceeds the amount incurred, then an **over-absorption** arises; the opposite is referred to as an **under-absorption**. The terms under-recovery and over-recovery are sometimes used.

Note: The above overhead absorption calculations would be different if the company was adopting standard costing. In standard costing, the overhead is not absorbed using the actual labour or machine hours, but is absorbed using the standard hours for the actual level of production. Standard costing is covered in detail in the standard costing and variance analysis chapter and under- and over-absorption of overheads using standing costing is covered in the integrated accounting systems chapter.

The problems caused by under- or over-absorption of overheads

If overheads are under-absorbed then managers have been working with unit rates for overheads which are too low. Prices may have been set too low and other similar decisions may have been taken based on inaccurate information. If the amount of under-absorption is significant, then this can have a dramatic effect on reported profit.

Do not make the common mistake of thinking that over-absorption is not such a bad thing because it leads to a boost in profits at the period end. If overhead rates have been unnecessarily high, then managers may have set selling prices unnecessarily high, leading to lost sales, for example.

It is possible to minimise the over-/under-adjustment necessary at the year end by conducting regular reviews of the actual expenditure and activity levels which are arising. The overhead absorption rate can be reviewed to check that it is still appropriate or whether it should be adjusted to reflect more recent estimates of activity and expenditure levels.

Test your understanding 7

Budgeted labour hours	8,500
Budgeted overheads	$148,750
Actual labour hours	7,928
Actual overheads	$146,200

(a) **What is the labour hour overhead absorption rate?**

    A $17.50 per hour

    B $17.20 per hour

    C $18.44 per hour

    D $18.76 per hour

(b) **What is the amount of overhead under-/over-absorbed?**

    A $2,550 under-absorbed

    B $7,460 over-absorbed

    C $2,550 over-absorbed

    D $7,460 under-absorbed

Test your understanding 8

Production overhead in department A is absorbed using a predetermined rate per machine hour. Last period, the production overhead in department A was under-absorbed.

Which of the following situations could have contributed to the under-absorption? (Tick all that apply.)

❑ the actual production overhead incurred was lower than budgeted

❑ the actual production overhead incurred was higher than budgeted

❑ the actual machine hours were lower than budgeted

❑ the actual machine hours were higher than budgeted

11 Practice in dealing with algebraic equations

In the equation method of reapportionment, algebra is used. This section recaps some of the basic aspects of rearranging and solving equations.

Practice in dealing with equations

Rearranging equations

If you are given the following equation and asked to rearrange it so that X can be calculated:

$2B = X - 500$

If you do the same to both sides of an equation, the equation will remain true. If we add 500 to both sides of our equation:

$2B + 500 = X - 500 + 500$

This leaves us with:

$2B + 500 = X$ or $X = 500 + 2B$

Solving equations

We have looked at the basics of rearranging equations, we will now look at how to solve them.

If we are given the following equation and asked to solve for A:

$A = 250 + 6B$

To work out the value of A we will firstly need the value of B. If we are told that B = 5:

$A = 250 + (6 \times 5)$

$A = 280$

Test your understanding 9

Rearrange the following so that Y can be calculated:

$5X - 200 = Y + 300$

Test your understanding 10

Solve the following equation for Y:

$5Y - 750 = Y + 1{,}250$

Simultaneous equation example

Now we have looked at the basics of rearranging equations, we have seen how we need to use simultaneous equations in the equation method of reciprocal servicing. With simultaneous equations, we are dealing with two equations which both have elements to be solved. In order to solve these equations, you must first combine the two equations into one with only one missing element which can then be solved. Once one of the missing elements has been solved, this can be used to help solve the other missing elements.

Consider the following two equations:

$V = 1,000 - 3Z$ (i)

$2Z = 400 + 2V$ (ii)

Solve the equations for V and Z.

Solution:

We firstly need to combine the two equations into one with only one missing element to allow us to solve it. The easiest way to do this in this example is to substitute one equation into the other.

If we substitute (i) into (ii):

In equation (ii), we change the V element to its value from equation (i):

$2Z = 400 + 2(1,000 - 3Z)$

Remove the brackets:

$2Z = 400 + 2,000 - 6Z$

We have now eliminated the V element and can rearrange this equation and solve for Z:

Add 6Z to both sides:

$8Z = 2,400$

$Z = 300$

We can now solve for V by using Z = 300 in equation (i):

$V = 1,000 - (3 \times 300)$

$V = 100$

So the solution is **Z = 300, V = 100**

Test your understanding 11

Solve the following for X and Y:

$X = 20 - 4Y$ (i)

$2Y = 32 + 5X$ (ii)

12 Chapter summary

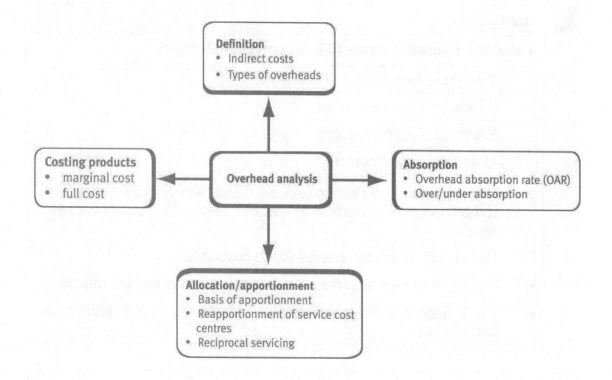

13 End of chapter questions

Question 1

Match the following terms to their correct definition.

Over-absorbed overhead
Overhead absorption rate
Overhead reapportionment
Overhead apportionment

This is a method of dealing with overheads which involves spreading common costs over cost centres on the basis of benefit received.

This is used to charge overheads to cost units.

This occurs when absorbed overheads exceed actual overheads.

This is used to share the costs of service cost centres to production cost centres.

Question 2

A management consultancy recovers overheads on chargeable consulting hours. Budgeted overheads were $615,000 and actual consulting hours were 32,150. Overheads were under-recovered by $35,000.

If actual overheads were $694,075, what was the budgeted overhead absorption rate per hour?

A $19.13

B $20.50

C $21.59

D $22.68

Budgeted
$$OAR = \frac{Total\ Overhead\ absorbed}{Budgeted\ quantity\ of\ absorption\ hours}$$

Overhead incurred = $694,075

overhead absorbed =
(694,075 − 35,000) $659,075

$$OAR = \frac{659,075}{32,150} = \$20.50$$

Question 3

ABC is a manufacturing company which produces a number of products. All products pass through ABC's three production departments.

Details for one unit of product CD are as follows:

	CD
Prime cost	$33
Direct labour hours:	
Cutting	②
Assembling	④
Finishing	4
Machine hours:	
Cutting	3.5
Assembling	②
Finishing	0.5

The following budgeted information is available for ABC's three production departments:

	Cutting	Assembling	Finishing
Production overheads	$87,505	$57,135	$46,537
Machine hours	40,700	15,000	5,400
Labour hours	25,500	29,300	17,300

Overheads in the Cutting department are absorbed on the basis of machine hours, while in Assembling and Finishing they are absorbed on the basis of labour hours.

Calculate the total production cost of one unit of product CD

$ ___51·62___

Prime cost   33

Product O/H   7·86
                                    7·53
Assembly (4 x 1·95)   2·69
Cutting (2·15 x 3·5)   ‾‾‾‾‾
Finishing (2·69 x 1·5)   51·02

1) OAR for cutting : 87505 → 2·15
                      ‾‾‾‾‾
                      40,700

OAR Assembly : 57,135 = 1·95
                ‾‾‾‾‾‾
                29,300

OAR : Finishing = 46,537 = 2·69
                   ‾‾‾‾‾‾
                   17,300

Question 4

A manufacturing organisation has two production departments (Machining and Finishing) and two service departments (Quality and Maintenance). After primary apportionment the overheads for the factory are as follows:

Machining	$220,000
Finishing	$160,000
Quality	$140,000
Maintenance	$113,000

Quality and Maintenance departments do work for each other as well as for the production departments as shown in the table below:

	Machining	Finishing	Quality	Maintenance
Work done by Quality	45%	35%	–	20%
Work done by Maintenance	30%	40%	30%	–

What is the total overhead to be apportioned to the Finishing department?

A $124,750

B $284,750

C $285,821

D $348,250

Question 5

Data for the machining cost centre are as follows:

Budgeted cost centre overhead	$210,000
Actual cost centre overhead	$230,000
Budgeted machine hours	42,000
Actual machine hours	43,000

Complete the following calculation.

             $

Overhead absorbed	
Actual overhead incurred	
Overhead under-/over-absorbed	

The overhead is under-/over-absorbed. *(delete as appropriate)*

Question 6

QRS has three main departments – Casting, Dressing and Assembly – and has prepared the following production overhead budgets for period 3.

	Casting	Dressing	Assembly
Production overheads	$225,000	$175,000	$93,000
Production hours	7,500	7,000	6,200

During period 3, actual results were as follows:

	Casting	Dressing	Assembly
Production overheads	$229,317	$182,875	$92,500
Production hours	7,950	7,280	6,696

Required:

(a) The departmental overhead absorption rates per production hour for period 3 are:

Casting $ _____ 30 _____

Dressing $ _____ 25 _____

Assembly $ _____ 15 _____

(b) (i) The overheads in the Casting department were (tick the correct box and insert the value of the over-/under-absorption):

under-absorbed ☐   over-absorbed ☑

by $ ___ 9182 ___

(ii) The overheads in the Dressing department were (tick the correct box and insert the value of the over-/under-absorption):

under-absorbed ☑   over-absorbed ☐

by $ ___ 875 ___

(c) The overheads in the Assembly department were over-absorbed. Which of the following factors contributed to the over-absorption?

☑ the actual overheads incurred were lower than budgeted.

☑ the actual production hours were higher than budgeted.

Question 7

After the initial overhead allocation and apportionment has been completed, the overhead analysis sheet for a car repair workshop is as follows:

Total overhead cost	Vehicle servicing	Crash repairs	Tyre fitting	Canteen and vending
$	$	$	$	$
233,000	82,000	74,000	61,000	16,000

The costs of the canteen and vending activity are to be reapportioned to the other activities on the basis of the number of personnel employed on each activity.

	Vehicle servicing	Crash repairs	Tyre fitting	Canteen and vending
Number of personnel	20	15	5	2

Required:

The canteen and vending cost to be apportioned to the crash repair activity is $ ___6000___ .

Question 8

ABC Hotel has completed its initial allocation and apportionment of overhead costs and has established that the total budgeted annual overhead cost of its linen services activity is $836,000.

The cost unit used to plan and control costs in the hotel is an occupied room night. The hotel expects the occupancy rate of its 400 rooms, which are available for 365 nights each year, to be 85% for the forthcoming year.

Required:

To the nearest cent, the overhead absorption rate for the linen services activity is $ ___6∙74___ per occupied room night.

Question 9

Which of the following statements regarding overheads is correct?

A   Allocation is used when overheads cannot be specifically attributed to a particular cost centre.

B   Apportionment is used to attribute the total cost of the production cost centres to the cost units.

C   The repeated distribution and equation methods are used to allocate costs to all production and service cost centres.

D   The overhead absorption rate is calculated by dividing the budgeted overhead by the budgeted quantity of the absorption base.

Question 10

For the following overhead costs, select the most appropriate apportionment base. Bases can be used more than once.

Overhead costs

- Rent

- Power

- Factory administration

- Canteen

- Cleaning

- Depreciation of factory machinery

Bases of apportionment

- Factory machinery at cost

- Number of employees

- Floor area

- Machine hours

Test your understanding and end of chapter answers

Test your understanding 1

(a)   Canteen costs – Number of employees

(b)   Cleaning of factory premises – Floor area

(c)   Power – Machine running hours

(d)   Rent – Floor area

(e)   Insurance of plant and machinery – Plant and equipment at cost

Test your understanding 2

Overhead cost item	Total $	Machining $	Assembly $	Finishing $
Maintenance cost	38,000	19,000	13,300	5,700

Working:

$$\text{Overhead cost per maintenance hour} = \frac{\$38,000}{(1,000 + 700 + 300)} = \$19$$

Maintenance cost for Machining = ($19 × 1,000) = **$19,000**

The other apportionments are calculated in the same way.

Test your understanding 3

The total production cost per unit of product M15 is **$54**

	$
Prime cost	25
Production overhead ($7.25* × 4)	29
	——
Total production cost	54
	——

* OAR = $184,875 ÷ 25,500 = $7.25

Test your understanding 4

B, D and E

	7Y
	$
Direct material (6 kg × $4.50)	27.00
Direct labour (1 + 2 + 1.5) × $12	54.00
	———
PRIME COST	81.00
Production overhead A ($2.59 × 2)	5.18
Production overhead B ($3.05 × 3.2)	9.76
Production overhead C ($1.40 × 1.5)	2.10
	———
TOTAL PRODUCTION COST	98.04
Selling and distribution overhead	2.50
	———
FULL COST	100.54
	———

Test your understanding 5

Machining: **$691,500**

Assembly: **$299,500**

Finishing: **$189,000**

Workings:

	Machining	Assembly	Finishing	Stores	Maintenance
	$000	$000	$000	$000	$000
Allocated costs	600.00	250.00	150.00	100.00	80.00
Stores apportionment	40.00	30.00	20.00	(100.00)	10.00
Maintenance apportionment	49.50	18.00	18.00	4.50	(90.00)
Stores apportionment	2.00	1.50	1.00	(4.50)	–
	———	———	———	———	———
Total	**691.50**	**299.50**	**189.00**	–	–
	———	———	———	———	———

Test your understanding 6

Total overheads:

Assembly: $30,103

Finishing: $36,417

First we have to produce two calculations that show the relationship between Maintenance and Canteen – the two service departments.

Maintenance = $18,600 (overhead already apportioned) + 20% of the Canteen overhead

Canteen = $6,600 (overhead already apportioned) + 10% of the Maintenance overhead

These can be shortened to:

M = 18,600 + 20%C

C = 6,600 + 10%M

Currently each formula has 2 unknowns – M and C. We can substitute one of the formulae into the other to calculate the unknowns:

M = 18,600 + 20%(6,600 + 10%M)

M is the only unknown

Change the % to decimals

M = 18,600 + 0.2(6,600 + 0.1 M)

Remove the brackets

M = 18,600 + (0.2 × 6,600) + (0.2 × 0.1 M)

M = 18,600 + 1,320 + 0.02M

Put the 'unknowns' together

M − 0.02M = 18,600 + 1,320

0.98M = 19,920

Therefore **M = 19,920/0.98 = $20,327**

We now know M so can substitute into the formula for C

C = 6,600 + 10%M

C = 6,600 + 0.1 × 20,327

C = $8,633

Final step is to then relate these amounts to the production centres:

Assembly = 17,350 + 0.5M + 0.3C

Assembly = 17,350 + (0.5 × 20,327) + (0.3 × 8,633)

Assembly = $30,103

Finishing = 23,970 + 0.4M + 0.5C

Finishing = 23,970 + (0.4 × 20,327) + (0.5 × 8,633)

Finishing = $36,417

Test your understanding 7

(a) **A**

Labour hour overhead absorption rate = $148,750 ÷ 8,500 = **$17.50 per hour**.

(b) **D**

	$
Overhead incurred	146,200
Overhead absorbed ($17.50 × 7,928 hours)	138,740
Under-absorption	**7,460**

Test your understanding 8

Two of the stated factors could have contributed to the under-absorption:

• **the actual production overhead incurred was higher than budgeted**; if this did happen then the predetermined absorption rate would be too low and there would be a potential under-absorption

• **the actual machine hours were lower than budgeted**; if this occurred then there would be fewer than expected hours to absorb the production overhead, potentially leading to under-absorption.

Test your understanding 9

Y = 5X − 500

Working:

5X − 200 = Y + 300

To get rid of the +300, we need to deduct 300 on the right hand side. To keep the equation true, we must do the same to the other side:

5X − 200 − 300 = Y + 300 − 300

This leaves:

5X − 500 = Y or **Y = 5X − 500**

Test your understanding 10

Y = 500

Working:

5Y − 750 = Y + 1,250

In this example we need to rearrange the equation so that all the Y elements are on one side and all the non-Y elements are on the other side. To remove the Y from the right hand side, deduct Y from both sides:

5Y − Y − 750 = Y − Y + 1,250

This gives us:

4Y − 750 = 1,250

Now, remove the 750 from the left hand side by adding 750 to both sides:

4Y − 750 + 750 = 1,250 + 750

This gives us:

4Y = 2,000

So, **Y = 500**

Test your understanding 11

Y = 6, X = –4

Workings:

Substitute (i) into (ii):

2Y = 32 + 5(20 – 4Y)

Remove the brackets:

2Y = 32 + 100 – 20Y

Rearrange:

22Y = 132

Y = 6

Substitute Y = 6 in equation (i):

X = 20 – (4 × 6)

X = –4

So the solution is **Y = 6, X = –4**

Question 1

Over-absorbed overhead	This occurs when absorbed overheads exceed actual overheads.
Overhead absorption rate	This is used to charge overheads to cost units.
Overhead reapportionment	This is used to share the costs of service cost centres to production cost centres.
Overhead apportionment	This is a method of dealing with overheads which involves spreading common costs over cost centres on the basis of benefit received.

Question 2

B

Let $x = budgeted overhead absorption rate per hour:

	$
Overhead incurred	694,075
Overhead absorbed ($694,075 – $35,000)	659,075
Under-absorption	35,000

$$\$x = \frac{659,075}{32,150} = \textbf{\$20.50}$$

Question 3

The total production cost per unit of product CD is **$51.02**

	$
Prime cost	33.00
Production overhead:	
Cutting ($2.15 × 3.5)	7.53
Assembling ($1.95 × 4)	7.80
Finishing ($2.69 × 1)	2.69
Total production cost	51.02

Production overhead absorption rates:

Overhead absorption rate for Cutting = $87,505 ÷ 40,700 = $2.15 per machine hour

Overhead absorption rate for Assembling = $57,135 ÷ 29,300 = $1.95 per labour hour

Overhead absorption rate for Finishing = $46,537 ÷ 17,300 = $2.69 per labour hour

Question 4

B

Q = 140,000 + 0.3M (1)

M = 113,000 + 0.2Q (2)

Substitute (1) in equation (2):

M = 113,000 + 0.2 (140,000 + 0.3M)

M = 113,000 + 28,000 + 0.06M

0.94M = 141,000

M = 150,000

Substituting this into equation (1)

Q = 140,000 + 0.3(150,000) = 185,000

Total overheads for departments

	Machining	Finishing
Primary apportionment	220,000	160,000
Share of Quality (45%/35%)	83,250	64,750
Share of Maintenance (30%/40%)	45,000	60,000
TOTAL	348,250	284,750

Question 5

	$
Overhead absorbed ($5* × 43,000)	215,000
Actual overhead incurred	230,000
Overhead under-/over-absorbed	**15,000**

The overhead is **under-absorbed.**

$$\text{* Overhead absorption rate} = \frac{\$210,000}{42,000} = \$5 \text{ per machine hour}$$

Question 6

(a) Predetermined departmental overhead absorption rates for period 3 (per production hour).

Casting	Dressing	Assembly
$\dfrac{\$225,000}{7,500} = \$30$	$\dfrac{\$175,000}{7,000} = \$25$	$\dfrac{\$93,000}{6,200} = \$15$

(b) (i) The overheads in the Casting department were **over-absorbed by $9,183.**

    (ii) The overheads in the Dressing department were **under-absorbed by $875.**

Workings:

	Casting $	Dressing $
Overheads absorbed:		
$30/hour × 7,950	238,500	
$25/hour × 7,280		182,000
Actual overheads	(229,317)	(182,875)
Over-/(Under)-absorption	**9,183**	**(875)**

(c) **Both factors would have contributed to the over-absorption.** The amount of overhead absorbed increased in line with the production hours, which would have led to over-absorption even if the overhead expenditure had remained constant. The fact that the overhead expenditure was below budget would have increased the amount of over-absorption.

Question 7

The canteen and vending cost to be apportioned to the crash repair activity is **$6,000.**

The canteen and vending cost per personnel member in production activities * =

$$\frac{\$16,000}{(20 + 15 + 5)} = \$400$$

* The canteen and vending personnel are not included because the canteen cannot give a charge to itself.

The canteen and vending cost apportioned to the crash repair activity is $400 × 15 = **$6,000.**

Question 8

The overhead absorption rate for the linen services activity is **$6.74 per occupied room night**.

Budgeted number of occupied room nights

= 400 rooms × 365 nights × 85% = 124,100 occupied room nights.

Overhead absorption rate for linen services activity = $836,000/124,100 = **$6.74** per occupied room night.

Question 9

D

A is incorrect as allocation is used when overheads can be specifically attributed to a particular cost centre.

B is incorrect as this is the definition of absorption.

C is incorrect as these methods are used to reapportion the costs from the service cost centres to the production cost centres.

Question 10

Overhead costs	Bases of apportionment
Rent	Floor area
Power	Machine hours
Factory administration	Number of employees
Canteen	Number of employees
Cleaning	Floor area
Depreciation of factory machinery	Factory machinery at cost

Marginal and absorption costing

Chapter learning objectives

After completing this chapter, you should be able to

- reconcile the differences between profits calculated using absorption costing and those calculated using marginal costing

- apply cost information in pricing decisions.

1 Session content diagram

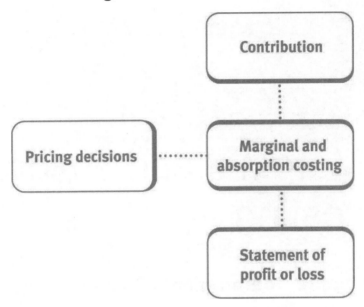

2 Marginal and absorption costing

Marginal and absorption costing are two different ways of valuing the cost of goods sold and finished goods in inventory which can affect the profit charged to the statement of profit or loss.

To understand absorption and marginal costing and the differences between them we need to revisit some of the cost classifications covered in the cost identification and classification chapter. When looking at marginal and absorption costing, we have to introduce a new cost classification and classify each cost as either a **period** or a **product** cost.

- Period costs are costs which are charged in full to the statement of profit or loss in the period in which they are incurred.

- Product costs are charged to the individual product and matched against the sales revenue they generate.

The main difference between marginal costing and absorption costing is the treatment of the **fixed production costs**:

Type of cost	Marginal costing	Absorption costing
Variable production cost	product cost	product cost
Fixed production cost	**period cost**	**product cost**
Variable non-production cost	period cost	period cost
Fixed non-production cost	period cost	period cost

For internal profit reporting in the management accounts, companies can choose whether to adopt marginal or absorption costing. The choice can affect:

- Inventory valuation (and therefore cost of sales in a period)

- The format of the statement of profit or loss.

3 Marginal costing

We saw in the cost identification and classification chapter that the **marginal** (or incremental) cost of a product is the additional cost incurred in producing one additional unit of the product. This will include the total of the **variable** costs, including direct materials, direct labour, direct expenses and variable overheads.

Note that fixed overheads are not included as the total fixed production overhead will not increase as a result of making one additional unit. Fixed overheads are treated as a period cost and deducted in full within the statement of profit or loss.

 Variable costs are sometimes referred to as marginal costs and the two terms are often used interchangeably.

 The marginal production cost is the cost of one unit of product or service which would be avoided if that unit were not produced, or which would increase if one extra unit were produced.

 The marginal production cost and the total marginal cost are not the same. Marginal **production** cost only include costs related to production which increase with each extra unit produced; it would not include other marginal costs, such as variable selling costs.

Marginal costing is the principal costing technique used in decision making. The key reason for this is that the marginal costing approach allows management's attention to be focused on the changes which result from the decision under consideration.

It is important to be able to calculate the marginal cost from a given set of data.

 Illustration 1 – Determining the marginal cost of a product

The following information about product CC is given below:

Selling price per unit	$140
Direct material per unit	6 kg
Direct labour per unit	4.5 hours
Direct expenses per unit	$3.75
Variable production overheads	$2.70 per labour hour
Fixed production overheads	$4.20 per labour hour
Variable non-production overheads	5% of selling price
Fixed non-production overheads per unit	$3.00

Direct material costs $2.60 per kg and direct labour is paid $12 per hour.

Calculate the marginal cost per unit of product CC.

Solution:

The marginal cost per unit of product CC is **$92.50**

Workings:

		$
Direct material	(6 kg × $2.60)	15.60
Direct labour	(4.5 hours × $12)	54.00
Direct expenses		3.75
Variable production overheads	(4.5 hours × $2.70)	12.15
Variable non-production overheads	(5% × $140)	7.00
		———
TOTAL MARGINAL COST		92.50
		———

Test your understanding 1

EFG manufactures a number of household electrical products. Details of its best-selling kettle and toaster are given below:

	Kettle	Toaster
Direct material per unit	$8.50	$9.00
Direct labour hours per unit	1.5	1.8
Machine hours per unit	0.6	0.4

The following additional information on overheads is given:

	Absorbed:
Variable production overheads	$2.70 per machine hour
Fixed production overheads	$4.20 per labour hour
Variable non-production overheads	$1.50 per labour hour
Fixed non-production overheads	$3.00 per unit

In addition a royalty of $2.50 per unit is paid to the designer of the kettle. Direct labour is paid $10 per hour.

Which of the following statements is correct?

A The marginal cost of a kettle is $27.37 and the marginal cost of a toaster is $30.78

B The marginal cost of a kettle is $29.87 and the marginal cost of a toaster is $30.78

C The marginal cost of a kettle is $33.92 and the marginal cost of a toaster is $35.64

D The marginal cost of a kettle is $39.17 and the marginal cost of a toaster is $41.34

The contribution concept

To understand marginal costing, we must understand the concept of **contribution**. The contribution concept lies at the heart of marginal costing. Contribution can be calculated as follows:

CONTRIBUTION = SALES VALUE – VARIABLE COSTS

You have already learned that variable costs are those that vary with the level of activity. If we can identify the variable costs associated with producing and selling a product or service we can calculate the contribution.

Contribution is so called because it literally does contribute towards fixed costs and profit. Once the contribution from a product or service has been calculated, the fixed costs associated with the product or service can be deducted to determine the profit for the period.

Illustration 2 – The concept of contribution

The following information relates to a company that makes a single product, a specialist lamp, which is used in the diamond-cutting business. The lamp sells for $600.

The costs for the lamp are as follows.

	$
Direct materials	200
Direct labour	150
Prime cost	350
Variable production overheads	50
Fixed production overheads	100
Total cost	500

Fixed costs have been estimated to be $120,000 based on a production level of 1,200 lamps.

Let us look at the costs and revenues involved when different volumes of lamps are sold.

Sales volume		1,200		1,500
		$		$
Sales revenue		720,000		900,000
Direct materials	240,000		300,000	
Direct labour	180,000		225,000	
Prime cost	420,000		525,000	
Variable production overheads	60,000		75,000	
Marginal cost of production		**480,000**		**600,000**
CONTRIBUTION		**240,000**		**300,000**
Fixed production overheads		120,000		120,000
Total profit		120,000		180,000

Contribution per unit	**200**	**200**
Profit per unit	100	120

- We can see that the profit per lamp has increased from **$100** when 1,200 lamps are sold to **$120** when 1,500 lamps are sold.

- This is because all of the variable costs (direct materials, direct labour, direct expenses and variable overheads) have increased but the fixed costs have remained constant at $120,000.

- Notice that **the contribution per unit remains constant at $200.**

Based on what we have seen above, the idea of profit is not a particularly useful one for decision making as it depends on how many units are sold. For this reason, the contribution concept is frequently employed by management accountants.

Benefits of contribution

- Contribution gives an idea of how much 'money' there is available to 'contribute' towards paying for the fixed costs of the organisation and generating profit.

- At varying levels of output and sales, contribution per unit is constant (while profit per unit varies).

- Contribution can be used to calculate profit:

  Total contribution = Contribution per unit × Sales volume.

  Profit = Total contribution – Fixed costs.

Test your understanding 2

Consider a product with a variable cost per unit of $26 and selling price of $42. Fixed costs for the period are $12,000.

Required:

(a)　What is the contribution per unit for the product?

(b)　If 1,000 units are sold, what is the total contribution?

(c)　What is the total profit and the profit per unit at this level of sales?

(d)　Calculate the total profit for the following levels of sales:

- 　　500 units

- 　　900 units

- 　　1,200 units

(e)　Calculate the contribution per unit and profit per unit for each level of sales.

 ## 4　Absorption costing

In absorption costing we build up a **full product cost**, including direct costs and a proportion of production overhead costs.

When we use absorption costing, the fixed production overhead is added to the cost of each unit, i.e. it is treated as a product cost rather than a period cost.

In the previous chapter we looked at how production overheads are absorbed into each cost unit. We noted that there are various methods which can be used for this and each can give different results.

This is not a problem with marginal costing where the fixed production overheads are treated as period costs, but it is a problem in absorption costing.

Recap of calculating a total product cost

GHI manufactures one product (A) and expects to make and sell 1,000 units in the next period. The direct cost of one unit is $35 and each is expected to sell for $60. Fixed production overheads are budgeted to be $10,000.

To calculate the total cost of each unit of product A, we add the direct costs and a share of the production overheads.

	$
Prime cost	35
Fixed production overhead *	10
Total unit cost	45

* In the previous chapter we saw that to calculate a fixed production cost per unit (overhead absorption rate) the budgeted fixed production costs are divided by the budgeted activity.

OAR = $10,000 ÷ 1,000 units = $10

From this total cost, we can calculate the total profit:

	$
Selling price per unit	60
Total unit cost	45
	——
Profit per unit	15
	——

Total profit = $15 × 1,000 = **$15,000**

5 Marginal and absorption costing profits

Marginal and absorption costing differ in their treatment of fixed production overheads. We can now compare the two methods using the following example.

BCD is a manufacturing company which manufactures two products, the X1 and the X2. Details for the two products for period 1 are:

	X1	X2
	$	$
Selling price per unit	150	180
Direct materials per unit	40	50
Direct labour per unit	30	40
Variable overheads per unit	10	15
Units produced and sold	500	300

Other information:

Fixed overheads for the period are $40,500 and are absorbed on the basis of direct labour hours. Direct labour is paid at a rate of $10 per hour.

Calculate the total profit for period 1 using both marginal and absorption costing.

Solution: Marginal costing

	X1	X2	Total
	$	$	$
Selling price	150	180	
Direct materials	40	50	
Direct labour	30	40	
Variable overheads	10	15	
Contribution per unit	70	75	
× units	× 500	× 300	
Total contribution	35,000	22,500	57,500
Less fixed overheads			40,500
Total profit			**17,000**

Solution: Absorption costing

	X1	X2	Total
	$	$	$
Selling price	150	180	
Direct materials	40	50	
Direct labour	30	40	
Variable overheads	10	15	
Fixed overheads (W1)	45	60	
Profit per unit	25	15	
	× 500	× 300	
Total profit	12,500	4,500	**17,000**

(W1) **Fixed overheads:**

X1 uses ($30 ÷ $10) = 3 hours per unit

X2 uses ($40 ÷ $10) = 4 hours per unit

Total labour hours = (3 × 500) + (4 × 300) = 2,700 hours

OAR = $40,500 ÷ 2,700 = $15

X1 absorbs fixed overhead per unit of $15 × 3 = **$45**

X2 absorbs fixed overhead per unit of $15 × 4 = **$60**

The differences between the two methods can be seen. Marginal costing highlights the contribution per unit and treats fixed production overheads as a period cost, deducting these in total from the total contribution.

Absorption costing treats fixed production overhead as a product cost and each unit of X1 and X2 absorbs a share of the fixed overhead.

The total profit is the same under both methods.

In our example there was no inventory, as the volume produced and the volume sold in the period was the same.

> **In cases where we make more or less than we sell in a period, inventory levels will change and the profits under marginal and absorption costing will differ.**

The reason for this is that marginal costing values inventory at the **total variable production cost** of a unit of product while absorption costing values inventory at the **full production cost** of a unit of product. This means that:

- Inventory values will be different at the beginning and end of a period under marginal and absorption costing.

- If inventory values are different, then this will have an effect on profits reported in the statement of profit or loss in a period.

Profits determined using marginal costing principles will therefore be different to those using absorption costing principles.

Absorption costing statement of profit or loss

In order to be able to prepare statements of profit or loss under absorption costing, you need to be able to complete the following proforma.

Statement of profit or loss – Absorption costing

	$	$
Sales		X
Less Cost of sales:		
Opening inventory	X	
Variable cost of production	X	
Fixed overhead absorbed	X	
Less Closing inventory	(X)	
		(X)
		X
(Under)/Over-absorption of overheads		(X)/X
Gross profit		X
Less Non-production costs		(X)
Profit/Loss		X

- **Valuation of inventory** – opening and closing inventory are valued at full production cost under absorption costing.

- **Under/Over-absorbed overhead** – an adjustment for under or over absorption of overheads is necessary in absorption costing statements of profit or loss.

Marginal costing statement of profit or loss

In order to be able to prepare statements of profit or loss under marginal costing, you need to be able to complete the following proforma.

Statement of profit or loss – Marginal costing

	$	$
Sales		X
Less Cost of sales:		
Opening inventory (note 1)	X	
Variable cost of production	X	
Less Closing inventory	(X)	
		(X)
		X
Less Other variable costs (note 2)		(X)
Contribution		X
Less Fixed costs (note 3)		(X)
Profit/Loss		X

Note 1: **Valuation of inventory** – opening and closing inventory are valued at marginal production cost under marginal costing.

Note 2: If there are **variable non-production costs** (i.e. selling costs) these would be deducted before contribution but not included in the cost of sales.

Note 3: The **fixed costs** actually incurred are deducted from contribution earned in order to determine the profit or loss for the period.

Illustration 3 – Impact of inventory on profit

PQR, a manufacturing company, commenced business on 1 March making one product only, the costs for which are as follows:

	$
Direct labour	5
Direct material	8
Variable production overhead	2
Fixed production overhead	5
Total production cost	20

The fixed production overhead figure has been calculated on the basis of a budgeted normal output of 36,000 units per annum. The fixed production overhead incurred in March was $15,000.

Selling, distribution and administration expenses are:

Fixed	$10,000 per month
Variable	15% of the sales value

The selling price per unit is $50 and the number of units produced and sold in March were:

Production	2,000
Sales	1,500

Prepare the absorption costing and marginal costing statements of profit or loss for March.

Absorption costing statement of profit or loss – March

	$	$
Sales		
Less Cost of sales:		
Opening inventory		
Variable cost of production		
Fixed overhead absorbed		
Less Closing inventory	____	
		____
(Under)/over-absorption		____
Gross profit		
Less Non-production costs		____
Profit/Loss		____

Value of closing inventory at the end of March (using absorption costing) $ [   ]

Marginal costing statement of profit or loss – March

	$	$
Sales		
Less Cost of sales:		
Opening inventory		
Variable cost of production		
Less Closing inventory	—	
		—
Less Other variable costs		
		—
Contribution		
Less Fixed costs (actually incurred)		
Less Non-production costs		
		—
Profit/Loss		
		—

Value of closing inventory at the end of March (using marginal costing)	$

Solution:

Absorption costing statement of profit or loss – March

	$	$
Sales (1,500 × $50)		75,000
Less Cost of sales:		
(valued at full production cost)		
Opening inventory	–	
Variable cost of production (2,000 × $15)	30,000	
Fixed overhead absorbed (2,000 × $5)	10,000	
Less Closing inventory (500 × $20)	(10,000)	
		(30,000)
		45,000
(Under)/over-absorption (W1)		(5,000)
Gross profit		40,000
Less Non-Production Costs (W2)		**(21,250)**
Profit		18,750

Value of closing inventory at the end of March (using absorption costing)	$10,000

Workings:

(W1) (Under)/over-absorption

	$
Overheads absorbed (2,000 × $5)	10,000
Overheads incurred in March	15,000
Under-absorption on overheads	(5,000)

(W2) Non-production costs

	$
Fixed	10,000
Variable (15% × $75,000)	11,250
Total	21,250

Marginal costing statement of profit or loss – March

	$	$
Sales (1,500 × $50)		75,000
Less Cost of sales: (marginal production costs only)		
Opening inventory	–	
Variable cost of production (2,000 × $15)	30,000	
Less Closing inventory (500 × $15)	(7,500)	
		(22,500)
		52,500
Less Other variable costs (15% × $75,000)		(11,250)
Contribution		41,250
Less Fixed costs actually incurred ($15,000 + $10,000)		(25,000)
Profit		16,250

Value of closing inventory at the end of March (using marginal costing)	$7,500

Impact of the over- or under-absorption of overheads

Notice how the under-absorption of has had no effect on the different profit figures reported under absorption and marginal costing. In the absorption costing system $10,000 of production overheads were recorded in cost of sales and then there was a $5,000 deduction for the under-absorption meaning that the total deduction was $15,000 (the actual fixed overheads). In the marginal costing system $15,000 was deducted for the actual fixed production overheads. Therefore the under-absorption in the absorption costing system simply ensured that the total deduction from profits for fixed overheads was the same for both systems.

The difference in the profit figures is wholly attributable due to the different inventory valuations.

Test your understanding 3

FGH makes and sells one product, the Alpha. The following information is available for period 3:

Production (units)	2,500
Sales (units)	2,300
Opening inventory (units)	0

	$
Unit selling price	90
Unit costs:	
Direct materials	15
Direct labour	18
Variable production overheads	12
Fixed production overheads	30

Fixed production overheads for the period were $52,500 and fixed administration overheads were $13,500. Variable selling overheads were $2,300.

Required:

(a) Prepare a Statement of profit or loss for period 3 based on marginal costing principles.

(b) Prepare a Statement of profit or loss for period 3 based on absorption costing principles.

6 Reconciling marginal and absorption costing profits

When inventory levels increase or decrease during a period then profits differ under absorption and marginal costing.

- **If inventory levels increase, absorption costing gives the higher profit.**

  This is because in absorption costing, fixed overheads held in closing inventory are carried forward to the next accounting period instead of being written off as a period cost in the current accounting period as in marginal costing.

- **If inventory levels decrease, marginal costing gives the higher profit.**

  This is because fixed overhead brought forward in opening inventory is released, thereby increasing cost of sales and reducing profits.

- **If inventory levels are constant, both methods give the same profit.**

Illustration 4 – Reconciling marginal and absorption costing

Using the same data for PQR as in Illustration 3:

	$
Direct labour	5
Direct material	8
Variable production overhead	2
Fixed production overhead	5
	___
Total production cost	20
	___

- Full (total) cost of production = $20.

- Marginal cost of production = $(5 + 8 + 2) = $15 (excludes the fixed production overhead).

- Difference in cost of production = $5 which is the fixed production overhead element of the full production cost.

- This means that each unit of opening and closing inventory will be valued at $5 more under absorption costing.

The number of units produced and sold in March was as follows.

Production	2,000
Sales	1,500

If   CI < OI |||

AC < MC
profit   profit

Closing inventory at the end of March is the difference between the number of units produced and the number of units sold, i.e. 500 units (2,000 – 1,500).

- Profit for March under absorption costing = $18,750 (as calculated in Illustration 3).

- Profit for March under marginal costing = $16,250 (as calculated in Illustration 3).

- Difference in profits = $18,750 – $16,250 = $2,500.

- This difference can be analysed as being due to the fixed overhead held in inventory, i.e. 500 units of inventory 'holding' at $5 fixed overhead per unit.

- 500 × $5 = $2,500 which is the difference between the profit in the profit statements under the different costing methods for March.

In an assessment question you may be told the profit under either marginal or absorption costing and be asked to calculate the alternative profit for the information provided.

 A good layout to use to reconcile the profits is shown below:

	$
Absorption costing profit	18,750
(Opening inventory – closing inventory) × OAR	
= (0–500) × 5	(2,500)
	————
Marginal costing profit	16,250
	————

Test your understanding 4

(a) In a period where opening inventory was 5,000 units and closing inventory was 3,000 units, a company had a profit of $92,000 using absorption costing.

   If the fixed overhead absorption rate was $9 per unit, calculate the profit using marginal costing.

(b) When opening inventory was 6,750 litres and closing inventory was 8,500 litres, a company had a profit of $62,100 using marginal costing.

   The fixed overhead absorption rate was $3 per litre. Calculate the profit using absorption costing.

7 Comparing absorption and marginal costing

Advantages of marginal costing	Advantages of absorption costing
• Contribution per unit is constant unlike profit per unit which varies with changes in volume.	• Absorption costing includes an element of fixed overheads in inventory values.
• There is no under/over-absorption of overheads (and hence no adjustment is required in the Statement of profit or loss).	• Analysing under/over-absorption of overheads is a useful exercise in controlling costs of an organisation.
• Fixed overheads are a period cost and are charged in full to the period under consideration.	• In small organisations, absorbing overheads into the costs of products is the best way of estimating job costs and profits on jobs.
• Marginal costing is useful in the decision-making process.	
• It is simple to operate.	

The main disadvantages of absorption costing are that it is more complex to operate than marginal costing and it does not provide any useful information for short-term decision making (like marginal costing does).

 Activity-based costing

Activity-based costing (ABC) is a more recent development in cost analysis. It is based on the idea that to use a single absorption base of either labour or machine hours does not accurately reflect the cause of the overhead costs being incurred.

Using an ABC approach, overhead costs are accumulated initially in activity **cost pools**. These might include, for example, order placing or material handling. Costs would then be collected and analysed for each activity cost pool and a **cost driver** would be identified for each activity. Cost drivers are the factors which cause the cost of an activity to increase.

Using estimates of the costs attributed to each activity cost pool and the number of cost drivers associated with it, a **cost driver rate** is calculated. This is similar in principle to the calculation of absorption rates.

For example, if the total cost of the activity of setting up a machine is $5,000 for a period and the number of machine set-ups for the period is 250, the cost per set-up is $20 ($5,000/250). Each product that requires the use of this machine is regarded as having incurred $20 of overhead cost each time the machine is set up for the product.

> This analysis of overhead costs into activities, and their absorption using a variety of cost drivers, is believed to produce more accurate product costs. The ABC technique can also be applied to non-production costs as well as to the determination of the costs of services provided.
>
> **Note:** ABC will be looked at in detail in later CIMA subjects. For *Fundamentals of Management Accounting* students are not expected to have a detailed knowledge of ABC, but should be aware of it.

8 The use of costing information in pricing decisions

We have now looked at marginal and absorption costing and how they are calculated. Both can be used when determining the selling price of a product. The way overheads are treated will have a big impact on the selling price calculated.

Marginal cost pricing

With marginal costing, we look at the cost of making and selling one additional unit. This can be very useful when deciding the selling price for a special order. The variable costs will be incurred if one additional unit is made, but the fixed cost may not change (if the unit to be made falls within the relevant range). Marginal cost is often thought of as variable cost.

Marginal costing is easier than absorption costing in that we do not have to absorb the overhead into the product cost. The problem with marginal cost pricing is that it is difficult to decide on the amount that must be added to the marginal cost in order to ensure that the other costs such as production and administration overheads are covered and that the organisation makes a profit.

Marginal cost pricing is useful in a one-off special price decision, but it does not help us to decide on the price to be charged in routine product pricing decisions, in order to cover all costs and earn a profit.

Full cost (absorption) pricing

With absorption costing, as we have seen, the overhead absorption rate can be used to trace indirect costs to cost units in order to obtain the unit's full cost.

The full cost of production can be used to determine the selling price.

Organisations need to decide whether to use marginal costing or full (absorption) costing to ascertain the selling price. They also have a choice in the method they use to calculate the selling price.

Organisations can use **mark-up** or **margin**. Firstly, the costs of the job will be estimated (either marginal or full cost) then the profit can be calculated using either mark-up or margin. The selling price can be calculated by adding the costs to the profit.

Profit mark-up

Profit mark-up is calculated as a **percentage of costs**. This can be marginal cost or total cost. This is also referred to as **cost-plus**.

Illustration 5 – Profit mark-up

ABC uses profit mark-up to calculate selling prices. The mark-up is 20% of total cost.

If the total cost of Job 35 is $8,400, what selling price would ABC quote for the job?

Solution:

Selling price = Total cost + 20%.

Total cost	$8,400	
Profit	$1,680	(20% of costs)
	_____	
Selling price	$10,080	
	_____	

Profit margin

Profit margin can calculated as a **percentage return on sales**, or it can be calculated as a **percentage return on investment**.

When using return on sales, the following formula can be used to calculate the profit:

$$\text{profit} = \text{total cost} \times \frac{\text{required margin}}{1 - \text{required margin}}$$

If you require to calculate the sales price, the following formula can be used:

$$\text{selling price} = \frac{\text{total cost}}{1 - \text{required margin}}$$

Illustration 6 – Return on sales

Full-cost pricing to achieve a specified return on sales

This pricing method involves determining the full cost of a cost unit and then adding a mark-up that represents a specified percentage of the final selling price.

WXY manufactures product A. Data for product A are as follows:

Direct material cost per unit	$7
Direct labour cost per unit	$18
Direct labour hours per unit	2 hours
Production overhead absorption rate	$6 per direct labour hour
Mark-up for non-production overhead costs	5% of total production cost

WXY requires a 15% return on sales revenue from all products.

Calculate the selling price for product A, to the nearest cent.

Solution:

	$ per unit
Direct material cost	7.00
Direct labour cost	18.00
Total direct cost	25.00
Production overhead absorbed (2 hours × $6)	12.00
Total production cost	37.00
Mark-up for non-production costs (5% × $37.00)	1.85
Full cost	38.85
Profit (15/85* × $38.85)	6.86
Selling price	45.71

*Always read the question carefully. The 15% required return is expressed as a percentage of the sales revenue, not as a percentage of the cost.

Test your understanding 5

A company has calculated its marginal cost of production for its bestselling product as $50 per unit and its full cost of production as $85 per unit.

Which two of the following statements are true?

A   If the company uses a mark-up of 20% on full cost, the selling price would be $106.25 per unit.

B   If the company uses a margin on sales of 25%, the selling price would be $113.33 per unit.

C   If the company uses a mark-up on marginal cost of 120%, the selling price will be $110 per unit.

D   If the company requires a margin on sales of 20%, the profit will be $17.00 per unit.

Illustration 7 – Return on investment

Full-cost pricing to achieve a specified return on investment

This method involves determining the amount of capital invested to support a product. For example, some non-current assets and certain elements of working capital such as inventory and trade receivables can be attributed to individual products.

The selling price is then set to achieve a specified return on the capital invested on behalf of the product. The following example will demonstrate how the method works.

EFG manufactures product B.

Data for product B are as follows:

Direct material cost per unit	$62
Direct labour cost per unit	$14
Direct labour hours per unit	4 hours
Production overhead absorption rate	$16 per direct labour hour
Mark-up for non-production overhead costs	8% of total production cost

EFG sells 1,000 units of product B each year. Product B requires an investment of $400,000 and the target rate of return on investment is 12% per annum.

Calculate the selling price for one unit of product B, to the nearest cent.

Solution:

	$ per unit
Direct material cost	62.00
Direct labour cost	14.00
Total direct cost	76.00
Production overhead absorbed (4 hours × $16)	64.00
Total production cost	140.00
Mark-up for non-production costs (8% × $140)	11.20
Full cost	151.20
Profit mark-up (see working)	48.00
Selling price	199.20

Working:

Target return on investment in product B = $400,000 × 12% = $48,000

Target return per unit of product B = $48,000/1,000 units = $48

Test your understanding 6

XYZ budgets to produce and sell 3,800 units of product R in the forthcoming year. The amount of capital investment attributable to product R will be $600,000 and XYZ requires a rate of return of 15% on all capital invested.

Further details concerning product R are as follows:

Direct material cost per unit	$14
Direct labour cost per unit	$19
Variable overhead cost per unit	$3
Machine hours per unit	8

Fixed overhead is absorbed at a rate of $11 per machine hour.

Calculate all answers to the nearest cent.

(a) The marginal cost of product R is $ _____ per unit.

(b) The total (full) cost of product R is $ _____ per unit.

(c) The selling price of product R which will achieve the specified return on investment is $ _____ per unit.

9   Chapter summary

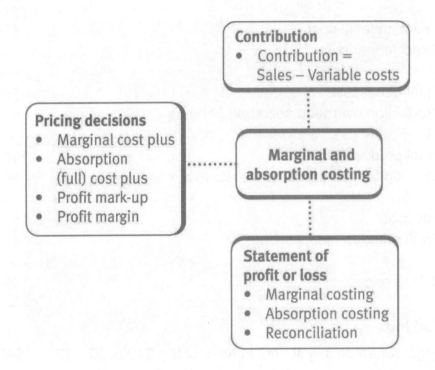

10 End of chapter questions

Question 1

ABC makes only one product, the unit costs of which are:

	$
Direct materials	3
Direct labour	6
Variable production overhead	2
Fixed production overhead	4
Variable selling cost	5
	20

The selling price of one unit is $21.

Budgeted fixed overheads are based on budgeted production of 5,000 units. Opening inventory was 1,000 units and closing inventory was 4,000 units.

Sales during the period were 3,000 units and actual fixed production overheads incurred were $25,000.

Required:

(a) Calculate the marginal cost per unit. $(3+6+ 2 3 +5) = 16$

$$cpu = 21-16$$
$$= \$ \times 3000$$
$$= 15,000$$

(b) Calculate the total contribution earned during the period.

(c) Calculate the total profit or loss for the period under marginal costing. $(15,000 - 25,000) = (10,000)$

(d) Calculate the total profit or loss for the period under absorption costing.

(e) Reconcile the profits calculated in parts (c) and (d).

Question 2

A company manufactures a range of products one of which, product Y, incurs a total cost of $20 per unit. The company incurs a total cost of $600,000 each period and the directors wish to achieve a return of 18% on the total capital of $800,000 invested in the company.

Required:

Based on this information the selling price of one unit of product Y should be $ _____ .

$800,000 \times 18\% = 144,000 \leftarrow$ required retn

$\dfrac{144,000}{600,000} = 24\%$

selly prc $= 20 + (24\% \times 20)$
$= 24.80$

CI LOI
AC LMC

Question 3

The number of units of finished goods inventory at the end of a period is greater than at the beginning.

What would the effect be of using the marginal costing method of inventory valuation?

A   less operating profit than the absorption costing method

B   the same operating profit as the absorption costing method

C   more operating profit than the absorption costing method

D   more or less operating profit than the absorption costing method depending on the ratio of fixed to variable costs

Question 4

GHI has just completed its first year of trading, manufacturing and selling product RT1. The following information has been collected from the accounting records.

Product RT1

Sales volume	70,000
	$
Selling price per unit	8.00
Variable cost per unit	
Production	6.00
Selling and administration	0.20
Fixed costs per unit	
Production overhead	1.20

The fixed production overhead cost was based on a budget of $90,000. Actual fixed production overheads and production volume were as budgeted.

GHI uses absorption costing.

Required:

If GHI used marginal rather than absorption costing, the profit will be $ _____ higher/lower.

Question 5

FGH makes only one product, which has the following costs per unit:

	$
Direct materials	3
Direct labour	6
Variable production overhead	2
Fixed production overhead	4
Variable selling cost	5

The selling price of one unit is $21.

Budgeted fixed overheads are based on budgeted production of 5,000 units. Actual production and sales were 6,000 and actual fixed production overheads incurred were $25,000.

Which THREE of the following statements are true?

A   Overheads were under-absorbed by $1,000.

B   Overheads were over-absorbed by $5,000.

C   The contribution earned was $30,000.

D   The marginal costing profit was $5,000.

E   The marginal costing profit would be higher than the absorption costing profit.

Question 6

LMN produced 24,000 units of product X in the last period. The total production cost was $40 per unit, 55% of which was variable. The product was sold at $55 per unit. The sales for the period were 20,000 units.

What will be the difference between the profit calculated using absorption costing principles and marginal costing principles?

A   Absorption costing profit will be higher by $72,000

B   Absorption costing profit will be lower by $72,000

C   Absorption costing profit will be higher by $88,000

D   Absorption costing profit will be lower by $88,000

Question 7

For the forthcoming year, EFG's variable costs are budgeted to be 60% of sales value and fixed costs are budgeted to be 10% of sales value.

If EFG increases its selling prices by 10%, but if fixed costs, variable costs per unit and sales volume remain unchanged, the effect on EFG's contribution would be:

A   a decrease of 2%

B   an increase of 5%

C   an increase of 10%

D   an increase of 25%

Question 8

XYZ is trying to cost its new product, the GX2. Details of the unit costs for the GX2 are given below:

	$
Direct materials	24
Direct labour (4 hours at $10 per hour)	40

Variable production overheads are absorbed at a rate of $4 per direct labour hour.

Fixed production overheads are absorbed at a rate of $8 per direct labour hour.

XYZ hopes to sell 2,000 units of the GX2 in the next period.

Calculate the selling price for the GX2 using the following pricing bases:

Based on full production costs:

(a)   Using a mark-up of 8%

(b)   Using a margin of 10%

Based on marginal production costs:

(c)   Using a mark-up of 45%

Using a return on investment method of pricing:

(d)   Product GX2 requires an investment of $300,000 and XYZ requires a return on investment of 15%

Question 9

Match the statements to whether they relate to marginal or absorption costing.

Absorption costing	Marginal costing

- This method treats fixed production cost as a period cost.

- A key concept of this approach is contribution.

- If inventory levels are increasing, this method will show the higher profit.

- This method values inventory at the variable cost of production.

Question 10

RST has been asked to quote for a job. Details are as follows:

- The estimated total variable production cost for the job is $250. Fixed production overheads for the company are budgeted to be $200,000 and are recovered on the basis of machine hours. There are 10,000 budgeted machine hours and this job is expected to take 2 machine hours.

- Other costs in relation to selling, distribution and administration are recovered at the rate of $30 per job.

- The company aims to make a profit margin of 25%.

The company quote for the job should be:

A $312.50

B $333.33

C $412.50

D $426.67

Test your understanding and end of chapter answers

Test your understanding 1

B

	Kettle		Toaster
	$		$
Direct material	8.50		9.00
Direct labour (1.5 hours × $10)	15.00	(1.8 hours × $10)	18.00
Direct expenses	2.50		
Variable production overheads (0.6 hours × $2.70)	1.62	(0.4 hours × $2.70)	1.08
Variable non-production overheads (1.5 hours × $1.50)	2.25	(1.8 hours × $1.50)	2.70
TOTAL MARGINAL COST	29.87		30.78

Test your understanding 2

(a) Contribution per unit = sales value – variable costs
$42 – $26 = **$16**

(b) Total contribution = contribution per unit × number of units
$16 × 1,000 = **$16,000**

(c) Total profit = total contribution – fixed costs
$16,000 – $12,000 = **$4,000**

Profit per unit = total profit/number of units
$4,000/1,000 = **$4**

(d) It is easier to use a table for these calculations:

Units	500	900	1,200
	$	$	$
Sales	21,000	37,800	50,400
Variable cost	13,000	23,400	31,200
Total contribution	8,000	14,400	19,200
Fixed costs	12,000	12,000	12,000
Total Profit/(Loss)	**(4,000)**	**2,400**	**7,200**

(e)

	500	900	1,200
Contribution per unit	**$16**	**$16**	**$16**
Profit per unit	**($8)**	**$2.67**	**$6**

You can see from this that the contribution per unit does not change, but that the profit per unit can change significantly as the volume changes. This makes contribution much more useful than profit in many decisions.

In the above example, it would have been quicker to start with contribution when working out the profit, as shown below. This saves some unnecessary calculations:

	$	$	$
Contribution per unit	16	16	16
× units	500	900	1,200
Total contribution	8,000	14,400	19,200
Fixed costs	12,000	12,000	12,000
Total Profit/(Loss)	**(4,000)**	**2,400**	**7,200**

Test your understanding 3

(a) Marginal costing – Statement of profit or loss

	$000	$000
Sales		207
Opening inventory	–	
Variable production cost (2,500 × 45)	112.5	
Closing inventory (200 × 45)	(9)	
		(103.5)
		103.5
Variable selling costs		(2.3)
Contribution		101.2
Fixed production overhead		(52.5)
Fixed administration overhead		(13.5)
Profit		35.2

(b) Absorption costing – Statement of profit or loss

	$000	$000
Sales		207
Opening inventory	–	
Full production costs (2,500 × 75)	187.5	
Closing inventory (200 × 75)	(15)	
		(172.5)
		34.5
Over-absorbed overhead (W1)		22.5
Gross profit		57
Less: Non-production overheads		
Variable selling overheads		(2.3)
Fixed administration overheads		(13.5)
Profit		41.2

(W1)

	$
Overhead absorbed (2,500 × $30)	75,000
Overheads incurred	52,500
Over-absorbed overhead	22,500

Test your understanding 4

(a)

Absorption costing profit	$92,000
Change in inventory × fixed cost per unit	
= (5,000 – 3,000) × $9	$18,000
	————
Marginal costing profit	**$110,000**
	————

Since inventory levels have fallen in the period, marginal costing shows the higher profit figure, therefore marginal costing profit will be $18,000 higher than the absorption costing profit, i.e. $110,000.

(b)

Absorption costing profit	**$67,350**
Change in inventory × fixed cost per unit	
= (6,750 – 8,500) × $3	($5,250)
	————
Marginal costing profit	$62,100
	————

Inventory levels have risen in the period and therefore marginal costing profits will be lower than absorption costing profits. Absorption costing profit is therefore $5,250 higher than the marginal costing profit.

Test your understanding 5

B and C are true.

A   If the company uses a mark-up of 20% on full cost, the selling price would be $106.25 per unit. This is false.

Using a mark-up of 20% on full cost of $85 per unit would give a selling price per unit of $85 × 1.2 = **$102 per unit**.

B   If the company uses a margin on sales of 25%, the selling price would be $113.33 per unit. This is true.

Selling price = $85 ÷ (1 – 0.25) = **$113.33 per unit**.

C   If the company uses a mark-up on marginal cost of 120%, the selling price will be $110 per unit. This is true.

Selling price = $50 + 120% = **$110 per unit**.

D   If the company requires a margin on sales of 20%, the profit will be $17 per unit. This is false.

Profit = $85 × (0.2 ÷ 0.8) = **$21.25 per unit**.

Test your understanding 6

(a) The variable cost per unit of product R is **$36.00** per unit.

Direct material $14 + direct labour $19 + variable overhead $3 = $36.

(b) The total (full) cost of product R is **$124.00** per unit.

Variable cost $36 + fixed overhead (8 hours × $11) = $124.

(c) The selling price of product R which will achieve the specified return on investment is **$147.68** per unit.

Working:

Required return from investment in product R

= $600,000 × 15% = $90,000

Required return per unit sold = $90,000/3,800 units = $23.68

Required selling price = $124.00 full cost + $23.68 = $147.68

Question 1

(a) The marginal cost per unit is **$16**.

Total marginal cost = total variable costs = $(3 + 6 + 2 + 5) = $16

(b) The total contribution earned during the period is **$15,000**.

Contribution per unit (selling price less total variable costs)
= $21 – $16 = $5

Total contribution earned = 3,000 × $5 = $15,000

(c) The total loss for the period under marginal costing is **$10,000**.

Total profit/(loss) = Total contribution – Fixed production overheads incurred

= $(15,000 – 25,000) = $(10,000)

(d) The total profit for the period under absorption costing is **$2,000**.

Total unit cost = $(3 + 6 + 2 + 5 + 4) = $20

Total profit per unit = $21 – $20 = $1

Gross profit ($1 × 3,000)	$3,000
Less under absorption of overheads (1)	$(1,000)
	———
Total profit	$2,000
	———

Note (1):

Overhead absorbed ($4 × 6,000 (2))	$24,000
Overhead incurred	$25,000
Under-absorbed overhead	$1,000

Note (2):

Sales	3,000
Opening inventory	(1,000)
Closing inventory	4,000
Production	6,000

(e) **Reconciliation**

Marginal costing loss	$(10,000)
Change in inventory × fixed overhead absorption rate (3,000 × $4)	$12,000
Absorption costing profit	$2,000

Question 2

The cost-plus selling price of one unit of product Y should be **$24.80**.

Required annual return = $800,000 × 18% = $144,000

Return as a percentage of total cost =144,000/$600,000 = 24%

Required cost-plus selling price = $20 + (24% × $20) = **$24.80**

Question 3

A

If the number of units of finished goods inventory at the end of a period is greater than at the beginning, marginal costing would give a lower operating profit than absorption costing.

Question 4

If GHI uses marginal rather than absorption costing, the profit will be **$6,000 lower**.

Working:

The difference between the marginal and absorption costing is:

Change in inventory × fixed overhead absorption rate

To find the change in inventory we need to know the production volume. We are told that this is as budgeted.

Budgeted production volume = Budgeted fixed production overhead ÷ fixed overhead absorption rate

$$= \frac{\$90,000}{\$1.20} = 75,000$$

Change in inventory = 75,000 – 70,000 = 5,000

As inventory is increasing, marginal profit will be lower by:

5,000 × $1.20 = $6,000.

Question 5

A, C and D are true.

A	Fixed production overheads absorbed (6,000 × $4)	$24,000
	Fixed production overheads incurred	$25,000
	Under absorption	**$1,000**

B is incorrect as overheads are under absorbed by $1,000

C	Variable costs = 3 + 6 + 2 + 5 = $16	
	Unit contribution = $21 – $16 = $5	
	Total contribution = 6,000 × $5 = **$30,000**	

D	Total contribution	$30,000
	Fixed cost	$25,000
	Profit	**$5,000**

E is incorrect. As there is no change in inventory levels, the profits under marginal and absorption costing would be the same.

Question 6

A

The difference in profit between marginal and absorption costing will be:

Change in inventory × fixed production cost per unit.

Change in inventory = an increase of 4,000

Fixed production cost per unit = 45% × $40 = $18

The difference in profit will be $18 × 4,000 = $72,000.

As inventory levels are increasing, absorption profit will be higher

Question 7

D

Fixed costs are not relevant because they do not affect contribution. Taking a selling price of, say, $100 per unit, the cost structures will look like this:

	Before change $ per unit	After change $ per unit
Sales price	100 + 10%	110
Variable cost	60	60
Contribution	40	50

Contribution per unit **increases by 25%.** If sales volume remains unchanged then total contribution will also increase by 25%.

Question 8

(a) Selling price = $120.96

	$
Direct materials	24.00
Direct labour	40.00
Variable overheads (4 hours × $4)	16.00
Marginal cost of production	80.00
Fixed overheads (4 hours × $8)	32.00
Full cost of production	112.00
Mark-up (8% × 112)	8.96
Selling price	120.96

(b) Selling price = $124.44

	$
Full cost of production (from (a))	112.00
Margin (10 ÷ 90 × 112)	12.44
Selling price	124.44

(c) Selling price = $116.00

	$
Marginal cost of production (from (a))	80.00
Mark-up (45% × 80)	36.00
Selling price	116.00

(d) Selling price = $134.50

Return required = $300,000 ×15% = $45,000

Return required per unit = $45,000 ÷ 2,000 = $22.50

Selling price = Full production cost + required return = $112.00 + $22.50 = $134.50

Question 9

Absorption costing	Marginal costing
• If inventory levels are increasing, this method will show the higher profit.	• This method treats fixed production cost as a period cost. • A key concept of this approach is contribution. • This method values inventory at the variable cost of production.

Question 10

D

	$
Variable production costs	250.00
Fixed production overheads ($200,000 ÷ 10,000) × 2	40.00
Selling, distribution and administration	30.00
	——
Total cost	320.00
Profit margin (320 × 0.25 ÷ 0.75)	106.67
	——
Quote	426.67
	——

Budgeting

Chapter learning objectives

After completing this chapter, you should be able to

- explain why organisations prepare forecasts and plans

- prepare functional budgets

- explain budget statements

- identify the impact of budgeted cash surpluses and shortfalls on business operations

- prepare a flexible budget

- calculate budget variances.

1 Session content diagram

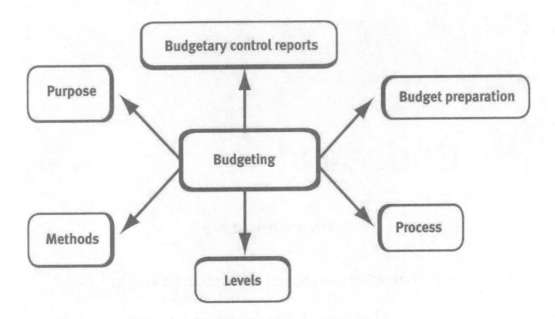

2 Budgeting

The main purposes of management accounting are planning, control and decision making. In the next few chapters we will look in detail at the planning and control aspects. Planning involves organisations looking ahead and trying to forecast what is likely to happen or what the organisation would like to happen in the future and control involves reviewing actual performance against these plans.

Most organisations, whether commercial or not-for-profit, plan using budgets. Budgeting is one of the most important roles undertaken by management accountants. A large amount of time and effort goes into budgeting. It is important to understand why organisations feel that budgeting is so worthwhile.

The purposes of budgeting

Budgets have several different purposes:

Planning – the budgeting process forces management to look ahead, set targets, anticipate problems and give the organisation purpose and direction.

Control – the budget provides the plan against which actual results can be compared.

Co-ordination – a sound budgeting system helps to co-ordinate the different activities of the business and to ensure that they are in harmony with each other.

Communication – budgets communicate targets to managers.

Motivation – the budget can influence behaviour and motivate managers.

Performance evaluation – the budget can be used to evaluate the performance of a manager.

Authorisation – budgets act as authority to spend.

More on the purposes of budgeting

Planning

Budgets force organisations to plan. Without the annual budgeting process the pressures of day-to-day operational problems may tempt managers not to plan for future operations. The budgeting process encourages managers to anticipate problems before they arise, and hasty decisions that are made on the spur of the moment, based on expediency rather than reasoned judgements, will be minimised. Corporate planners would regard budgeting as an important technique whereby long-term strategies are converted into shorter-term action plans.

Control

The budget acts as a comparator for current performance, by providing a yardstick against which current activities can be monitored. Those results which are out-of-line with the budget can be further investigated and corrected. The comparison of actual results with a budgetary plan, and the taking of action to correct deviations, is known as **feedback control**.

Appropriate control action can be taken if necessary to correct any deviations from the plan.

Co-ordination

The budget serves as a vehicle through which the actions of the different parts of an organisation can be brought together and reconciled into a common plan. Without any guidance managers may each make their own decisions believing that they are working in the best interests of the organisation. Budgeting forces managers to appreciate how their activities relate to those of other managers within the organisation.

Communication

Through the budget, top management communicates its expectations to lower-level management so that all members of the organisation may understand these expectations and can co-ordinate their activities to attain them.

Motivation

The budget can be a useful device for influencing managerial behaviour and motivating managers to perform in line with the organisational objectives.

Performance evaluation

The performance of managers is often evaluated by measuring their success in achieving their budgets. The budget might quite possibly be the only quantitative reference point available.

Consider two divisions within a company, A and B. You are told that both achieved profits of $1 million during the year. If you are now told that division A had a budgeted profit of $2 million and division B had budgeted for a profit of $500,000, you now have much more information about the two divisions and their performances.

Authorisation

A budget may act as formal authorisation to a manager for expenditure, the hiring of staff and the pursuit of the plans contained in the budget.

 ## What is a budget?

The *CIMA Terminology* defines a **budget** as 'a quantitative expression of a plan for a defined period of time'

The definition goes on to explain that budgets can be set for sales volumes and revenues, resource quantities, costs and expenses, assets, liabilities and cash flows.

For a budget to be useful it must be **quantified**. For example:

'We plan to spend as little as possible in running the printing department this year'

would not be particularly useful.

This is simply a vague indicator of intended direction; it is not a quantified plan and would not provide much assistance in management's task of planning and controlling the organisation.

'Budgeted revenue expenditure for the printing department for the year to 31st December 20X7 is $60,000'

is much better.

The quantification of the budgets has provided:

- a definite target for planning purposes; and
- a yardstick for control purposes.

The budget period

The time period for which a budget is prepared and used is called the **budget period**. It can be any length to suit management purposes but it is usually one year.

The length of time chosen for the budget period will depend on many factors, including:

- the nature of the organisation
- the type of item being considered.

Each budget period can be subdivided into control periods, of varying lengths, depending on the level of control which management wishes to exercise. The usual length of a control period is one month.

3 Levels of budgeting

It is useful at this stage to distinguish in broad terms between three different types of planning:

(1) Strategic planning

(2) Budgetary planning

(3) Operational planning.

These three forms of planning are interrelated. The main distinction between them relates to their time span which may be short-term, medium-term or long-term.

The short-term for one organisation may be the medium- or long-term for another, depending on the type of activity in which it is involved.

Strategic planning

Strategic planning is concerned with preparing long-term action plans to attain the organisation's objectives.

Strategic planning is also known as corporate planning or long-range planning.

Budgetary planning

Budgetary planning is concerned with preparing the short- to medium-term plans of the organisation. It will be carried out within the framework of the strategic plan. An organisation's annual budget could be seen as an interim step towards achieving the long-term or strategic plan.

Operational planning

Operational planning refers to the short-term or day-to-day planning process. It is concerned with planning the utilisation of resources and will be carried out within the framework set by the budgetary plan.

4 The budget process

The process of preparing and using budgets will differ from organisation to organisation. However there are a number of key requirements in the budgetary planning process.

The budget committee

The need for coordination in the planning process is paramount. For example, the purchasing budget cannot be prepared without reference to the production budget. The best way to achieve this coordination is to set up a budget committee. The budget committee should comprise representatives from all functions in the organisation.

The budget committee should meet regularly to review the progress of the budgetary planning process and to resolve problems that have arisen. These meetings will effectively bring together the whole organisation in one room, to ensure a coordinated approach to budget preparation.

The budget manual

Effective budgetary planning relies on the provision of adequate information to the individuals involved in the planning process.

A budget manual is a collection of documents which contain key information for those involved in the planning process.

 The contents of the budget manual

Typical contents could include the following:

- **The budget process**. An introductory explanation of the budgetary planning and control process including a statement of the budgetary objective and desired results.

  Participants should be made aware of the advantages to them and to the organisation of an efficient planning and control process. This introduction should give participants an understanding of the workings of the planning process, and of the sort of information that they can expect to receive as part of the control process.

- **Organisation chart**. A form of organisation chart to show who is responsible for the preparation of each functional budget and the way in which the budgets are inter-related.

- **Budget timetable**. This will prevent the formation of a 'bottleneck', with the late preparation of one budget holding up the preparation of all others.

- **Proformas**. Copies of all forms to be completed by those responsible for preparing budgets, with explanations concerning their completion.

- **Account codes**. A list of the organisation's account codes, with full explanations of how to use them.

- **Key assumptions**. Information concerning key assumptions to be made by managers in their budgets, for example, the rate of inflation, key exchange rates, etc.

- **Budget Officer**. The name and location of the person to be contacted concerning any problems encountered in preparing budgetary plans. This will usually be the coordinator of the budget committee (the budget officer) and will probably be a senior accountant.

The principal budget factor

The principal budget factor (key factor) is the factor which limits the activities of the organisation. The principal budget factor is also known as the **limiting factor**.

The early identification of this factor is important in the budgetary planning process because it indicates which budget should be prepared first.

For example, if sales volume is the principal budget factor, then the sales budget must be prepared first. All other budgets should then be linked to this.

Failure to identify the principal budget factor at an early stage could lead to delays at a later stage when managers realise that the targets they have been working with are not feasible.

 The inter-relationship of budgets

The critical importance of the principal budget factor stems from the fact that all budgets are inter-related. For example, if sales is the principal budget factor this is the first budget to be prepared. This will then provide the basis for the preparation of several other budgets including the selling expenses budget and the production budget.

The budget committee, with representatives from all areas of the organisation should help to ensure the coordination of all budgets within the organisation.

Using computers in budget preparation

A vast amount of data can be involved in the budgetary planning process and managing this volume of data in a manual system is a cumbersome task.

A computerised budgetary planning system will have the following advantages over a manual system:

- computers can easily handle the volume of data involved

- a computerised system can process the data more rapidly than a manual system

- a computerised system can process the data more accurately than a manual system

- computers can quickly and accurately access and manipulate the data in the system.

Organisations may use specially designed budgeting software. Alternatively, a well-designed spreadsheet model can take account of all of the budget inter-relationships described above.

The model will contain variables for all of the factors about which decisions must be made in the planning process, for example, sales volume, unit costs, credit periods and inventory volumes.

If managers wish to assess the effect on the budget results of a change in one of the decision variables, this can be accommodated easily by amending the relevant variable in the spreadsheet model. The effect of the change on all of the budgets will be calculated instantly so that managers can make better informed planning decisions.

> This process of reviewing the effect of changes in the decision variables is called '**what-if?**' analysis. For example, managers can rapidly obtain the answer to the question, 'What if sales volumes are 10% lower than expected?'.

Budgetary planning is an iterative process. Once the first set of budgets has been prepared, those budgets will be considered by senior management. The criteria used to assess the suitability of budgets may include adherence to the organisation's long-term objectives, profitability and liquidity. Computerised spreadsheet models provide managers with the ability to amend the budgets rapidly, and adjust decision variables until they feel that they have achieved the optimum plan for the organisation for the forthcoming period.

5   Functional budgets and the master budget

A master budget for the entire organisation brings together the departmental or activity budgets for all the departments or responsibility centres within the organisation.

 The master budget is a summary of all the functional budgets. It usually comprises the budgeted statement of profit or loss, budgeted statement of financial position and budgeted cash flow statement (cash budget).

It is this master budget which is submitted to senior management for approval because they should not be burdened with an excessive amount of detail. The master budget is designed to give the summarised information that they need to determine whether the budget is an acceptable plan for the forthcoming period.

The structure of a budget depends on the nature of the organisation and its operations. In a manufacturing organisation, the budgeting process will probably consist of preparing several functional budgets, often beginning with a sales budget. (Sales volume is very often the principal budget factor but this should not be assumed.)

Budget preparation

The stages in budget preparation for a manufacturing company are illustrated in the following diagram.

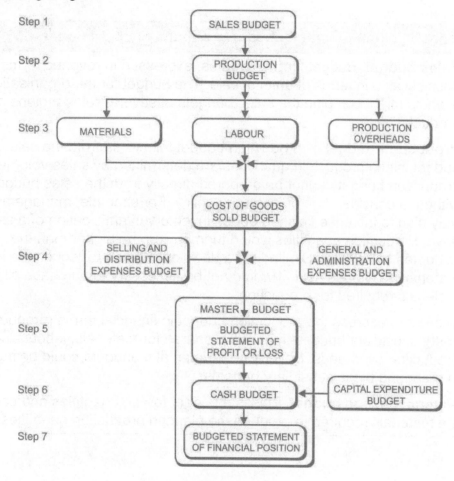

You can see from this that the principal budget factor is the starting point in the process. It is often sales, as shown in the diagram.

Step 1: The sales budget considers how many units can be sold.

Step 2: The production budget considers how many units must be produced to meet the budgeted sales level.

Note: The difference between the sales and the production budgets is the inventory of finished goods.

Step 3: The material, labour and overhead budgets can be established, based on the production budget.

Note: The material budget is generally calculated in two parts, firstly the quantity of material required in production, then the quantity of material required to be purchased. The difference between these will be the inventory of raw materials.

Material losses in production and idle time must be taken account of in the material and labour budgets.

Step 4: Non-production budgets. Budgets for non-production costs, such as selling and distribution costs, must also be considered.

Steps 5, 6 and 7: The master budget, comprising the statement of profit or loss, cash budget and statement of financial position can be pulled together from the individual budgets.

More detail on functional budgets and the master budget

Sales budget. Budget for future sales, expressed in revenue terms and possibly also in terms of units of sale. The budget for the organisation as a whole might combine the sales budgets of several sales regions or products.

Production budget. A production budget follows on from the sales budget, since production quantities are determined by sales volume. The production budget cannot be prepared directly from the sales budget without a consideration of inventory policy. For example, management may plan to increase finished goods inventory in anticipation of a sales drive. Production quantities would then have to be higher than the budgeted sales level. Similarly, if a decision is taken to reduce the level of material inventories held, it would not be necessary to purchase all of the materials required for production.

In order to express the production budget in financial terms (production cost), subsidiary budgets must be prepared for materials, labour and production overheads. Several departmental managers could be involved in preparing these subsidiary budgets.

Materials usage budget. This is a budget for the quantities and cost of the materials required to produce the planned production quantities.

Materials purchasing budget. This is a budget for the cost of the materials to be purchased in the period. The materials purchased budget will differ from the material usage budget if there is a planned increase or decrease in direct materials inventory. The material purchases budget should also include the purchase costs of indirect materials.

Direct labour budget. This is a budget of the direct labour costs of production. If direct labour is a variable cost, it is calculated by multiplying the production quantities (in units) by the budgeted direct labour cost per unit. If direct labour is a fixed cost, it can be calculated by estimating the payroll cost for the period.

Production overhead budget. Budgets can be produced for production overhead costs. Where a system of absorption costing is used, overheads are allocated and apportioned, and budgeted absorption rates are determined.

Administration and Selling and distribution overhead budgets. Other overhead costs should also be budgeted.

Capital expenditure and depreciation budgets. Organisations will also prepare a separate capital expenditure budget. This would be based on the approved capital expenditure proposals for the period. Capital expenditure would include the purchase of or improvements to non-current assets, such as buildings, machinery, vehicles etc. and can involve substantial sums of money. Organisations must carefully plan for this expenditure as it can affect other budgets such as the cash budget and depreciation budget.

The depreciation budget will be prepared based on the organisation's depreciation policies and covers the writing down of the value of non-current assets. The depreciation budget becomes an input to the relevant overhead cost budget (production overhead, administration or selling and distribution overhead) depending on the nature of the non-current asset but it is not an input to the cash budget, as it is not a cash flow.

The master budget

Budgeted statement of profit or loss, cash budget and budgeted statement of financial position. Having prepared the functional budgets for sales and costs, the master budget can be summarised as a statement of profit or loss for the period, a cash budget (or cash flow forecast) and a statement of financial position as at the end of the budget period.

If the budgeted statement of profit or loss, cash budget or statement of financial position are unsatisfactory, the budgets should be revised until a satisfactory planned outcome is achieved.

The best way to see how budgets are prepared is to work through an example.

Illustration 1 – Budget preparation

A company manufactures two products, Aye and Bee. Expected cost data for the products for next year are as follows:

	Product Aye per unit	Product Bee per unit
Direct materials:		
X at $2 per kg	24 kg	30 kg
Y at $5 per kg	10 kg	8 kg
Z at $6 per kg	5 kg	10 kg
Direct labour:		
Unskilled at $6 per hour	10 hours	5 hours
Skilled at $10 per hour	6 hours	5 hours

Budgeted inventories for next year are as follows:

	Product Aye units	Product Bee units
Opening	400	800
Closing	500	1,100

	Material X kg	Material Y kg	Material Z kg
Opening	30,000	25,000	12,000
Closing	35,000	27,000	12,500

Budgeted sales for next year: product Aye 2,400 units; product Bee 3,200 units.

Prepare the following budgets for next year:

(a)   production budget, in units

(b)   material usage budget, in kgs

(c)   material purchases budget, in kgs and $

(d)   direct labour budget, in hours and $.

Solution:

(a) Production budget

	Product Aye units	Product Bee units
Sales units required	2,400	3,200
Closing inventory	500	1,100
	2,900	4,300
Less opening inventory	400	800
Production units required	**2,500**	**3,500**

(b) Material usage budget

	Material X kg	Material Y kg	Material Z kg
Requirements for production:			
Product Aye (W1)	60,000	25,000	12,500
Product Bee	105,000	28,000	35,000
Total material usage	**165,000**	**53,000**	**47,500**

   (W1) Material X for product Aye:

     2,500 units produced × 24 kg = 60,000 kg

     The other material requirements are calculated in the same way.

(c) Material purchases budget

	Material X kg	Material Y kg	Material Z kg
Material required for production (from (b))	165,000	53,000	47,500
Closing inventory	35,000	27,000	12,500
Less opening inventory	(30,000)	(25,000)	(12,000)
Material purchases (kg)	**170,000**	**55,000**	**48,000**
× Standard price per kg	$2	$5	$6
Material purchases ($)	**$340,000**	**$275,000**	**$288,000**

Total material purchases = $(340,000 + 275,000 + 288,000) = **$903,000**.

(d) Direct labour budget

	Unskilled labour hours	Skilled labour hours	Total
Requirements for production:			
Product Aye (W2)	25,000	15,000	
Product Bee	17,500	17,500	
Total hours required	42,500	32,500	
× Standard rate per hour	$6	$10	
Direct labour cost	**$255,000**	**$325,000**	**$580,000**

(W2) Unskilled labour for product Aye:

2,500 units produced × 10 hours = 25,000 hours

The other labour requirements are calculated in the same way.

Test your understanding 1

An ice cream manufacturer is in the process of preparing budgets for the next few months, and the following draft figures are available:

Sales forecast:

June	6,000 cases
July	7,500 cases
August	8,500 cases
September	7,000 cases
October	6,500 cases

Each case uses 2.5 kg of ingredients and it is policy to have inventories of ingredients at the end of each month to cover 50% of next month's production.

There are 600 cases of finished ice cream in inventory on 1 June and it is policy to have inventories at the end of each month to cover 10% of the next month's sales.

Required:

(a) The production budget (in cases) for June and July will be:

June: _____ cases

July: _____ cases

(b) The ingredient purchases budget (in kg) for August will be _____ kg

6   The cash budget

The cash budget is one of the most vital planning documents in an organisation. It will show the cash effect of all of the decisions taken in the planning process.

Management decisions will have been taken concerning such factors as inventory policy, credit policy, selling price policy and so on. All of these plans will be designed to meet the objectives of the organisation. However, if there are insufficient cash resources to finance the plans, they may need to be modified or perhaps action might require to be taken to alleviate the cash constraint.

A cash budget can give forewarning of potential problems that could arise so that managers can be prepared for the situation or take action to avoid it.

Cash budgets are prepared for each period (typically monthly). In a period the cash budget could show more outgoings than receipts. This is known as a **shortfall**, or **deficit**. In this situation there is a danger that the organisation will have insufficient cash to meet any payments which are due. They may be unable to pay wages or pay suppliers. This is not a sustainable position and the organisation would have to take action to avoid, or at least manage, the situation.

Alternatively the cash budget could show higher receipts than payments in the period. This is known as a cash **surplus**. Identifying surpluses can help an organisation to plan its operations. For example it may change the timing of purchases or use the surplus in one period to alleviate a shortfall in another period. Surpluses can also offer the organisation opportunities for investment.

 The use of forecasts to modify actions so that potential threats are avoided or opportunities exploited is known as **feedforward control**.

There are four possible cash positions that could arise:

	Possible management action
Short-term deficit	Arrange a bank overdraft, reduce receivables and inventories, increase payables.
Long-term deficit	Raise long-term finance, such as long-term loan capital or share capital.
Short-term surplus	Invest short term, increase receivables and inventories to boost sales, pay suppliers early to obtain cash discount.
Long-term surplus	Expand or diversify operations, replace or update non-current assets.

Notice that the type of action taken by management will depend not only on whether a deficit or a surplus is expected, but also on how long the situation is expected to last.

For example, management would not wish to use surplus cash to purchase non-current assets, if the surplus was only short-term and the cash would soon be required again for day-to-day operations.

Preparing cash budgets

A few basic principles when preparing cash budgets:

- **The format for cash budgets**

  There is no definitive format which should be used for a cash budget. However, whichever format you decide to use it should include the following:

  (i) **A clear distinction between the cash receipts and cash payments for each period** and a subtotal clearly shown for each.

  (ii) **A figure for the net cash flow for each period**. This makes the cash budget easier to prepare and use. In practice, managers find the figure for the net cash flow helps to draw attention to the cash flow implications of their actions during the period.

  (iii) **The closing cash balance for each period**. The closing balance for each period will be the opening balance for the following period.

- **Depreciation is not included in cash budgets**

  Remember that depreciation is not a cash flow. It may be included in your data for overheads and must therefore be excluded before the overheads are inserted into the cash budget. Only cash flows are included in the cash budget.

- **Allowance must be made for bad and doubtful debts**

  Bad debts will never be received, and doubtful debts may not be received. When you are forecasting the cash receipts from customers you must remember to adjust for these items – this normally means that sales receipts have be reduced to remove these items from actual sales.

- **Include ALL cash flows**

  The cash budget does not just reflect sales revenue and production costs, but all movements of cash including cash flows for financial items such as inflows from the sale of shares or grants received and outflows such as the purchase of a non-current asset or the repayment of a loan.

Illustration 2 – Cash budget

WXY is preparing budgets for the next quarter. The following information has been prepared so far:

Sales value		
	June	$12,500
	July	$13,600
	August	$17,000
	September	$16,800
Direct wages	$1,300 per month	
Direct material purchases	June	$3,450
	July	$3,780
	August	$2,890
	September	$3,150

Other information

- WXY sells 10% of its goods for cash. The remainder of customers receive one month's credit.

- Payments to material suppliers are made in the month following purchase.

- Wages are paid as they are incurred.

- WXY takes one month's credit on all overheads.

- Production overheads are $3,200 per month.

- Selling, distribution and administration overheads amount to $1,890 per month.

- Included in the amounts for overhead given above are depreciation charges of $300 and $190, respectively.

- WXY expects to purchase a delivery vehicle in August for a cash payment of $9,870.

- The cash balance at the end of June is forecast to be $1,235.

Prepare a cash budget for July, August and September.

Solution:

WXY cash budget for July to September

	July $	August $	September $
Receipts:			
Cash sales (10% in month)	1,360	1,700	1,680
Credit sales (90% of previous month)	11,250	12,240	15,300
Total receipts	12,610	13,940	16,980
Payments:			
Material purchases (one month credit)	3,450	3,780	2,890
Direct wages	1,300	1,300	1,300
Production overheads (1)	2,900	2,900	2,900
Selling, distribution and administration overhead (1)	1,700	1,700	1,700
Delivery vehicle	–	9,870	–
Total payments	9,350	19,550	8,790
Net cash inflow/(outflow)	3,260	(5,610)	8,190
Opening cash balance	1,235	4,495	(1,115)
Closing cash balance	4,495	(1,115)	7,075

Note 1: Depreciation has been excluded from the overhead figures because it is not a cash item.

Interpretation of the cash budget

The cash budget produced for WXY forewarns the management that their plans will lead to a cash deficit of $1,115 at the end of August. They can also see that it will be a short-term deficit and can take appropriate action.

They may decide to delay the purchase of the delivery vehicle or perhaps negotiate a period of credit before the payment will be due. Alternatively overdraft facilities may be arranged for the appropriate period.

The important point to appreciate is that management should take appropriate action if they forecast a short-term deficit. For example, it would not be appropriate to arrange a five year loan to manage a cash deficit that is expected to last for only one month.

If it is decided that overdraft facilities are to be arranged, it is important that account is taken of the timing of the receipts and payments within each month.

For example, all of the payments in August may be made at the beginning of the month but receipts may not be expected until nearer the end of the month. The cash deficit could then be considerably greater than it appears from looking only at the month-end balance.

If the worst possible situation arose, the overdrawn balance during August could become as large as $4,495 – $19,550 = $15,055. If management had used the month-end balances as a guide to the overdraft requirement during the period then they would not have arranged a large enough overdraft facility with the bank. It is important therefore, that they look in detail at the information revealed by the cash budget, and not simply at the closing cash balances.

Test your understanding 2

The following details have been extracted from the receivables records of ABC:

Invoice paid in the month after sale	60%
Invoice paid in the second month after sale	25%
Invoice paid in the third month after sale	12%
Bad debts	3%

Invoices are issued on the last day of each month.

Customers paying in the month after sale are entitled to deduct a 2% settlement discount.

Credit sales for June to September are budgeted as follows:

June	July	August	September
$35,000	$40,000	$60,000	$45,000

The amount budgeted to be received from credit sales in September is:

A $47,280

B $47,680

C $48,850

D $49,480

Test your understanding 3

Note: This is a comprehensive question. It is much bigger than you will see in your assessment but it is useful to work through examples like this to improve your understanding.

BCD is preparing its budgets for year 2. The company's year end is 31st December.

The following information is available:

Budgeted statement of profit or loss for the year ended 31 December, year 2

	$	$
Revenue		1,203,500
Opening inventory of raw materials	32,000	
Purchases of raw materials	253,700	
	─────	
	285,700	
Closing inventory of raw materials	17,000	
	─────	
	268,700	
Direct wages	448,500	
Production overhead *	200,000	
	─────	
Production cost of goods completed	917,200	
Opening inventory of finished goods	25,000	
	─────	
	942,200	
Closing inventory of finished goods	37,800	
	─────	
Production cost of goods sold		904,400
		─────
Gross profit		299,100
Selling and administration overhead *		75,000
		─────
Net profit before taxation		224,100
Taxation		67,230
		─────
		156,870
Retained earnings b/f		103,000
		─────
Retained earnings c/f		259,870
		─────

* Included in the production overhead cost is $25,000 for depreciation of property and equipment. Selling and administration overhead includes $5,000 for depreciation of equipment.

A quarterly cash flow forecast has already been partly completed for year 2 and is set out below:

Quarter	1	2	3	4
	$	$	$	$
Receipts	196,000	224,000	238,000	336,000
Payments:				
Materials	22,000	37,000	40,000	60,000
Direct wages	100,000	110,500	121,000	117,000
Overhead	45,000	50,000	70,000	65,000
Taxation	5,000			

In addition to the above, the company plans to purchase a new machine during the year which will cost $120,000. This will be paid for in quarter 3.

The company's statement of financial position as at 31st December, year 1, is expected to be as follows:

	$ Cost	$ Depreciation	$ Net
Assets			
Non-current assets			
Land	50,000	–	50,000
Buildings and equipment	400,000	75,000	325,000
	450,000	75,000	375,000
Current assets			
Inventories			
– raw materials	32,000		
– finished goods	25,000		
		57,000	
Receivables		25,000	
Cash at bank		10,000	
			92,000
			467,000

Capital and liabilities		
Capital		
Share capital		350,000
Retained earnings		103,000
		453,000
Current liabilities		
Payables	9,000	
Taxation	5,000	
		14,000
		467,000

No changes to share capital will be made during the year.

Prepare the company's quarterly cash budget for the year ended 31st December, year 2 and a budgeted statement of financial position as at 31 December, year 2.

7 Approaches to budgeting

There are many approaches used in budgeting. It is useful to think of these in pairs:

- Rolling and periodic budgets

- Incremental and zero-based budgeting (ZBB)

- Participative and imposed budgeting.

Rolling budgets

The *CIMA Terminology* defines a **rolling budget** as a 'budget continuously updated by adding a further accounting period (month or quarter) when the earliest accounting period has expired. Its use is particularly beneficial where future costs and/or activities cannot be forecast accurately.'

For example, a budget may initially be prepared for January to December. At the end of the first quarter, that is, at the end of March, year 1, the first quarter's budget is deleted. A further quarter is then added to the end of the remaining budget, for January to March, year 2. The remaining portion of the original budget is updated to reflect current conditions. This means that managers have a full year's budget always available and the rolling process forces them continually to plan ahead.

A system of rolling budgets is **also known as continuous budgeting**.

Advantages

- Budgeting should be more accurate, uncertainties should be reduced.

- Managers are forced to reconsider their budgets on a much more regular basis, taking into account current conditions.

- Planning and control are based on a more recent, more realistic budget.

- There is always a budget extending 9 – 12 months into the future.

Disadvantages

- Budgets are prepared several times a year meaning more time, money and effort in budget preparation.

- Managers doubt the usefulness of preparing one budget after another.

In practice, most organisations carry out some form of updating process on their budgets, so that the budgets represent a realistic target for planning and control purposes. The formalised budgetary planning process will still be performed on a regular basis to ensure a coordinated approach to budgetary planning.

Periodic budget

A periodic budget shows the costs and revenue for one period of time, e.g. one year and is updated on a periodic basis, e.g. every 12 months.

 Incremental budgeting

The *CIMA Terminology* defines **incremental budgeting** as 'a method of budgeting based on the previous budget or actual results, adjusting for known changes and inflation, for example'.

The traditional approach to budgeting is to take the previous year's budget and to add on a percentage to allow for inflation and other cost increases. In addition there may be other adjustments for specific items such as an extra worker or extra machine.

In times of recession, the opposite process will take place, i.e. last year's budget minus a certain percentage.

Advantages

- Relatively easy to do, even for non-accountants.

- Can be performed relatively quickly.

- Less likely to miss required items.

Disadvantages

- Consideration will not be given to the justification for each activity. They will be undertaken merely because they were undertaken the previous year. Different ways of achieving the objective will not be examined.

- Past inefficiencies will be continued and it may result in **budget slack**, which is unnecessary expenditure being built into the budget.

- Managers know that if they fail to spend their budget, it is likely to be reduced next period. They therefore try to spend the whole budget, regardless of whether or not the expenditure is justified.

Zero-based budgeting

Zero-based budgeting (ZBB) was developed as an alternative to the incremental approach.

 The *CIMA Terminology* defines **zero-based budgeting** as a 'method of budgeting that requires all costs to be specifically justified by the benefits expected.'

Zero-based budgeting is so called because it requires each budget to be prepared and justified from zero, instead of simply using last year's budget or actual results as a base. Incremental levels of expenditure on each activity are evaluated according to the resulting incremental benefits. Available resources are then allocated where they can be used most effectively.

The major advantage of ZBB is that managers are forced to consider alternative ways of achieving the objectives for their activity and they are required to justify the activities which they currently undertake. This helps to eliminate or reduce the incidence of budget slack.

 Advantages and disadvantages of ZBB

Advantages

- Inefficient or obsolete operations can be identified and discontinued.

- It creates an inquisitorial attitude, rather than one which assumes current practices represent value for money.

- Wasteful expenditure is avoided.

- Managers are forced to consider alternative methods of achieving their objectives.

- Knowledge and understanding of the cost behaviour patterns of the organisation will be enhanced.

- Resources should be allocated efficiently and economically.

Disadvantages

- The time involved and the cost of preparing the budget is much greater than for less elaborate budgeting methods.

- It may emphasise short-term benefits to the detriment of long-term benefits.

- There is a need for management to possess skills that may not be present in the organisation.

- It is difficult to compare and rank completely different types of activity.

- The budgeting process may become too rigid and the company may not be able to react to unforeseen opportunities or threats.

- Incremental costs and benefits of alternative courses of action are difficult to quantify accurately.

Note: A detailed discussion of ZBB is outside the scope of your *Fundamentals of Management Accounting* syllabus, but you should be aware that there are a number of different approaches to budgetary planning.

Participative budgeting

 The *CIMA Terminology* defines **participative budgeting** as a 'budgeting process where all budget holders have the opportunity to participate in setting their own budgets'.

This may also be referred to as '**bottom-up budgeting**'.

Advantages

- Improved quality of forecasts to use as the basis for the budget. Managers who are doing a job on a day-to-day basis are likely to have a better idea of what is achievable, what is likely to happen in the forthcoming period, local trading conditions, etc.

- Improved motivation. Budget holders are more likely to want to work to achieve a budget that they have been involved in setting themselves, rather than one that has been imposed on them by more senior managers. They will own the budget and accept responsibility for the achievement of the targets contained.

Disadvantages

- Extended and complex budgetary process. It is a lengthy process to get every manager's input to the process.

- Slack may be built in to the budget. Where managers are involved in setting their own budgets, they may deliberately make the budgets easier to achieve.

Imposed budgeting

 The *CIMA Terminology* defines **imposed budgeting** as 'A budget allowance which is set without permitting the ultimate budget holder to have the opportunity to participate in the budgeting process'.

This may also be referred to as '**top down budgeting**'.

Advantages

* Involving managers in the setting of budgets is more time consuming than if senior managers simply imposed the budgets.

* Managers may not have the skills or motivation to participate usefully in the budgeting process.

* Senior managers have a better overall view of the company and its resources and may be better placed to create a budget which utilises those scarce resources to best effect. They may offer a more objective, fresher perspective.

Disadvantages

* Lack of ownership of the budget. Managers may resent the budget being imposed and therefore may not try hard to meet it.

* Lack of detailed knowledge of each business area may result in an unrealistic budget.

Note: The behavioural aspects of budgeting is outside the scope of the *Fundamentals of Management Accounting* syllabus.

> **Test your understanding 4**
>
> **The term 'budget slack' refers to:**
>
> A   the extended lead time between the preparation of the functional budgets and the master budget
>
> B   the difference between the budgeted output and the breakeven output
>
> C   the additional capacity available which can be budgeted for
>
> D   the deliberate over-estimation of costs and under-estimation of revenues in a budget

Test your understanding 5

Match the descriptions to the type of budgeting system being described.

- A method of budgeting based on the previous budget or actual results, adjusted for any anticipated changes.

- A method of budgeting requiring all costs to be specifically justified by the benefits expected.

- A budget prepared for a fixed period of time.

- A system of budgeting whereby the budget is continuously updated by adding a further accounting period when the earliest accounting period has expired.

Type of budgeting
Zero-based
Periodic
Rolling
Incremental

8 Budgetary control

Once budgets have been set, they can be used for control.

Budgetary control is achieved by comparing the actual results with the budget. The differences are calculated as **variances** and management action may be taken to investigate and correct the variances if necessary or appropriate.

- If costs are higher or revenues are lower than the budget, then the difference is an **adverse variance**.

- If costs are lower or revenues are higher than the budget, then the difference is a **favourable variance**.

Budget centres

The *CIMA Terminology* defines a **budget centre** as a 'section of an entity for which control may be exercised through prepared budgets'

Each budget centre is often a **responsibility centre**. Each centre will have its own budget and a manager will be responsible for managing the centre and controlling the budget. This manager is often referred to as the budget holder. Regular budgetary control reports will be sent to each budget holder so that they may monitor their centre's activities and take control action if necessary.

There are four classifications for responsibility centres, depending on what the manager of the centre has responsibility for:

- **Cost centre** – manager is responsible for operating costs.

- **Revenue centre** – manager is responsible for revenue.

- **Profit centre** – manager is responsible for operating costs and revenue and the resulting profit.

- **Investment centre** – manager is responsible for profit and the return on any investment made.

Budgetary control reports

If managers are to use budgets to control their areas effectively, they must receive regular control information.

The budgetary reporting system should ideally be based on the **exception principle** which means that management attention is focused on those areas where performance is significantly different from budget. Subsidiary information could be provided on those items which are not in line with the budget.

Attributes of budgetary control reports

Budgetary control reports should be:

- **Timely**. The information should be made available as soon as possible after the end of the control period. Corrective action will be much more effective if it is taken soon after the event, and adverse trends could continue unchecked if budgetary reporting systems are slow.

- **Accurate**. Inaccurate control information could lead to inappropriate management action. There is often a conflict between the need for timeliness and the need for accuracy. More accurate information might take longer to produce. The design of budgetary reporting systems should allow for sufficient accuracy for the purpose to be fulfilled.

- **Relevant to the recipient**. Busy managers should not be swamped with information that is not relevant to them. They should not need to search through a lot of irrelevant information to reach the part which relates to their area of responsibility. The natural reaction of managers in this situation could be to ignore the information altogether.

- **Communicated to the correct manager**. Control information should be directed to the manager who has the responsibility and authority to act on it. If the information is communicated to the wrong manager its value will be immediately lost and any adverse trends may continue uncorrected. Individual budget holders' responsibilities must be clearly defined and kept up to date in respect of any changes.

Many control reports also segregate controllable and non-controllable costs and revenues, that is, the costs and revenues over which managers can exercise control are highlighted separately in the reports from those over which they have no control.

A number of accounting packages have the facility to record actual and budget details against each account code for each budget centre. These may then be printed in the form of a report.

9 Fixed and flexible budgets

When managers are comparing the actual results with the budget for a period, it is important to ensure that they are making a valid comparison. The use of flexible budgets can help to ensure that actual results are monitored against realistic targets.

Illustration 3 – Flexible budgets

A company manufactures a single product and the following data show the actual results for costs for the month of April compared with the budgeted figures.

Operating statement for April

	Budget	Actual	Variance
Units produced	1,200	1,000	(200)
	$	$	$
Direct material	19,200	16,490	2,710
Direct labour	13,200	12,380	820
Production overhead	24,000	24,120	(120)
Administration overhead	21,000	21,600	(600)
Selling overhead	16,400	16,200	200
Total cost	93,800	90,790	3,010

Note: Variances in brackets are adverse.

Looking at the costs incurred in April, a cost saving of $3,010 has been made compared with the budget. However, the number of units produced was 200 less than budget so some savings in expenditure might be expected. It is not possible to tell from this comparison how much of the saving is due to efficient cost control, and how much is the result of the reduction in activity.

The type of budget being used here is a **fixed budget**. A fixed budget is one which remains **unchanged regardless of the actual level of activity**. In situations where activity levels are likely to change, and there is a significant proportion of variable costs, it is difficult to control expenditure satisfactorily with a fixed budget.

If costs are mostly fixed, then changes in activity levels will not cause problems for cost comparisons with fixed budgets.

A **flexible budget** can help managers to make more valid comparisons. It is designed to show the allowed expenditure for the actual number of units produced and sold. Comparing this flexible budget with the actual expenditure, it is possible to distinguish genuine efficiencies and inefficiencies.

Preparing a flexible budget

Before a flexible budget can be prepared, managers must identify the cost behaviour, i.e. which costs are fixed, which are variable and which are semi-variable. The allowed expenditure on variable costs can then be increased or decreased as the level of activity changes. You will recall that fixed costs are those costs which will not increase or decrease over the relevant range of activity. The allowance for these items will therefore remain constant. Semi-variable costs have both a fixed and a variable element.

We can now continue with the example.

Management has identified that the following budgeted costs are fixed:

	$
Direct labour	8,400
Production overhead	18,000
Administration overhead	21,000
Selling overhead	14,000

It is now possible to identify the expected variable cost per unit produced.

	Original budget (a)	Fixed cost (b)	Variable cost (c) = (a) − (b)	Variable cost per unit (c) ÷ 1,200
Units produced	1,200			
	$	$	$	$
Direct material	19,200	–	19,200	16
Direct labour	13,200	8,400	4,800	4
Production overhead	24,000	18,000	6,000	5
Admin overhead	21,000	21,000	–	–
Selling overhead	16,400	14,000	2,400	2
	93,800	61,400	32,400	27

From this you can see that:

- administration overhead is fixed

- direct material is variable

- direct labour, production overhead and selling and distribution overheads are semi-variable.

Now that managers are aware of the fixed costs and the variable costs per unit it is possible to '**flex**' the original budget to produce a budget cost allowance for the actual 1,000 units produced.

The budget cost allowance (or flexed budget) for each item is calculated as follows:

> Budget cost allowance = Budgeted fixed cost + (number of units produced × variable cost per unit)

The budget cost allowances can be calculated as follows:

Direct material = 0 + (1,000 × 16) = $16,000

Direct labour = 8,400 + (1,000 × 4) = $12,400

Production overhead = 18,000 + (1,000 × 5) = $23,000

Administration overhead = 21,000 + 0 = $21,000

Selling overhead = 14,000 + (1,000 × 2) = $16,000

A flexible budget statement can now be produced:

Flexible budget comparison for April

	Flexed budget	Actual cost	Budget variance
	$	$	$
Direct material	16,000	16,490	(490)
Direct labour	12,400	12,380	20
Production overhead	23,000	24,120	(1,120)
Administration overhead	21,000	21,600	(600)
Selling overhead	16,000	16,200	(200)
Total cost	88,400	90,790	(2,390)

Note: Variances in brackets are adverse.

This revised analysis shows that in fact the cost was $2,390 higher than would have been expected from a production volume of 1,000 units.

The cost variances in the flexible budget comparison are almost all adverse. These overspendings were not revealed when the fixed budget was used and managers may have been under the false impression that costs were being adequately controlled.

The total cost variance

If we now produce a statement showing the fixed budget, the flexible budget and the actual results together, it is possible to analyse the total cost variance between the original budget and the actual results.

	Fixed budget $	Flexible budget $	Actual results $	Budget variances $
Direct material	19,200	16,000	16,490	(490)
Direct labour	13,200	12,400	12,380	20
Production o/h	24,000	23,000	24,120	(1,120)
Administrative o/h	21,000	21,000	21,600	(600)
Selling o/h	16,400	16,000	16,200	(200)
	93,800	88,400	90,790	(2,390)

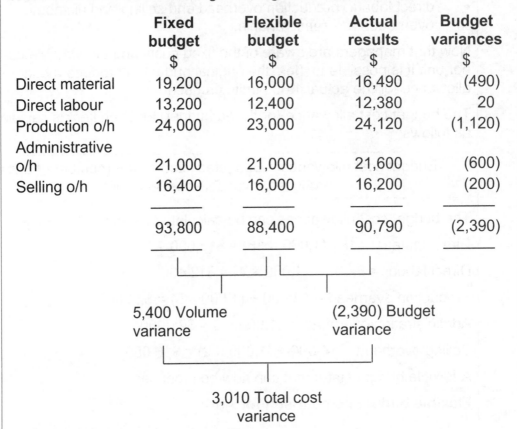

5,400 Volume variance

(2,390) Budget variance

3,010 Total cost variance

The total cost variance is therefore made up of two parts:

(1) the volume variance of $5,400 favourable, which is the expected cost saving resulting from producing 200 units less than budgeted

(2) the budget variance of $2,390 adverse, which is the net total of the over- and under-expenditure on each of the costs for the actual output of 1,000 units.

Notice that the volume variance is the saving in standard variable cost: 200 units × $27 per unit = $5,400.

Using flexible budgets for planning

You should appreciate that while flexible budgets can be useful for control purposes they are not particularly useful for planning. The original budget must contain a single target level of activity so that managers can plan such factors as the resource requirements and the product pricing policy. This would not be possible if they were faced with a range of possible activity levels, although managers will of course consider a range of possible activity levels before they select the target budgeted activity level.

The budget can be designed so that the fixed costs are distinguished from the variable costs. This will facilitate the preparation of a budget cost allowance (flexed budget) for control purposes at the end of each period, when the actual activity is known.

Test your understanding 6

EFG produces and sells a single product. The budget for the latest period is as follows.

	$
Sales revenue (12,600 units)	277,200
Variable costs:	
Direct material	75,600
Direct labour	50,400
Production overhead	12,600
Fixed costs:	
Production overhead	13,450
Other overhead	10,220
	162,270
Budgeted profit	114,930

The actual results for the period were as follows.

	$
Sales revenue (13,200 units)	303,600
Variable costs:	
Direct material	78,350
Direct labour	51,700
Production overhead	14,160
Fixed costs:	
Production overhead	13,710
Other overhead	10,160
	168,080
Actual profit	135,520

Prepare a flexible budget control statement and calculate the variances.

Test your understanding 7

A flexible budget is:

A   a budget which, by recognising different cost behaviour patterns, is designed to change as the volume of activity changes.

B   a budget for a defined period of time which includes planned revenues, expenses, assets, liabilities and cash flow.

C   a budget which is prepared for a period of one year which is reviewed monthly, whereby each time actual results are reported, a further forecast period is added and the intermediate period forecasts are updated.

D   a budget of semi-variable production costs only.

10 Reconciling actual contribution with budgeted contribution

We can use the variances calculated in the budgetary control statements to reconcile the actual contribution with the budgeted contribution for the period.

Illustration 4 – Reconciling actual contribution with budgeted

ABG has a budgeted contribution for May of $368,000. The following variances were calculated for the period:

Direct material total variance	$12,500 adverse
Direct labour total variance	$17,900 favourable
Variable production overhead total variance	$11,850 favourable

Calculate the actual contribution for May.

Solution:

	$
Budgeted contribution	368,000
Direct material total variance	(12,500)
Direct labour total variance	17,900
Variable production overhead total variance	11,850
	———
Actual contribution	385,250
	———

Test your understanding 8

The budgeted contribution for last month was $45,500. The following variances arose:

	$	
Sales total variance	3,100	adverse
Direct material total variance	1,986	favourable
Direct labour total variance	1,090	adverse
Variable overhead total variance	465	adverse

Required:

The actual contribution for last month was $ _____

11 Chapter summary

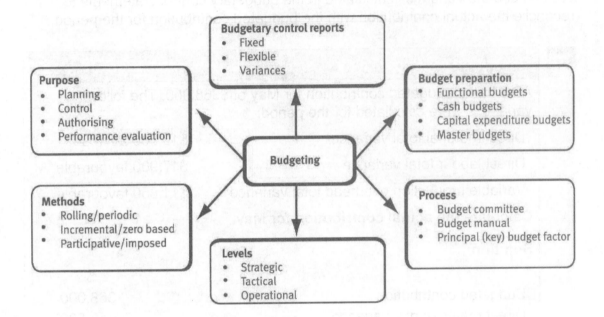

12 End of chapter questions

Question 1

A job requires 2,400 actual labour hours for completion and it is anticipated that there will be 20% idle time *.

* Idle time refers to hours for which the employees are being paid but are not actively working. In some cases the idle time will be charged to a specific job and the cost passed to the customer, but this is not always the case.

If the wage rate is $10 per hour, what is the budgeted labour cost for the job?

A $19,200

B $24,000

C $28,800

D $30,000

Question 2

Which of the following items of information would be contained in the budget manual? (Tick all that are correct.)

(a)   An organisation chart.   ❏

(b)   The timetable for budget preparation.   ❏

(c)   The master budget.   ❏

(d)   A list of account codes.   ❏

(e)   Sample forms to be completed during the budgetary
        process.   ❏

Question 3

A company specialises in food testing for restaurants and supermarkets.

For the year just ended it was hoped that it could secure a new contract with a large supermarket chain, therefore it had produced cost budgets for 12,000 and 18,000 tests. The following labour costs were budgeted:

	$000
12,000 tests	1,440
18,000 tests	2,160

It did not secure the contract with the large supermarket but did manage to take on work for several smaller supermarkets. Its actual results for the year are:

Tests	15,000
Labour costs	$1,875

Calculate the budget variance for labour cost for the period.

$ _____ adverse/favourable

Question 4

Assuming that sales volume is the principal budget factor, place the following budgets in the order that they would be prepared in the budgetary planning process. Indicate the correct order by writing 1, 2, 3, etc. in the boxes provided.

	Sales budget
	Materials purchases budget
	Materials inventory budget
	Production budget
	Finished goods inventory budget
	Materials usage budget

Question 5

Each finished unit of product H contains 3 litres of liquid L. 10% of the input of liquid L is lost through evaporation in the production process. Budgeted output of product H for June is 3,000 units. Budgeted inventories of liquid L are:

- Opening inventory   1,200 litres

- Closing inventory   900 litres

Required:

The required purchases of liquid L for June are _____ litres.

Question 6

A small manufacturing company is to commence operations on 1 July. The following estimates have been prepared:

	July	August	September
Sales (units)	10	36	60
Production (units)	40	50	50

It is planned to have raw material inventories of $10,000 at the end of July, and to maintain inventories at that level thereafter. There is no opening inventory.

Selling prices, costs and other information:

	Per unit
	$
Selling price	900
Material cost	280
Labour cost	160
Variable overheads	40

Fixed overheads are expected to be $5,000 per month, including $1,000 depreciation.

10% of sales are in cash, the balance payable the month following sale.

Labour is paid in the month incurred, and all other expenditures the following month.

Required:

(a) The budgeted cash receipts from sales are:

July	$	
August	$	
September	$	

(b) The budgeted cash payments for raw materials are:

July	$	
August	$	
September	$	

(c) The total of the budgeted cash payments for labour and overhead in August is $ _____.

(d) A cash budget can be used to give forewarning of potential cash problems that could arise so that managers can take action to avoid them. This is known as:

feedforward control ☐

feedback control ☐

(e) A cash budget is continuously updated to reflect recent events and changes to forecast events. This type of budget is known as a:

flexible budget ☐

rolling budget ☐

Question 7

JKL Hotel operates a budgeting system and budgets expenditure over eight budget centres as shown below. Analysis of past expenditure patterns indicates that variable costs in some budget centres vary according to occupied room nights (ORN), while in others the variable proportion of costs varies according to the number of visitors (V).

The budgeted expenditures for a period with 2,000 ORN and 4,300 V were as follows:

Budget centre	Variable costs vary with:	Budgeted expenditure $	Budget notes:
Cleaning	ORN	13,250	$2.50 per ORN
Laundry	V	15,025	$1.75 per V
Reception	ORN	13,100	$12,100 fixed
Maintenance	ORN	11,100	$0.80 per ORN
Housekeeping	V	19,600	$11,000 fixed
Administration	ORN	7,700	$0.20 per ORN
Catering	V	21,460	$2.20 per V
Overheads	–	11,250	all fixed
		112,485	

In period 9, with 1,850 ORN and 4,575 V, actual expenditures were as follows:

Budget centre	Actual expenditure $
Cleaning	13,292
Laundry	14,574
Reception	13,855
Maintenance	10,462
Housekeeping	19,580
Administration	7,930
Catering	23,053
Overheads	11,325
	114,071

Required:

(a) The total budget cost allowances (to the nearest $) for the following costs for period 9 are:

	$
Cleaning	
Laundry	
Reception	
Maintenance	
Housekeeping	
General overheads	

(b) The total budget cost allowance in the flexible budget for period 9 is $113,521.

The total budget variance for period 9 is $ _____. The variance is:

adverse ☐

favourable ☐

Question 8

PQR's cash budget forewarns of a short-term surplus.

Which of the following would be appropriate actions to take in this situation? Select all that are correct.

(a) Increase receivables ☐

(b) Purchase new non-current assets ☐

(c) Repay long-term loans ☐

(d) Pay suppliers early to obtain a cash discount ☐

(e) Arrange a bank overdraft ☐

(f) Reduce inventory ☐

Question 9

LMN operates a system of flexible budgets. The flexed budgets for expenditure for the first two quarters of year 3 are given below.

Assuming the cost structures in quarters 1 and 2 continue, complete the statement of the budget cost allowances for quarter 3, when production was 15,000 units.

	Quarter 1	Quarter 2	Quarter 3
Production units	**10,000**	**13,000**	**15,000**
Budget cost allowances:	$	$	$
Direct materials	130,000	169,000	195,000
Direct labour	74,000	96,200	A
Production overhead	88,000	109,000	B
Administration overhead	26,000	26,000	26,000
Total budget cost allowance	318,000	400,200	C

Question 10

Use some of the following words to complete the sentences below.

Participative budgeting	Periodic budgets	Imposed budgeting
Continuous budgeting	Zero-based budgeting	Incremental budgeting

RST and XYZ are two manufacturing companies. RST involves all the managers in the budget process. Each manager is asked to prepare a budget from scratch, justifying all items with a business case. XYZ takes a different approach to budgeting. The budget for XYZ is prepared by the finance director. He prepares the budget by taking last year's actual results and adjusting it for any changes expected for the next period.

RST uses _____ and _____,

while XYZ uses _____ and _____.

Test your understanding and end of chapter answers

Test your understanding 1

(a)   June: **6,150 cases**

      July: **7,600 cases**

(b)   August: **19,125 kg**

Use a clear columnar layout for your budget workings. Although your workings will not earn marks, clear workings help you to avoid arithmetical errors because 100% accuracy is vital.

Do not forget to adjust for the budgeted movement in inventory in parts (a) and (b). A common error is to get the opening and closing inventory calculations the wrong way round.

Workings:

(a)   **Production budget (in cases)**

	June	July	August	September
Sales	6,000	7,500	8,500	7,000
Closing inventory (1)	750	850	700	650
Opening inventory	(600)	(750)	(850)	(700)
Production budget	**6,150**	**7,600**	**8,350**	**6,950**

> **Note 1:** Closing inventory for June is calculated as 10% of July sales (7,500 × 10%) = 750. All other months are calculated in the same way.

(b)   **Ingredients purchases budget (in kg)**

		August
Quantity to be used in production	(8,350 × 2.5 kg)	20,875
Closing inventory	(6,950 × 2.5 kg × 50%)	8,687.5
Opening inventory	(8,350 × 2.5 kg × 50%)	(10,437.5)
Ingredients purchases budget		**19,125 kg**

Test your understanding 2

D

Amount to be received in September is:

	$
60% of August sales less 2% discount: ($60,000 × 60% × 98%)	35,280
25% of July sales: ($40,000 × 25%)	10,000
12% of June sales: ($35,000 × 12%)	4,200
	49,480

Test your understanding 3

Cash budget for the year ended 31st December, year 2

Quarter	1	2	3	4
	$	$	$	$
Receipts	196,000	224,000	238,000	336,000
Payments:				
Materials	22,000	37,000	40,000	60,000
Direct wages	100,000	110,500	121,000	117,000
Overhead	45,000	50,000	70,000	65,000
Taxation	5,000			
Machinery purchase			120,000	
Total payments	172,000	197,500	351,000	242,000
Net cash inflow/ (outflow)	24,000	26,500	(113,000)	94,000
Balance b/fwd (1)	10,000	34,000	60,500	(52,500)
Balance c/fwd	34,000	60,500	(52,500)	41,500

Note 1: The balance b/fwd in quarter 1 is the cash at bank on the estimated statement of financial position for 31st December, year 1.

Budgeted statement of financial position at 31st December, year 2

	Cost $	Deprec'n $	Net $
Assets			
Non-current assets			
Land	50,000	–	50,000
Buildings and equipment (2)	520,000	105,000	415,000
	570,000	105,000	465,000
Current assets			
Inventories			
– raw materials	17,000		
– finished goods	37,800		
		54,800	
Receivables (3)		234,500	
Cash at bank		41,500	
			330,800
			795,800
Capital and liabilities			
Capital			
Share capital			350,000
Retained earnings			259,870
			609,870
Current liabilities			
Payables (4)		118,700	
Taxation		67,230	
			185,930
			795,800

Note 2: Buildings and equipment	$
Opening cost balance	400,000
Purchases during year	120,000
	520,000

Depreciation	$
Opening depreciation balance	75,000
Production depreciation	25,000
Selling depreciation	5,000
	105,000

Note 3: Receivables	$
Opening balance	25,000
Sales	1,203,500
Receipts (from cash budget)	(994,000)
Closing balance of receivables	**234,500**

Note 4: Payables	$
Opening balance of payables	9,000
Material purchases	253,700
Overhead, excluding depreciation:*	
Production	175,000
Selling and administration	70,000
	507,700
Less payments (from cash budget):	
Materials	159,000
Overhead	230,000
Closing balance of payables	**118,700**

* The depreciation must be excluded from the overhead because it is not a cash item, i.e. it is not a payment which is made to suppliers.

Test your understanding 4

D

A manager might build some slack into a budget to provide some 'leeway' to disguise unnecessary spending.

Test your understanding 5

The correct matching is:

- A method of budgeting based on the previous budget or actual results, adjusted for any anticipated changes. This describes **Incremental** budgeting.

- A method of budgeting requiring all costs to be specifically justified by the benefits expected. This describes **Zero-based** budgeting.

- A budget prepared for a fixed period of time. This describes **Periodic** budgeting.

- A system of budgeting whereby the budget is continuously updated by adding a further accounting period when the earliest accounting period has expired. This describes **Rolling** budgeting.

Test your understanding 6

Flexible budget control statement for the latest period

	Original budget	Flexed budget	Actual results	Budget variance
Activity (units)	12,600	13,200	13,200	
	$	$	$	$
Sales revenue	277,200	290,400	303,600	13,200
Variable costs:				
Direct material	75,600	79,200	78,350	850
Direct labour	50,400	52,800	51,700	1,100
Production overhead	12,600	13,200	14,160	(960)
Fixed costs:				
Production overhead	13,450	13,450	13,710	(260)
Other overhead	10,220	10,220	10,160	60
	162,270	168,870	168,080	790
Profit	114,930	121,530	135,520	13,990

Note: Variances in brackets are adverse.

Comments

(1) The total variance can be analysed as follows.

	$	$
Sales volume variance ($121,530 – $114,930)		6,600
Sales price variance	13,200	
Budget variance	790	
		13,990
Total variance ($135,520 – $114,930)		20,590

(2) The favourable sales price variance indicates that a higher selling price than standard was charged for the units sold. Despite the higher price, the sales volume achieved was higher than budgeted.

(3) Expenditure on direct material, direct labour and other overhead costs was lower than the budget cost allowance for the activity level achieved. It is not possible to tell from the data provided whether the savings were achieved as a result of a lower price or a lower usage of resources.

(4) Expenditure on production overhead costs, both fixed and variable, was higher than the budget cost allowance for the activity level achieved.

Test your understanding 7

A

A flexible budget is designed to show the budgeted costs and revenues at different levels of activity.

Test your understanding 8

The actual contribution for last month was **$42,831**.

	$
Budgeted contribution	45,500
Sales variance	(3,100)
Direct material variance	1,986
Direct labour variance	(1,090)
Variable production overhead variance	(465)
Actual contribution	**42,831**

Question 1

D

Idle time is 20% of the total hours to be paid for.

Therefore, hours to be paid for = 2,400/0.8 = 3,000. Budgeted labour cost = 3,000 × $10 = **$30,000**.

Question 2

(a), (b), (d) and **(e)** would be contained in a budget manual.

The master budget (c) is the end result of the budgetary planning process.

Question 3

The budget variance for labour cost for the period was **$75,000 adverse**.

The unit labour cost for 12,000 units is $1,440,000 ÷ 12,000 = $120 and for 18,000 units is $2,160,000 ÷ 18,000 = $120. So labour is a variable cost.

The budget cost allowance for labour for 15,000 units is $120 × 15,000 = $1,800,000.

Actual labour cost was $1,875,000, therefore the budget variance for labour = $1,875,000 – $1,800,000 = **$75,000 adverse**.

Question 4

1	Sales budget
6	Materials purchases budget
5	Materials inventory budget
3	Production budget
2	Finished goods inventory budget
4	Materials usage budget

Question 5

The required purchases of liquid L for June are **9,700 litres**.

	Litres
Liquid L required (3,000 × 3 litres)	9,000
Evaporation loss (9,000 × 10/90)*	1,000
Total required input of liquid L	10,000
Closing inventory	900
Less: opening inventory	(1,200)
Required purchases of liquid L	**9,700**

* evaporation loss is 10 % of input

Question 6

(a) July   **$900**

August   **$11,340**

September   **$34,560**

Workings:

		$	$
July:	10% × (10 × $900)		900
August:	90% × July sales (10 × $900)	8,100	
	10% × August sales (36 × $900)	3,240	
			11,340
September:	90% × August sales (36 × $900)	29,160	
	10% × September sales (60 × $900)	5,400	
			34,560

(b) July   **$0**

     August   **$21,200**

     September   **$14,000**

     Workings:

     Cash payments each month are for the previous month's purchases. Therefore, no payments are made in July.

		$	$
August:	Payment for July closing inventory	10,000	
	Payment for July usage (40 × $280)	11,200	
		————	
			21,200
September:	Payment for August usage		
	(50 × $280)		14,000

(c) **$13,600**

     Workings:

	$
August labour cost paid in month incurred (50 × $160)	8,000
July variable overhead cost paid in August (40 × $40)	1,600
Fixed overhead cash cost ($5,000 – $1,000 depreciation)	4,000
	————
	13,600
	————

(d) This is known as **feedforward** control.

(e) This type of budget is known as a **rolling** budget.

Question 7

(a)

	$
Cleaning	**12,875**
Laundry	**15,506**
Reception	**13,025**
Maintenance	**10,980**
Housekeeping	**20,150**
Overheads	**11,250**

Workings:

	Activity (ORN/V)	Variable cost per unit	Variable cost allowance	Fixed cost allowance	Total budget cost allowance
		$	$	$	$
Cleaning (1)	1,850	2.50	4,625	8,250	12,875
Laundry (2)	4,575	1.75	8,006	7,500	15,506
Reception (3)	1,850	0.50	925	12,100	13,025
Maintenance (4)	1,850	0.80	1,480	9,500	10,980
H/keeping (5)	4,575	2.00	9,150	11,000	20,150
Overheads	–	–	–	11,250	11,250

Notes:

		$
(1)	Total budget cost allowance for 2,000 ORN	13,250
	Less variable allowance (2,000 × $2.50)	5,000
	Fixed cost allowance	8,250

(2) $15,025 − (4,300 × $1.75) = $7,500

(3)

	$
Total budget cost allowance for 2,000 ORN	13,100
Less fixed allowance	12,100
Variable cost allowance for 2,000 ORN	1,000

Variable cost allowance per ORN $\dfrac{\$1,000}{2,000}$ = $0.50 per ORN

(4) $11,100 − (2,000 × $0.80) = $9,500

(5)

	$
Total budget cost allowance for 4,300 V	19,600
Less fixed allowance	11,000
Variable cost allowance for 4,300 V	8,600

Variable cost allowance per V: $\dfrac{\$8,600}{4,300}$ = $2 per visitor

(b) **$550 adverse**

Workings:

	$
Flexible budget expenditure	113,251
Actual expenditure	114,071
Budget variance	550 adverse

Question 8

(a) and (d) would be appropriate actions in this situation. Actions **(b)** and **(c)** would not be appropriate because they would involve investing the surplus funds for too long. **(e)** and **(f)** would be appropriate for a short-term deficit.

Question 9

A = $111,000

B = $123,000

C = $455,000

	Quarter 1	Quarter 2	Quarter 3
Production units	**10,000**	**13,000**	**15,000**
Budget cost allowances:	$	$	$
Direct materials	130,000	169,000	195,000
Direct labour	74,000	96,200	**111,000**
Production overhead	88,000	109,000	**123,000**
Administration overhead	26,000	26,000	26,000
Total budget cost allowance	318,000	400,200	**455,000**

Workings:

In this example you will need to investigate the cost behaviour patterns to determine which costs are fixed, which are variable and which are semi-variable.

The first step in investigating cost behaviour patterns is to look at the cost data. You should be able to easily spot any fixed costs because they remain constant when activity levels change. You can see that administration overhead is fixed.

The easiest way to identify the behaviour patterns of non-fixed costs is to divide each cost figure by the related activity level. If the cost is a linear variable cost, then the cost per unit will remain constant. For a semi-variable cost the unit rate will reduce as the activity level increases, because the same basic amount of fixed costs is being spread over a greater number of units.

Direct material and direct labour are variable costs. The cost for direct materials has been given:

Direct material has a cost per unit of $13, so for 15,000 units the cost will be (15,000 × $13) = **$195,000**

Calculate the cost for direct labour:

Direct labour has a cost per unit of $7.40, so for 15,000 units the cost will be (15,000 × $7.40) = **$111,000**

Production overhead is a semi-variable cost.

You will need to use the high–low method to determine the fixed and variable elements of production overheads.

Production overhead

	Production, units	**$**
Quarter 2	13,000	109,000
Quarter 1	10,000	88,000
Change	3,000	21,000

$$\text{Variable cost per unit} = \frac{\$21,000}{3,000} = \$7 \text{ per unit}$$

Fixed cost= $109,000 – ($7 × 13,000) = $18,000

So, for 15,000 units the cost will be 18,000 + (15,000 × 7) = **$123,000**

Question 10

RST uses **participative budgeting** and **zero-based budgeting**, while XYZ uses **imposed budgeting** and **incremental budgeting**.

Standard costing and variance analysis

Chapter learning objectives

After completing this chapter, you should be able to

- explain why planned standard costs, prices and volumes are useful

- calculate variances for materials, labour, variable overheads, sales prices and sales volumes

- prepare a statement that reconciles budgeted profit with actual profit calculated using marginal costing

- explain why variances could have arisen and the inter-relationships between variances.

1 Session content diagram

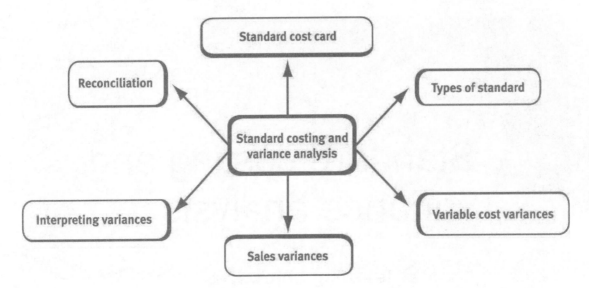

2 Standard costing

In the budgeting chapter we looked at the preparation of budgets within an organisation. These budgets were prepared at a total level and became a target against which actual results could be measured. In this chapter we will look at another control technique known as standard costing. Standard costing also produces a target against which we can measure actual results, but in standard costing the targets are set at a unit level.

 The *CIMA Terminology* defines **standard costing** as a 'control technique that reports variances by comparing actual costs to pre-set standards facilitating action through management by exception'.

A standard cost is a carefully **pre-determined** unit cost which is prepared for each cost unit. It contains details of the standard amount and price of each resource that will be utilised in providing the service or manufacturing the product.

The standard becomes a **target** against which performance can be measured.

The actual costs incurred are measured after the event and compared to the pre-determined standards.

The difference between the standard and the actual is known as a **variance**. Analysing variances can help managers focus on the areas of the business requiring the most attention. This is known as **management by exception**.

3   Standard cost card

Once standard costs for a product or service have been set, they are presented in a **standard cost card**.

A standard cost card for a product, showing the variable elements of production cost, might look like this.

Standard cost card: product 176

	$ per unit
Direct materials: 30 kg @ $4.30	129.00
Direct labour: 12 hours @ $11.80	141.60
	————
Prime cost	270.60
Variable production overhead:	
12 hours @ $0.75	9.00
	————
Variable production cost	279.60
	————

 Look at each item in detail; it is essential that you recognise the detail given on the standard cost card. Ensure you learn the terminology used.

For each of the variable costs, the standard amount and the standard price are given.

Direct material is $129.00 per unit, made up of:	**standard quantity** (30 kg) × **standard price** ($4.30 per kg)
Direct labour is $141.60 per unit, made up of:	**standard hours** (12 hours) × **standard rate** ($11.80 per hour)
Variable production overheads are $9.00 per unit, made up of:	**standard hours** (12 hours) × **standard rate** ($0.75 per hour)

Note: The standard hours for labour and overheads are usually the same as we normally assume that variable overheads vary in direct proportion to the number of direct labour hours worked, unless told otherwise.

Some standard cost cards will also include the fixed overhead and the standard selling price.

These standard data provide the information for a detailed variance analysis, as long as the actual data are collected at the same level of detail.

Measurable cost units

In order to be able to apply standard costing it must be possible to identify a **measurable cost unit**. This can be a unit of product or service but it must be capable of being standardised, for example standardised tasks must be involved in its creation. The cost units themselves do not necessarily have to be identical. For example, standard costing can be applied in situations such as costing plumbing jobs for customers where every job is unique. However, the plumbing jobs must include standardised tasks for which a standard time and cost can be determined for monitoring purposes.

> Standard costing can also be used for services although it can be more difficult to apply in some types of service organisation, where cost units may not be standardised and they are more difficult to measure.

The standard cost may be stored on a physical card, but nowadays it is more likely to be stored on a computer, perhaps in a database. Alternatively it may be stored as part of a spreadsheet so that it can be used in the calculation of variances.

Illustration 1 – Standard cost card

The following data are given for one unit of product K.

  Direct materials: 40 m^2 @ $6.48/m^2

  Direct labour: Bonding department – 48 hours @ $12.50/hour

  Direct labour: Finishing department – 30 hours @ $11.90/hour

The following are the budgeted costs and labour hours per annum for variable production overhead:

	$	hours
Bonding department	375,000	500,000
Finishing department	150,000	300,000

From the information given, prepare a standard cost card extract for one unit of product K showing the subtotals for prime cost and variable production cost.

Solution:

Product K – Standard cost card extract

		$ per unit
Direct materials: 40 m^2 @ $6.48		259.20
Direct labour:		
Bonding – 48 hours @ $12.50		600.00
Finishing – 30 hours @ $11.90		357.00
Prime cost		**1,216.20**
Variable production overhead:		
Bonding – 48 hours @ $0.75 (1)	36.00	
Finishing – 30 hours @ $0.50 (2)	15.00	51.00
Variable production cost		**1,267.20**

(1) Bonding department OAR = $375,000/500,000 hours = $0.75

(2) Finishing department OAR = $150,000/300,000 hours = $0.50

Information for setting standard costs

Setting standard costs

Each element of a unit's standard cost has details of the price and quantity of the resources to be used. In this section, we will list some of the sources of information which may be used in setting the standard costs.

Standard material price

Sources of information include:

(a) quotations and estimates received from potential suppliers

(b) trend information obtained from past data on material prices

(c) details of any bulk discounts which may be available

(d) information on any charges which will be made for packaging and carriage inwards

(e) the quality of material to be used: this may affect the price to be paid

(f) for internally manufactured components, the pre-determined standard cost for the component will be used as the standard price.

Standard material usage

Sources of information include:

(a)   the basis to be used for the level of performance

(b)   if an attainable standard is to be used, the allowance to be made for losses, wastage, etc.

(c)   technical specifications of the material to be used.

Standard labour rate

Sources of information include:

(a)   the HR department, for the wage rates for employees of the required grades with the required skills

(b)   forecasts of the likely outcome of any trades union negotiations currently in progress

(c)   details of any bonus schemes in operation. For example, employees may be paid a bonus if higher levels of output are achieved.

Standard labour times

Sources of information include:

(a)   the basis to be used for the level of performance

(b)   if an attainable standard is to be used, the allowance to be made for downtime, etc.

(c)   technical specifications of the tasks required to manufacture the product or provide the service

(d)   the results of work study exercises which are set up to determine the standard time to perform the required tasks and the grades of labour to be employed.

Variable production overhead costs

In the overhead analysis chapter you learned how pre-determined hourly rates were derived for production overhead. These overhead absorption rates represent the standard hourly rates for overhead in each cost centre. They can be applied to the standard labour hours or machine hours for each cost unit.

The overheads will be analysed into their fixed and variable components so that a separate rate is available for fixed production overhead and for variable production overhead. This is necessary to achieve adequate control over the variable and fixed elements.

The *Fundamentals of Management Accounting* syllabus requires you to deal only with standard variable overhead costs.

> **Test your understanding 1**
>
> **A standard cost is:**
>
> A   the planned unit cost of a product, component or service in a period
>
> B   the budgeted cost for the level of activity achieved in a budget centre in a control period
>
> C   the budgeted production cost for the level of activity in a budget period
>
> D   the budgeted non-production cost for a product, component or service in a period

4 Types of standards

The *CIMA Terminology* defines a **standard** as a 'benchmark measurement of resource usage or revenue or profit generation, set in defined conditions'.

There are four main types of standards:

Ideal standard

Standards may be set at ideal levels, which make no allowance for inefficiencies such as losses, waste and machine downtime. This type of standard is achievable only under the most favourable conditions and can be used if managers wish to highlight and monitor the full cost of factors such as waste, etc. However, this type of standard will almost always result in adverse variances since a certain amount of waste, etc., is usually unavoidable. This can be very demotivating for individuals who feel that an adverse variance suggests that they have performed badly.

Attainable standard

Standards may be set at attainable levels which assume efficient levels of operation, but which include allowances for factors such as losses, waste and machine downtime. This type of standard does not have the negative motivational impact that can arise with an ideal standard because it makes some allowance for unavoidable inefficiencies. Adverse variances will reveal whether inefficiencies have exceeded this unavoidable amount.

Current standard

Standards based on current performance levels (current wastage, current inefficiencies) are known as current standards. Their disadvantage is that they do not encourage any attempt to improve on current levels of efficiency.

Basic standard

Standards set for the long term and remain unchanged over a period of years. This standard is often retained as a minimum standard and can be used for long term comparisons of performance.

Bases for setting standards

CIMA's definition of standards goes on to describe a number of bases which can be used to set the standard. These bases include:

- a prior period level of performance by the same organisation

- the level of performance achieved by comparable organisations

- the level of performance required to meet organisational objectives.

Use of the first basis indicates that management feels that performance levels in a prior period have been acceptable. They will then use this performance level as a target and control level for the forthcoming period.

When using the second basis management is being more outward looking, perhaps attempting to monitor their organisation's performance against 'the best of the rest'.

The third basis sets a performance level which will be sufficient to achieve the objectives which the organisation has set for itself.

Test your understanding 2

Complete the sentences below using some of the following words:

- Attainable standards

- Basic standards

- Ideal standards

- Current standards

Standards which remain unchanged over a period of years are known as _____.

Standards which assume efficient levels of operation, but which includes allowances for factors such as waste and machine downtime, are known as _____.

5 Standard costing in the modern business environment

There has recently been some criticism of the appropriateness of standard costing in the modern business environment. The main criticisms include the following:

- Standard costing was developed when business environments were more stable. In the present dynamic environment, such stable conditions cannot be assumed. If conditions are not stable, then it is difficult to set a standard cost which can be used to control costs over a period of time.

- Attainment of standard used to be judged as satisfactory, but in today's climate, continuous improvement must be aimed for in order to remain competitive.

- The emphasis on labour variances is no longer appropriate with the increasing use of automated production methods.

Using standards

The main purpose of standard costing is to provide a yardstick or benchmark against which actual performance can be monitored. If the comparison between actual and standard cost is to be meaningful, then the standard must be valid and relevant.

It follows that the standard cost should be kept as up to date as possible. This may necessitate frequent updating of standards to ensure that they fairly represent the latest methods and operations, and the latest prices which must be paid for the resources being used.

The standards may not be updated for every small change however any significant changes should be adjusted for as soon as they are known.

Standard costing can be used in most organisations, whether they are involved with manufacturing, or with services such as hospitals or insurance. For example, a pre-determined standard could be set for the labour time to process an insurance claim. This would help in planning and controlling the cost of processing insurance claims.

Standard costing may still be useful even where the final product or service is not standardised. It may be possible to identify a number of standard components and activities for which standards may be set and used effectively for planning and control purposes. In addition, the use of demanding performance levels in standard costs may help to encourage continuous improvement.

6 Variance analysis

In budgetary control, we saw that variances were calculated by comparing the actual costs to the flexed budget cost. In standard costing, variances are calculated in the same way, although more detailed variance analysis is possible.

Total cost variances can be broken down to explain how much of it is caused by the usage of resources being different from the standard, and how much of it is caused by the price of resources being different from the standard.

If resource price or usage is above standard, or if sales volume or selling price is below standard, an **adverse** variance will result. If resource price or usage is below standard, or if sales volume or selling price is above standard, a **favourable** variance will result.

Variable cost variances

There are six main variable cost variances as shown below:

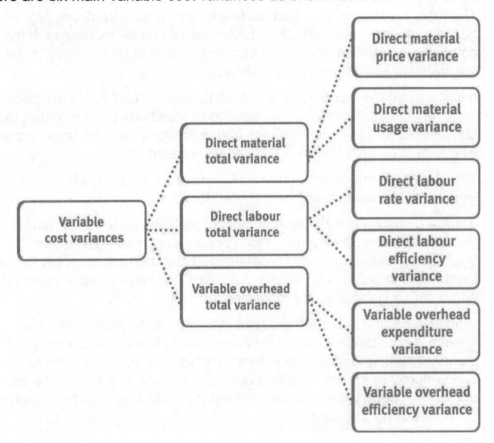

> **Ensure you learn the names of the six variable cost variances as questions may ask you to calculate just one or two variances.**

We will use a simple example to demonstrate how the variances are calculated for direct material, direct labour and variable overhead.

Illustration 2

A company manufactures a single product. The standard cost card for one unit of the product is given:

	$ per unit
Direct material: 81 kg × $7 per kg	567
Direct labour: 97 hours × $8 per hour	776
Variable overhead: 97 hours × $3 per hour	291
	1,634

For January, the company had budgeted to produce 550 units, but 530 units were actually produced and the costs incurred were as follows:

Direct material:	42,845 kg purchased and used at a cost of $308,484
Direct labour:	51,380 hours worked at a cost of $400,764
Variable overhead:	$156,709

Calculate the variable cost variances for January.

You can see that the company had budgeted to produce 550 units but only produced 530 units. The budgeted volume is not relevant when calculating the cost variances. All total cost variances are calculated by comparing the actual cost to the standard cost for the actual level of production (the flexed budget).

Direct material cost variances

(a) **Direct material total variance**

	$	
530 units should cost (530 × 567)	300,510	
But did cost	308,484	
Total direct material cost variance	$7,974	adverse

> **You should always remember to indicate whether a variance is adverse or favourable.**

This direct material total variance can now be analysed into its 'price' and 'quantity' elements. For material, the 'price' element is called the material price variance and the 'quantity' element is called the material usage variance.

(b) **Direct material price variance**

The direct material price variance reveals how much of the direct material total variance was caused by paying a different price for the materials purchased.

	$
42,845 kg purchased should have cost (× $7)	299,915
But did cost	308,484
Direct material price variance	$8,569 adverse

The adverse price variance indicates that expenditure was $8,569 more than standard because a higher than standard price was paid for each kilogram of material.

(c) **Direct material usage variance**

The direct material usage variance reveals how much of the direct material total variance was caused by using a different quantity of material, compared with the standard allowance for the production achieved.

	kg
530 units produced should have used (× 81 kg)	42,930
But did use	42,845
Variance in kg	85 favourable
× standard price per kg ($7): Direct material usage variance	$595 favourable

The favourable usage variance of $595 is the saving in material cost (at standard prices) resulting from using a lower amount of material than the standard expected for this level of output.

Check: $8,569 adverse + $595 favourable = $7,974 adverse (the correct total variance).

 All of the 'quantity' variances are always valued at the **standard** price. Later in this example you will see that the 'quantity' variances for labour and for variable overhead – the efficiency variances – are valued at the **standard** rate per hour.

Test your understanding 3

The standard cost card for product F shows that each unit requires 3 kg of material at a standard price of $9 per kilogram. Last period, 200 units of F were produced and $5,518 was paid for 620 kg of material that was bought and used.

Calculate the following variances and tick the correct box to indicate whether each variance is adverse or favourable.

		Adverse	Favourable
(a)	the direct material price variance is $	❑	❑
(b)	the direct material usage variance is $	❑	❑

Direct labour cost variances

(a) Direct labour total variance

	$
530 units should cost (× $776)	411,280
But did cost	400,764
Total direct labour cost variance	$10,516 favourable

This variance can now be analysed into its 'price' and 'quantity' elements. For labour, the 'price' part is called the labour rate variance and the 'quantity' part is called the labour efficiency variance.

(b) Direct labour rate variance

The direct labour rate variance reveals how much of the direct labour total variance was caused by paying a different rate per hour for the labour hours worked.

	$
51,380 hours should have cost (× $8)	411,040
But did cost	400,764
Direct labour rate variance	10,276 favourable

The favourable rate variance indicates that expenditure was $10,276 less than standard because a lower than standard rate was paid for each hour of labour.

> **Notice the similarity between the method used to calculate the labour rate variance and the method used to calculate the material price variance.**

(c) **Direct labour efficiency variance**

The direct labour efficiency variance reveals how much of the direct labour total variance was caused by using a different number of hours of labour, compared with the standard allowance for the production achieved.

	Hours	
530 units produced should take (× 97 hours)	51,410	
But did take	51,380	
Variance in hours	30	favourable
× standard labour rate per hour ($8)		
Direct labour efficiency variance	$240	favourable

The favourable efficiency variance of $240 is the saving in labour cost (at standard rates) resulting from using fewer labour hours than the standard expected for this level of output.

Check: $10,276 favourable + $240 favourable = $10,516 favourable (the correct total variance).

Variable overhead cost variances

(a) **Variable overhead total variance**

	$	
530 units should cost (× $291)	154,230	
But did cost	156,709	
Total variable overhead cost variance	$2,479	adverse

This variance can now be analysed into its 'price' and 'quantity' elements. The 'price' part is called the variable overhead expenditure variance and the 'quantity' part is called the variable overhead efficiency variance.

(b) **Variable overhead expenditure variance**

The variable overhead expenditure variance reveals how much of the variable overhead total variance was caused by paying a different hourly rate of overhead for the hours worked.

	$	
51,380 hrs of variable overhead should cost (× $3)	154,140	
But did cost	156,709	
Variable overhead expenditure variance	$2,569	adverse

The adverse expenditure variance indicates that expenditure was $2,569 more than standard because a higher than standard hourly rate was paid for variable overhead.

(c) **Variable overhead efficiency variance**

The variable overhead efficiency variance reveals how much of the variable overhead total variance was caused by using a different number of hours of labour, compared with the standard allowance for the production achieved. Its calculation is very similar to the calculation of the labour efficiency variance.

Variance in hours (from labour efficiency variance)	30	favourable
× standard variable overhead rate per hour ($3)		
Variable overhead efficiency variance	$90	favourable

The favourable efficiency variance of $90 is the saving in variable overhead cost (at standard rates) resulting from using fewer labour hours than the standard expected for this level of output.

Check: $2,569 adverse + $90 favourable = $2,479 adverse (the correct total variance)

Test your understanding 4

Budgeted production of product V is 650 units each period. The standard cost card for product V contains the following information.

		$ per unit
Ingredients	12 litres @ $4 per litre	48
Direct labour	3 hours @ $9 per hour	27
Variable production overhead	3 hours @ $2 per hour	6

During the latest period 670 units of product V were produced. The actual results recorded were as follows:

Ingredients purchased and used	8,015 litres	$33,663
Direct labour	2,090 hours	$17,765
Variable production overhead		$5,434

(a) **The ingredients price variance is:**

- A $1,503 favourable
- B $1,503 adverse
- C $1,603 favourable
- D $1,603 adverse

(b)   **The ingredients usage variance is:**

    A $100 favourable

    B $100 adverse

    C $105 favourable

    D $860 adverse

(c)   **The labour rate variance is**

    A $325 favourable

    B $325 adverse

    C $1,045 favourable

    D $1,045 adverse

(d)   **The labour efficiency variance is**

    A $680 adverse

    B $720 adverse

    C $720 favourable

    D $1,260 adverse (e)   **The variable overhead expenditure variance is:**

    A $1,254 favourable

    B $1,254 adverse

    C $1,534 favourable

    D $1,534 adverse

(f)   **The variable overhead efficiency variance is:**

    A $151 adverse

    B $160 adverse

    C $160 favourable

    D $280 adverse

Standard selling price

We will now consider sales. Once standard costs have been set, these can be used to help set the standard selling price of the product or service. The standard cost card will show the total unit cost of the product or service and a calculation based on mark-up or margin can be carried out to establish a suitable standard selling price. With the standard selling price set, the standard contribution per unit can be calculated. The standard selling price will be set taking account of budgeted production and sales volumes. These may be the same, but could be different if the company is changing its inventory levels.

A full set of standard data can be produced for a product or service showing standard selling price, standard costs, standard contribution and budgeted production and sales volumes.

For example, the following gives an example of all the standard data you may be presented with for a product:

Budgeted production	1,500 units
Budgeted sales	1,200 units

	$ per unit
Direct material (4 kg × $ 3.50 per kg)	14
Direct labour (20 minutes × $12 per hour)	4
Variable overheads (20 minutes × $24 per hour)	8
Total variable costs	26
Selling price	32
Standard contribution	6

Sales variances

We can now turn our attention to calculating the sales variances. The *Fundamentals of Management Accounting* syllabus requires you to be able to calculate two variances for sales: the sales price variance and the sales volume contribution variance:

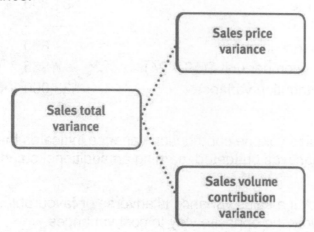

We will demonstrate the calculation of these variances using the following data.

Budget		
	Sales and production volume	81,600 units
	Standard selling price	$59 per unit
	Standard variable cost	$24 per unit
Actual results		
	Sales and production volume	82,400 units
	Actual selling price	$57 per unit
	Actual variable cost	$23 per unit

Sales price variance

The sales price variance reveals the difference in total revenue caused by charging a different selling price from standard.

	$	
82,400 units should sell for (× $59)	4,861,600	
But did sell for (82,400 units × $57)	4,696,800	
Sales price variance	164,800	adverse

The adverse sales price variance indicates that the 82,400 units were sold for a lower price than standard, which we can see from the basic data.

Sales volume contribution variance

The sales volume contribution variance reveals the contribution difference which is caused by selling a different quantity from that budgeted.

Note: In all the cost variance calculations we saw that the budgeted volume was irrelevant. However, the budgeted sales volume is used in the sales volume variance.

Actual sales volume	82,400	units
Budget sales volume	81,600	units
Sales volume variance in units	800	favourable
× standard contribution per unit $(59 – 24)	× $35	
Sales volume contribution variance	$28,000	favourable

The favourable sales volume contribution variance indicates that 800 additional units were sold than was budgeted, earning an additional standard contribution of $28,000.

Be careful to check if a sales variance is adverse or favourable. Remember, sales variances work the opposite way to cost variances.

Test your understanding 5

The following data relate to product R for the latest period.

Budgeted sales revenue	$250,000
Standard selling price per unit	$12.50
Standard contribution per unit	$5.00
Actual sales volume (units)	19,500
Actual sales revenue	$257,400

The sales variances for the period are:

		Adverse	Favourable
(a)	Sales price variance $	❑	❑
(b)	Sales volume contribution variance $	❑	❑

Remember: The sales volume variance is calculated using the budgeted sales volume, while the cost variances used flexed budget, i.e. standard usage for actual level of production.

7 Variances working backwards

It is essential that you are comfortable with the calculation of variances. In some questions the variance will already have been calculated and you will be asked to work back to one of the components of the calculation such as the actual material used, or the actual hours worked.

Illustration 3 – Variances working backwards

XYZ uses standard costing. It makes a product for which the following standard data are available:

Standard labour hours per unit	24
Standard labour cost per hour	$8

During a period 850 units were made, there was a nil direct labour rate variance and an adverse direct labour efficiency variance of $4,400.

How many actual labour hours were worked?

Solution:

You are given the direct labour efficiency variance and the item you are looking for, the actual hours worked, is part of that calculation. Put all the information you have into your calculation and 'work back' to the part that is missing.

850 units should take (850 × 24)	20,400 hours
Did take	?
Variance in hours	?
× standard labour rate per hour (× $8)	
Direct labour efficiency variance	$4,400 adverse

Work back – the variance in hours must have been 4,400/8 = 550 hours adverse.

Therefore the actual hours must have been 20,400 + 550 = **20,950 hours**.

Test your understanding 6

ABC uses standard costing. It purchases a small component for which the following information is available:

Actual purchase quantity	6,800 units
Standard price	$0.85 per unit
Material price variance (adverse)	($544)

What was the actual purchase price per unit?

A $0.75

B $0.77

C $0.93

D $0.95

Test your understanding 7

During a period 17,500 labour hours were worked at a standard cost of $6.50 per hour. The labour efficiency variance was $7,800 favourable.

The number of standard labour hours expected for the output achieved was:

A   1,200

B   16,300

C   17,500

D   18,700

8   Reconciling actual contribution with budgeted contribution

Now that you have seen how to calculate the variable cost and sales variances, you should be in a position to produce a statement which reconciles the actual and budget contribution for the period.

Illustration 4 – Operating statement

LMN has calculated the following variances for Period 4:

	$
Direct material price	1,954 A
Direct material usage	580 A
Direct labour rate	4,361 F
Direct labour efficiency	168 F
Variable production overhead expenditure	8,772 A
Variable production overhead efficiency	56 F
Sales price	8,750 F
Sales volume contribution	14,500 A

The budgeted contribution for period 4 was $116,000 and the actual contribution for the period was $103,579.

Present the variances in a statement which reconciles the budget and actual contribution for Period 4.

Solution:

A reconciliation statement, known as an **operating statement**, begins with the original budgeted contribution. It then adds or subtracts the variances (depending on whether they are favourable or adverse) to arrive at the actual contribution for the month.

Operating statement Period 4

	$
Original budgeted contribution	116,000
Sales volume contribution variance	14,500 A
	————
Standard contribution from actual sales volume	101,500
Sales price variance	8,750 F
	————
	110,250

	$	$	$
Cost variances:	**Fav**	**Adv**	
Direct material price		1,954	
Direct material usage		580	
Direct labour rate	4,361		
Direct labour efficiency	168		
Variable overhead expenditure		8,722	
Variable overhead efficiency	56		
	___	___	
Total cost variances			6,671 A
			___
Actual contribution			103,579
			___

Illustration 5 – Full worked example

We will now try a full example working out each variance and then preparing an operating statement to reconcile the budgeted contribution to the actual contribution.

FGH produces a single product, the RG2. The company operates a standard costing system.

The standard production cost details per unit of product RG2 are:

	$
Materials (5 kg at $20 per kg)	100
Labour (4 hours at $10 per hr)	40
Variable overheads (4 hours at $5 per hr)	20
	___
	160
	___

Variable overheads are absorbed on the basis of labour hours.

The budgeted selling price of the RG2 is $250 and FGH has budgeted production and sales in July to be 1,400 units.

Actual data for product RG2 for July are as follows:

Production and sales	1,600 units
Selling price	$240 per unit
Direct materials (7,300 kg)	$153,300
Direct labour (5,080 hours)	$58,300
Variable overheads	$25,400

Produce a statement that reconciles the budgeted and actual contribution for product RG2 for July showing the variances in as much detail as possible.

Solution:

Operating statement July

	$	$	$
Original budgeted contribution (W1)			126,000
Sales volume contribution variance (W2)			18,000 F
Standard contribution from actual sales volume			144,000
Sales price variance (W3)			16,000 A
			128,000

Cost variances:	**Fav**	**Adv**	
Direct material price (W4)		7,300	
Direct material usage (W5)	14,000		
Direct labour rate (W6)		7,500	
Direct labour efficiency (W7)	13,200		
Variable overhead expenditure (W8)	0		
Variable overhead efficiency (W9)	6,600		
Total cost variances	33,800	14,800	19,000 F
Actual contribution (W10)			147,000

Workings:

(W1) Budgeted contribution

Budgeted contribution per unit = $250 − $160 = $90

Budgeted total contribution for July = $90 × 1,400 = **$126,000**.

(W2) Sales volume contribution variance

Actual sales volume (units)	1,600
Budgeted sales volume (units)	1,400
Sales volume variance in units	200
× Standard contribution per unit	$90
Variance	**$18,000** Fav

(W3) Sales price variance

	$	
1,600 units should have sold for (1,600 × $250)	400,000	
But did sell for (1,600 × $240)	384,000	
Variance	**$16,000**	**Adv**

(W4) Materials price variance

	$	
7,300 kg should have cost (× $20/kg)	146,000	
But did cost	153,300	
Variance	**$7,300**	**Adv**

(W5) Materials usage variance

1,600 units produced should have used (5 kgs × 1,600)	8,000	kg
But did use	7,300	kg
Variance in kgs	700	
× Standard price	$20	
Variance	**$14,000**	**Fav**

(W6) Labour rate variance

	$	
5,080 hours should have cost (× $10/hr)	50,800	
But did cost	58,300	
Variance	**$7,500**	**Adv**

(W7) Labour efficiency variance

1,600 units produced should have taken (1,600 × 4 hrs)	6,400	hours
But did take	5,080	hours
Variance in hrs	1,320	
× Standard rate	$10	
Variance	**$13,200**	**Fav**

(W8) Variable overhead expenditure variance

	$
5,080 hours should have cost (× $5/hr)	25,400
But did cost	25,400
Variance	**$ 0**

(W9) Variable overhead efficiency variance

1,600 units produced should have taken (4 hrs × 1,600)	6,400	hours
But did take	5,080	hours
Variance in hrs	1,320	
× Standard rate	$5	
Variance	**$6,600**	**Fav**

(W10) Actual contribution

	$	$
Sales		384,000
Cost of sales:		
Materials	153,300	
Labour	58,300	
Variable overheads	25,400	
		(237,000)
Actual contribution		**$147,000**

Test your understanding 8

The budgeted contribution for last month was $43,900 but the following variances arose:

	$	
Sales price variance	3,100	adverse
Sales volume contribution variance	1,100	adverse
Direct material price variance	1,986	favourable
Direct material usage variance	2,200	adverse
Direct labour rate variance	1,090	adverse
Direct labour efficiency variance	512	adverse
Variable overhead expenditure variance	1,216	favourable
Variable overhead efficiency variance	465	adverse

Required:

The actual contribution for last month was $ _____.

Reconciling budgeted profit to actual profit

In the above examples we have reconciled budgeted contribution to actual contribution. In some cases we will be required to reconcile budgeted profit to actual profit. To do this we will need to know the actual and budgeted fixed overhead.

We can still use the operating statement format only we start with budgeted profit rather than budgeted contribution as we did before. Starting from the budgeted profit we **add the budgeted fixed overhead** which will leave us with the budgeted contribution. The sales and cost variances are then added and deducted as before giving us actual contribution. From this we can **deduct the actual fixed overhead** which will give us actual profit.

9 Interpreting variances

Now that we have seen how to calculate variances and use these to explain the difference between budgeted and actual contribution, we can look at the variances in more detail and try to interpret them to give us more understanding about what could have caused them. Understanding the causes of the variances will help organisations take appropriate corrective action. It is worth remembering that one possible cause of a variance is that the standard was set too high or too low in the first instance.

Using the FGH example from Illustration 5 we will consider the variances and try to establish what could have caused them. When interpreting variances it is important to recognise that the variances are inter-related and that one issue could affect a number of variances.

The variances calculated were:

	$	
Direct material price	7,300	Adv
Direct material usage	14,000	Fav
Direct labour rate	7,500	Adv
Direct labour efficiency	13,200	Fav
Variable overhead expenditure	0	
Variable overhead efficiency	6,600	Fav
Sales price variance	16,000	Adv
Sales volume contribution variance	18,000	Fav

Now let's consider what may have caused these variances.

Material

The adverse material price variance suggests that FGH paid more per kg of material than it expected. From the standard cost card we can see that FGH expected to pay $20 per kg, but they actually paid $153,300 for 7,300 kg which works out at $21 per kg. There are many possible reasons for this. For example, there could have been a shortage of this material which caused suppliers to raise their prices, or FGH could have used a new, more expensive, supplier.

The material usage variance was favourable which means that less material was used in production than was expected. For 1,600 units, FGH expected to use 8,000 kg (1,600 × 5 kg) but only used 7,300 kg. This could have been due to the level of wastage being lower than expected.

If we look at these two variances together we can see that it could be that FGH paid more for material because it was a higher quality material and this could be a reason for the wastage being less. Better quality material may cause fewer problems during production.

Labour

Looking at the labour variances, we have an adverse rate variance of $7,500 and a favourable efficiency variance of $13,200. The rate variance means that FX paid a higher wage rate that it expected. The standard cost card suggested a wage rate of $10 per hour, but the actual rate paid was $11.48 ($58,000 ÷ 5,080 hours). This could have been as a result of a shortage of staff, resulting in FGH having to pay more to attract workers, or it could be that FGH decided to employ more experienced staff and had to pay them a higher rate.

The favourable efficiency variance suggests that the time taken producing the goods was less than expected. FGH expected 1,600 units to take 6,400 hours (1,600 × 4 hours) to produce but they only took 5,080 hours. This could tie in with the adverse rate variance. If the reason for the adverse rate variance was that more experienced staff were used, then these staff could have worked faster and more efficiently causing a favourable efficiency variance.

This could also tie in to the favourable material usage variance. More experienced staff may cause less wastage in production, contributing to a favourable material usage variance.

You should see from this that it is important to look at variances together to try to establish a clear picture of what has happened.

Variable overhead

In the FGH example, the variable overhead expenditure variance was zero, suggesting that the overhead was, unusually, exactly as expected. The variable overhead expenditure variance is caused by the standard absorption rate being set at too high, or too low a level.

When interpreting the variable overhead expenditure variance, remember that overheads consist of a number of items: indirect materials, indirect labour, maintenance costs, power, etc., which may change because of rate changes or variations in consumption. Consequently, any meaningful interpretation of the variable overhead expenditure variance must focus on individual cost items.

As variable overheads were absorbed on the basis of direct labour hours, then the variable overhead efficiency variance will be affected by all of the same factors as the labour efficiency variance. If fewer hours were worked, a lower amount of overhead would be absorbed resulting in a favourable variance. Remember the overhead could be absorbed on another basis, such as machine hours in which case an alternative explanation would be required.

Sales

Now we will look at the sales variances. An adverse sales price variance suggests that the actual selling price was lower than expected. FGH expected the selling price to be $250 per unit, but the actual selling price was $240. The lower price could have been set to be more competitive in the market place, or to encourage higher sales volume.

The favourable sales volume contribution variance means that the actual volume of sales was higher than expected. Sales of 1,600 units were achieved, compared to the budgeted 1,400 units. The higher volume of sales is likely to be directly linked to the lower sales price as a lower selling price will generally encourage more customers to buy the product. Sales price and volume of sales generally have an inverse relationship.

Possible causes of variances

There are many possible causes of variances, ranging from errors in setting the standards to efficiencies and inefficiencies of operations. The following is a useful list of some of the possible causes of variances.

Variance	Favourable	Adverse
Material price	• Standard price set too high	• Standard price set too low
	• Lower quality material used	• Higher quality material used
	• Unexpected discounts available	• Unexpected price increase
Material usage	• Standard usage set too high	• Standard usage set too low
	• Higher quality material used	• Lower quality material used
	• More skilled workers	• Less skilled workers
	• Stricter quality control	• Theft
Labour rate	• Standard rate set too high	• Standard rate set too low
	• Lower pay rises	• Higher pay rises
Labour efficiency	• Standard hours set too high	• Standard hours set too low
	• More skilled workers	• Less skilled workers
	• Higher grade of material	• Lower grade of material
	• More efficient working	• Less efficient working
Sales price	• Higher quality product	• Increased competition
	• Higher selling price	• Lower selling price
Sales volume contribution	• Increased marketing activity	• Quality control problems
	• Higher sales volume	• Lower sales volume

In an assessment question, you should review the information given and select any feasible cause that is consistent with the variance in question: that is, if the variance is favourable you must select a cause that would result in a favourable variance.

The inter-relationships between variances

We can see from the FGH example that one variance can be related to another. Adverse variances in one area of the organisation may be interrelated with favourable variances elsewhere, or vice versa. For example, if cheaper material is purchased this may produce a favourable material price variance. However, if the cheaper material is of lower quality and difficult to process, this could result in adverse variances for material usage and labour efficiency. There could also be an impact on the sales variances if the cheaper material affects the overall quality of the final product. Sales volume could reduce resulting in an adverse sales volume contribution variance, or the sales price may have to be reduced which would result in an adverse sales price variance.

> **It is important that students can identify any inter-relationships between variances.**

Test your understanding 9

The direct material usage variance for last period was $3,400 adverse.

Which of the following reasons could have contributed to this variance? Select all that apply.

(a) Output was higher than budgeted ☐

(b) The purchasing department bought poor quality material ☐

(c) The original standard usage was set too high ☐

(d) Market prices for the material were higher than expected ☐

(e) An old, inefficient machine was causing excess wastage ☐

Standard hour

Sometimes it can be difficult to measure the output of an organisation which manufactures a variety of dissimilar items. For example, if a company manufactures metal saucepans, utensils and candlesticks, it would not be meaningful to add together these dissimilar items to determine the total number of units produced. It is likely that each of the items takes a different amount of time to produce and utilises a different amount of resource.

A standard hour is a useful way of measuring output when a number of dissimilar items are manufactured. A standard hour is the amount of work achievable, at standard efficiency levels, in an hour.

The best way to see how this works is to look at an example.

Example

A company manufactures tables, chairs and shelf units. The standard labour times allowed to manufacture one unit of each of these are as follows:

	Standard labour hours per unit
Table	3
Chair	1
Shelf unit	5

Production output during the first two periods of this year was as follows:

	Units produced	
	Period 1	Period 2
Table	7	4
Chair	5	2
Shelf unit	3	5

It would be difficult to monitor the trend in total production output based on the number of units produced. We can see that 15 units were produced in total in period 1 and 11 units in period 2. However, it is not particularly meaningful to add together tables, chairs and shelf units because they are such dissimilar items. You can see that the mix of the three products changed over the two periods and the effect of this is not revealed by simply monitoring the total number of units produced.

Standard hours present a useful output measure which is not affected by the mix of products. The standard hours of output for the two periods can be calculated as follows:

		Period 1		Period 2	
	Standard hours per unit	Units produced	Standard hours	Units produced	Standard hours
Table	3	7	21	4	12
Chair	1	5	5	2	2
Shelf unit	5	3	15	5	25
			——		——
Total standard labour hrs			41		39
			——		——

Expressing the output in terms of standard labour hours shows that in fact the output level for period 2 was very similar to that for period 1.

It is important to realise that the actual labour hours worked during each of these periods was probably different from the standard labour hours produced. The standard hours figure is simply an expression of how long the output should have taken to produce, to provide a common basis for measuring output.

The difference between the actual labour hours worked and the standard labour hours produced will be evaluated as the labour efficiency variance.

10   Chapter summary

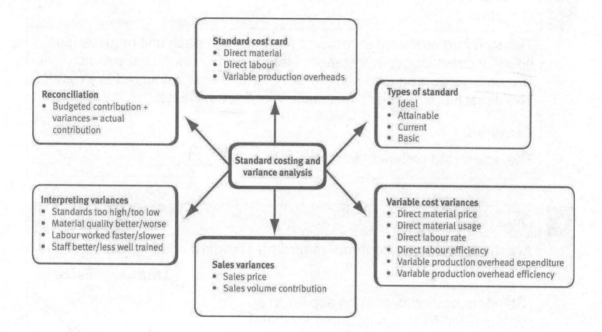

11 End of chapter questions

Question 1

The standard cost card for product K shows that each unit requires <u>four hours</u> of direct labour at a standard rate of $8 per hour. Last period, 420 units were produced and the direct labour cost amounted to $15,300. The direct labour efficiency variance was $160 adverse.

Required:

The actual rate paid per direct labour hour is $ ____9____ .

Question 2

Are the following statements regarding standard costing true or false?

	True	False
Standard costing cannot be applied in an organisation that manufactures specialist furniture to customers' specifications because every cost unit is unique.	☐	☑
A standard is a benchmark measurement of resource usage or profit generation, set in defined conditions.	☑	☐
To reconcile the budgeted contribution to the actual contribution, deduct adverse cost variances and favourable sales variances and add on favourable cost variances and adverse sales variances.	☐	☑

Question 3

The direct labour efficiency variance for the latest period was adverse.

Which TWO of the following reasons could have contributed to this variance? Select all that apply.

(a) Output was higher than budgeted ☐

(b) The purchasing department bought poor quality material which was difficult to process ☑

(c) The original standard time for the output was set too low ☑

(d) The hourly labour rate was higher than had been expected when the standard was set ☐

(e) Employees were more skilled than specified in the standard ☐

Question 4

VWX produces product H. The standard cost card indicates that each unit of H requires 4 kg of material W and 2 kg of material X at a standard price of $1 and $5 per kg, respectively.

Direct labour cost per unit is $112. Direct labour is paid a rate of $8 per hour. Variable production overheads are absorbed at a rate of $4 per direct labour hour. The standard contribution for a unit of product H is $32.

Required:

Calculate the standard selling price of one unit of product H.

$ _____.

Question 5

X, Y and Z are manufacturing companies and all use standard costing.

X has set a standard cost which allows for 90% efficiency. This allows for machine downtime and the level of wastage normally experienced during production.

Y's standards were set several years ago. The managers of Y find it useful to compare current performance against these standards to measure the improvements which have been made.

Z has set standards which assume 100% efficiency will be achieved and no losses will be incurred during production.

Match each of the companies to the types of standards they are using:

- Ideal standards
- Basic standards
- Attainable standards

Question 6

If employees are more skilled than had been allowed for in the original standard cost, which of the following variances are most likely to result? Select all that apply.

(a) favourable material usage ☑

(b) adverse material usage ☐

(c) favourable labour efficiency ☑

(d) adverse labour efficiency ☐

(e) favourable labour rate ☐

(f) adverse labour rate ☑

(g) favourable variable overhead efficiency ☑

(h) adverse variable overhead efficiency ☐

Question 7

PQR has prepared the following standard cost information for one unit of product X:

Direct materials	2 kg @ $13/kg	$26.00
Direct labour	3.3 hours @ $12/hour	$39.60
Variable overheads	3.3 hours @ $2.50	$8.25

Actual results for the period were recorded as follows:

Production	12,000 units
Materials – 26,400 kg	$336,600
Labour – 40,200 hours	$506,520
Variable overheads	$107,250

(a) **The direct material price and usage variances are:**

	Material price	Material usage
A	$6,600F	$31,200A
B	$6,600F	$31,200F
C	$31,200F	$6,600A
D	$31,200A	$6,600A

(b)   **The direct labour rate and efficiency variances are**

	Labour rate	Labour efficiency
A	$24,120F	$7,200F
B	$24,120A	$7,200A
C	$24,120A	$7,560A
D	$31,320A	$7,200A

(c)   **The variable overhead expenditure and efficiency variances are:**

	Expenditure	Efficiency
A	$6,750A	$1,500A
B	$6,750A	$1,500F
C	$8,250A	$1,500A
D	$8,250F	$1,500F

Question 8

Budgeted sales of product V are 4,800 units per month. The standard selling price and variable cost of product V are $45 per unit and $22 per unit respectively.

During June the sales revenue achieved from actual sales of 4,390 units of product V amounted to $231,900.

Required:

(a)   The sales price variance for product V for June was $ _____ adverse/favourable (delete as appropriate).

(b)   The sales volume contribution variance for product V for June was $ _____ adverse/favourable (delete as appropriate).

Question 9

The following variances have been calculated for the latest period:

	$
Sales volume contribution variance	11,245 (F)
Material usage variance	6,025 (F)
Labour rate variance	3,100 (A)
Variable overhead expenditure variance	2,415 (A)

All other variances were zero. The budgeted contribution for the period was $48,000.

Required:

The actual contribution reported for the period was $ _____.

Question 10

The standard cost of providing a meal in a fast food restaurant is as follows:

	$
Ingredient cost	1.80
Direct labour cost	0.30
Variable overhead cost	0.20

The standard price of the meal is $4.50 and the budgeted sales volume is 4,650 meals each period.

During period 9 a total of 4,720 meals were sold for $20,768. The actual total variable cost per meal was $2.30.

(a) **The sales price variance for period 9 was:**

    A $465 favourable

    B $465 adverse

    C $472 favourable

    D $472 adverse

(b) **The sales volume contribution variance for period 9 was:**

    A $147 favourable

    B $147 adverse

    C $154 favourable

    D $154 adverse

Test your understanding and end of chapter answers

Test your understanding 1

A

A standard cost is a carefully pre-determined unit cost which is prepared for each cost unit.

Test your understanding 2

Standards which remain unchanged over a period of years are known as **basic standards**.

Standards which assume efficient levels of operation, but which includes allowances for factors such as waste and machine downtime, are known as **attainable standards**.

Ideal standards are set at ideal levels, making no allowances for inefficiencies, loss or wastage.

Current standards are based on current performance levels.

Test your understanding 3

(a)   the direct material price variance is **$62 favourable**.

(b)   the direct material usage variance is **$180 adverse**.

	$	
620 kg should have cost (× $9)	5,580	
But did cost	5,518	
Direct material price variance	**$62**	**favourable**

	kg	
200 units produced should have used (× 3 kg)	600	
But did use	620	
Variance in kg	20	adverse

× standard price per kg ($9):

Direct material usage variance	**$180**	**adverse**

Test your understanding 4

(a) **D**

8,015 litres should cost (× $4)	32,060
But did cost	33,663
Ingredients price variance	**$1,603** adverse

(b) **A**

	Litres	
670 units produced should use (× 12)	8,040	
But did use	8,015	
Variance in litres	25	favourable
× standard price per litre ($4)		
Ingredients usage variance	**$100**	**favourable**

(c) **C**

	$	
2,090 hours should cost (× $9)	18,810	
But did cost	17,765	
Labour rate variance	**$1,045**	**favourable**

(d) **B**

	Hours	
670 units produced should take (× 3)	2,010	
But did take	2,090	
Variance in hours	80	adverse
× standard labour rate per hour ($9)		
Labour efficiency variance	**$720**	**adverse**

(e) **B**

	$	
2,090 hours should cost (× $2)	4,180	
But did cost	5,434	
Variable overhead expenditure variance	**$1,254**	**adverse**

(f) **B**

	$	
Variance in hours (from labour efficiency variance) × standard variable overhead rate per hour ($2)	80	adverse
Variable overhead efficiency variance	**$160**	**adverse**

Test your understanding 5

(a) the sales price variance is **$13,650 favourable**.

(b) the sales volume contribution variance is **$2,500 adverse**.

	$	
19,500 units should sell for ($12.50)	243,750	
But did sell for	257,400	
Sales price variance	**$13,650**	**favourable**
Actual sales volume	19,500	
Budget sales volume ($250,000/$12.50)	20,000	
Sales volume variance in units	500	adverse
× standard contribution per unit	× $5	
Sales volume contribution variance	**$2,500**	**adverse**

Test your understanding 6

C

	$	
6,800 litres should cost (× $0.85)	5,780	
But did cost	?	
Material price variance	544	adverse

Working back, materials must have cost ($5,780 + $544) = $6,324

Therefore the actual purchase price per unit = material cost ÷ actual quantity purchased

Actual purchase price per unit = $6,324 ÷ 6,800 = **$0.93 per unit.**

Test your understanding 7

D

X units should take	?	
Did take	17,500	hours
Variance in hours	?	
× standard labour rate per hour (× $6.50)		
Direct labour efficiency variance	$7,800	F

Working backwards, the variance in hours must have been $7,800/$6.50 = 1,200 hours favourable

The actual hours were 17,500, therefore the standard hours expected must have been 17,500 + 1,200 = **18,700 hours**.

Test your understanding 8

The actual contribution for last month was **$38,635**.

Workings:

When working from the budgeted contribution to the actual contribution, adverse variances are deducted from the budgeted contribution and favourable variances are added.

The actual contribution for last month was $(43,900 − 3,100 − 1,100 + 1,986 − 2,200 − 1,090 − 512 + 1,216 − 465) = **$38,635**.

Test your understanding 9

The reasons which could have contributed to the adverse direct material usage variance are:

(b)   Poor quality material could have led to higher wastage.

(e)   Excess wastage causes an adverse material usage variance.

(a)   A higher output would not in itself cause an adverse usage variance, because the expected usage of material would be based on the actual output achieved.

(c)   Setting the original standard usage too high is likely to lead to favourable usage variances.

(d)   Higher market prices would cause adverse material price variances.

Question 1

The actual rate paid per direct labour hour is **$9 per hour**.

420 units should take (420 × 4)	1,680	hours
Did take	?	
Variance in hours	?	

× standard labour rate per hour (× $8)		
Direct labour efficiency variance	$160	adverse

Work back – the variance in hours must have been 160/8 = 20 hours adverse

Therefore the actual hours must have been 1,680 + 20 = 1,700 hours.

If the actual direct labour cost was $15,300 for 1,700 hours. The actual rate must have been ($15,300/1,700) = $9 per hour.

Question 2

Standard costing cannot be applied in an organisation that manufactures specialist furniture to customers' specifications because every cost unit is unique is **False**. Even though each cost unit is unique, each could involve standardised tasks for which a standard time and/or cost can be determined for control purposes.

A standard is a benchmark measurement of resource usage or profit generation, set in defined conditions is **True**.

To reconcile the budgeted contribution to the actual contribution, deduct adverse cost variances and favourable sales variances and add on favourable cost variances and adverse sales variances is **False**. To reconcile the budgeted contribution to the actual contribution, deduct all adverse variances and add on all favourable variances.

Question 3

Only **(b)** and **(c)** could have contributed to an adverse direct labour efficiency variance.

(a) Higher output would not in itself cause an adverse efficiency variance. In calculating the efficiency variance the expected labour hours would be flexed according to the actual output achieved.

(b) If material was difficult to process the number of labour hours taken might have been higher than standard. This would result in an adverse labour efficiency variance.

(c) If the original standard time was set too low then actual times are likely to be higher than standard, thus resulting in an adverse labour efficiency variance.

(d) A higher hourly labour rate would cause an adverse labour rate variance, not an adverse efficiency variance.

(e) Using employees who are more skilled than specified in the standard is more likely to result in a favourable direct labour efficiency variance.

Question 4

The standard selling price of one unit of product H is **$214**.

		$ per unit
Direct material W	(4 kg × $1)	4
Direct material X	(2 kg × $5)	10
Direct labour	(14 × $8)	112
Variable production overhead	(14 × $4)	56
Total variable production cost		**182**

Standard contribution = standard selling price – standard variable cost.

Standard selling price = standard contribution + standard variable cost = $32 + $182 = **$214**

Question 5

X is using **attainable standards**.

Y is using **basic standards**.

Z is using **ideal standards**.

Question 6

(a), (c), (f) and (g) are most likely.

(a)   Highly skilled employees may use material more efficiently.

(c)   Highly skilled employees may work more quickly.

(f)   Highly skilled employees are likely to be paid a higher hourly rate.

(g)   Highly skilled employees may work more quickly.

Question 7

(a)   **A**

Material price variance	$	
Standard cost of materials used		
26,400 kg × $13	343,200	
Actual cost	336,600	
Material price variance	**$6,600**	**favourable**

Material usage variance	kg	
Standard usage 12,000 units × 2 kg	24,000	
Actual usage	26,000	
Material usage variance in kg	2,400	adverse
× standard price per kg	× $13	
Material usage variance	**$31,200**	**adverse**

(b)   **B**

Labour rate variance	$	
Standard cost of hours used		
40,200 × $12	482,400	
Actual labour cost	506,520	
Labour rate variance	**$24,120**	**adverse**

Labour efficiency variance	Hours	
Standard time 12,000 units × 3.3 hours	39,600	
Actual time	40,200	
Labour efficiency variance in hours	600	adverse
× standard rate per hour	× $12	
Labour efficiency variance	**$7,200**	**adverse**

(c) **A**

	$	
Variable overhead expenditure variance		
40,200 hours of variable overhead should cost (× $2.50)	100,500	
But did cost	107,250	
Variable overhead expenditure variance	**$6,750**	**adverse**
Variable overhead efficiency variance		
Efficiency variance in hours, from labour efficiency variance	600	adverse
× standard variable overhead rate per hour	× $2.50	
Variable overhead efficiency variance	**$1,500**	**adverse**

Question 8

(a) The sales price variance for product V for June was **$34,350 favourable.**

(b) The sales volume contribution variance for product V for June was **$9,430 adverse**.

	$	
4,390 units should sell for (× $45)	197,550	
But did sell for	231,900	
Sales price variance	**$34,350**	**favourable**
Actual sales volume	4,390	units
Budget sales volume	4,800	units
Sales volume variance in units	410	adverse
× standard contribution per unit $(45 – 22)	× $23	
Sales volume contribution variance	**$9,430**	**adverse**

Question 9

The actual contribution reported for the period was **$59,755**.

Adverse variances are deducted from the budgeted contribution to derive the actual contribution. Favourable variances are added because they would increase the contribution above the budgeted level.

$48,000 + $(11,245 + 6,025 − 3,100 − 2,415) = $59,755.

Question 10

(a) **D**

	$
4,720 meals should sell for (× $4.50)	21,240
But did sell for	20,768
Sales price variance	**$472** **adverse**

(b) **C**

Actual sales volume	4,720	meals
Budget sales volume	4,650	meals
Sales volume variance in meals	70	favourable
× standard contribution per meal *	× $2.20	
Sales volume contribution variance	**$154**	**favourable**

* standard contribution = $(4.50 − 1.80 − 0.30 − 0.20) = $2.20

Integrated accounting systems

Chapter learning objectives

After completing this chapter, you should be able to

- explain the integration of the cost accounts with the financial accounting system

- prepare a set of integrated accounts, showing standard cost variances.

1   Session content diagram

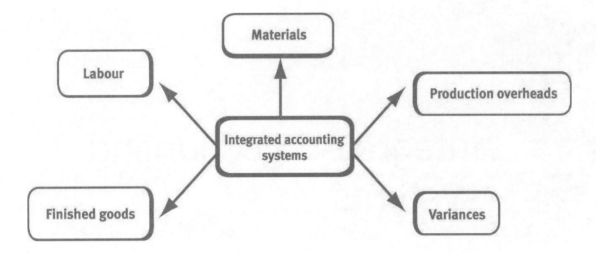

2   Integrated accounting systems

Each organisation will design its accounting system to suit its own needs, taking into account factors such as statutory accounting requirements and management information needs. The accounting systems that are in use range from very simple manual systems to sophisticated computerised systems capable of producing detailed reports as required by management.

In an integrated system the cost accounting function and the financial accounting function are combined in one system, rather than separating the two sets of accounts in two separate ledgers.

 The *CIMA Terminology* defines **integrated accounts** as a 'set of accounting records that integrates both financial and cost accounts using a common input of data for all accounting purposes'.

Accounts required for an integrated accounting system:

- Raw materials control account
- Wages control account
- Production overhead control account
- Administration overhead control account
- Selling and distribution overhead control account
- Work in progress control account
- Finished goods control account

- Cost of sales control account
- Other accounts:
  - Sales account
  - Under-/over-absorption account
  - Statement of profit or loss.

Control accounts are total or summary accounts. For example, the raw materials control account records the total materials received and the total materials issued.

Advantages of an integrated system

The main advantages of integrated systems are as follows:

- Duplication of effort is avoided and there is less work involved in maintaining the system than if two sets of accounts are kept.

- There is no need for the periodic reconciliation of the two sets of accounts which is necessary with non-integrated systems.

- Maintaining a single set of accounts avoids the confusion that can arise when two sets of accounts are in existence which each contain different profit figures.

The main disadvantage of integrated accounts is that a single system is used to provide information both for external and internal reporting requirements. The need to provide information for statutory purposes may influence the quality of information which can be made available for management purposes.

Financial accounting is required to record all transactions for the accounting period and to allow the organisation to produce the statutory accounts at the end of the period. Financial accounting is viewed as external in nature.

Management accounting is the production of information for management of a company to aid planning, control and decision making. It is internal in nature and needs to be more detailed than financial accounting.

3 Accounting for the cost of labour

Before looking at integrated accounts in operation, we need to discuss the detail of accounting for the cost of labour.

The cost of labour is made up of a number of components. It is important to recognise how these components are accounted for. Some will be treated as **direct** labour costs and some will be treated as **indirect** labour costs.

Gross wages

The total amount of pay for each employee is known as a **gross wage**. This is the total amount of pay, but this is not the amount received by the employee as a number of deductions are made first. Employees receive a **net wage**.

> ### Net wage = Gross wage – Deductions

Deductions from employees' wages

Employers often make deductions from employee gross wages for items such as pension contributions, child support payments, income and/or social security taxes, and trade union membership fees. These deductions may be required by law or, in areas such as pension contributions, may be made at the request of the employee.

The employer may also make additional benefit contributions on behalf of employees. For example, the employer may make extra payments into the employee's pension scheme over-and-above the gross wage.

Some organisations treat these additional benefit contributions as an indirect cost. However, others regard this related employment cost as part of the wage cost of each direct employee and would share it among the tasks completed by adding it to the gross wages value, thus treating it as part of direct wages cost.

Overtime premium

It is common for hours worked in excess of the basic working week to be paid at a higher rate per hour. The extra amount is usually referred to as **overtime premium**. The treatment of overtime premium depends on the reason for the overtime.

- **Specific customer request**. Where a customer requires a job to be completed early or at a specific time, they should be advised that overtime would be required and that this cost would be charged to them. In this situation the overtime premium is treated as a direct cost.

- **General circumstances**. Overtime may be required as a result of the organisation's need to complete work which would not be finished without the working of overtime. In his case the cost of the overtime premium is regarded as an indirect cost, even the premium that is paid to direct workers, because it cannot be identified with a specific cost unit.

Bonus earnings

The earning of bonuses, if paid on an individual task basis, can be clearly attributed to a particular task and so would be a direct labour cost of this task. However, if the bonus system accumulates the total standard time and hours worked for a particular pay period and then calculates the bonus based on these totals, any bonus will usually be treated as an indirect cost.

Idle time

Idle time payments are made when an employee is available for work and is being paid, but is not carrying out any productive work. Idle time can arise for various reasons including machine breakdown, lack of orders or unavailability of materials. Idle time must be recorded carefully and management must ensure that it is kept to a minimum. Idle time payments are treated as indirect costs in the analysis of wages.

Illustration 1 – Direct and indirect labour costs

The wages analysis for cost centre 456 shows the following summary of gross pay:

		Direct employees $	Indirect employees $
Basic pay	ordinary hours	48,500	31,800
Overtime pay	basic rate	1,600	2,800
	premium	800	1,400
Bonuses paid		5,400	8,700
Total gross pay		56,300	44,700

Direct employees are those directly involved in production, while indirect employees may be involved indirectly with production, or in support functions. Remember, direct labour costs can be associated directly with an individual cost unit but indirect labour costs cannot.

Which of these costs are direct labour costs and which are indirect labour costs?

Solution:

There is no indication that the overtime and bonuses can be specifically identified with any particular cost unit. Therefore, the overtime premium and the bonuses are indirect costs, even the amounts which were paid to direct employees.

The wages can be analysed as follows:

		Direct labour cost $	Indirect labour cost $
Basic pay		48,500	31,800
Overtime pay	basic rate	1,600	2,800
	premium		2,200
Bonuses paid			14,100
		50,100	50,900

It would not be 'fair' to charge the overtime premium of direct workers to the cost unit which happened to be worked on during overtime hours if this unit did not specifically cause the overtime to be incurred. Therefore, the premium is treated as an indirect cost of all units produced in the period.

The direct labour cost of $50,100 can be directly identified with cost units and will be charged to these units based on the analysis of labour time. The indirect costs cannot be identified with any particular cost unit and will be shared out over all units, using the overhead absorption methods described in the overhead analysis chapter.

Test your understanding 1

Gross wages incurred in department 1 in June were $54,000. The wages analysis shows the following summary breakdown of the gross pay:

	Paid to direct labour $	Paid to indirect labour $
Ordinary time	25,185	11,900
Overtime		
basic pay	5,440	3,500
premium	1,360	875
Shift allowance	2,700	1,360
Sick pay	1,380	300
	36,065	17,935

What is the direct wages cost for department 1 in June?

A $25,185

B $30,625

C $34,685

D $36,065

Test your understanding 2

FGH has two production departments, A and B. Workers in department A are considered direct workers and workers in department B are considered indirect workers.

In the last week department A worked 40 hours of overtime, 30 at the specific request of a customer and the remaining at the request of management. Department B worked 15 hours of overtime, 5 of which were at the specific request of a customer.

All workers in department A are paid at a rate of $12 per hour and workers in department B are paid at a rate of $10 per hour. All overtime is paid at time and a half.

Calculate the total overtime pay for the week, split between direct and indirect cost.

Direct overtime cost $ _____

Indirect overtime cost $ _____

Total overtime cost $ _____

4   Accounting entries

Double entry

To understand integrated accounting you will need an understanding of double entry, which you will cover in more detail in your financial accounting studies.

All transactions undertaken by the organisation must be recorded. They are recorded using **double entry**.

Each transaction is entered into a **ledger** (this is the name we give for each account). A ledger exists for each type of cost or income which the organisation wishes to gather information about. Each ledger has two sides, **debit** and **credit**. All entries must have two equal parts, a debit and a credit. At the end of the period all of the entries in each ledger are added up and the ledgers are balanced. The balances end up in the Statement of financial position (SOFP) or the Statement of profit or loss (SOPL).

> **A debit is an asset (in the SOFP) or an expense (in the SOPL) and a credit is a liability (in the SOFP) or an income (in the SOPL).**

We normally draw our ledgers as '**T-accounts**' and show the name of the account at the top, the debits on the left and the credits on the right.

Ledger name

Debit	Credit

Example

Purchase $500 of material by cash. The two ledger accounts are material and cash. In this case, we would debit the materials accounts and credit the cash account. We write the name of the other side of the entry as the description.

Material

	$		$
Cash	500		

Cash

	$		$
		Material	500

If we then purchased $6,000 of materials on credit (pay later), we would debit the materials account and credit the payables account. The material account would now show:

Material

	$		$
Cash	500		
Payables	6,000		

And the payables account would show:

Payables

	$		$
		Material	6,000

Balancing a ledger

Assume we have the following entries in the production overhead ledger at the end of the period:

Production overhead

	$		$
Bank	5,000	Work in progress	27,000
Wages control	10,000		
Raw materials control	9,000		

To balance the account, add up both sides, in this case the debit total is $24,000 and the credit total is $27,000. Put the largest total at the bottom of BOTH columns.

Production overhead

	$		$
Bank	5,000	Work in progress	27,000
Wages control	10,000		
Raw materials control	9,000		
Balance c/d	**3,000**		
	———		———
	27,000		27,000
	———		———

To make the account balance, $3,000 must be added to the debit side of the account. This is the closing balance of the account and we show it as Balance c/d (carried down) or c/f (carried forward). This means that when we start the next period we start with a balance of $3,000 in the production overhead ledger.

Illustration 2 – Integrated accounting example

The following example will demonstrate the double-entry principles involved in an integrated system. Make sure that you understand which accounts are used to record each type of transaction, before you move on to the next example.

The main accounting entries in an integrated system

The following shows the flow of accounting entries within an integrated system. The numbers in brackets refer to the numbers of the transactions described in the following pages (it is best to work through the transactions in order and to refer back to these accounts so that you can see where each transaction has been recorded):

Raw materials control					Payables control			
10,000	(1)	8,000	(2)				10,000	(1)
		1,000	(3)				5,000	(8)

Work in progress control					Production overhead control			
8,000	(2)	50,000	(13)		1,000	(3)	20,000	(11)
22,000	(6)				10,000	(7)		
20,000	(11)				5,000	(8)		
					4,000	(9)		

Wages control					Cash/bank			
25,000	(4)	22,000	(6)				25,000	(4)
8,000	(5)	10,000	(7)				1,500	(10)

Employee deductions payable

	8,000 (5)

Provision for depreciation

	4,000 (9)

Administration overhead control

1,500 (10)	1,500 (16)

Receivables control

80,000 (12)	

Sales account

80,000 (17)	80,000 (12)

Finished goods control

50,000 (13)	50,000 (14)

Cost of sales account

50,000 (14)	50,000 (15)

Statement of profit or loss

50,000 (15)	80,000 (17)
1,500 (16)	

(1) The purchase of $10,000 worth of raw materials on credit terms.

Debit   Raw materials control

Credit   Payables control

The cost of raw materials purchased is debited to the raw material control account.

(2) The issue of $8,000 worth of direct materials to production.

Debit   Work in progress control

Credit   Raw materials control

Direct materials costs are charged to the work in progress account.

(3) The issue of $1,000 worth of indirect materials to production overheads.

Debit   Production overhead control

Credit   Raw materials control

Indirect production costs (in this case indirect materials costs) are collected in the production overhead control account for later absorption into production costs.

From (2) and (3) you can see that the materials purchased in (1) have been split between direct (posted to work in progress control) and indirect (posted to production overhead control).

(4) A cash payment of net wages of $25,000.

Debit   Wages control

Credit   Cash/Bank

Wages control is debited with the net amount of wages actually paid, after deductions.

(5) **There are employee deductions of $8,000 to be made from employee wages and paid to other parties (such as tax authorities and pension funds)**

Debit   Wages control

Credit   Employee deductions payable

The total deductions are credited to the Employee deductions payable account. This amount will be paid to the authorities/relevant party at a later date.

The wages control account has now been debited with the gross amount of total wages. This gross amount must then be charged out according to whether it is direct or indirect wages:

(6) **The direct wages of $22,000 are charged to work in progress.**

Debit   Work in progress control

Credit   Wages control

Work in progress control is debited with the amount of direct wages.

(7) **The indirect wage costs of $10,000 are collected in the production overhead control account.**

Debit   Production overhead control

Credit   Wages control

We have now dealt with labour and materials; we will now deal with other expenses:

(8) **Electricity of $5,000 for production purposes, obtained on credit.**

Debit   Production overhead control

Credit   Payables control

(9) **Depreciation of machinery used for production of $4,000.**

Debit   Production overhead control

Credit   Provision for depreciation

These last two items are both production overhead costs which are being accumulated for later absorption into production costs.

(10) **Cash of $1,500 paid for office expenses.**

Debit   Administration overhead control

Credit   Cash account

Once all of the production overhead has been accumulated in the overhead control account, a predetermined rate is used to absorb it into the cost of work in progress.

(11) Absorption of production overhead, using a predetermined rate.

Debit   Work in progress control

Credit Production overhead control. The work in progress account now contains charges for direct costs and for absorbed production overheads. Assuming no over or under absorption, this will amount to $20,000.

(12) The sale, on credit, of all goods produced in the month for $80,000.

Debit   Receivables control

Credit   Sales account

(13) The transfer of completed goods to the finished goods account.

Debit   Finished goods control

Credit   Work in progress control

This is usually done in stages as production is completed during the month. For demonstration purposes this has been simplified to show one transfer of $50,000 at the end of the month.

(14) The transfer of finished goods from the inventory account to cost of sales.

Debit   Cost of sales account

Credit   Finished goods control

This is also usually done in stages as inventory is sold during the month but for simplicity we will show one transfer of $50,000.

The summary statement of profit or loss is prepared for the month.

(15) Transfer the costs of goods sold for the month, $50,000, from the cost of sales to the statement of profit or loss.

Debit   Statement of profit or loss

Credit   Cost of sales account

(16) Transfer the $1,500 administration costs for the month from the administration overhead control account to the statement of profit or loss.

Debit   Statement of profit or loss

Credit   Administration overhead control

(Alternatively, the administration overhead control account balance may first be transferred to the cost of sales account and from there to the statement of profit or loss).

(17) **The transfer of sales revenue of $80,000 to the statement of profit or loss.**

Debit   Sales account

Credit   Statement of profit or loss

The costs in the statement of profit or loss can now be offset against the sales revenue, and the profit for the period can be calculated.

In this example the profit would be $80,000 – $50,000 – $1,500 = $28,500.

You can see that there are amounts left in the raw materials control account and the wages control account. These amounts would be the balances carried forward to the next period.

This illustration has been simplified to demonstrate the main accounting flows. For example, in practice there would be more items of production overhead and administration overhead. There would also be expenditure on other types of overhead such as selling and distribution costs. Control accounts would be opened for these costs and they would be dealt with in the same way as the administration overhead in this example.

The important thing about this example is that you can see the standard entries which are made to record each aspect of the process. You must learn these. For example, a purchase of raw materials on credit will always be a debit to the raw material control account and a credit to the payables control account.

Test your understanding 3

An entity operates an integrated accounting system. It is issuing $40,000 worth of direct materials to production.

In an integrated accounting system, the accounting entries to record an issue of direct materials to production would be:

	Debit	Credit
A	Work in progress control account	Material control account
B	Finished goods account	Material control account
C	Material control account	Work in progress control account
D	Cost of sales account	Work in progress control account

Test your understanding 4

During a period $35,750 was incurred for indirect labour.

In an integrated accounting system, the accounting entries to record the indirect labour cost incurred in a period would be:

	Debit	Credit
A	Wages control account	Overhead control account
B	WIP control account	Wages control account
C	Overhead control account	Wages control account
D	Wages control account	WIP control account

Test your understanding 5

In an integrated accounting system, the accounting entries required when a company absorbs production overhead would be:

	Debit	Credit
A	Work in progress control account	Overhead control account
B	Overhead control account	Work in progress control account
C	Overhead control account	Cost of sales account
D	Cost of sales account	Overhead control account

5   Accounting for under or over absorbed overheads

Take a moment to look back at the production overhead control account in Illustration 2.

You will see that the production overhead control account has acted as a collecting place for the production overheads incurred during the period. In this simplified example the account has been debited with the following overhead costs:

- indirect materials issued from stores ($1,000)

- the wages cost of indirect workers associated with production ($10,000)

- the cost of electricity for production purposes ($5,000)

- the depreciation of machinery used for production ($4,000).

At the end of the period the production overhead cost is absorbed into work in progress costs using the predetermined overhead absorption rate. The amount absorbed is credited in the production overhead control account and debited in the work in progress account.

In our example above we assumed that $20,000 would be debited to WIP leaving a zero balance on the production overhead account.

Where there is a remaining balance on the production overhead control account, this represents the amount of production overhead which is under-absorbed (debit balance) or over-absorbed (credit balance).

If overheads are over- or under-absorbed it effectively means that product costs have been overstated or understated.

 Over/under absorption

When there has been an over or under absorption of overheads, it is not usually considered necessary to adjust individual unit costs and therefore inventory values are not altered. However, the cost of units sold will have been overstated or understated.

We saw in the marginal and absorption costing chapter that with absorption costing, any under-absorption is charged to the statement of profit or loss for the period. The reverse is true for any over absorption, which is credited in the statement of profit or loss for the period.

The over or under absorption is not taken straight to the statement of profit or loss, but is gathered in an over absorption or under absorption account first.

Some organisations do not charge or credit the under- or over-absorption to the statement of profit or loss every period. Instead, the balance is carried forward in the control account and at the end of the year the net balance is transferred to the statement of profit or loss. This procedure is particularly appropriate when activity fluctuations cause under and over absorptions which tend to cancel each other out over the course of the year.

Illustration 3 – Overhead control account example

ABC absorbs overheads on the basis of machine hours. The following data are available for period 2:

Budgeted production overhead	$120,000
Budgeted machine hours	60,000
Budgeted output units	10,000

During period 2, actual output was 8,500 units and actual machine hours were 55,000.

ABC incurred the following production overheads in period 2:

	$
Indirect materials	40,300
Indirect labour	25,600
Utilities	14,200
Depreciation of machinery	10,700
Other production overheads	12,400
Total	103,200

In the overhead analysis chapter we looked at over- and under-absorption. To recap:

Over-/under-absorption is calculated as the difference between the overheads absorbed and overheads incurred.

To calculate the overheads absorbed we need the overhead absorption rate (OAR). Remember this is a pre-determined rate based on budgeted figures. In this example overheads are absorbed on the basis of machine hours so:

OAR = budgeted overhead ÷ budgeted machine hours = $120,000 ÷ 60,000 = $2 per machine hour.

To calculate the overheads absorbed we multiply the OAR by the actual machine hours (or the actual of whichever basis is being used).

	$
Overhead incurred	103,200
Overhead absorbed ($2 × 55,000 hours)	110,000
Over-absorption	**6,800**

Prepare the production overhead control account and the over-/under-absorption account for period 2.

Solution:

(1) Debit all of the actual production overheads to the production overhead control account.

(2) Absorb the production overhead to WIP using the pre-determined OAR.

(3) The production overhead control account is balanced to either the production overhead over-absorption account or the production overhead under-absorption account. In this example we have an over-absorption of $6,800.

Production overhead control account

	$		$
(1) Indirect materials	40,300	(2) Work in progress	110,000
(1) Indirect labour	25,600		
(1) Utilities	14,200		
(1) Depreciation of machinery	10,700		
(1) Other production overheads	12,400		
(3) Over-absorption	6,800		
	110,000		110,000

Production overhead over-absorption account

	$		$
		(3) Production overhead control	6,800

To take this over-absorption to the statement of profit or loss, the entry would be:

Debit Production overhead over-absorption account

Credit Statement of profit or loss

A credit to the statement of profit or loss reduces the cost which makes sense as we have absorbed too much overhead.

Note: If there is no production overhead over-absorption account, the over-absorption can be taken straight to the statement of profit or loss. The entry to record the over-absorption would be:

Debit Production overhead control account

Credit Statement of profit or loss

Illustration 4 – Example using standard costing

Using the same example as in the last illustration, we will look at the same question except where **standard costing** is being used. In this case the overhead will not be absorbed on the basis of actual machine hours but on the **standard machine hours for the actual production level**.

The standard machine hours per unit were: 60,000 machine hours ÷ 10,000 units = 6 machine hours.

The overhead absorbed would be the standard machine hours for the actual production level × OAR.

	$
Overhead incurred	103,200
Overhead absorbed (6 × 8,500 units × $2)	102,000
Under-absorption	**1,200**

The entries in the accounts would be:

Production overhead control account

	$		$
Indirect materials	40,300	Work in progress	102,000
Indirect labour	25,600	Under-absorption	1,200
Utilities	14,200		
Depreciation of machinery	10,700		
Other production overheads	12,400		
	103,200		103,200

Production overhead under-absorption account

	$		$
Production overhead control	1,200		

To take this under-absorption to the statement of profit or loss, the entry would be:

Debit Statement of profit or loss

Credit Production overhead under-absorption account

A debit to the statement of profit or loss increases the cost which makes sense as we have absorbed too little overhead.

Note: If there is no production overhead under-absorption account, the under-absorption can be taken straight to the statement of profit or loss. The entry to record the under-absorption would be:

Debit Statement of profit or loss

Credit Production overhead control account

If you look back at the variance calculations in the standard costing and variance analysis chapter you will see that all of the total cost variances are calculated by comparing the actual cost with the standard quantity (hours/kg etc) for the actual level of production.

When using standard costing, the actual hours are not used.

Test your understanding 6

FGH uses standard costing. It has produced the following data for period 3:

	Budget	Actual
Production overhead	$900,000	$950,000
Production units	20,000	22,000
Labour hours	180,000	185,000

Production overheads are absorbed on the basis of labour hours.

Required:

(a) Calculate the under- or over-absorption of production overheads and show the entries required in the production overhead control account and the production overhead over- or under-absorption account.

(b) Calculate the under- or over-absorption if FGH was not using standard costing.

Test your understanding 7

At the end of a period, in an integrated accounting system the accounting entries for $18,000 overheads under-absorbed would be:

	Debit	Credit
A	Work in progress control account	Overhead control account
B	Statement of profit or loss	Work in progress control account
C	Statement of profit or loss	Overhead control account
D	Overhead control account	Statement of profit or loss

6 Recording variances in the ledger accounts

To be able to study this section effectively you must have a sound understanding of:

- the workings of an integrated accounting system
- the calculation of cost variances in a standard costing system.

If you are not confident that you have a sound understanding of both of these subjects, then you should return and study them carefully before you begin on this section of the chapter.

General rules for recording variances

Although variations do exist, you will find the following general rules useful when you are recording variances in the ledger accounts:

- Variances are entered in the accounts **at the point at which they arise**.
- The materials price variance is recorded in the materials control account.
- The labour rate variance is recorded in the wages control account.
- The 'quantity' variances, that is, material usage, labour efficiency and variable production overhead efficiency, are recorded in the work in progress account.
- The variance for variable production overhead expenditure is usually recorded in the production overhead control account.
- Sales values are usually recorded at actual amounts and the sales variances are not shown in the ledger accounts.

> The amount of the variance is recorded in the relevant variance account:
>
> **a debit for an adverse variance and**
> **a credit for a favourable variance**

Recording variances in ledgers

A ledger account is usually kept for each cost variance. As a general rule, all **variances are entered in the accounts at the point at which they arise**. For example:

- **labour rate variances** arise when the wages are paid. Therefore, they are entered in the **wages control account**. An adverse variance is debited in the account for wage rate variance and credited in the wages control account. For a favourable variance the entries would be the opposite way round

- **labour efficiency variances** arise as the employees are working. Therefore, the efficiency variance is entered in the **work in progress account**. An adverse variance is debited in the account for labour efficiency variance and credited in the work in progress account. For a favourable variance the entries would be the opposite way round.

Illustration 5 – Recording material variances

Material variances

1,000 kg of material is purchased at $5 per kg on 1st March and issued to production at the standard cost of $6 per kg on 10th March.

If the standard usage for producing the actual quantity of finished goods was 900 kg (but 1,000 kgs were actually consumed) then the entries in the raw material control account and the work in progress control account would be:

Raw material control

(1) payables (1,000 × $5)	5,000	(2) work in progress (1,000 × $6)	6,000
(4) material price variance	1,000		

Work in progress

(2) raw material control	6,000	(3) finished goods (900 × $6)	5,400
		(5) material usage variance	600

Material price variance		
	(4) raw material control	1,000

Material usage variance		
(5) work in progress	600	

(1) The actual purchases are debited to raw materials and credited to payables (1,000 × $5).

(2) The issues to production are credited to the raw material account and debited to the work in progress account. Actual quantity at standard price (1,000 × $6).

(3) Work in progress is transferred to finished goods. Standard quantity at standard price (900 × $6).

(4) The material price variance can be calculated as the balance on the raw material control account. This is transferred to the material price variance account. It is a **credit balance** on the variance account, therefore it is **favourable**.

(5) The material usage can be calculated as the balance on the work in progress account. This is transferred to the material usage variance account. It is a **debit balance** on the variance account, therefore it is **adverse**.

The statement of profit or loss

You will see that all of the variances are eliminated before any entries are made in the finished goods inventory account. The finished goods inventory is therefore held at standard cost and the transfer to the cost of sales account and to the statement of profit or loss will be made at standard cost.

At the end of the period the variance accounts are totalled and transferred to the statement of profit or loss. **Adverse variances are debited to the statement of profit or loss and favourable variances are credited**. In this way the actual cost (standard cost, plus or minus the variances) is charged against the sales value in the statement of profit or loss for the period.

Full worked example with variances

Work carefully through the following example of integrated standard cost bookkeeping. It will also give you some useful practice at calculating cost variances.

JKL produces and sells one product only, product J, the standard variable cost of which is as follows for one unit:

	$
Direct material X: 10 kg at $20	200
Direct material Y: 5 litres at $6	30
Direct wages: 5 hours at $6	30
Variable production overhead	10
	___
Total standard variable cost	270
Standard contribution	130
	___
Standard selling price	400
	___

During April, the first month of the financial year, the following were the actual results for production and sales of 800 units

	$
Sales on credit: 800 units at $400	320,000
Direct materials:	
X: 9,000 kg	184,500
Y: 5,000 litres	27,500
Direct wages: 4,200 hours	24,150
Variable production overhead	10,500

The raw materials stores control account is maintained at standard prices. Assume no opening inventories, and no opening bank balance.

All wages and production overhead costs were paid from the bank during April.

Required:

(a) Calculate the variable cost variances for the month of April.

(b) Show all the accounting ledger entries for the month of April. The work in progress account should be maintained at standard variable cost and each balance on the separate variance accounts is to be transferred to the statement of profit or loss (SOPL) which you are also required to show.

Solution:

(a) **Direct material price variance**

Material X	$
9,000 kg should have cost (× $20)	180,000
But did cost (9,000 × $20.50)	184,500
Direct material price variance	$4,500 adverse

Material Y	$
5,000 litres should have cost (× $6)	30,000
But did cost (5,000 × $5.50)	27,500
Direct material price variance	$2,500 favourable

Direct material usage variance

Material X	kg
800 units should have used (× 10 kg)	8,000
But did use	9,000
Variance in kg	1,000 adverse
× standard price per kg ($20)	
Direct material usage variance	$20,000 adverse

Material Y	Litres
800 units should have used (× 5 litres)	4,000
But did use	5,000
Variance in litres	1,000 adverse
× standard price per litre ($6)	
Direct material usage variance	$6,000 adverse

Direct labour rate variance

	$	
4,200 hours should have cost (× $6)	25,200	
But did cost	24,150	
Direct labour rate variance	$1,050	favourable

Direct labour efficiency variance

	Hours	
800 units should have taken		
(× 5 hours)	4,000	
But did take	4,200	
Variance in hours	200	adverse
× standard labour rate per hour ($6)		
Direct labour efficiency variance	$1,200	adverse

Variable overhead expenditure variance

	$	
4,200 hours should cost (× $2)	8,400	
But did cost	10,500	
Variable overhead expenditure variance	$2,100	adverse

Variable overhead efficiency variance

	$	
Variance in hours (from labour efficiency variance)	200	adverse
× standard variable overhead rate per hour	× $2	
Variable overhead efficiency variance	$400	adverse

(b) The easiest way to approach this question is probably to follow the production through: deal first with the purchase and then the issue of the material; then move on to deal with the information about the wages. Lastly, prepare the control account for overheads, before dealing with the transfer from the work in progress account.

Numbers in brackets refer to the notes following the accounts.

Raw materials stores control

	$		$
Payables: material X (1)	184,500	Direct material price variance: material X (1)	4,500
Payables: material Y (2)	27,500	Work in progress (3)	
Direct material price		material X (9,000 × $20)	180,000
variance: material Y (2)	2,500	material Y (5,000 × $6)	30,000
	214,500		214,500

Payables

	$		$
		Raw materials stores control (1)	184,500
Balance c/f	212,000	Raw materials stores control (2)	27,500
	212,000		212,000

Work in progress control

	$		$
Raw material stores: (3)		Direct material usage variance: (3)	
material X	180,000	material X	20,000
material Y	30,000	material Y	6,000
Wages control (5)	25,200	Direct labour efficiency variance (6)	1,200
Production overhead control (7)	8,400	Variable overhead efficiency variance (7)	400
		Finished goods: (8)	
		800 units × $270	216,000
	243,600		243,600

Wages control

	$		$
Bank (4)	24,150	Work in progress	
Labour rate variance (5)	1,050	(4,200 × $6) (5)	25,200
	25,200		25,200

Bank

	$		$
		Wages control (4)	24,150
		Production overhead	
		control (7)	10,500

Production overhead control

	$		$
Bank (7)	10,500	Work in progress (7)	
		(4,200 × $2)	8,400
		Variable overhead	
		expenditure variance (7)	2,100
	10,500		10,500

Finished goods control

	$		$
Work in progress (8)	216,000	Cost of sales (8)	216,000

Cost of sales

	$		$
Finished goods (8)	216,000	SOPL (8)	216,000

Sales

	$		$
SOPL	320,000	Receivables	320,000

Receivables

	$		$
Sales	320,000		

Direct material price variance

	$		$
Raw material stores control (1)	4,500	Raw material stores control (2)	2,500
		SOPL (9)	2,000
	4,500		4,500

Direct material usage variance

	$		$
Work in progress:		SOPL (9)	26,000
material X (3)	20,000		
material Y (3)	6,000		
	26,000		26,000

Direct labour rate variance

	$		$
SOPL (9)	1,050	Wages control (5)	1,050

Direct labour efficiency variance

	$		$
Work in progress control (6)	1,200	SOPL (9)	1,200

Variable overhead expenditure variance

	$		$
Production overhead control (7)	2,100	SOPL (9)	2,100

Variable overhead efficiency variance

	$		$
Production overhead control (7)	400	SOPL (9)	400

The statement of profit or loss could also be shown as a T-account. However, a vertical presentation is probably preferable.

Statement of profit or loss for April (extract)

	$	$	$
Sales			320,000
Cost of sales (8)			216,000
			104,000
Cost variances			
Direct material price	(2,000)		
Direct material usage	(26,000)		
		(28,000)	
Direct labour rate	1,050		
Direct labour efficiency	(1,200)		
		(150)	
Variable production overhead expenditure	(2,100)		
Variable production overhead efficiency	(400)		
		(2,500)	
			(30,650)
Contribution			73,350

Note: Variances in brackets are adverse.

Explanatory notes:

(1) The actual cost of material X purchases is debited to the raw materials stores control and credited to payables. The adverse price variance is credited to the raw materials stores control and debited to the variance account. The net effect of these two entries is that the material is held in the stores account at standard cost.

(2) The actual cost of material Y purchases is debited to the raw materials stores control and credited to payables. To bring the inventory value of material Y up to standard cost, the favourable price variance is debited to the stores control account and credited to the variance account.

(3) The standard cost of the actual material usage is transferred from the raw materials inventory to work in progress. The usage variances are transferred from work in progress to the material usage variance account. An adverse variance is debited to the variance account and credited to work in progress. The net balance for materials cost in the work in progress account is now equal to the standard material cost for 800 units. Check this for yourself.

(4) The wages paid are collected in the control account.

(5) The standard wages cost of the hours worked is debited to work in progress. The favourable labour rate variance is credited to the variance account.

(6) The adverse labour efficiency variance is transferred from work in progress to the relevant variance account. The net balance for wages cost in the work in progress account is now equal to the standard wages cost for 800 units. Check this for yourself.

(7) The variable production overhead paid is collected in the production overhead control account. The standard variable overhead cost of the hours worked is then debited to work in progress. The adverse variable overhead expenditure variance is debited to the variance account. The adverse variable overhead efficiency variance is transferred from work in progress to the relevant variance account. Notice the similarity between the accounting entries for labour and for variable overhead.

(8) The standard variable production cost of 800 units (800 × $270 = $216,000) is transferred from work in progress to finished goods. Since no finished goods inventories are held (production is equal to sales), this amount is transferred at the end of the month to cost of sales, and from there to the statement of profit or loss.

(9) At the end of April, the balances on the variance accounts are transferred to the statement of profit or loss.

Test your understanding 8

An entity uses standard costing and an integrated accounting system.

The double entry for an adverse material usage variance is:

	Debit	Credit
A	Material control account	Work in progress control account
B	Material usage variance account	Material control account
C	Work in progress control account	Material usage variance account
D	Material usage variance account	Work in progress control account

7 Chapter summary

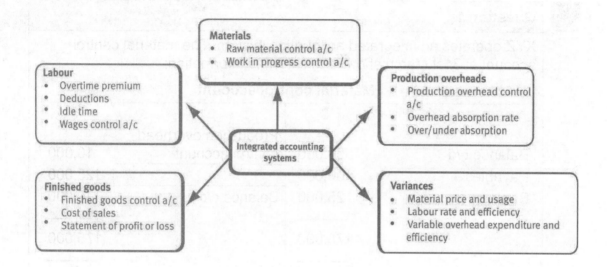

8   End of chapter questions

Question 1

XYZ operates an integrated accounting system. The material control account at 31st March shows the following information:

Material control account

	$		$
		Production overhead	
Balance b/d	50,000	control account	10,000
Payables	100,000		125,000
Bank	25,000	Balance c/d	40,000
	175,000		175,000

Drag the correct account from the list below to complete the ledger account.

- Cost of sales account

- Finished goods account

- Statement of profit or loss

- Work in progress account

(handwritten notes: Materials either: - direct → WIP - indirect → O/H)

Question 2

A company purchased materials costing $30,000. Of these, materials worth $1,000 were issued to the maintenance department and materials worth $22,000 were issued to the production department. *(handwritten: indirect)*

(handwritten: WIP ←)

Which of the following accounting entries would arise as a result of these transactions? Select all that apply.

			$	
(a)	Debit	Raw materials control	29,000	☐
(b)	Debit	Raw materials control	30,000	☑
(c)	Debit	Work in progress control	22,000	☑
(d)	Debit	Work in progress control	23,000	☐
(e)	Debit	Work in progress control	30,000	☐
(f)	Debit	Production overhead control	1,000	☑
(g)	Credit	Raw materials control	23,000	☑
(h)	Credit	Raw materials control	30,000	☐

Question 3

Look at the wages control account and identify whether the following statements are true or false.

Wages control account

	$		$
Bank	82,500	Work in progress control	52,500
Employee deductions payable	9,500	Production overhead control	39,500
	92,000		92,000

	True	False
(a) Gross wages for the period amounted to $82,500.	☐	☑
(b) Indirect wages incurred amounted to $39,500.	☑	☐
(c) Direct wages incurred amounted to $92,000.	☐	☑

Question 4

Details of the production wages for a company last period are as follows:

	Gross wages $000	Employee deductions $000	Net wages $000
Direct wages paid	40	10	30
Indirect wages paid	20	6	14

Post the entries required to record the wages for the period in the following ledger accounts:

- Wages control
- Work in progress
- Production overhead control
- Bank
- Employee deductions payable

Question 5

DEF operates an integrated accounting system. Balances at 31 October were:

	$	
Raw material control account	34,789	Dr
Wages control account	5,862	Cr
Production overhead control account	3,674	Cr
Work in progress control account	13,479	Dr

During the first week of November the following transactions occurred:

	$
Purchased materials on credit	4,320
Incurred wages	6,450
Issued direct materials to production	2,890
Issued indirect materials to production	560
Incurred production overheads on credit	1,870
Absorbed production overhead cost	3,800
Cost of units completed	12,480
Paid wages	5,900

An analysis of the wages incurred shows that direct wages were $5,200.

Required:

(a) The balance shown on the production overhead control account means that the production overhead at 31 October was:

under-absorbed ☐

over-absorbed ☐

(b) The raw material control account has been prepared for the first week of November:

Raw material control account

	$		$
Balance b/d	34,789	Work in progress	B
Payables	A	Production overhead	C
		Balance c/d	35,659

The values that would be entered as A, B and C would be:

A	$	
B	$	
C	$	

(c) The wages control account has been prepared for the first week of November:

Wages control account

	$		$
Bank	A	Balance b/d	5,862
		Work in progress	B
Balance c/d	6,412	Production overhead	C
	————		————
	————		————

The values that would be entered as A, B and C would be:

A $ _____

B $ _____

C $ _____

(d) At the end of the week, the balance brought down on the production overhead control account will be a:

debit balance ☐

credit balance ☐

The value of the balance will be $ _____.

(e) The work in progress control account has been prepared for the first week of November:

Work in progress control account

	$		$
Balance b/d	13,479	Finished goods	D
Raw materials	A	Balance c/d	12,889
Wages	B		
Production overhead	C		
	————		————
	————		————

The values shown in the account as A, B, C and D are:

A $ _____

B $ _____

C $ _____

D $ _____

Question 6

A manufacturing company is very busy and overtime is being worked.

The amount of overtime premium contained in direct wages would normally be classified as:

A   part of prime cost

B   production overheads

C   direct labour costs

D   administrative overheads

Question 7

Data for the finishing department for the last quarter are as follows:

Budgeted cost centre overhead	$320,000
Actual cost centre overhead	$311,250
Budgeted direct labour hours	40,000
Actual direct labour hours	41,500

The accounting entries to record the under- or over-absorbed overhead for the quarter would be:

		Debit		Credit	
A	Overhead control account		$20,750	Statement of profit or loss	$20,750
B	Overhead control account		$8,750	Statement of profit or loss	$8,750
C	Statement of profit or loss		$20,750	Overhead control account	$20,750
D	Statement of profit or loss		$8,750	Overhead control account	$8,750

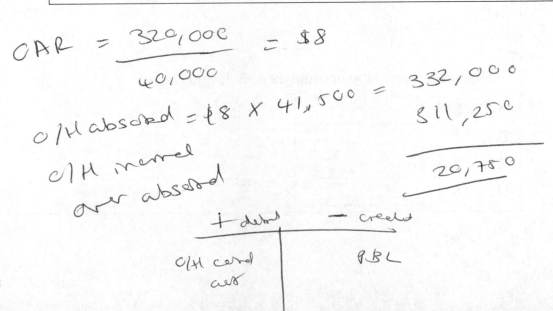

Question 8

The production overhead absorption rate is $3 per direct labour hour. During the period 23,000 direct labour hours were worked.

Production overhead control account

	$		$
		Work in progress	
Wages control	44,000	control	A
Bank	22,000		
Depreciation	8,000		
Raw materials control	2,000		
	‾‾‾‾‾		
	76,000		
	‾‾‾‾‾		

[handwritten annotations:] 76,000 incurred; 69,000 absorbed; 7,000

Required:

(a) In the production overhead control account for the period shown above, the value to be inserted at A is $ _(3×23,000) = $69,000_

[handwritten: 69,000]

(b) Production overhead for the period was:

   under-absorbed   ☑

   over-absorbed   ☐

(c) The value of the under-/over-absorption was $ _____

Question 9

QRS uses an integrated standard costing system. In October, when 2,400 units of the finished product were made, the actual material cost details were:

Material purchased 5,000 units @ $4.50 each

Material used   4,850 units

The standard cost details are that two units of the material should be used for each unit of the completed product, and the standard price of each material unit is $4.70.

The entries made in the variance accounts would be:

	Material price variance account	Material usage variance account
A	Debit $970	Debit $225
B	Debit $1,000	Debit $225
C	Credit $970	Debit $235
D	Credit $1,000	Debit $235

Question 10

RST operates an integrated accounting system and wants to make entries for the following transactions in its accounting system:

- Absorbed production overheads from work in progress

- A labour efficiency variance

- A labour rate variance

Each of these would be credited to one of the accounts below. Match the entries to the correct account:

Cr Work in progress	
Cr Wages control account	
Cr Production overhead control	

Test your understanding and end of chapter answers

Test your understanding 1

B

$25,185 + $5,440 = **$30,625**. The only direct costs are the wages paid to direct workers for ordinary time, plus the basic pay for overtime.

Overtime premium and shift allowances are usually treated as indirect costs. However, if and when the overtime and shift work are incurred specifically for a particular cost unit, they are classified as direct costs of that cost unit. Sick pay is treated as an overhead and is therefore classified as an indirect cost.

Test your understanding 2

Direct overtime cost **$735**

Indirect overtime cost **$210**

Total overtime cost **$945**

		Direct cost $	Indirect cost $
A	Specific overtime (30 × $18)	540	
	General overtime (10 × $12)	120	
	General overtime (10 × $6)		60
B	Specific overtime (5 × $15)	75	
	General overtime (10 × $15)		150
	Total cost	735	210

Where overtime is worked for a specific customer request, the overtime is treated as a direct cost, even that worked by indirect workers.

Where overtime is worked for general circumstances, the overtime worked by indirect workers is treated as an indirect cost. For direct workers, the overtime hours at normal rate are treated as a direct cost and the overtime premium is treated as an indirect cost.

Test your understanding 3

A

Direct costs of production are debited to the work in progress control account and credited to the material control account.

Test your understanding 4

C

Indirect costs, including indirect labour, are collected in the debit side of the overhead control account pending their later absorption into work in progress. To record the indirect labour, the production overhead control account would be debited and the wages control account would be credited.

Test your understanding 5

A

The production overhead is first collected in the overhead control account. It is then absorbed into production costs by debiting the work in progress account using the predetermined overhead absorption rate.

Test your understanding 6

(a)   **Over-absorption of $40,000**

(b)   **Under-absorption of $25,000**

The overhead absorption rate (OAR) = budgeted overhead ÷ budgeted labour hours. $900,000 ÷ 180,000 = $5 per labour hour.

The standard labour hours per unit were: 180,000 machine hours ÷ 20,000 units = 9 labour hours.

The overhead absorbed would be the standard labour hours for the actual production level × OAR.

	$
Overhead incurred	950,000
Overhead absorbed (9 × 22,000 units × $5)	990,000
	————
Over-absorption	**40,000**
	————

The entries in the accounts would be:

Production overhead control account

	$		$
Production overheads	950,000	Work in progress	990,000
Over-absorption	40,000		
	———		———
	990,000		990,000
	———		———

Production overhead over-absorption account

	$		$
		Production overhead control	40,000
	———		———

To take this over-absorption to the Statement of profit or loss, the entry would be:

Debit Production overhead over-absorption account

Credit Statement of profit or loss

If FGH was not using standard costing then the overheads would be absorbed based on actual labour hours:

Overheads absorbed = 185,000 labour hours × $5 = $925,000

Overheads incurred = $950,000

Therefore we have an under-absorption of $925,000 – $950,000 = **$25,000**.

Test your understanding 7

C

Under-absorbed overhead is transferred from the overhead control account as a debit to the statement of profit or loss.

Test your understanding 8

D

An adverse variance is debited to the relevant variance account. This leaves us with options (B) or (D). The usage variance is eliminated where it arises, that is, in the work in progress account. Therefore, (D) is the correct answer.

Question 1

The completed ledger is shown below:

Material control account

	$		$
Balance b/d	50,000	Production overhead control account	10,000
Payables	100,000	Work in progress account	125,000
Bank	25,000	Balance c/d	40,000
	175,000		175,000

Materials are issued from stores as either direct materials (to work in progress) or indirect materials (charged to the production overhead control account). The entry for the issue of indirect materials is already shown ($10,000 to production overhead). Therefore, the $125,000 must be the value of the issue of direct materials to work in progress.

Question 2

The correct entries are (b), (c), (f) and (g):

(b)   The purchased materials are debited in the raw materials control account.

(c)   The direct materials are issued to the production department (work in progress).

(f)   Materials issued to maintenance are indirect materials, debited to the production overhead control account.

(g)   The total amount of materials issued is credited in the materials control account.

Question 3

(a)   **False**. Gross wages are $92,000.

(b)   **True**. Indirect wages are transferred to the production overhead control account.

(b)   **False**. Direct wages are $52,500: the amount transferred to work in progress.

Question 4

Wages control

	$		$
(1) Bank	44,000	(3) Work in progress	40,000
(2) Employee deductions payable	16,000	(4) Production overhead	20,000

Bank

	$		$
		(1) Wages control	44,000

Employee deductions payable

	$		$
		(2) Wages control	16,000

Work in progress

	$		$
(3) Wages control	40,000		

Production overhead control

	$		$
(4) Wages control	20,000		

(1) Net wages paid credited to the Bank

(2) Employee deductions credited to the Employee deductions payable account

(3) Direct wages debited to the Work in progress account

(4) Indirect wages debited to the production overhead account

Question 5

(a) The credit balance shown on the production overhead control account means that there was **over-absorption** of production overhead at 31 October. A debit balance would have indicated an under absorption of production overheads at that date.

(b) A **$4,320**

B **$2,890**

C **$560**

(c) A **$5,900**

B **$5,200**

C **$1,250**

Workings:

	$
Wages incurred	6,450
Direct wages to WIP	5,200
Indirect wages to production overhead	1,250

(d) At the end of the week, the balance on the production overhead control account will be a **credit** balance of **$3,794**.

Workings:

Production overhead control account

	$		$
Raw materials	560	Balance b/d	3,674
Wages	1,250	Work in progress*	3,800
Payables	1,870		
Balance c/d	3,794		
	7,474		7,474

*Production overhead absorbed is transferred to work in progress. The over-absorbed balance is now $3,794, which is carried down to the next week.

(e) A **$2,890**

B **$5,200**

C **$3,800**

D **$12,480**

Work in progress control account

	$		$
Balance b/d	13,479	Finished goods	12,480
Raw materials	2,890	Balance c/d	12,889
Wages	5,200		
Production overhead	3,800		
	25,369		25,369

Question 6

B

Overtime premium is usually treated as an overhead cost if the overtime cannot be specifically identified with a particular cost unit.

Question 7

A

Overhead absorption rate = $320,000/40,000 = $8 per direct labour hour

	$
Overhead absorbed = $8 × 41,500	332,000
Overhead incurred	311,250
Over absorption	**20,750**

The over absorption is credited to the statement of profit or loss and debited to the overhead control account.

Question 8

(a) **$69,000** ($3 × 23,000 hours)

(b) Production overhead for the period was **under-absorbed** (see workings in (c)).

		$
(c)	Overhead incurred	76,000
	Overhead absorbed into production	69,000
	Overhead under-absorbed	**7,000**

Integrated accounting systems

Question 9

D

Price variance	**$**
5,000 units should cost (5,000 × 4.70)	23,500
But did cost	22,500
Price variance	1,000 Fav

This variance will be credited to the variance account

Usage variance	**Material units**
2,400 finished units should use (× 2)	4,800
But did use	4,850
Variance in units	50 Adv
× standard price	4.70
Usage variance	$235 Adv

This variance will be debited to the variance account.

Question 10

The correct accounts are:

Cr Work in progress	A labour efficiency variance
Cr Wages control account	A labour rate variance
Cr Production overhead control	Absorbed production overheads from work in progress

Performance measurement

Chapter learning objectives

After completing this chapter, you should be able to

- explain the need for appropriate performance measures
- calculate appropriate financial and non-financial performance measures in a variety of contexts.

1 Session content diagram

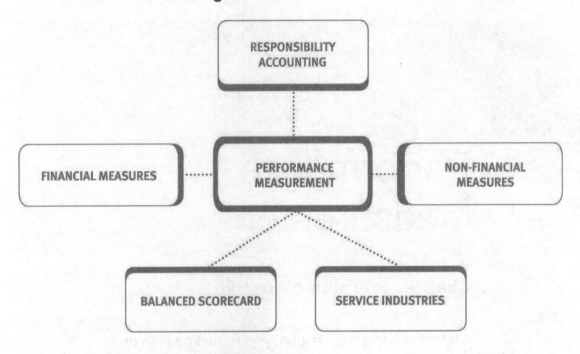

2 Performance measurement

Performance measurement is the monitoring of budgets or targets against actual results to establish how well the business and its employees are functioning as a whole and as individuals.

Performance measurement is a very important aspect of management accounting. Management accountants get involved in setting targets, measuring the actual performance against those targets and providing information to management regarding the outcome. This information will be used by management to make decisions about the organisation.

Performance measurement is very important as it can affect behaviour, so it is crucial when setting performance targets that we consider what behaviour we are looking to encourage. Setting poor performance targets can lead to dysfunctional behaviour which is behaviour that is not in the best interests of the organisation as a whole.

Performance can be measured at an individual, departmental or organisation level and the types of measurements used will depend on the area being measured.

Responsibility accounting

Responsibility centres were covered in the budgeting chapter. This is an important area when it comes to performance management and presenting management information. In responsibility reporting, costs and revenues are grouped according to which individual manager or management team is responsible for their control. It is worth recapping on the definitions of the types of responsibility centres and what the managers of each type of centre may require.

Cost centre managers might be interested in assessing the costs incurred by a particular responsibility centre within their area.

Profit centre managers might be interested in assessing the profitability of a particular product or service, in which case, costs might be classified by nature so that they can be traced to individual products or services.

Investment centre managers will be interested in assessing the return being made by a product or service centre in relation to the capital outlay for that product or service.

Different types of organisations require different types of performance measures and different areas within an organisation require different measures.

Objectives and goals of a business or business area will vary depending on the type of business that is being operated. For example:

- A commercial organisation's overall goal will be to maximise their shareholders wealth so they will want to monitor profitability (based on increasing sales and reducing costs) and growth of market share compared to competitors.

- A not-for-profit organisation, for example a government department, will want to provide the best service possible for the lowest cost so that the residents being cared for achieve value for money from the taxes they pay.

Within organisations, the objectives and goals in a production centre would be different to those in a call centre. For example:

- A production centre manager will be interested in maximising volume of output or reducing the level of wastage.

- A call centre manager will be interested in answering as many calls as possible or minimising the percentage of calls unanswered.

What these businesses or business areas have in common is that they will have long term (strategic) goals or objectives. These long term goals will be broken down into tactical and operational targets which will need to be monitored. To be able to do this they will identify **critical success factors** (those things which must be done correctly) and from this they will look for measures (**key performance indicators**) which will help them assess if they have met the critical success factors.

A performance measure will be particularly relevant if it is **controllable** by the manager for whom it has been set, that is if the manager is able to take action to influence the measure, and if an improvement in the performance measure would improve the performance of the responsibility centre or the organisation overall.

Financial performance measures

Financial performance measures are used to monitor the inflows (revenue) and outflows (costs) and the overall management of money in the business. These measures focus on information available from the statement of profit or loss and statement of financial position of a business.

Financial measures can be used to record the performance of cost centres, profit centres and investment centres within a responsibility accounting system but they can also be used to assess the overall performance of the organisation as a whole. For example, if cost reduction or cost control is important to an organisation, cost based performance measures might be appropriate performance indicators to use.

Cost based performance measures can be calculated as a simple cost per unit of output. The organisation will have to determine its policy for establishing cost per unit for performance measurement purposes.

3 Common financial performance measures

Let us look now at a number of common financial performance measures

- gross revenue
- contribution
- gross profit/margin
- operating (net) profit/margin
- return on capital.

Gross revenue

The total sales achieved by a company is known as gross revenue. This is the total of all sales transactions made by the company. This is a useful figure for the sales director of a company who needs to know how many customers their products or services have reached.

However, for various reasons, not all sales are successful and companies can experience returns from customers or goods could be lost in transit. It is important that these deductions are made from the gross revenue figure to give another meaningful measure called **sales revenue**.

Contribution

Contribution is an important measure within management decision making. It is calculated as follows:

> **Contribution = sales revenue – variable costs**

Contribution is often highlighted in management reports when it is important for managers to be able to see whether individual cost objects are generating sufficient revenue to cover the variable costs they incur.

Highlighting contribution can also help managers to see the potential effect on profit of an increase or decrease in activity.

Gross profit/margin

Other measures which may be useful to managers are gross profit and gross margin. Gross profit is calculated as follows:

> **Gross profit = sales revenue – cost of sales/cost of goods sold**

Where:

Cost of sales for a retailer = purchase cost of goods sold

Cost of sales for a manufacturer = total production cost of goods sold

This is a useful measure which shows how effective the company's trading activity is. It shows if the sales revenue is enough to cover the cost of the item sold.

Gross margin can be more useful as it is shown as a percentage. This measure is widely used in reporting. It is calculated as follows:

$$\text{Gross margin} = \frac{\text{Gross profit}}{\text{Sales revenue}} \times 100$$

Gross margin helps to highlight the relationship between sales revenues and production/purchase costs.

A high gross profit margin is desirable. It indicates that either sales prices/volumes are high or that production/purchase costs are being kept well under control.

As it is a % measure, it can be used to compare the performance of different areas of the business or different products.

Operating (Net) profit/margin

Operating or Net profit can then be calculated by deducting all other expenses from the gross profit. These other expenses will include administration and sales and distribution overheads. For a manufacturing company, this will be all non-production costs.

This is a useful measure which shows how much profit the company has generated in the period. It shows if the sales revenue is enough to cover the cost of the item sold and all expenses.

> **Note: Operating profit and net profit are the same thing. This may also be called earnings before interest and tax (EBIT) in the financial statements.**

The operating margin is also a useful measure in reporting. It is calculated as follows:

$$\text{Operating margin} = \frac{\text{Operating profit}}{\text{Sales revenue}} \times 100$$

It can be useful to compare the gross margin and operating margin as it helps to see how well the business is controlling its expenses.

Return on capital

Capital is the investment in an entity; it is often referred to as capital employed.

Capital employed is calculated as total assets less current liabilities.

There are a number of measures which can be used to calculate the return on capital, the main one is return on capital employed (ROCE). It is calculated as follows:

$$\text{Return on capital employed (ROCE)} = \frac{\text{Operating profit}}{\text{Capital employed}}$$

This measure helps to highlight the productivity of the capital employed.

You can see from the above that the performance measurements used will depend on the needs of the individual manager.

Not all of these measures are suitable for all types of responsibility centres, for example ROCE is only suitable in investment centres where managers are responsible for the level of investment.

Cost centre managers are only responsible for costs, so are most likely to use variance analysis to measure performance. This was covered in detail in the budgeting and standard costing and variance analysis chapters.

The following table shows which measures would be suitable for each type of centre:

	Cost centre	Profit centre	Investment centre
Variance analysis	✓	✓	✓
Gross revenue		✓	✓
Contribution		✓	✓
Gross/Net margin		✓	✓
ROCE			✓

Test your understanding 1

JKL has two production divisions, X and Y which operate as investment centres. A report for July has been prepared for the two divisions and extracts are shown below:

	X	Y
	$000	$000
Sales revenue	300	550
Direct costs of production	−160	−230
Indirect costs of production	− 50	−160
Non-production costs	25	32
Capital employed	500	1,300

Calculate the following for divisions X and Y: $300 - 166 - 50 = \quad 90$

A Gross margin $\rightarrow \dfrac{90}{300} \times 100 =$

B ROCE

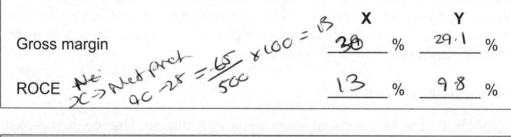

	X	Y
Gross margin	30 %	29.1 %
ROCE	13 %	98 %

ROCE $X \rightarrow$ Net profit $\dfrac{65}{500} \times 100 = 13$
Net profit $90 - 25 = 65$

Test your understanding 2

Companies XYZ and ABC are both involved in retailing.

Relevant information for the year ended 30 September 20X5 was as follows:

	XYZ	ABC
	$000	$000
Sales revenue	50,000	200,000
Operating profit	10,000	10,000
Capital employed	50,000	50,000

Prepare the following ratios for both companies and comment on the results:

(a) ROCE

(b) Operating margin

4 Problems with using only financial performance indicators

All of the measures we have looked at so far have concentrated on the financial performance of the business. Many of these ratios may be used to assess the performance of a division and of the manager in charge of that division.

Achievement of these target ratios (financial performance indicators) may be linked to a reward system in order to motivate managers to improve financial performance.

However, there are a number of problems associated with the use of financial performance indicators alone to monitor performance:

Short-termism vs long term performance

Linking rewards to financial performance may tempt managers to make decisions that will improve short-term financial performance but may have a negative impact on long-term profitability. For example, they may decide to cut investment or to purchase cheaper but poorer quality materials to reduce costs.

As mentioned at the start of this chapter any targets that are set at the different planning levels should all aim towards achieving the overall aim or mission of the business. There should be goal congruence to reduce the risk of a short-termist view being taken by the managers.

Manipulation of results

In order to achieve the target financial performance and hence their reward, managers may be tempted to manipulate results. For example:

- **Accelerating revenue**. Revenue earned in one year may be wrongly included in the previous year in order to improve the financial performance for the earlier year.

- **Delaying costs**. Costs incurred in one year may be wrongly recorded in the next year's accounts in order to improve performance and meet targets for the earlier year.

- **Understating a provision or accrual**. This would improve the financial performance and may result in the targets being achieved.

- **Manipulation of accounting policies**. This could include overstating closing inventory values resulting in an increase in profits for the year.

Do not convey the full picture

The use of only financial performance indicators has limited benefit to the company as it does not convey the full picture regarding the factors that will drive long-term profitability, for example customer satisfaction or quality. They are also focusing on the past as they are calculated from historical data. They are therefore not always the best indicator of future performance.

Therefore, when monitoring performance, a broader range of measures should be used.

5   Non-financial performance measures

Information provided by management accountants needs to be both financial and non-financial. Financial information is important for management because many objectives of an organisation are financial in nature, such as making profits. While profit cannot be ignored as it is the main objective of commercial organisations, performance measures should not focus on profit alone. Managers also need information of a non-financial nature.

Examples of non-financial performance measures include:

- measurements of customer satisfaction, for example returning customers or reduction in complaints

- resource utilisation, for example, are the machines being operated for all the available hours and producing output as efficiently as possible?

- measurement of quality, for example, reduction in production losses or number of rejected units.

Most organisations accept that a range of performance indicators should be used and these should be a mix of financial and non-financial measures. In fact many would argue that non-financial measures are more valuable to managers. For example, in an accountancy training business, sales and market share (financial issues) are often driven by non-financial issues such as student pass rates, student satisfaction, class sizes, tutor quality, etc. If performance in these non-financial measures begins to fall, it will not be long before the financial measures deteriorate as well.

While financial measures tend to be backward looking and report what has happened in the past, non-financial measures have the advantage of being forward looking. That is, they are likely to highlight factors that suggest how well or badly the business will perform in the future.

The large variety in types of businesses means that there are many non-financial measures which could be used. Each business and business unit will have its own set of non-financial measures which are relevant to their type of operation; however they are often grouped together into the broad headings of **productivity** or **quality**.

As with any performance indicator, a non-financial measure has to be viewed in some context in order to be most meaningful. Measures should be expressed in terms of a deviation from target, relative to an industry benchmark or as part of a trend analysis covering comparable earlier periods. Further, it is best to consider a range of financial and non-financial performance indicators as part of a package to give a multi-dimensional impression of how the organisation is performing.

An organisation's success usually involves focussing on a small number of critical areas that they must excel at. These factors vary from business to business. If we consider a manufacturing company, the important factors could be:

- Having a wide range of products that people want.

- Having a strong brand name or image.

- Offering quality products at low prices.

- Quick delivery of products to customers.

- Customer satisfaction, perhaps through high quality.

Most of these are best assessed using non-financial performance indicators. Financial performance appraisal often reveals the ultimate effect of operational factors and decisions but non-financial indicators are needed to monitor the causes.

For example, the company may have found using its financial performance measures that operating profit margin and ROCE have fallen. These measures are not very useful in explaining the reasons for this deterioration.

Looking at the non-financial measures may highlight issues such as falling customer numbers. Looking at why this may be, it may be found that there has been an increase in customer complaints regarding delivery times.

This will help management to highlight the issues quickly and help them to focus on the main problem areas.

 Examples of non-financial measures

Non-financial measures vary depending on the area being measured and the nature of the operation. There is no one list of suitable measures; each area must construct measures which are suitable for their own purposes. Here are some examples of non-financial measures for a variety of areas to give you a feel for the different of measures which could be used.

Production department

- Wastage levels

- Internal re-working of finished products

- Meeting government targets on emissions.

Sales department

- Repeat sales

- Number of new customers

- Staff cost per customer.

Call centre

- Average length of time of calls

- Staff absences

- Number of abandoned calls.

Distribution centre

- Speed of delivery

- Accuracy of delivery

- Customer complaints.

Test your understanding 3

RST Hospice is a charity which collects funds and donations and utilises these in the care of terminally ill patients. The governing body has set the manager three performance objectives for the three months to 30 June 20X7:

- to achieve a level of donations of $150,000 over the 3 month period

- to keep administration costs to no more than 8% of donations per month

- to achieve 80% of respite care requested from the community.

Actual results were as follows:

	April	May	June
Donations ($)	35,000	65,000	55,000
Administration costs ($)	2,450	5,850	4,400
Respite care requests (days)	560	570	600
Respite care provided (days)	392	430	510

Calculate appropriate performance measures to evaluate the manager's performance.

---

6 Advantages and disadvantages of non-financial performance indicators

The use of non-financial performance measures such as those mentioned is now common place, and brings many advantages, such as:

- they offer a wider view of performance than using financial measures alone

- they can be easy to understand as they measure the aspects of the business area that the manager is interested in, e.g. the number of calls answered in a call centre

- they are not distorted by inflation and are therefore directly comparable year on year

- they focus management's attention on potential problem areas

- they can offer positive motivational implications.

However, they are not without their problems:

- Setting up and operating a system involving a wide range of performance indicators can be time-consuming and costly.

- It can be a complex system that managers may find difficult to understand.

- There is no clear set of non-financial performance indicators that the organisation must use. Each will have to select those that seem to be most appropriate.

- It can be difficult to measure some aspects such as customer satisfaction. In this case measures such as the number of customer complaints can be used. e.g. a reduction in customer complaints can be taken as an increase in customer satisfaction.

- The scope for comparison with other organisations is limited as few businesses may use precisely the same non-financial performance indicators as the organisation under review.

- It can lead to indicator overload.

7 The balanced scorecard

To get an effective system of performance appraisal a business should use a combination of financial and non-financial measures.

One of the major developments in performance measurement techniques in recent years that has been widely adopted is the balanced scorecard.

The concept was developed by Kaplan and Norton, 1993 at Harvard. It is a device for planning that enables managers to set a range of targets linked with appropriate objectives and performance measures.

The four perspectives

The framework looks at the strategy and performance of an organisation from four points of view, known in the model as four perspectives:

- financial

- customer

- internal business processes

- learning and growth.

The approach is shown in the following diagram:

BALANCED SCORECARD
STRATEGIC PERSPECTIVES

Financial perspective

This focuses on traditional financial measures.

Performance measures could include:

- operating margin
- return on capital employed
- return on shareholders' funds.

Customer perspective

This is an attempt to measure customers' view of the organisation by measuring customer satisfaction.

Performance measures could include:

- number of customer complaints
- % of returning customers
- new customers as a % of total customers.

Internal business processes perspective

This aims to measure the organisation's output in terms of technical excellence and consumer needs.

Performance measures could include:

- unit costs
- capacity utilisation %
- number of units rejected.

Learning and growth perspective

This perspective can also be known as Innovation and learning. This focuses on the need for continual improvement of existing products and techniques and developing new ones to meet customers' changing needs.

Performance measures could include:

- % of revenue attributable to new products

- number of new products launched in the period

- number of staff training days undertaken.

Note: A detailed knowledge of the balanced scorecard is not required but you need to be aware of it and understand the benefits it provides. The following example shows types of financial and non-financial measures for a company, presented using a balanced scorecard format.

8   Performance measurement in service industries

There are many different types of organisation which can broadly be placed into one the following groups:

- Manufacturing industry

- Service industry

- Not-for-profit organisation (charities, government departments).

Each of these business sectors will have different objectives, for example:

- Manufacturing – reduce the cost of the product or increase the contribution per product

- Service – improve the quality of the service

- Not-for-profit organisation – meet the demands of the 'customer' and operate within a tight budget.

Each business will need to monitor the performance of their objectives to ensure they are able to succeed in their chosen field but each will face their own difficulties in deciding on appropriate measures to use.

So far we have focused largely on manufacturing. We will now look at issues with performance measurement when dealing with service industries. Not-for-profit organisations also have difficulties deciding on performance measures, as traditional profit measures are not appropriate. This will be looked at in the next chapter.

In many western economies one of the major changes that has taken place in recent years has been a change in the structure of those economies – the manufacturing sector has declined in size and significance and the service sector has grown in importance. The service sector consists of banks, airlines, transport companies, accountancy and consultancy firms and service shops.

Measurement of performance for a service provider can be difficult due to the nature of services.

Services have four main features:

- **Intangibility**. Services are activities undertaken by the organisation on behalf of its customers and therefore cannot be packaged for the customer to take away with them. They often have few, if any, physical aspects. For example, a taxi driver provides a service, carrying customers from one location to another. The customers do not have a permanent, tangible product they can keep.

- **Variability**. Each service is unique and cannot usually be repeated in exactly the same way, making offering a standardised service to customers very difficult.

- **Simultaneous production and consumption**. Services are often created by the organisation at the same time as they are consumed by the customer. For example, a restaurant meal is cooked as it is ordered by the customer. This brings with it particular management problems of planning and control but it does mean that the incidence of work in progress is very low, that is, it is rarely necessary to value part-finished units of service at the end of an accounting period.

- **Perishability**. Services cannot be stored for later. For example, if a cinema seat is vacant when a film is showing it cannot be stored in inventory for a later sale. Therefore, capacity utilisation becomes a very important issue for managers in many service organisations.

There is a wide variety of service organisations, ranging from private sector organisations such as hotels and courier services, to public sector organisations such as hospitals and schools.

One aspect of service organisations that can present difficulties for the information provider is establishing a suitable cost unit.

Establishing a suitable cost unit

Many service organisations produce an intangible 'output', that is, their output has no physical substance and it cannot be physically seen and touched. In order to maintain effective cost control it is essential to establish a measurable cost unit for which we can ascertain and monitor the costs.

In the cost identification and classification chapter we saw how **composite cost units** are often used to monitor and control the costs in service operations. Any cost unit can be used as long as it can be objectively measured and its cost can be determined and compared from one period to another and if possible from one organisation to another.

Composite cost units that could be used in each of these service organisations:

- Hotel — bed-night or room-night

- Hospital — in-patient day

- Haulage contractor — tonne-kilometre.

Establishing the cost per unit

Once a suitable cost unit has been selected, the cost for each unit can be determined using an averaging method:

> **Average cost per units of service** = $\dfrac{\textbf{Total cost incurred in period}}{\textbf{Units of service supplied in the period}}$

Test your understanding 4

Records for a passenger limousine company reveal the following data for last period:

No. of passengers	Miles travelled
80	4
40	5
90	6
100	7
140	8
180	9
150	10

The drivers' wages cost incurred was $1,100.

The drivers' wages cost per passenger mile was (to the nearest cent):

A $0.03

B $0.18

C $1.41

D $22.45

Now that we have looked at the difficulties of calculating cost units in service industries we can look at performance measurement in these industries. Many of the basic principles which we have looked at for the manufacturing industries will also apply in service industries, so service companies will set objectives and goals and identify the critical success factors and key performance indicators as would a manufacturing company, but the application of these performance measures will require special attention if they are to be useful in assessing performance.

We shall consider two main aspects of performance in relation to service organisations:

- Financial performance

- Service quality.

Quality is seen to be a particularly important non-financial performance indicator in the service sector.

Financial performance

Conventional financial analysis as looked at earlier can be used in service organisations and can be useful as long as it involves comparisons with past trends and/or competitors' ratios. Typical ratios that could be used by a service organisation include:

- gross revenue
- revenue per 'service'
- revenue per 'principal' or partner in, say, a management consultancy
- staff costs as a % of revenue
- space costs as a % of revenue
- training costs as a % of revenue
- operating (net) margin.

Financial ratio analysis is of limited use due to the 'human' nature of a service provider. The quality of the service also needs to be considered.

Service quality

Service quality is going to be critical in a service company as there is no tangible product, the company will be judged on that service.

Consider a large hotel chain. Customer satisfaction is critical if the hotel is going to survive in the long-term. Customer service is difficult to measure, so the hotel chain could use the following to assess customer satisfaction.

- the length of time to be served at reception
- the availability of facilities in the hotel
- the cleanliness of the rooms
- the quality of the food
- the helpfulness of its staff.

In some of these cases, the item cannot be directly measured but could be judged from customer feedback surveys where direct questions about certain aspects of their stay could be asked and a rating system used to analyse the results. For example the measure for cleanliness of the rooms could be that 95% of customers ranked the cleanliness of the room as 'excellent'. These could also be measured using mystery shoppers. Mystery shopping involves getting another member of staff, or an independent party to use the facilities as if they were a customer and report back on their findings.

Cleanliness of common areas or the condition of service facilities could be measured by the regular completion of detailed checklists showing when each area has been cleaned or maintained.

Note: The above list is not exhaustive; any suitable measure which can help determine customer satisfaction and can be measured could be used. The way customer service is measured will vary between different types of organisations, but for most organisations it is something that they want to measure.

Internal quality measurement

Inspection and monitoring of the inputs to the service process is important for all organisations. The quality of the solicitors in a practice or the number and grades of staff available in a consultancy organisation are crucial to the provision of service quality.

Many service companies use internal mechanisms to measure service quality during the process of service delivery.

The quality of the service may be measured after the event by measuring the output of the service against the target output for the period.

We can see that for service organisations, quality performance measurements are more useful than financial measures.

Illustration 1 – Performance measures in a service company

We will use the following example to consider quality performance measures in a service company.

RST operates a chain of coffee shops, located in prime high street locations, motorway service stations, railway stations and airports. The company has expanded rapidly since its first shop was opened five years ago.

The following information has been provided for RST:

	Current year	Previous year
Sales revenue	$3,670,100	$3,001,200
Gross profit	$975,300	$744,400
Operating profit	$622,700	$457,400
Number of customers	1,243,000	912,000
% of customers who complained	17%	8%
% returning customers	43%	64%
Time to receive order	11 minutes	3 minutes
Staff turnover per year	33%	11%
% of staff time spent on training	2%	10%
% of revenue from new products	2%	33%

Industry averages for the current year are:

Gross profit margin 22.4%

Operating profit margin 13.4%

As RST is a coffee shop, factors which will be critical to its success will include:

- Good range and quality of products

- Efficient service

- Helpful and knowledgeable staff

- Cleanliness and comfort of the premises.

It is important for RST to find ways of measuring these factors.

If we start by looking at the financial performance of RST. We can calculate the following financial measures:

	Current year	Previous year	Industry average
Gross profit margin = gross profit/revenue × 100	26.6%	24.8%	22.4%
Operating profit margin = operating profit/ revenue × 100	17.0%	15.2%	13.4%

Overall, the company's current year financial performance is favourable when compared to the previous years and to the industry average.

However, as we saw before financial indicators tell us where the company has been, but are poor at identifying why performance has improved or declined. They show effects but not causes. Non-financial measures can provide a better guide to future performance since they measure attributes which are essential to the long term success of a business, such as quality.

We will now look at some of the non-financial measures to help us get a clearer picture of how RST is performing in relation to the quality service measures which we highlighted.

Good range and quality of products

The percentage of revenue from new products has fallen from 33% to only 2%. The high level of competition in the industry together with the demanding needs of the modern customer make innovation a key driver of long-term profitability. Customers may choose other coffee shops if this matter is not addressed.

Efficient service

Waiting times have risen dramatically year on year and customers are now waiting almost four times as long to receive their order. Customers will expect to be served quickly and therefore the long waiting times may lead to a loss in customers in the long-term.

Helpful and knowledgeable staff

Staff turnover has increased three fold year on year to 33%. This may have resulted in a large number of inexperienced staff who are unable to deliver the high quality service that is demanded by the modern customer. The reason for the high staff turnover must be investigated in order to reduce the turnover rate, improve the morale of remaining employees and maintain long-term profitability.

Staff training time has dropped significantly from 10% to 2%. Poorly trained staff will not be able to provide such a high quality service and morale may fall if staff feel that their training needs are not being met. This could be a factor in the increased staff turnover.

Cleanliness and comfort of the premises

There is no data available to measure this directly, but we know that the % returning customers has fallen year on year by approximately one third from 64% to 43%. This indicates that the business is struggling to maintain customer loyalty. This may be a factor of the premises, or could be due to the inexperienced staff and increased waiting times.

In total the number of customers has increased year on year from 912,000 to 1,243,000. This may have contributed towards the increase in sales revenue and profit; however the % customer complaints have more than doubled year on year to 17%. This is a significant movement and may be linked to the high staff turnover and the increased waiting times. This increase in customer complaints must be addressed in order to ensure that the business can thrive in the long-term.

Overall, while RST's financial indicators are strong, looking at the non-financial indicators shows that there are a number of problem areas which must be addressed. RST must consider the issues surrounding these non-financial objectives immediately. Otherwise, the current financial performance will not be maintained.

9 Chapter summary

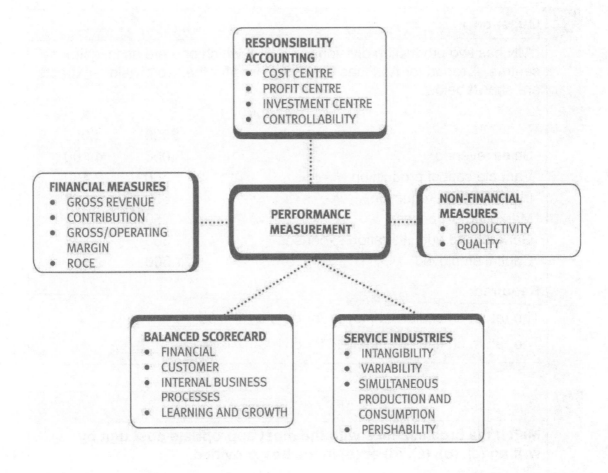

10　End of chapter questions

Question 1

LMN has two production divisions, Y and X which operate as investment centres. A report for April has been prepared for the two division, extracts are shown below:

	Y	X
	$000	$000
Sales revenue	3,000	4,100
Variable cost of production	1,560	2,430
Fixed cost of production	650	860
Marketing expenses	250	320
General and administration expenses	365	128
Capital employed	1,500	2,700

Required:

The return on capital employed for division Y is % _____.

The return on capital employed for division X is % _____.

Question 2

Match the organisations with the most appropriate cost unit by writing (a), (b), (c), (d) or (e) in the box provided.

Organisation:

Hotel

Transport service

College

Restaurant

Accountancy service

Cost unit:

(a)　Enrolled student

(b)　Meal served

(c)　Chargeable hour

(d)　Room night

(e)　Tonne-kilometre

Question 3

FGH hotel has 345 rooms. During the latest week, the following data were collected concerning unoccupied rooms.

	Number of unoccupied rooms
Monday	77
Tuesday	43
Wednesday	26
Thursday	31
Friday	17
Saturday	12
Sunday	88

Which of the following statements is INCORRECT?

(a)   The total number of available room nights in the week was 2,415.

(b)   The number of occupied room nights during the week was 2,121.

(c)   The unoccupied room rate in the week was 85%.

(d)   The overall percentage room occupancy rate during the week 88%.

Question 4

LMN Hotel is used for conference bookings and private guest bookings. Conference bookings use some bedrooms each week, the balance being available for private guests.

Data have been collected relating to private guest bookings which are summarised below for a 10-week period.

Week	Double rooms available for private guest bookings	Number of guests	Average stay (nights)
1	55	198	2.1
2	60	170	2.6
3	72	462	1.4
4	80	381	3.2
5	44	83	5.6
6	62	164	3.4
7	80	348	2.6
8	54	205	1.7
9	80	442	1.8
10	24	84	3.2

Some of the costs for private guest bookings vary with the number of guests, regardless of the length of their stay, while others vary with the number of rooms available in any week.

Variable cost per guest	$17.50
Variable cost per week per room available	$56.00

The general fixed cost for private guest bookings per week is $8,100.

Required:

(a) To the nearest cent, the total costs for private guests' bookings for the 10-week period is $ _____.

(b) To the nearest whole number, the number of private guest-nights achieved in the 10-week period is _____.

(c) The number of private guest-nights available for the 10-week period is _____.

Question 5

The balanced scorecard model, shown below, has four perspectives. Within each perspective of the model, key financial and non-financial performance measures are used.

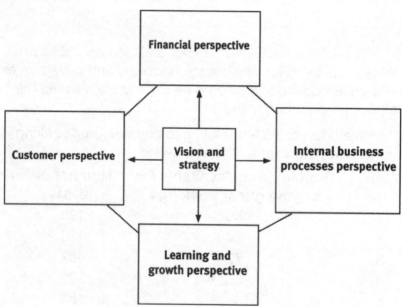

Drag the following measures to the most appropriate perspective on the model.

- Number of customer complaints
- ROCE
- Number of new products launched
- % productivity
- Repeat customer visits

Question 6

The following is ABC's statement of profit or loss for year ended 20X6, together with additional analysis of revenue and costs.

From this summary we can develop a series of performance indicators relevant to the four perspectives used by the balanced scorecard.

Statement of profit or loss for ABC for the year ended X6

	$m
Revenue	1.35
Cost of sales	0.83
	–––––
Gross profit	0.52
Admin and distribution costs	0.15
	–––––
Operating profit	0.37
Taxation	0.04
	–––––
Profit after taxation	0.33
Dividends	0.13
	–––––
Profit for the period	0.20
	–––––
Total assets less current liabilities	2.40

An analysis of revenue and costs show:

Revenue	$m
Existing products	1.03
New products	0.32
Sales to existing customers	0.82
Sales to new customers	0.53

Included in the cost structure is:	$m
Research and development	0.08
Training	0.14
Customer support costs	0.04
Quality assurance	0.03

A number of potential performance indicators have been suggested.

Note: This list is not exhaustive – there will other indicators that ABC could calculate for each of the four perspectives.

Calculate the following measures for ABC:

(a) **Financial perspective**

Return on capital employed

Operating margin

(b) **Customer perspective**

Customer support as % of revenue

% of business from existing customers

(c) **Learning and growth perspective**

Training costs as % of total costs

% of revenue from new products

(d) **Internal business process perspective**

Quality assurance % of revenue

Admin and distribution costs % of revenue

Question 7

The following figures are extracted from the accounts of RST, a company selling gourmet homemade soups.

	20X9	20X8
	$	$
Gross profit	3,006,000	2,582,000
Operating profit	590,000	574,000
Total capital employed	5,790,000	5,722,000
Total revenue	9,544,000	7,664,000

Select the correct word to complete the sentences regarding the financial performance of RST between 20X8 and 20X9.

(a) Gross margin has improved/deteriorated.

(b) Operating margin has improved/deteriorated.

(c) ROCE has improved/deteriorated.

Question 8

Match the financial performance measure to the responsibility centre to which it would be most appropriate.

Responsibility centre	Measure
Cost centre	Return on capital employed
Profit centre	Total cost
Investment centre	Operating margin

Question 9

In the context of a balanced scorecard approach to the provision of management information, which THREE of the following measures might be appropriate for monitoring the innovation and learning perspective?

A   Training days per employee

B   Level of wastage

C   Cost income ratio

D   Percentage of revenue generated by new products and services

E   Labour turnover rate

Question 10

Which THREE of the following statements relating to financial and non-financial performance measures are correct?

A   With financial performance measures there is a risk that managers will take a more short-term view.

B   Financial performance measures tend to be more forward looking than non-financial performance measures.

C   A disadvantage of non-financial measures is that it can be costly and time consuming to gather the required information.

D   Non-financial measures are not affected by inflation and are therefore directly comparable year on year.

E   Financial measures are more applicable to manufacturing industries.

Test your understanding and end of chapter answers

Test your understanding 1

	X	Y
Gross margin	**30%**	**29.1%**
ROCE	**13%**	**9.8%**

	X	Y
	$000	$000
Sales revenue	300	550
Direct costs of production	160	230
Indirect costs of production	50	160
Gross profit	90	160
Non-production costs	25	32
Operating profit	65	128

$$\textbf{Gross margin} = \frac{\textbf{Gross profit}}{\textbf{Sales revenue}} \times \textbf{100}$$

Gross margin % (X) = (90 ÷ 300) × 100 = **30%**

Gross margin % (Y) = (160 ÷ 550) × 100 = **29.1%**

$$\textbf{Return on capital employed (ROCE)} = \frac{\textbf{Operating profit}}{\textbf{Capital employed}} \times \textbf{100}$$

ROCE (X) = (65 ÷ 500) × 100 = **13%**

ROCE (Y) = (128 ÷ 1,300) × 100 = **9.8%**

Test your understanding 2

	XYZ	ABC
ROCE	$\dfrac{10,000}{50,000} \times 100\%$	$\dfrac{10,000}{50,000} \times 100\%$
	= **20%**	= **20%**
Operating margin	$\dfrac{10,000}{50,000} \times 100\%$	$\dfrac{10,000}{200,000} \times 100\%$
	= **20%**	= **5%**

The ROCE for both companies is the same. XYZ has a higher profit margin, whilst ABC shows a more efficient use of assets.

Test your understanding 3

	April	May	June
Administration costs as a % of donations	7%	9%	8%
Respite care provided as a % of care requested	70%	75.4%	85%

Total donations of $155,000 have been received which exceeds the target for the period.

Administration costs have been within the target of 8% in April and June but exceeded the target in May.

There has been a steady improvement in the level of respite care provided and in June the target was exceeded.

Test your understanding 4

B

No. of passengers	Miles travelled	Passenger miles
80	4	320
40	5	200
90	6	540
100	7	700
140	8	1,120
180	9	1,620
150	10	1,500
		―――
	Total passenger miles	6,000
		―――

Drivers' wages cost per passenger mile = $1,100/6,000 = **$0.18**

Question 1

The return on capital employed for division Y is **11.7%**.

The return on capital employed for division X is **13.4%**.

	Y $000	X $000
Sales revenue	3,000	4,100
Variable cost of production	1,560	2,430
Fixed cost of production	650	860
Marketing expense	250	320
General and administration expenses	365	128
Operating profit	175	362

$$\text{Return on capital employed (ROCE)} = \frac{\text{Operating profit}}{\text{Capital employed}} \times 100$$

ROCE (Y) = (175 ÷ 1,500) × 100 = **11.7%**

ROCE (X) = (362 ÷ 2,700) × 100 = **13.4%**

Question 2

Hotel	(d)	Room night
Transport service	(e)	Tonne-kilometre
College	(a)	Enrolled student
Restaurant	(b)	Meal served
Accountancy service	(c)	Chargeable hour

Question 3

(c) **is incorrect**

(a) The total number of available room nights in the week was 345 × 7 = **2,415**

(b) Total number of unoccupied room nights = 294
Number of occupied room nights = 2,415 – 294 = **2,121**

(c) The unoccupied room rate in the week = 294 ÷ 2,415 = **12%**

(d) Percentage occupancy = 2,121/2,415 = **88%**

Question 4

(a) **$159,613.50**

(b) **6,064 private guest-nights achieved**

(c) **8,554 private guest-nights available**

You will be using a composite cost unit in this question: a guest-night. The cost per guest night is the cost incurred by the hotel for one guest to stay for one night. In this example, the number of guest-nights is calculated as:

Guest-nights = number of guests × average number of nights stayed

Week	Rooms	Guests	Average stay	Guest-nights
1	55	198	2.1	415.8
2	60	170	2.6	442.0
3	72	462	1.4	646.8
4	80	381	3.2	1,219.2
5	44	83	5.6	464.8
6	62	164	3.4	557.6
7	80	348	2.6	904.8
8	54	205	1.7	348.5
9	80	442	1.8	795.6
10	24	84	3.2	268.8
	611	2,537		6,063.9

(a) Total costs for private guests' bookings: $

    Variable cost per room (611 × $56)   34,216.00

    Variable cost per guest (2,537 × $17.50)   44,397.50

    Fixed costs (10 × $8,100)   81,000.00

     159,613.50

(b) Guest-nights achieved (from above table) = **6,064**

(c) Guest-nights available = (611 rooms × 7 nights × 2 guests) = **8,554**

Question 5

The completed model is shown below:

Financial perspective

ROCE

Customer perspective

Number of customer complaints

Repeat customer visits

Vision and strategy

Internal business process perspective

% productivity

Learning and growth perspective

Number of new products launched

Question 6

(a) **Financial perspective**

Return on capital employed = (0.37/2.40) × 100 = **15.42%**

Profit from operations margin = (0.37/1.35) × 100 = **27.41%**

(b) **Customer perspective**

Customer support as % of revenue = (0.04/1.35) × 100 = **2.96%**

% of business from existing customers = (0.82/1.35) × 100 = **60.74%**

(d) **Learning and growth perspective**

Training costs as % of total costs = 0.14/(0.15 + 0.83) × 100 = **14.29%**

% of revenue from new products = (0.32/1.35) × 100 = **23.70%**

(d) **Internal business process perspective**

Quality assurance % of revenue = (0.03/1.35) × 100 = **2.22%**

Admin and distribution costs % of revenue = (0.15/1.35) × 100 = **11.11%**

To be useful these performance indicators would need to be compared with benchmarked or target levels for the current period and undergo analysis with previous years.

Question 7

(a)　Gross margin has **deteriorated**.

(b)　Operating margin has **deteriorated**.

(c)　ROCE has **improved**.

Workings:

	20X9	20X8
Gross margin = gross profit/revenue (%)	31.50%	33.69%
Operating margin = operating profit/revenue (%)	6.18%	7.49%
ROCE = operating profit/capital employed (%)	10.19%	10.03%

Question 8

The most appropriate measure for each responsibility centre would be:

Responsibility centre	Measure
Cost centre	Total cost
Profit centre	Operating margin
Investment centre	Return on capital employed

Question 9

A, D and E

In principle, the more training days an employee receives the more knowledgeable and skilful he or she becomes.

A target for the percentage of total sales revenue earned from new products focuses on innovation. The higher the target percentage, the more innovative the organisation might be with new product development.

Labour turnover rate could be a suitable target. The rate at which staff leave and are replaced provides a measure of the loss of existing employee skills, and possibly also the recruitment of new staff with new ideas.

Question 10

A, C and D

Financial performance measures tend to be more forward looking than non-financial performance measures. This is incorrect. Non-financial performance measures tend to be more forward looking than financial performance measures.

Financial measures are more applicable to manufacturing industries. This is incorrect. Both financial and non-financial measures are required by all types of organisations.

Preparing accounts and reports for management

Chapter learning objectives

After completing this chapter, you should be able to

- prepare appropriate accounts for job and batch costing
- prepare reports in a range of organisations.

1 Session content diagram

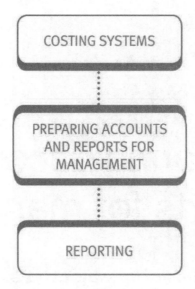

COSTING SYSTEMS

PREPARING ACCOUNTS
AND REPORTS FOR
MANAGEMENT

REPORTING

2 Management reporting

Management accounting reports are used by management for:

- planning
- controlling
- decision making.

It is essential that these reports are presented clearly and effectively.

In the context of management accounting chapter we looked at the characteristics of good information and how information needs differed at different levels of the organisation. It is worth recapping on these areas before considering management reporting.

In the previous chapter we looked at various performance measurements, both financial and non-financial which could be used to measure the performance of individuals, departments or companies and considered the particular difficulties when measuring performance in a service organisation.

We will now look at how we can use these measures in reports to management. Remember the purpose of management reports is to inform management and provide them with the information they require to make good decisions.

We will look at a variety of organisations in this chapter:

- Manufacturing
- Service
- Not-for-profit.

You will already be familiar with many aspects of these types of organisations from previous chapters.

3   Costing systems

Firstly we will consider costing systems and how these are used to gather information which will be used to produce reports for management.

Most organisations will have a costing system which is used to gather the cost information for the organisation together. An organisation's costing system is the foundation of the internal financial information system for managers. It provides the information that management needs to plan and control the organisation's activities and to make decisions about the future.

Every organisation's costing system will have characteristics which are unique to that particular system. However, although each system might be different, the basic costing method used by the organisation is likely to depend on the type of activity that the organisation is engaged in. The costing system would have the same basic characteristics as the systems of other organisations which are engaged in similar activities.

Examples of the type of information provided by a costing system and the uses to which it might be put include the following:

- **Actual unit costs** for the latest period; could be used for cost control by comparing with a predetermined unit cost. Could also be used as the basis for decisions about pricing and production levels. For example, a manager cannot make a decision about the price to be charged to a customer without information which tells the manager how much it costs to produce and distribute the product to the customer.

- **Actual costs of operating a department** for the latest period; could be used for cost control by comparing with a predetermined budget for the department. Could also be used as the basis for decisions such as outsourcing. For example, a manager might be considering the closure of the packing department and instead outsourcing the packing operations to another organisation. In order to make this decision the manager needs to know, amongst other things, the actual cost of operating the packing department.

- **The forecast costs to be incurred at different levels of activity**. Could be used for planning, for decision making and as a part of cost control by comparing the actual costs with the forecasts. For example, a manager cannot make a well-informed decision about the appropriate production level for the forthcoming period unless information is available about the costs that will be incurred at various possible output levels.

This is by no means an exhaustive list of the information that is provided by a costing system. However, it should serve to demonstrate that organisations need costing systems that will provide the basic information that management requires for **planning, control and decision-making**.

The way information for reporting is gathered is linked to the nature of the organisation. In organisations which work on unique jobs for each customer, job costing is used.

Job costing

Job costing applies where work is undertaken according to specific orders from customers. For example, a customer may request the manufacture of a single machine to the customer's own specification. Job costing can also be applied in service organisations, for example the repair of a vehicle or the preparation of a set of accounts for a client.

The way information is gathered and processed in job costing is useful for performance measurement such as:

- cost control
- time management.

The type of organisation that is using job costing will influence the type of measure used, for example:

- Accountants may want to measure a ratio of chargeable time for a job to total time required to complete the job
- Garages may want to measure the average age of inventories of spares
- Printers may want to measure the cost per printed page
- Fruit juice producers may want to measure the time taken to pick and process the fruit.

Job cost sheets

The main feature of a job costing system is the use of a **job cost sheet** or **job card** which is a detailed record used to collect the costs of each job. In practice this would probably be a file in a computerised system but the essential feature is that each job would be given a **specific job number** which identifies it from all other jobs. Costs would be allocated to this number as they are incurred on behalf of the job. Since the sales value of each job can also be separately identified, it is then possible to determine the profit or loss on each job.

Illustration 1 – Job cost sheet

| JOB COST SHEET | | | | | | | | | | Job no.: 472 | |

| Estimate no.: | 897 | | | | Job description: | | Instal shower Model no. 5856 | | | | |

Details: Mrs. P. Johnson
01734 692174
30 Hillside, Whyteham
Price estimate: £330

Date started: 15 June 20 ×6

MATERIALS					LABOUR						PRODUCTION OVERHEAD		
Date	Req. no.	Qty	Price $	Value $	Date	Emp. no.	Cost ctr	Hrs	Rate	$	Hours	Overhead absorption rate	$
14/6	641	1	128.00	128.00	15/6	17	4	8	10	80.00	9	4.50	40.50
15/6	644	2	3.10	6.20	15/6	12	3	1	10	10.00			
			Total c/f	134.20				Total c/f		90.00		Total c/f	40.50

EXPENSES				JOB COST SUMMARY		
Description	Cost $			Cost element	Actual $	Estimate $
				Direct materials b/f	134.20	150.00
				Direct labour b/f	90.00	80.00
				Direct expenses b/f	–	–
				Total direct cost	224.20	230.00
				Production o/h b/f	40.50	36.00
Total c/f				Total production cost	264.70	266.00
				Admin. o/h (5%)	13.24	13.30
				Total cost	277.94	279.30
				Price estimate	330.00	330.00
				Job profit/(loss)	52.06	50.70

Job card completed by: *Genny*

The job cost sheet would record details of the job as it proceeds. The items recorded would include:

- job number

- description of the job; specifications, etc.

- customer details

- estimated cost, analysed by cost element

- selling price, and hence estimated profit

- delivery date promised

- actual costs to date, analysed by cost element

- actual delivery date, once the job is completed

- sales details, for example delivery note no., invoice no.

The sheet has a separate section to record the details of each cost element. There is also a summary section where the actual costs incurred are compared with the original estimate. This helps managers to control costs and to refine their estimating process.

Completing the job cost sheet

Direct labour

The correct analysis of labour costs and their attribution to specific jobs depends on the existence of an efficient time recording and analysis system. For example, daily or weekly timesheets may be used to record how each employee's time is spent, using job numbers where appropriate to indicate the time spent on each job. The wages cost can then be charged to specific job numbers (or to overhead costs, if the employee was engaged on indirect tasks). In the job cost sheet shown in Illustration 1, a total of nine direct labour hours were worked by two different employees.

Direct material

All documentation used to record movements of material within the organisation should indicate the job number to which it relates.

For example a **material requisition note**, which is a formal request for items to be issued from stores, should have a space to record the number of the job for which the material is being requisitioned. If any of this material is returned to stores, then the material returned note should indicate the original job number which is to be credited with the cost of the returned material. In the job cost sheet shown in Illustration 1, two separate material requisitions were raised for material used on job number 472.

Sometimes items of material might be purchased specifically for an individual job. In this situation the job number must be recorded on the supplier's invoice or on the relevant cash records. This will ensure that the correct job is charged with the cost of the material purchased.

Direct expenses

Although direct expenses are not as common as direct material and direct labour costs, it is still essential to analyse them and ensure that they are charged against the correct job number.

For example, if a machine is hired to complete a particular job, then this is a direct expense of the job. The supplier's invoice should be coded to ensure that the expense is charged to the job. Alternatively, if cash is paid, then the cash book analysis will show the job number which is to be charged with the cost. We can see from the job cost sheet shown in Illustration 1 that no direct expenses were incurred on behalf of job number 472.

Production overheads

The successful attribution of production overhead costs to cost units depends on the existence of well-defined cost centres and appropriate absorption bases for the overhead costs of each cost centre.

It must be possible to record accurately the units of the absorption base which are applicable to each job. For example, if machine hours are to be used as the absorption base, then the number of machine hours spent on each job must be recorded on the job cost sheet. The relevant cost centre absorption rate can then be applied to produce a fair overhead charge for the job.

The production overhead section of the job cost sheet for job 472 shows that the absorption rate is $4.50 per labour hour. The labour analysis shows that 9 hours were worked on this job, therefore the amount of production overhead absorbed by the job is $40.50.

Non-production overheads

The level of accuracy achieved in attributing costs such as selling, distribution and administration overheads to jobs will depend on the level of cost analysis which an organisation uses.

Many organisations simply use a predetermined percentage to absorb such costs, based on estimated levels of activity for the forthcoming period. The use of predetermined rates will lead to the problems of under- or over- absorbed overhead which we discussed in the overhead analysis chapter. The rates should therefore be carefully monitored throughout the period to check that they do not require adjusting to more accurately reflect recent trends in costs and activity.

Administrative overheads

For Job 472, administrative overheads have been included. These have been calculated as 5% of total production cost.

Preparing ledgers in job costing

In job costing systems a separate work in progress account is maintained for each job, as well as a summary work in progress control account for all jobs worked on in the period.

The best way to see how this is done is to work carefully through the following example and ensure that you understand each entry that is made in every account. You will need to apply the principles of integrated accounts.

Example

JKL operates a job costing system. All jobs are carried out on JKL's own premises and then delivered to customers as soon as they are completed.

Direct employees are paid $10 per hour and production overhead is absorbed into job costs using a predetermined absorption rate of $24 per labour hour. General overhead is charged to the statement of profit or loss on completed jobs using a rate of 12% of total production cost.

Details of work done during the latest period are as follows:

Work in progress at beginning of period

Job number 308 was in progress at the beginning of the period.

Cost incurred up to beginning of period:

	$
Direct material	1,790
Direct labour	960
Production overhead absorbed	2,304
Production cost incurred up to beginning of period	5,054

Activity during the period

Job numbers 309 and 310 commenced during the period.

The following details are available concerning all work done in the period.

Job number:	308	309	310
Direct materials issued from stores	$169	$2,153	$452
Excess materials returned to stores	–	$23	–
Direct labour hours worked	82	53	28
Invoice value	$9,900	$6,870	–

Jobs 308 and 309 were completed in the period.

Further information:

Cost of material transferred from job 309 to job 310	$43
Production overhead cost incurred on credit	$4,590
General overhead cost incurred on credit	$1,312

Required:

(a) Prepare the ledger account for the period for each job, showing the production cost of sales transferred on completed jobs.

(b) Prepare the following accounts for the period:

- work in progress control

- production overhead control

- general overhead control

- overhead under- or over absorbed control

- statement of profit or loss.

(c) Calculate the profit on each of the completed jobs.

Solution:

(a)

Job 308

	$		$
Balance b/f (1)	5,054	Production cost of sales	8,011
Material stores	169		
Wages control (82 × $10)	820		
Production overhead (82 × $24)	1,968		
	8,011		8,011

Job 309

	$		$
Material stores	2,153	Material stores (2)	23
Wages control (53 × $10)	530	Job 310 (3)	43
Production overhead (53 × $24)	1,272	Production cost of sales	3,889
	3,955		3,955

Job 310

	$		$
Job 309 (3)	43	Balance c/f (4)	1,447
Material stores	452		
Wages control (28 × $10)	280		
Production overhead (28 × $24)	672		
	1,447		1,447

(b)

Work in progress control

	$		$
Balance b/f (1)	5,054	Material stores (2)	23
		Production cost of sales to statement of	
Material stores control (5)	2,774	profit or loss (6)	11,900
Wages control (163 hours × $10)	1,630		
Production overhead (9) (163 × $24)	3,912	Balance c/f (7)	1,447
	13,370		13,370

Production overhead control

	$		$
		Work in progress control (9)	3,912
Payables control (8)	4,590		
		Overhead under-/over-absorbed control (10)	678
	4,590		4,590

General overhead control

	$		$
		General overhead cost to statement of profit or	
Payables control (8)	1,312	loss (11)	1,428
Overhead under-/over-absorbed control (10)	116		
	1,428		1,428

Overhead under-/over-absorbed control

	$		$
Production overhead control (10)	678	General overhead control (10)	116
		Statement of profit or loss	562
	———		———
	678		678
	———		———

Statement of profit or loss

	$		$
Production cost of sales (6)	11,900	Sales (9,900 + 6,870)	16,770
General overhead control (11)	1,428		
Under-absorbed overhead	562		
Profit for the period	2,880		
	———		———
	16,770		16,770
	———		———

Notes:

(1) The cost of the opening work in progress is shown as a brought forward balance in the individual job account and in the work in progress control account.

(2) The cost of materials returned to stores is credited in the individual job account and in the work in progress control account.

(3) The cost of materials transferred between jobs is credited to the job from which the material is transferred and debited to the job that actually uses the material.

(4) Job 310 is incomplete. The production cost incurred this period is carried down as an opening work in progress balance for next period.

(5) The total cost of all materials issued is debited to the work in progress control account.

(6) The production cost of both completed jobs ($3,889 + $8,011) is transferred to the statement of profit or loss.

(7) The balance carried forward to next period is the cost of the work in progress represented by job 310.

(8) The overhead costs incurred are debited in the control accounts.

(9) The production overhead absorbed into work in progress is credited to the overhead control account and debited to the work in progress account.

(10) Production overhead is under-absorbed and general overhead is over absorbed this period.

(11) The general overhead cost charged to the statement of profit or loss on completed jobs =12% × $(3,889 + 8,011) = $1,428.

(c)

	Job 308	Job 309
	$	$
Production cost	8,011.00	3,889.00
General overhead absorbed at 12%	961.32	466.68
	8,972.32	4,355.68
Invoice value	9,900.00	6,870.00
Profit	**927.68**	**2,514.32**

The total profit on the two jobs is $3,442. The difference of $562 between this total and the profit shown in the statement of profit or loss is the result of the under absorbed overhead of $562.

Illustration 2 – Cost and profit analysis

JHI manufactures precision tools to its customers' own specifications. The manufacturing operations are divided into three cost centres: A, B and C.

Job number 32 was manufactured during the period and its job cost sheet reveals the following information relating to the job:

Direct material requisitioned	$6,780.10
Direct material returned to stores	$39.60

Direct labour recorded against job number 32:

Cost centre A:	146 hours at $4.80 per hour
Cost centre B:	39 hours at $5.70 per hour
Cost centre C:	279 hours at $6.10 per hour

A special machine was hired for job 32 costing $59.00.

Machine hours recorded against job number 32:

Cost centre A:	411 hours
Cost centre B:	657 hours
Price quoted and charged to customer, including delivery	$17,200

Production overheads from the three cost centres are absorbed using the following overhead absorption rates:

Cost centre A:	$1.75 per machine hour
Cost centre B:	$3.80 per machine hour
Cost centre C:	$0.98 per labour hour

JHI absorbs non-production overhead using the following pre-determined overhead absorption rates:

Administration and general overhead	10% of total production cost
Selling and distribution overhead	12% of selling price

Present an analysis of the total cost and profit or loss attributable to job number 32.

Solution:

Cost and profit analysis: job number 32	$	$
Direct material (1)		6,740.50
Direct labour:		
Cost centre A (146 hours × $4.80)	700.80	
Cost centre B (39 hours × $5.70)	222.30	
Cost centre C (279 hours × $6.10)	1,701.90	
		2,625.00
Direct expenses: hire of machine		59.00
Prime cost		9,424.50
Production overhead absorbed:		
Cost centre A (411 hours × $1.75)	719.25	
Cost centre B (657 hours × $3.80)	2,496.60	
Cost centre C (279 hours × $0.98)	273.42	
		3,489.27
Total production cost		12,913.77

	$	$
Administration and general overhead (10% × $12,913.77)		1,291.38
Selling and distribution overhead (12% × $17,200)		2,064.00
Total cost		16,269.15
Operating profit		930.85
Selling price		17,200.00

Note (1): The figure for material requisitioned has been reduced by the amount of returns to give the correct value of the materials actually used for the job. ($6,780.10 – $39.60) = $6,740.50.

Test your understanding 1

GRO uses job costing.

Three jobs were worked on during a period, the details of which were:

	Job 1 $	Job 2 $	Job 3 $
Opening work in progress	8,500	0	46,000
Material in period	17,150	29,025	0
Labour in period	12,500	23,000	4,500

The overheads for the period were exactly as budgeted: $140,000 and are absorbed on the basis of direct labour cost.

Jobs 1 and 2 were incomplete at the end of the period.

What was the value of closing work in progress?

A $81,900

B $90,175

C $140,675

D $214,425

Test your understanding 2

A company which uses job costing is pricing 3 jobs, details of which are as follows:

	Production cost	Pricing method
Job A	$45	Mark-up 25%
Job B	$38	Mark-up 20%
Job C	$75	Margin 15%

10% has to be added to production cost to absorb general overheads.

Calculate the selling prices for jobs A, B and C.

Job A: $ _____

Job B: $ _____

Job C: $ _____

Batch costing

The *CIMA Terminology* defines a **batch** as a 'group of similar units which maintains its identity throughout one or more stages of production and is treated as a cost unit'. An example would be a batch of printed leaflets.

Batch costing is very similar in nature to job costing. It is a separately identifiable cost unit for which it is possible to collect and monitor the costs. The only difference is that a number of items are being costed together as a single unit, instead of a single item or service.

Once the cost of the batch has been determined, the cost per item within the batch can be calculated by dividing the total cost by the number of items produced.

Batch costing can be applied in many situations, including the manufacture of furniture, clothing and components. It can also be applied when manufacturing is carried out for the organisation's own internal purposes, for example, in the production of a batch of components to be used in production.

Batch costing example

LMN makes hand embroidered sweatshirts to customer specifications.

The following detail is available from the company's budget.

Cost centre	Overheads	Activity
Cutting and sewing	$93,000	37,200 machine hours
Embroidering and packing	$64,000	16,000 direct labour hours

Administration, selling and distribution overhead is absorbed into batch costs at a rate of 8% of total production cost. Selling prices are set to achieve a rate of return of 15% of the selling price.

Batch number 92 (an order for 45 shirts) has been produced. Details of activity on this batch are as follows:

Direct materials	$113.90
Direct labour	
Cutting and sewing (0.5 labour hours at $9 per hour)	$4.50
Embroidering and packing (29 labour hours at $11 per hour)	$319.00
Machine hours worked in cutting and sewing	2
Fee paid to designer of logo for sweat shirts	$140.00

Calculate the selling price per shirt in batch number 92.

Solution:

Batch No. 92

	$	$
Direct material		113.90
Direct labour:		
Cutting and sewing	4.50	
Embroidering and packing	319.00	
		323.50
Direct expense: design costs		140.00
Total direct cost		577.40

	$	$
Production overhead absorbed:		
Cutting and sewing (1)		
2 machine hours × $2.50	5.00	
Embroidering and packing (1)		
29 labour hours × $4	116.00	
		121.00
Total production cost		698.40
Administration, etc. overhead ($698.40 × 8%)		55.87
Total cost		754.27
Profit margin 15/85 × $754.27		133.11
Total selling price of batch		887.38
Selling price per shirt $887.38/45		$19.72

Note (1):

Calculation of production overhead absorption rates: _OAR_

Cutting and sewing = $93,000/37,200 = $2.50 per machine hour

Embroidering and packing = $64,000/16,000 = $4 per direct labour hour

---

Test your understanding 3

Using the data given in Test your understanding 1.

GRO has just completed Job 3 which consisted of a batch of 2,400 identical circuit boards. GRO adds 50% to total production costs to arrive at a selling price.

What is the selling price of a circuit board?

A   It cannot be calculated without more information

B $31.56

C $41.41

D $58.33

Job and batch costing are **specific order costing** methods. These methods are appropriate for organisations which produce cost units which are separately identifiable from one another.

4 Preparing reports for a range of organisations

The usefulness of any management report is greatly enhanced if it highlights subtotals, totals and performance measures that are relevant to the recipient. We looked at performance measures in detail in the performance measurement chapter.

This enables the manager who receives the information to focus on the most relevant information from the point of view of management action. The same information may be used in reports to different managers but it may be presented with different sub totals to highlight different points of interest.

A performance measure will be particularly relevant if it is **controllable** by the manager for whom the report is prepared, that is if the manager is able to take action to influence the measure and if an improvement in the performance measure would improve the performance of the responsibility centre or the organisation overall.

Controllable costs are generally assumed to be variable costs, and directly attributable fixed costs. These are fixed costs that can be allocated in full to a cost of the centre. However this assumption is not entirely correct and it should be used with caution. Some items treated as variable costs cannot be influenced or controlled in the short term.

It is important to remember that an item that is uncontrollable for one manager could be controllable by another. In the long term, all costs are controllable.

Illustration 3 – Controllability of costs

Consider the following profit report prepared for the three profit centres of FGH.

	Profit centre 1	Profit centre 2	Profit centre 3	Total
	$000	$000	$000	$000
Revenue	100	200	150	450
Material costs	20	60	30	110
Labour costs	50	60	50	160
Other costs	40	40	40	120
Operating profit	(10)	40	30	60

The profit centre managers are responsible for all material purchases. Profit centre 1 requires specially trained workers. These workers are recruited by the profit centre manager. Profit centres 2 and 3 use less skilled workers and these are taken from a pool of workers recruited by head office.

Of the $120,000 other costs, $20,000 can be directly attributed to profit centre 2 and $15,000 can be directly attributed to profit centre 3. The remainder are general overheads and are treated as head office costs.

Prepare a revised profit report highlighting the controllable profit for the three cost centres.

	Profit centre 1	Profit centre 2	Profit centre 3	Total
	$000	$000	$000	$000
Revenue	100	200	150	450
Material costs	20	60	30	110
Labour costs	50			50
Directly attributable costs		20	15	35
	———	———	———	———
Controllable profit	30	120	105	255
Head office costs				195
	———	———	———	———
Operating profit				60
	———	———	———	———

Head office costs is made up of the labour costs of profit centres 2 and 3 ($60,000 + $50,000) and the other costs excluding the directly attributable costs for profit centres 2 and 3 ($120,000 – $20,000 – $15,000).

In the rest of the chapter we will look at examples of reports for a range of organisations. These examples are not exhaustive and each organisation will produce reports suitable for their own purposes.

5   Reports in a manufacturing organisation

Manufacturing organisations may be interested in how well each of their products is performing. A suitable report to show this might be to focus on the contribution earned by each product.

Illustration 4 – Product contribution analysis

This example will demonstrate why it might be important to highlight the contribution earned by each product.

	Product A	Product B	Product C	Total
	$000	$000	$000	$000
Gross revenue	931	244	954	2,129
Variable costs:				
Direct material and labour	547	87	432	1,066
Variable production overhead	54	58	179	291
Variable marketing expense	9	3	7	19
Total variable cost	610	148	618	1,376
Contribution	**321**	**96**	**336**	**753**
Fixed production overhead	43	35	34	112
Fixed marketing expense	38	10	40	88
Fixed general expense	60	56	60	176
Operating profit/(loss)	180	(5)	202	377
Contribution to sales (PV) ratio	**34.5%**	**39.3%**	**35.2%**	

This product contribution analysis reveals the following:

- Product B appears to be incurring a loss. Its contribution is not sufficient to cover the fixed production, marketing, general and administration expenses attributed to it.

- However the product is earning a contribution. If the fixed costs attributed to product B are costs that would be incurred anyway, even if product B was discontinued, then it may be worth continuing production of product B since it does earn a contribution of $96,000 towards these fixed costs. If product B was discontinued then this $96,000 contribution would be forgone.

- Although product B is earning a contribution, it does not at present generate sufficient contribution to cover its fair share of support costs such as marketing and general overheads. The profitability of product B does require management attention.

- Product B earns the highest contribution to sales ratio. This means that if gross sales revenue of product B can be increased without affecting the fixed costs, the resulting increase in contribution will be higher than with the same sales increase on products A and C. Thus the key to product B's profitability might be to increase the volume sold.

Alternatively a manufacturing company may want to focus more on gross margin and how this is changing over time.

 Illustration 5 – Gross margin analysis

The following extract is taken from the monthly managerial report of DEF.

	Month 1	Month 2	Month 3	Month 4
	$000	$000	$000	$000
Gross sales revenue	896	911	919	935
Direct cost of goods sold	699	713	722	737
Gross profit	**197**	**198**	**197**	**198**
Gross margin	**22.0%**	**21.7%**	**21.4%**	**21.2%**

This gross margin analysis focuses managers' attention on the relationship between the sales value and the direct cost of sales, before indirect costs or overheads are taken into account. This analysis reveals the following:

- Although the gross sales revenue is steadily increasing, the gross profit is relatively constant each month.

- The gross margin is steadily decreasing each month. If the gross margin percentage could have been maintained at 22% the total gross profit earned would have been higher.

- Perhaps selling prices are being increased but the reduction in the gross margin might be the result of a failure to increase selling prices sufficiently in line with increasing direct costs.

- Alternatively the sales volume might be increasing but direct costs are not being controlled as sales increase.

6   Reports in a service organisation

The features of a service organisation were looked at in the performance measurement chapter. The management of a service organisation may require different reports, highlighting different aspects to that of a manufacturing organisation.

Illustration 6 – Managerial reporting in a consultancy business

As you read through this example, notice that we are applying all of the principles of cost analysis that you have already learned about. The only difference is that the principles are being applied to determine the cost of intangible services, rather than of tangible products.

Mr G and Mr H have recently formed a consultancy business and they wish to establish the following rates to charge clients:

- an hourly rate for productive client work

- an hourly rate for time spent travelling to/from the clients' premises

- a rate per mile for expenses incurred in travelling to/from the clients' premises.

Pricing policy

Mr G and Mr H have decided that their pricing policy will be based on the cost per hour plus a 5% profit mark-up. Travelling time will be charged to clients at one-third of the normal hourly rate. Travelling expenses will be charged to clients at cost.

Activity estimates

Mr G and Mr H each expect to work for 8 hours per day, 5 days per week, 45 weeks per year. They refer to this as 'available time'.

- 25% of the available time will be spent dealing with administrative matters relating to the general running of the business.

- In the first year, 22.5% of the available time will be idle, that is, no work will be done in this time.

- The remainder of the available time is expected to be chargeable to clients.

- Travelling time will amount to 25% of the chargeable time, during which a total of 18,000 miles will be travelled.

Cost estimates

- Mr G and Mr H each wish to receive a salary of $25,000 in the first year of trading.

- Other costs to be incurred in the first year of trading:

	$
Electricity	1,200
Fuel for vehicles	1,800
Depreciation of vehicles	6,000
Insurance – professional liability and office	600
Vehicle insurance and road tax	1,080
Office rent and rates	8,400
Telephone expenses	3,000
General office expenses	8,900
Servicing and repair of vehicles	1,200

Calculate the three client charge rates that Mr G and Mr H wish to establish.

Solution:

Rate per mile for travelling expenses	**$0.56**
Hourly rate for productive client work	**$48.07**
Hourly rate for travelling time	**$16.02**

Workings:

We firstly need to classify the costs provided to determine the total cost associated with travelling, and that associated with providing consultancy services.

	Consultancy	Travelling
	$	$
Salaries	50,000	
Electricity	1,200	
Fuel		1,800
Depreciation		6,000
Insurance	600	
Vehicle insurance, etc.		1,080
Office rent and rates	8,400	
Telephone expenses	3,000	
General office expenses	8,900	
Servicing vehicles, etc.		1,200
	72,100	10,080

Now we need to determine the number of units of service by which each of these cost totals is to be divided.

The calculation of the rate per mile for travelling expenses is relatively straightforward:

$$\text{Rate per mile} = \frac{\text{Total travelling expenses}}{\text{Miles travelled}} = \frac{\$10,080}{18,000} = \textbf{\$0.56 per mile}$$

The calculation of the hourly rate for productive work and travelling time is a little more complicated. The first step is to determine the number of units of service supplied, that is, the chargeable hours. We need to look at the activity estimates provided in order to analyse the available time.

Total available hours for the first year:

		Hours
(2 people × 8 hours × 5 days × 45 weeks)		3,600
Less: Administration time	25.0%	
Less: Idle time	22.5%	
	47.5% × 3,600	(1,710)
Time chargeable to clients		1,890
Productive time spent with clients (75%)		1,417.5
Travelling time (25%)		472.5

Travelling time will be charged at one-third of the normal hourly rate, therefore we need to calculate a 'weighted' figure for chargeable time.

$$\text{Weighted chargeable hour} = 1,417.5 + \frac{472.5}{3} = 1,575 \text{ hours}$$

Now we can combine the consultancy services costs and the weighted chargeable time to determine an hourly rate for each type of work.

$$\text{Cost per chargeable hour} = \frac{\$72,100}{1,575} = \$45.78$$

Hourly rate for productive client work = $45.78 + 5% profit mark-up = **$48.07 per hour**

$$\text{Hourly rate for travelling time} = \frac{\$48.07}{3} = \textbf{\$16.02 per hour}$$

7 Reports in a not-for-profit organisation

Not-for-profit organisations such as local authorities and charities have their own rules and requirements in terms of accounting. Some of the financial measures we have looked at so far (gross margin, contribution, ROCE) will not always be appropriate in a not-for-profit organisation.

There are two main problems involved in assessing performance of these organisations:

- the problem of identifying and measuring objectives
- the problem of identifying and measuring outputs.

Objectives

One of the issues in performance evaluation, in any sector, is defining organisational objectives. Once that is done, performance indicators can be devised that indicate the extent to which such objectives have been achieved.

In not-for-profit organisations the objectives may be much more varied, reflecting the variety of organisations included in the sector:

- charities
- professional institutions
- educational establishments
- government bodies.

Although the detail will vary depending on the organisation involved, we could suggest that the general objective of not-for-profit organisations is to provide the best possible service within a limited resource budget:

- **Charities** will have a limited amount of funds available – they will seek to use these funds to provide services to as many of their beneficiaries as possible. It will be important not to waste money or any other resources.

- A central **government department** (health or education for example) or a local authority typically has a limited amount of finance available. Its objective will be to provide the best possible service to the community with the financial constraints imposed upon it.

The problems of output measurement

Outputs of organisations in these sectors are often not valued in monetary terms. How do we measure the output of a school or hospital?

Output targets can be set in these situations, but they will always be open to debate and argument.

The not-for-profit sector incorporates a diverse range of operations including national government, local government and charities etc. The critical thing about such operations is that they are **not** motivated by a desire to maximise profit.

Many, if not all, of the benefits arising from expenditure by these bodies are non-quantifiable (certainly not in monetary terms, e.g. social welfare). The same can be true of costs. So any cost/benefit analysis is necessarily quite judgemental, i.e. social benefits versus social costs as well as financial benefits versus financial costs. The danger is that if benefits cannot be quantified, then they might be ignored.

Another problem is that these organisations often do not generate revenue but simply have a fixed budget for spending within which they have to keep.

Illustration 7 – Output measures of schools

In many countries, governments set targets for schools in the form of examination pass rates – a form of output for the school. League tables are then published which rank schools based on their pupils' examination results but:

- There are many people who argue that the output of a school cannot be measured by examination results. They argue the output is a wider concept than this such as the concept of value added education. This would look at the improvement in knowledge and ability of pupils over their life at the school. But how do we measure this?

- Comparing schools performance by publishing league tables of examination results is also open to question. It is of course an attempt to carry out comparative analysis of performance allowing one school to be measured against another. However, many people make the point that the tables do not compare like with like. Different schools have children from different social backgrounds for example, which may be reflected in examination results.

The 3Es concept

The 3Es concept is also known as the value for money (VFM) concept. This has been developed as a useful means of assessing performance in an organisation which is not seeking profit.

The value for money in these organisations is measured through the 3Es, as follows:

- **Economy** (an input measure). This measures the relationship between money spent and the inputs. Are the resources used the cheapest possible for the quality required?

- **Efficiency** (link inputs with outputs). This measures whether the maximum output is being achieved from the resources used.

- **Effectiveness** (links outputs with objectives). This measures to what extent the outputs generated achieve the objectives of the organisation.

You should note that VFM still focuses on financial performance. Not-for-profit organisations will also need to consider non-financial performance measurements, particularly quality.

Illustration 8 – Examples of performance measures using the 3Es

Hospitals

(1) **Economy**

Comparing the standard cost of drugs used in treatments with the actual cost of drugs.

(2) **Efficiency**

Comparing the number of beds in use in a ward with the number of beds available in the ward.

(3) **Effectiveness**

Comparing the current waiting time for patients with the desired waiting time for patients.

Colleges or universities

(1) **Economy**

Comparing the standard cost of tutors with the actual cost of the tutors.

(2) **Efficiency**

Comparing actual tutor utilisation in hours with planned tutor utilisation in hours.

(3) **Effectiveness**

Comparing actual exam results (% over a certain grade or percentage passes) with desired exam results.

Test your understanding 4

A government is looking at assessing state schools by reference to a range of both financial and non-financial factors, one of which is average class sizes.

Which of the three E's best describes the above measure?

A   Economy

B   Effectiveness

C   Efficiency

D   Externality

Example of a managerial report for a charity

TUV is a charity. It has just completed an overseas aid programme to assist homeless orphans. Cost and revenue data concerning the programme are as follows.

	$
Income from donations	157,750
Grants received from government and others	62,000
Fundraising costs	23,900
Direct staff costs, including travel and insurance	68,800
Medical supplies and temporary accommodation	78,120
Food, blankets and clothes	17,100
Transport costs	24,300
Other direct costs	9,800
Apportioned administrative support costs	13,200

Prepare a statement to enable managers to monitor the total net cost of the aid programme, highlighting any subtotals that you think may be useful to the managers.

Solution:

TUV: Report on overseas aid programme

	$	$
Income from donations		157,750
Grants received from government and others		62,000
		———
Gross revenue		**219,750**
Less fundraising costs		23,900
		———
Net revenue		195,850
Direct staff costs, including travel and insurance	68,800	
Medical supplies and temporary accommodation	78,120	
Food, blankets, clothes	17,100	
Transport costs	24,300	
Other direct costs	9,800	
	———	
Total direct cost		198,120
		———
Net direct cost of programme		**2,270**
Apportioned administrative support costs		13,200
		———
Total net cost of programme		**15,470**
		———

Points to note about the statement are as follows.

- The fundraising costs are netted off against the gross revenue. Managers can use the resulting net revenue to monitor the effectiveness of the fundraising activities undertaken.

- Direct costs of the programme are highlighted separately. Managers are able to see whether the net revenue from the fundraising efforts was sufficient to cover the directly identifiable costs of undertaking the programme. In this case, the direct costs exceeded the net fundraising revenue by $2,270.

- Administrative support costs are apportioned so that managers can see the final net impact of this programme on the charity's resources.

Test your understanding 5

As part of its fundraising and awareness-raising activities a charity operates a number of retail shops, selling new and donated second-hand goods.

Data for the latest period are as follows.

	$
Sales income	
New goods	6,790
Donated goods sold to customers	4,880
Purchase cost of new goods	3,332
Cost of laundering and cleaning selected donated goods	120
Delivery cost paid for new goods	290
Other income: low-quality donated goods sold for recycling	88
Salary costs	810
Amount paid to valuer to assess selected donated items	30
General overhead costs	1,220

Complete the managerial report for the charity.

Second-hand donated goods

	$	$	$
Sales income			
Sold to customers	⬜		
Sold for recycling	88		
	⎯⎯		
		⬜	
Cost of laundering, etc	120		
Valuation costs	30		
	⎯⎯		
		150	
		⎯⎯	

Gross profit for second-hand goods | | | ⬜ |

New Goods

Sales income		⬜	
Less: purchase cost	3,332		
delivery cost	290		
	⎯⎯⎯		
		3,622	
		⎯⎯⎯	

Gross profit for new goods | | | ⬜ |

Total gross profit | | | ⬜ |

| Salary costs | | | 810 |
| General overheads | | | 1,220 |

Operating profit | | | ⬜ |

8 Chapter summary

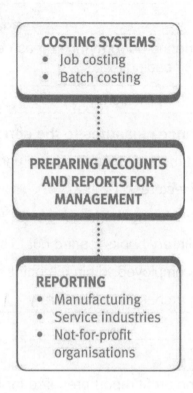

COSTING SYSTEMS
- Job costing
- Batch costing

PREPARING ACCOUNTS AND REPORTS FOR MANAGEMENT

REPORTING
- Manufacturing
- Service industries
- Not-for-profit organisations

9   End of chapter questions

Question 1

A university is considering performance measures which it could include under each of the 3E headings.

Economy ı	Efficiency ∿	Effectiveness ૩

Match the performance measures to the correct 3E heading.

- % of lecturer's time spent teaching and undertaking research ²
- Salary costs of lecturers ı
- % of students achieving the target grade *a* ૩
- How often are library books loaned out to students ૨
- % of graduates employed within 6 months ૩
- Cost of books purchased for the library ı

Question 2

Consider the following profit report prepared for the three divisions of ABC.

	Division 1	Division 2	Division 3	Total
	$000	$000	$000	$000
Revenue	400	600	250	1,250
Material costs	175	290	80	545
Labour costs	*ıʒo*			240
General costs	125	125	125	375
Operating profit	100	185	45	90

Each division purchases its own material. The labour cost is made up of the salaries of the three divisional managers (each is paid $40,000). The rest of the labour cost is a pool of labour which is recruited centrally and used by each of the three divisions as required.

Of the general costs, $150,000 relates to a machine used only by division 3 and $20,000 is the cost of the premises rented and used only by division 2. The remainder are general overheads and are treated as head office costs.

↗ Remove General costs, #only specific

Redo the report and calculate the following:

(a)   The controllable profit for Division 1. $ _____

(b)   The controllable profit for Division 2. $ _____

(c)   The controllable profit for Division 3. $ _____

(d)   The total head office cost. $ _____

Question 3

Match the organisational activities below to the most appropriate costing method by writing Job costing or Batch Costing in the boxes provided.

Organisational activities

- Accounting and taxation services
- Leaflet printing
- Plumbing and heating repairs
- Building maintenance and repairs

Question 4

A commercial decorating company budgets for 4% idle time on all its jobs. That is time that is being paid for but is not productive.

The estimated number of active labour hours required to complete decorating job D47 is 120 hours. The hourly labour rate is $11.

Required:

The estimated labour cost of job D47 is (to the nearest $) $ _____ .

Question 5

A company calculates the prices of jobs by adding overheads to the prime cost and adding 30% to total costs as a profit mark-up.

Complete the following job cost summary information:

Job Y256	$
Prime cost	
Overheads	694
Total cost	
Profit mark up	
Selling price	1,690

Question 6

JKL specialises in printing advertising leaflets and is in the process of preparing its price list. The most popular requirement is for a folded leaflet made from a single sheet of A4 paper. From past records and budgeted figures, the following data have been estimated for a typical batch of 10,000 leaflets.

Artwork	$65
Machine setting	4 hours at $22 per hour
Paper	$12.50 per 1,000 sheets
Ink and consumables	$40
Printers' wages	4 hours at $8 per hour

(Note: Printers' wages vary with volume.)

General fixed overheads are $15,000 per period, during which a total of 600 labour hours are expected to be worked.

The company wishes to achieve 30% profit on sales.

The selling prices (to the nearest $) per thousand leaflets for quantities of:

(a)   10,000 leaflets is $ _____.

(b)   20,000 leaflets is $ _____.

Question 7

Job cost sheets are used to record the work carried out on particular jobs. Consider the following elements:

(i) Actual direct material cost

(ii) Actual production overheads

(iii) Absorbed production overheads

(iv) Actual direct labour cost

Which of the above elements would be contained in a typical job cost sheet?

A (i), (ii) and (iv) only

B (i), and (iv) only

C (i), (iii) and (iv) only

D All of them

Question 8

Which of the following are characteristics of service organisations? Select all that apply.

A a low incidence of work in progress at the end of a period

B difficulty in identifying and measuring objectives

C a focus on contribution

D the use of composite cost units

Question 9

A government is looking at assessing the performance of teachers in a state school by reference to a range of both financial and non-financial factors, one of which is pass rates.

Which of the three E's best describes the above measure?

A Economy

B Effectiveness

C Efficiency

D Externality

Question 10

LMN has three main divisions – a motor-cycle courier service, a domestic parcel delivery service, and a bulk parcel service for industry.

The following information is available for a period:

	Courier service	Domestic parcels	Bulk parcels
Sales ($000)	205	316	262
Distance travelled (000km)	168	82	54

Variable costs vary both with the distance travelled and also the type of vehicle used, and are $307,800 for the company as a whole. A technical estimate shows that the various vehicles used for the three services incur variable costs per kilometre in the ratio of 1:3:5, respectively, for the courier service, domestic parcels and bulk parcels.

The contribution for each service for the period is:

(a)　courier service:　　　　　　$ _____

(b)　domestic parcels:　　　　　$ _____

(c)　bulk parcels:　　　　　　　$ _____

Test your understanding and end of chapter answers

Test your understanding 1

D

Total direct labour cost = (12,500) + (23,000) + (4,500) = $40,000

Overhead absorption rate $= \dfrac{\$140,000}{\$40,000} \times 100\% = 350\%$ of direct labour.

Work in progress valuation	$	$
Costs given in question:		
Job 1	38,150	
Job 2	52,025	
	———	
		90,175
Overhead absorbed:		
Job 1 $12,500 × 350%	43,750	
Job 2 $23,000 × 350%	80,500	
	———	
		124,250
		———
		214,425
		———

Test your understanding 2

Job A: Selling price = ($45 + 10%) = $49.50 + 25% = **$61.88**

Job B: Selling price = ($38 + 10%) = $41.80 + 20% = **$50.16**

Job C: Selling price = ($75 + 10%) = $82.50 × (100/85) = **$97.06**

Remember: Profit margin is based on sales and mark-up is based on cost.

Test your understanding 3

C

	$
Costs given in question	50,500
Overhead absorbed: $4,500 × 350%	15,750
Total production cost	66,250
Mark up 50%	33,125
Sales value of batch	99,375

Selling price per circuit board $\dfrac{99,375}{2,400}$ = **$41.41**

Test your understanding 4

C

Class sizes are the result of the number of pupils educated (output), the number of teachers employed (input) and how well the timetable is organised in using those teachers. Therefore this is a measure of efficiency.

Test your understanding 5

Second-hand donated goods

Sales income	$	$	$
Sold to customers	4,880		
Sold for recycling	88		
		4,968	
Cost of laundering, etc.	120		
Valuation costs	30		
		150	
Gross profit for second-hand goods		**4,818**	

	$	$	$
New goods			
Sales income		6,790	
Less: purchase cost	3,332		
delivery cost	290		
		3,622	
Gross profit for new goods			**3,168**
Total gross profit			7,986
Salary costs			810
General overheads			1,220
Operating profit			**5,956**

Question 1

Economy:

- Salary costs of lecturers

- Cost of books purchased for the library.

Efficiency:

- % of lecturer's time spent teaching and undertaking research

- How often are library books loaned out to students.

Effectiveness:

- % of students achieving the target grade

- % of graduates employed within 6 months.

Economy is about balancing the cost with the quality of the resources.

Efficiency focuses on the efficient use of any resources acquired.

Effectiveness measures the achievement of the organisation's objectives.

Question 2

(a)   The controllable profit for Division 1 is **$185,000**

(b)   The controllable profit for Division 2 is **$250,000**

(c)   The controllable profit for Division 3 is **($20,000)**

(d)   The total head office cost is **$325,000**

	Division 1	Division 2	Division 3	Total
	$000	$000	$000	$000
Revenue	400	600	250	1,250
Material costs	175	290	80	545
Specific labour costs	40	40	40	120
Specific costs		20	150	170
Controllable profit	185	250	(20)	415
Head office costs				325
Operating profit				90

Question 3

• Accounting and taxation services	**Job costing**
• Leaflet printing	**Batch costing**
• Plumbing and heating repairs	**Job costing**
• Building maintenance and repairs	**Job costing**

Question 4

The estimated labour cost of job D47 is **$1,375**.

Workings:

The idle time would be stated as a percentage of the **paid** labour hours.

	Hours
Active labour hours required	120
Idle time (× 4/96)	5
Total paid hours required	125
Labour cost × $11 per hour	**$1,375**

Question 5

In this question the profit is calculated as a percentage of cost. Calculate the total cost first, then the remaining answers can be calculated as balancing figures.

Job Y256	$
Prime cost	**606**
Overheads	694
TOTAL COST (1,690 × 100/130)	**1,300**
Profit mark-up	**390**
Selling price	1,690

Question 6

The selling prices (to the nearest $) per thousand leaflets for quantities of:

(a)   10,000 leaflets is **$ 64**.

(b)   20,000 leaflets is **$ 53**.

Workings:

	Cost of batch 10,000 leaflets	Cost of batch 20,000 leaflets
	$	$
Artwork (1)	65.00	65.00
Machine setting (1)	88.00	88.00
Paper	125.00	250.00
Ink and consumables	40.00	80.00
Printers' wages ($8/hour)	32.00	64.00
	350.00	547.00
General fixed o/head (2)	100.00	200.00
Total cost	450.00	747.00
Profit ((30/70) × cost)	192.86	320.14
Sales revenue required	642.86	1,067.14
Selling price per 1,000	**$64.00**	**$53.00**

Notes:

(1)   Machine setting (4 × $22) and artwork costs are not affected by the size of the batch.

(2)   General fixed overhead = $15,000/600 = $25 per hour.

Question 7

C

Job cost sheets would include the actual direct labour and direct material costs for the job. Production overheads are absorbed into the cost of each job using a predetermined overhead absorption rate. The actual production overhead would not be included in the job cost sheet.

Question 8

A and D

Many services are consumed as soon as they are made available to the customer. They cannot be held in inventory for sale at a later date. Therefore there is a low incidence of work in progress at the end of a period.

Composite cost units are often used because they are more useful for control purposes, for example in a haulage company a cost per tonne-mile might be more useful for planning and control purposes than a simple cost per tonne.

Difficulty in identifying and measuring objectives would be a feature of a not-for-profit organisation.

There is more likely to be a focus on contribution in a manufacturing organisation as service organisations tend to have a very high proportion of indirect costs making contribution less useful.

Question 9

B

Pass rates (objective) are the result of how well the teachers educate the pupils (output). Therefore this is a measure of effectiveness.

Question 10

(a) Courier service   **$129,400**

(b) Domestic parcels   **$205,300**

(c) Bulk parcels   **$140,500**

Workings:

Weighted total kilometres travelled

Weight	Distance km	Weighted km
1	168,000	168,000
3	82,000	246,000
5	54,000	270,000
		684,000

Total variable costs = $307,800

Variable costs per weighted km =

$$\frac{\$307,800}{684,000} = \$0.45 \text{ per weighted km}$$

Variable cost per service is therefore:

	$
Courier service: 168,000 × 0.45	75,600
Domestic parcels: 246,000 × 0.45	110,700
Bulk parcels: 270,000 × 0.45	121,500
	307,800

Thus, contribution per service is:

	Courier $	Domestic $	Bulk $
Sales	205,000	316,000	262,000
Variable costs	(75,600)	(110,700)	(121,500)
Contribution	**129,400**	**205,300**	**140,500**

- We are told that the various vehicles incur variable costs per kilometre in the ratio 1:3:5. Therefore, we need to calculate a weighted total number of kilometres travelled, in order to fairly share out the total variable costs incurred. We cannot simply calculate the variable cost per kilometre as (costs incurred ÷ kilometres travelled), because a kilometre travelled by a motor-cycle costs less than a kilometre travelled by a bulk parcel van or lorry.

Risk 1 – Summarising and analysing data

Chapter learning objectives

After completing this chapter, you should be able to

- explain the concepts of risk and uncertainty

- calculate summary measures of central tendency and dispersion for both grouped and ungrouped data.

1 Session content diagram

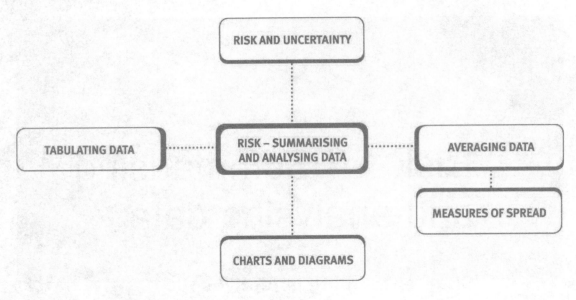

2 Introduction to risk and uncertainty

We have looked at the planning and control aspects of the management accountant's role. In the remaining four chapters we will consider the decision making role in more detail.

We will start by considering the impact of risk and uncertainty in decision making, then move on to short-term and long-term decision making techniques.

We know that risk is an important concept in decision making. Most decisions involve looking to the future and estimating future costs or benefits. These estimates will inevitably involve uncertainties and assumptions. For example a company may be considering investing in upgrading its production machinery in order to increase its production capacity and produce a new range of products. The level of perceived risk involved in this investment will have an impact on the return required from the investment. The higher the risk, the higher the return required to compensate for the level of risk.

Consideration of risk is therefore important. We have to be able to reflect this risk and uncertainty in our financial evaluations relating to these decisions.

In everyday speech most people use the terms 'risk' and 'uncertainty' as though they were interchangeable. As far as your CIMA studies are concerned, however, there is a distinction.

The term 'risk' is used to describe a scenario when we know the different possible outcomes and can estimate their associated probabilities.

 The *CIMA Terminology* defines **risk** as 'condition in which there exists a quantifiable dispersion in the possible outcomes from any activity'.

The term 'uncertainty' is used when we do not know the possible outcomes and/or their associated probabilities. Uncertainty is essentially a matter of ignorance. The future cannot be predicted because there is insufficient information about what the future outcomes might be. Decisions under conditions of uncertainty are often a matter of guesswork.

 The *CIMA Terminology* defines **uncertainty** as 'inability to predict the outcome from an activity due to lack of information about the required input/output relationships or about the environment within which the activity takes place'.

The difference between these is therefore that **risk is quantifiable while uncertainty is unquantifiable.**

For example, we may budget for sales of 100,000 units for the next period but could anticipate sales being anywhere between 80,000 and 130,000 units. From past experience we may be able to assign probabilities to these potential outcomes. However, in any industry and any business there is uncertainty. A change in the law, a change in consumer preference, availability of a new similar product could occur in the next period and affect the level of sales. These events are uncertain, they could happen but we are not able to assign a probability to them. We do however have to be aware of them in our decision making.

 Illustration on risk and uncertainty

Risk: There are a number of possible outcomes and the probability of each outcome is known.

For example, based on past experience of digging for oil in a particular area, an oil company may be able to estimate the probability (% chance) of finding oil.

Uncertainty: There are a number of possible outcomes but the probability of each outcome is not known.

For example, the same oil company may dig for oil in a previously unexplored area. The company knows that it is possible for them to either find or not find oil but it does not know the probabilities of each of these outcomes.

Dealing with risk and uncertainty is a major topic in your future studies. Understanding probabilities is thus essential to fully understanding risk and uncertainty. This will be looked at in detail in the next chapter.

Before we look at probability in detail we must be comfortable with some basic mathematical concepts concerning data. In the context of management accounting chapter we learned about data and information. We know that we need good information to make good decisions. In order for data to become information, we must be able to summarise and analyse it.

Management accountants must be able to analyse a large amount of data so that it becomes meaningful and useful information.

In this chapter we will look at some mathematical techniques which can be used to analyse data. In practice much of this type of analysis would be done using computers.

- Tabulating data (Tallying/Frequency distributions)

- Charts and diagrams (Pie charts/Bar charts/Histograms and ogives)

- Averaging (Arithmetic mean/Median/Mode)

- Measures of spread (Range/Variance/Standard deviation/Coefficient of variation).

Tabulating data: This is a good technique which helps us present raw data in a way which makes it easier to understand and therefore more useful for decision making.

Charts and diagrams: Once tabulated and grouped, we can then use charts and diagrams to present the data in an even more user friendly way. If a company is interested in reducing costs, a diagram showing the breakdown of where costs are incurred throughout the organisation would be very useful.

Remember, as management accountants we need to be able to analyse and present many different types of information, both financial such as costs and sales, but also non-financial such as staff numbers, customer orders, complaints etc. Being able to tabulate data and depict it graphically will help us to provide more meaningful reports to management.

Averaging: Being able to calculate basic averaging figures will also enhance our ability to provide meaningful information to management. For example we may say that sales are $4,000 per day or we receive 200 orders per day. It is unlikely that sales are exactly $4,000 each day or that we receive exactly 200 orders each day. These are average figures.

Spread: Related to the calculations of averages, we will look at techniques to measure spread. Measures of spread give us more information relating to the averages we have calculated.

All of these techniques will aid the production of good information which will aid decision making.

3 Tabulating data – Tallying

Tallying is one way of converting raw data into a more concise format to make it easier to use.

Illustration 1 – Processing raw data

In order to monitor the efficiency of his department, the head of the finance section of a large company spot-checks the number of invoices left unprocessed at the end of each day. At the end of the first period of this check (26 working days), he has collected the following data:

1	5	3	3	2
3	0	4	1	4
3	3	2	1	2
1	1	0	3	6
5	0	3	4	2
3				

Collate this raw data into a more meaningful form.

Solution:

The data given is not particularly useful so we will tally it to make it easier to use and understand.

By scanning the table we can see that all the values lie between 0 and 6 inclusive so we set up a table showing the possible values of 0 – 6. It might be useful to find out how often each value in this range occurs in the table. This could be achieved simply by counting, but there are no safeguards against human error in doing this. Instead we use a tallying procedure, which is more accurate than counting, especially with large tables of figures. Go along the top row of the table and mark when each number occurs. After going along the first row, the tally will look like:

Number of invoices left unprocessed	Tally
0	
1	I
2	I
3	II
4	
5	I
6	

As we go through the table, one 'notch' is put against the appropriate number each time it appears. For ease of counting, when each fifth notch is reached, it is often separated out or crossed to make adding easier.

So four tallies would be shown as IIII, five would be IIIII or ℍℍ and 6 would be IIIII I or ℍℍ I, etc.

Number of invoices left unprocessed	Tally	Total
0	III	3
1	IIIII	5
2	IIII	4
3	IIIII III	8
4	III	3
5	II	2
6	I	1
		___
		26
		___

The 'totals' in the above table are called **frequencies** and the table is called the **frequency distribution** of the sample. Thus the frequency of 0 invoices is 3 and so on.

Test your understanding 1

The daily absentee rate at a small factory is recorded for one calendar month (22 working days):

Number of employees absent:

6 8 7 8 5 5 6 8 2 4 5
7 6 2 3 3 4 8 3 5 4 7

Tally these data into a frequency distribution.

2 – 8

2	II
3	IIII
4	III
5	IIII
6	III
7	III
8	III

4 Tabulating data – Grouped distributions

In some cases if we try to tally using each possible measurement taken, then we will still have too many values to be really useful.

A far more sensible approach is to tally the number of values in a certain range or **class**. The choice of classes is somewhat arbitrary, but should be such that they are neither too narrow, which could result in most of the frequencies being zero, nor too wide, which could produce only a small number of classes and thereby tell us little.

As a rough guide, between four and twelve groups are often used.

Illustration 2 – Grouped distributions

In order to assist management negotiations with the trade unions over piecework rates, the management services department of a factory is asked to obtain information on how long it takes for a certain operation to be completed. Consequently, the members of the department measure the time it takes to complete 30 repetitions of the operation, at random occasions during a month. The times are recorded to the nearest tenth of a minute.

19.8	21.3	24.6	18.7	19.1	15.3
20.6	22.1	19.9	17.2	24.1	23.0
20.1	18.3	19.8	16.5	22.8	18.0
20.0	21.6	19.7	25.9	22.2	17.9
21.1	20.8	19.5	21.6	15.6	23.1

Form the frequency distribution of this sample.

Solution:

A scan of the table shows that the smallest value is 15.3 minutes and the largest 25.9 minutes. If we tallied as in the previous illustration we would have to show a large number of values.

Time (minutes)	Tally
15.3	
15.4	
15.5	
...	
...	
25.9	

This would provide a format of little more use than the original data, because most of the frequencies would be 0, interspersed by the occasional frequency of 1. Using ranges or classes we could tally as follows:

Time (minutes)	Tally	Frequency
15 – under 17	III	3
17 – under 19	IIIII	5
19 – under 21	IIIII IIIII	10
21 – under 23	IIIII II	7
23 – under 25	IIIII	4
25 – under 27	I	1
		30

Even though some precision has been lost, this grouped frequency distribution is of considerably more use to the management services department than the raw data, because, for example, we can see at a glance where the bulk of the times lie, how often the time exceeds some target figure such as 23 minutes, say, and so on.

When grouping data, take care when defining the classes so that it is clear where each observation will fit, e.g. 10 – below 20, 20 – below 30 etc. Be careful of using confusing groupings such as 10 – 20, 20 – 30 etc.

Test your understanding 2

For one month, the daily outputs, in units, of a certain product (A) are recorded:

Daily output, units

			49	47
33	58	56	59	45
39	53	51	44	49
37	53	48	47	40
36	50	55	44	42

Tally these data into a frequency distribution using the intervals 30 – under 35; 35 – under 40; and so on.

Continuous and discrete data

Discrete variables

Discrete variables can only consist of certain values. For example the number of invoices could be

> 0 or 1 or 2 or ...

but never   1.6, 2.3 and so on.

Continuous variables

On the other hand, the time taken to undertake a certain operation can theoretically take a value to any level of precision, depending on the degree of accuracy to which the management requires to measure.

> 20.2 minutes
>
> 20.19 minutes
>
> 20.186 minutes
>
> 20.1864 minutes and so on.

However, a number of invoices cannot be measured any more accurately than in whole numbers.

Tallying

This distinction has a number of consequences. Here, it can affect the way we tally. Continuous variables, such as the times to undertake a certain operation, can rarely be tallied as individual values, since few of them will coincide to give meaningfully large frequencies.

Classifying is therefore almost always necessary with continuous variables.

5 Tabulating data – Cumulative frequency distributions

It is sometimes helpful to develop the idea of frequency further and to look at **cumulative frequencies**. These are the number of data values up to (or up to and including) a certain point. They can easily be compiled as running totals from the corresponding frequency distribution.

Illustration 3 – Cumulative frequency distributions

Form the frequency distributions in Illustrations 1 and 2.

Estimate:

(a)   for Illustration 1, how often there are more than four invoices left unprocessed at the end of the day

(b)   for Illustration 2, how often the time taken beats the target of 23 minutes

To answer these questions, we will firstly obtain the cumulative frequency distributions for each.

Solution:

(a)   From Illustration 1, the frequency distribution of the number of unprocessed invoices can be used to obtain the following cumulative frequency distribution:

Number of invoices left unprocessed (less than or equal)	Frequency	Cumulative frequency	
0	3	3	(simply the frequency of '0')
1	5	8	(i.e. 3 + 5)
2	4	12	(i.e. 8 + 4)
3	8	20	
4	3	23	
5	2	25	
6	1	26	

We can now use this to estimate how often more than 4 invoices remain unprocessed:

26 – 23 = 3 occasions out of 26: that is, **11.5%.**

(b) We can now do the same for Illustration 2 so that we can estimate how often the time taken beats the target of 23 minutes.

Time (minutes) (less than)	Frequency	Cumulative frequency
15	0 *	0
17	3	3
19	5	8
21	10	18
23	7	25
25	4	29
27	1	30

Note: There are no values below 15 minutes.

In this example, we have to take the upper limit of each class to ensure that all the values in the class are definitely less than it. We must use 'less than' as opposed to 'less than or equal' here because it corresponds to the way the frequency table has been compiled.

We can now estimate how often the time taken beats the target of 23 minutes:

25 occasions out of 30: that is, **83.3%**.

How reliable these estimates are depends on how typical or representative is the period or month in which the samples are taken.

We shall see further applications of cumulative frequency throughout the chapter.

> ### Test your understanding 3
>
> **Using the data given in Test your understanding 2 you obtained the following distribution:**
>
> | Output of A units | No. of days (frequency) |
> |---|---|
> | 30 – under 35 | 1 |
> | 35 – under 40 | 3 |
> | 40 – under 45 | 4 |
> | 45 – under 50 | 6 |
> | 50 – under 55 | 4 |
> | 55 – under 60 | 4 |
>
> **Required:**
>
> Form the **cumulative** frequency distribution for this data.

6   Charts and diagrams – Pie charts

Many people find it easier to understand numerical information if it is presented in a pictorial form, rather than as a table of figures.

There are a number of simple charts and graphs commonly used to represent business data. In this section we look at one of the most basic: pie charts.

Pie charts are a very easily understood way of depicting the percentage or proportional breakdown of a total into various categories. They are so called because the total is represented by a circle, with each component shown as a sector with area proportional to percentage. Overall, the chart looks rather like a 'pie' with 'slices' in it.

Sometimes two pie charts are used to compare two totals, along with the manner in which they are broken down. The sections, or slices, of the pie are proportional to the total frequencies which aids comparisons between two charts.

Illustration 4 – Pie charts

A company trades in five distinct geographical markets. In the last financial year, its turnover was:

	$m
UK	59.3
EU, outside UK	61.6
Europe, outside EU	10.3
North America	15.8
Australasia	9.9
Total	156.9

Display these turnover figures as a pie chart.

Solution:

The first step is to calculate the percentage of the total turnover for each region:

	%
UK: (59.3/156.9) =	37.8
EU	39.3
Europe	6.6
North America	10.1
Australasia	6.3

Second, in order to make each 'slice' of the 'pie' proportional in area to these percentages, the whole circle (360°) has to be apportioned into five sections:

	Angle,°
UK: 37.8% of 360° =	136.1
EU	141.5
Europe	23.8
North America	36.4
Australasia	22.7

Alternatively, the angles can be calculated directly as proportions of 360°, for example,

360° × (59.3/156.9) = 136.1°

360° × (61.6/156.9) = 141.5°, etc

Note: There can be slight rounding in these figures.

The resulting pie chart is.

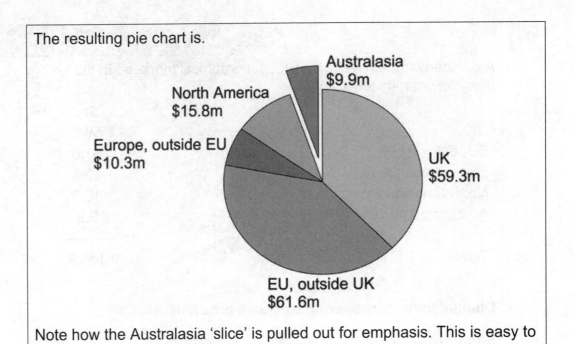

Note how the Australasia 'slice' is pulled out for emphasis. This is easy to do when using a computer.

Test your understanding 4

Display the following data using a pie chart:

Sales of furniture	($000)
Settees	34
Armchairs	27
Dining sets	38
Shelving	18
Others	12

7 Charts and diagrams – Bar charts

Bar charts are another simple way of representing actual data pictorially.
A chart is drawn where labels for the observations are shown on the horizontal (x) axis and the frequencies of each are shown on the vertical (y) axis subject to the following rules:

- Distances against the vertical axis are measurements and represent numerical data.

- Horizontal distances have no meaning. There is no horizontal axis or scale, there are only labels.

Bar charts are very useful for making comparisons between different data items, data sets and so on.

Illustration 5 – Bar charts

Represent the data from Illustration 4 as a bar chart.

Solution:

For this example we want to illustrate the difference in turnover between the various geographical markets.

To draw this chart, it is simply a matter of drawing five vertical 'bars', with heights to represent the various turnover figures, and just labels for regions in the horizontal direction.

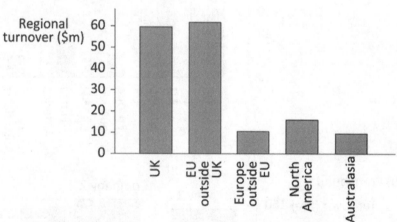

Using this chart it is easy to see, for example, that revenue is highest in the EU outside the UK. This is closely followed by the UK. This could also be seen on the pie chart but it is clearer on the bar chart.

There are a number of variations on such a basic bar chart which can be used to display more data or more complex data. The following example will show a multiple bar chart and a compound (or stacked) bar chart.

Illustration 6 – Multiple and Compound bar charts

A rival company to the one mentioned earlier trades in the same five geographical markets. Its turnover in the last financial year was:

	$m
UK	60.2
EU, outside UK	69.0
Europe, outside EU	11.1
North America	18.0
Australasia	8.8
Total	167.1

Display the turnover figures for both companies on a single chart.

There are at least two types of bar chart which can be used here: a **multiple bar chart** and a **compound (or component or stacked)** bar chart:

(a) Multiple

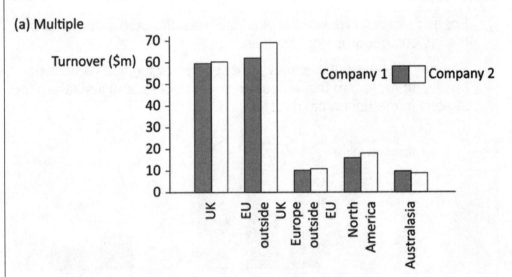

(b) Compound

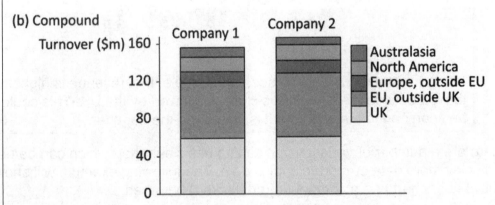

The multiple bar chart readily displays how well the two companies have performed in each market, but not so clearly in total. Conversely, the relative total performance of the two companies can be seen easily from the compound bar chart, but not so the breakdown by region.

You cannot be asked to actually draw charts during a computer-based assessment. Exam questions therefore take the form of labelling charts, calculating particular values, selecting a type of chart appropriate to particular data and drawing conclusions from charts.

Test your understanding 5

The following are percentage distributions of household income in two regions:

Income ($000)	Region A	Region B
0 – less than 10	25	15
10 – less than 20	30	29
20 – less than 30	32	38
30 – less than 40	10	9
40 or more	3	9
Total	100	100

Display the data by the following bar charts:

(a) region A by a simple bar chart

(b) region A by a compound bar chart

(c) both regions by a multiple bar chart.

8 Charts and diagrams – Histograms and ogives

Histograms

When we looked at bar charts we saw that the vertical **height** of the bar represented the frequency while the horizontal (x) axis simply showed the labels of the items or classes. With histograms the frequency is represented by the **area** of a block or rectangle.

More specifically, a histogram is a diagram consisting of rectangles whose area is proportional to the frequency of a variable and whose width is equal to the class interval. The x-axis is the variable being measured and the y-axis is the corresponding frequency.

Illustration 7 – Histograms

Draw a histogram for the following data from Illustration 2.

Time (minutes)	Frequency
15 – under 17	3
17 – under 19	5
19 – under 21	10
21 – under 23	7
23 – under 25	4
25 – under 27	1
	30

At first glance this looks no different from what we have seen before. However, when we look at examples with uneven class sizes, we will see that representing frequency by height alone can be misleading and a switch to areas (histograms) gives a fairer representation of the underlying data. This is discussed in more detail later in the chapter.

Ogives

An ogive is a graph of the cumulative frequency distributions met earlier.

As with bar charts, the x-axis is the variable being measured and the y-axis is the corresponding cumulative frequency, the x- and y-values are plotted as follows.

With a discrete variable, intermediate x-values have no meaning in reality (recall 1.6 invoices) and so the ogive would consist of a series of discrete points. It is usual therefore not to draw it. With a continuous variable, the intermediate values do have a meaning, and so it makes sense to join the plotted points.

This can be done with a series of straight lines, which is effectively assumes that the values are evenly spread throughout their classes.

Illustration 8 – Ogives

Draw an ogive for the data in Illustration 2.

Solution:

The cumulative frequency distribution was

Time (minutes) (less than)	Cumulative frequency
15	0
17	3
19	8
21	18
23	25
25	29
27	30

This gives the following ogive:

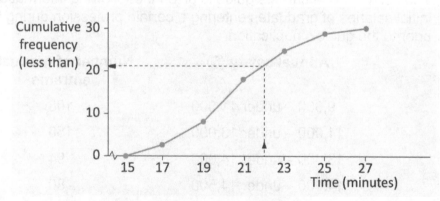

Note: The horizontal axis has been started at 15 rather than 0 to make it easier to read. Having part of the of axis missing like this is known as a **broken scale**.

Once we have an ogive we can use it to estimate probabilities.

Example

Suppose the management wishes to reduce the target time for the operation to 22 minutes. Assuming the distribution of times remains unaltered, how often will this target be met?

> **Solution:**
>
> First of all, it is not possible to answer this as a straight reading from the cumulative frequency distribution, as 22 minutes does not correspond to a value in the table. If we look at the ogive, however, we can estimate how many of the 30 occasions took less than 22 minutes, by reading off the graph, as shown.
>
> Thus, we estimate that the target will be met on 21 out of every 30 occasions: that is, **70%** of the time.

Unequal class sizes

Up till now, we have used examples with equal class sizes, but this is not always the case.

In some questions the class sizes are not constant. If we draw block heights equal to frequencies, we exaggerate those with larger class widths. In a case where there are unequal class widths, we must compensate by adjusting the heights of some of the blocks.

Instead of the height it is now the **area** of each block that reflects the frequency.

Illustration 9 – Unequal class sizes

The compiler of a careers guide is given the following information on the initial salaries of graduates entering a certain profession during the year prior to the guide's publication.

Annual salary ($)	Number of graduate entrants
9,000 – under 11,000	108
11,000 – under 13,000	156
13,000 – under 14,000	94
14,000 – under 14,500	80
14,500 – under 15,000	25

In order to convey the information in a quickly assimilated form, the compiler decides to represent it as a histogram.

In this illustration we will draw the histogram in two ways:

(a) incorrectly using the methods we have looked at so far

(b) correctly recognising the unequal class widths

If we draw the histograms, we obtain the following:

(a) incorrect

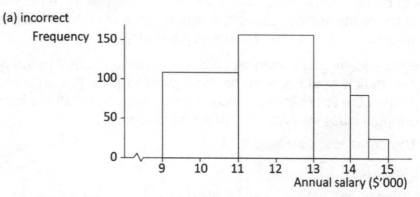

Close inspection of this will show that some discrepancies have arisen.

For example, the left-hand block is supposed to represent approximately four times more graduates than the right-hand block, and yet the ratio of the size of these two blocks is nearer to 16. There are other examples of disproportion in the size of the blocks, the underlying reason being that, by drawing block heights equal to frequencies, we exaggerate those with larger class widths.

Thus, in a case like this, where there are unequal class widths, one must compensate by adjusting the heights of some of the blocks:

13,000-under 14,000 is half the width of the first two, so
Height = 94 × 2 = 188

14,000-under 14,500 is quarter the width, Height = 80 × 4 = 320

14,500-under 15,000 Height = 25 × 4 = 100

(Alternatively, we could leave the frequencies of the last two classes unaltered, and divide the frequency of the first class by four and so on.)

This would leave the shape of the histogram as:

(b) correct

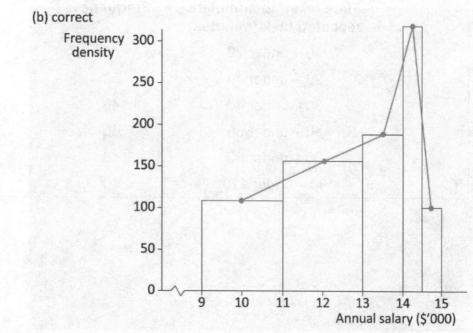

Formally, it is the area of the block that is proportional to the frequency. It will be noted that the areas of the blocks are now in the correct proportion and that the vertical axis of the graph can no longer be labelled 'frequency', but is now '**frequency density**'.

Before leaving this example, it is worth pointing out that the ogive of this distribution would present no extra problems. As this consists only of plotting the upper limit of each class against cumulative frequency, the unequal class intervals do not affect matters.

The ogive is shown below:

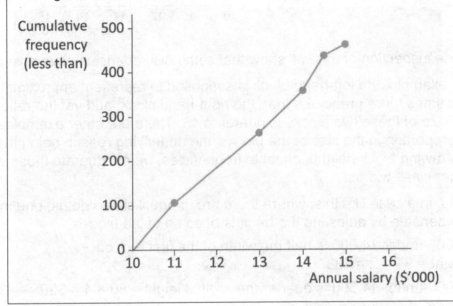

Test your understanding 6

Plot the histogram for the following distribution:

Time taken to complete repeated task (minutes)	Frequency
10 – under 20	63
20 – under 30	52
30 – under 40	46
40 – under 60	60
60 – under 80	48
80 – under 120	40

Test your understanding 7

In a histogram, the common class width is $10.00. For analysis purposes, the analyst has set one class width at $12.50 and the frequency recorded is 80 respondents.

To maintain the accuracy of the histogram, the score that must be plotted for the $12.50 class width is:

A   48

B   64

C   80

D   100

9   Averaging data – The arithmetic mean

We have looked at diagrams and charts which make data easier to use and understand. We will now look at some common mathematical concepts which help us to analyse and understand our data.

The first concept to look at is the average. Most people would understand an 'average' to be the value obtained by dividing the sum of the values in question by the number of values.

So if you had the following set of numbers:

12, 14, 17, 19, 15

The simple average would be (12 + 14 + 17 + 19 + 15) ÷ 5 = **15.4**

This measure is the **arithmetic mean**, or, where there is no possibility of confusion, simply the mean.

In mathematics there are different measures of average. We are going to look at three: mean, median and mode.

Sample means

Suppose you wanted to determine the mean weight of 5 year old children as part of an investigation into childhood obesity. It would be impractical to measure every child, so you would most likely pick a sample of 5 year olds and measure them instead.

Having calculated a 'sample mean', you could use this to comment on the likely mean of the whole population of 5 year olds. For such statements to retain credibility it is vital that the sample is considered to be representative, e.g. did it contain the same proportions of boys to girls present in the population as a whole? One way of trying to make the sample representative is to use a large sample, say, over 1,000 children.

Illustration 10 – Calculating the mean

A shopkeeper is about to put his shop up for sale. As part of the details of the business, he wishes to quote the average weekly takings. The takings in each of the last 6 weeks are:

$1,120 $990 $1,040 $1,030 $1,105 $1,015

Determine the mean weekly takings that the shopkeeper could quote.

Solution:

If the weekly takings are denoted by the variable x, then the sample mean value of x, pronounced 'x-bar' and written as $\overline{x}$, is given by:

$$\overline{x} = \frac{\text{Sum of the values of x}}{\text{Number of values of x}}$$

or $\overline{x} = \dfrac{\Sigma x}{n}$

where Σ, a Greek capital letter 'sigma', is the mathematical symbol for 'add up', and n is the number of values of x.

Note: The mathematical symbol used to denote the mean is μ.

In this example:

$$\overline{x} = \frac{1,120 + 990 + 1,040 + 1,030 + 1,105 + 1,015}{6} = \frac{6,300}{6} = 1,050$$

The shopkeeper could therefore quote a sample mean weekly takings figure of $1,050.

As we can see, this formula is very easy to apply and, as indicated above, merely reflects the arithmetical procedures most people would recognise as the determination of an average. It will, however, need some modification before it can be used to determine the mean from a **frequency distribution**, a form in which many data sets appear.

Illustration 11 – The mean from a frequency distribution

A company is implementing an efficiency drive and, as part of a leaflet it is to distribute to its employees, it wishes to point out the average daily absenteeism rate. The following data is collated from the records of a sample of 200 working days.

Compute the sample mean number of absentees per day.

Number of absentees per day (x)	Number of days (f)
0	9
1	28
2	51
3	43
4	29
5	18
6	10
7	7
8	5

It should be noted that the 'number of days' column simply gives the frequency of the corresponding x values, and so we shall denote this quantity by f. Now, to find the sample mean, the above formula can be applied in a straightforward manner.

Solution:

When calculating the total for x, we can see that we have 9 values of 0, 28 values of 1 etc.

Thus

$$= \frac{(9 \times 0)+(28 \times 1)+(51 \times 2)+(43 \times 3)+(29 \times 4)+(18 \times 5)+(10 \times 6)+(7 \times 7)+(5 \times 8)}{200}$$

$$= \frac{614}{200} = 3.07$$

The mean number of absentees in the sample is 3.07 per day.

Note how, in general, each x-value is multiplied by its corresponding frequency, f, and the products are then summed. That is, we evaluate the product fx for each x-value and then add all the values of fx. As we are denoting addition by 'Σ" this sum can be written as **Σfx**. The formula for the sample mean from a frequency distribution is thus:

$$\bar{x} = \frac{\Sigma fx}{\Sigma f}$$

$$= \frac{614}{200} = 3.07$$

The denominator of this expression Σf is simply the sum of the frequencies, which is, of course, the same as n in the earlier expression for x.

Test your understanding 8

The following distribution shows the number of employees absent per day for a company over a 22 day period.

No. of employees absent	No. of days (frequency)
2	2
3	4
4	3
5	4
6	3
7	3
8	3

Find the arithmetic mean for the above distribution.

The following illustration demonstrates how to calculate the mean in the slightly more complex case where we have grouped data.

Illustration 12 – Calculating the mean from grouped data

As part of its preparation for a wage negotiation, the HR manager of a company has collated the following data from a sample of payslips. She wishes to be able to use the average weekly wage figure in the negotiations.

Evaluate the mean of the sample.

Weekly wage ($)	Number of employees (f)
180 – under 185	41
185 – under 190	57
190 – under 195	27
195 – under 200	23
200 – under 205	15
205 – under 210	7

Solution:

The extra difficulty in this problem is clear: as the data has been collated into classes, a certain amount of detail has been lost and hence the values of the variable x to be used in the calculation of the mean are not clearly specified. Short of actually having the raw data, the actual wages of the employees in the sample, we can only approximate the value of the mean. To do this, we adopt the obvious approach of taking x to be a representative value of each class, the most plausible being the **mid-point**.

Doing this, we have

x	f	fx
182.50	41	7,482.5
187.50	57	10,687.5
192.50	27	5,197.5
197.50	23	4,542.5
202.50	15	3,037.5
207.50	7	1,452.5
	170	32,400.0

It is advisable to set out such statistical calculations in the way shown: very often figures have to be summed, and so they are best arranged in columns.

Now we have:

$$\bar{x} = \frac{\Sigma fx}{\Sigma f} = \frac{32,400}{170} = 190.60, \text{ approx.}$$

Hence, the manager can use an average weekly wage of $190.60 in the negotiations.

Test your understanding 9

The output levels of product Q have been given in the following distribution:

Output of Q (kg)	No. of days (frequency)
350 – under 360	4
360 – under 370	6
370 – under 380	5
380 – under 390	4
390 – under 400	3

Find the arithmetic mean for the above distribution (to two dp).

10 Averaging data – The median

So far we have dealt with the most commonly used average, the mean. We now consider another widely used average, the median.

In Illustration 12, we computed a mean weekly wage of $190.60 which the HR manager could quote in the wage negotiations. An impartial commentator could argue (and the manager might agree) that this is a rather high figure for a supposedly representative average. As 98 out of the sampled 170 people (i.e. 58%) actually earn less than $190 per week.

If we look at this wage distribution, shown below, it is easy to see the cause of this phenomenon. The two highest frequencies occur at the lowest wage classes and then the frequencies decrease slowly as the wages increase. The relatively small number of large wages has caused the mean value to be so large.

Distributions of this type are said to be **skewed**, i.e. the frequency distribution does not look (even roughly) symmetric. It is a criticism of the mean as an average that very skewed distributions can have mean values that appear unrepresentative, in that they are higher or lower than a great deal of the distribution.

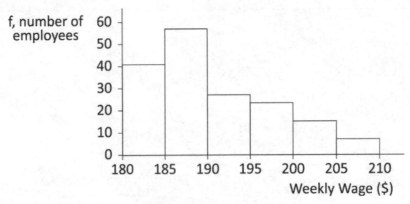

To address this problem, we introduce another measure of average, the **median**. This is defined as the middle of a set of values, when arranged in ascending (or descending) order. This overcomes the above problem, since the median has half the distribution above it, and half below.

Similarly the median is unaffected by any particularly large or unusual individual measurements whereas the mean would be.

We leave the wage distribution for now, and look at a simpler exercise.

Illustration 13 – Calculating the median

In Illustration 10 we saw that a shop's weekly takings were given by the following sample over six weeks. The sample has an arithmetic mean of $1,050.

| $1,120 | $990 | $1,040 | $1,030 | $1,105 | $1,015 |

A prospective purchaser of the business notices that the mean is higher than the takings in four of the 6 weeks.

Calculate the median for him.

Solution:

First of all, we arrange the takings figures in ascending order:

| $990 | $1,015 | **$1,030** | **$1,040** | $1,105 | $1,120 |

The question now is: what is the middle number of a list of six? With a little thought, you can see that there are two 'middle' values, the third and fourth. The median is thus taken to be the mean of these two values.

$$\text{Median} = \frac{(1,030 + 1,040)}{2} = 1,035$$

Hence, the median weekly takings figure that the prospective purchaser could quote is $1,035.

After this example, it is clear that, in the case of an odd number of values, the determination of the median is even easier, as there is a clear **single** middle item in an odd number of values. In general, if there are n observations, the position of the median is given by **(n + 1)/2**. With six observations, this gives 7/2 = 3.5, which is the position halfway between the third and fourth observations.

Test your understanding 10

(a) Calculate the median of the following data:

| 25 | 52 | 18 | 43 | 27 |

(b) Calculate the median of the data on staff absences (hint: use cumulative frequencies).

No. of employees absent	No. of days (f)
2	2
3	4
4	3
5	4
6	3
7	3
8	3

In the case of frequency distributions, the determination of the median is not as straightforward, but can be illustrated by returning to the earlier wage distribution from Illustration 12.

Illustration 14 – Calculating the median from a diagram

Using the data from Illustration 12, find the more representative median weekly wage figure that the HR manager could argue in the wage negotiations.

Solution:

It is clear that the middle wage figure in a set of 170 is halfway between the 85th and 86th. Unfortunately, we do not have the raw data from which the frequency distribution was compiled, and so cannot tell what these two wage figures are. It is therefore necessary to make an assumption about the wage distribution and to deduce an approximate value from the assumption.

If we consider the wage values to be evenly spread throughout their classes, then we can draw the ogive and then estimate the median from a construction based on this ogive. First of all, we need the cumulative frequency distribution.

Weekly wage ($): (less than)	Frequency	Cumulative frequency
185	41	41
190	57	98
195	27	125
200	23	148
205	15	163
210	7	170

The ogive of this cumulative frequency distribution is shown as follows.

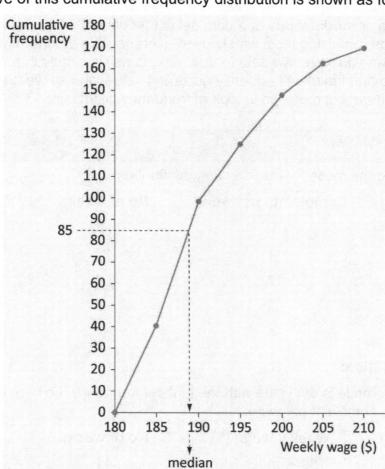

Now, as the median has the property that half of the wage figures lie below it, and half above it, the construction shown on the ogive, drawn at a cumulative frequency of 85 (half of 170), gives the approximate median weekly wage as $188.80. This value is arguably more representative of the sample than the earlier mean value of $190.60, precisely because half the wages lie below and half above it.

Test your understanding 11

Draw the ogive for the following data on the output of product Q and find the median from the ogive.

Output of Q (kg)	No. of days (frequency)
350 – under 360	4
360 – under 370	6
370 – under 380	5
380 – under 390	4
390 – under 400	3

11   Averaging data – The mode

The **mode** or **modal value** of a data set is that value that occurs most often, and it is the remaining most widely used average. The determination of this value, when you have raw data to deal with, consists simply of a counting process to find the most frequently occurring value, and so we do not dwell on this case here, but move on to look at frequency distributions.

Illustration 15 – Calculating the mode

Find the mode for the following distributions:

(a)

Complaints per week	No of weeks
0	5
1	12
2	7
3	2
4	1

Solution:

The mode is the value with the highest frequency, so here the mode is one complaint per week.

(b)

Weekly wage ($)	No of weeks
180 – under 185	41
185 – under 190	57
190 – under 195	27
195 – under 200	23
200 – under 205	15
205 – under 210	7

Solution:

The frequency distribution in this case shows that the **modal class** (that one with the highest frequency) is $185 to under $190.

The following graph shows a way of finding a single value to represent the mode. On the highest modal class, draw two lines as shown to the next observations. Where the two lines intersect gives an estimate of the mode.

The figure shows that the **modal weekly wage** is approximately **$186.60**.

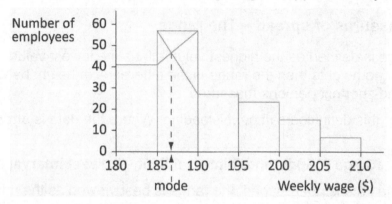

This construction can still be used when there are unequal class intervals.

Test your understanding 12

Find the mode of the following data on the output of product Q.

Output of Q (kg)	No. of days (frequency)
350 – under 360	4
360 – under 370	6
370 – under 380	5
380 – under 390	4
390 – under 400	3

In your assessment you cannot be asked to draw the histograms or ogives so you just have to know how to obtain the mode from it. It is possible to calculate the mode using formulae but this is not required in your syllabus.

Now we have looked at averages we will look at **measures of spread**.

Having obtained an average value to represent a set of data, it is natural to question the extent to which the single value is representative of the whole set. Through a simple example we shall see that part of the answer to this lies in how 'spread out' the individual values are around the average. In particular, we shall study four measures of **spread**, or **dispersion**, as it is sometimes called:

- the range
- the standard deviation and variance
- the coefficient of variation.

12 Measures of spread – The range

The range is defined as the highest value minus the lowest value. For example, if measuring heights then the range is the difference in height between the tallest and shortest persons measured.

However, this definition can be misleading. Where the data is arranged in classes:

Range = Upper most interval limit – Lowest interval limit

Where the data is not grouped, the range is best viewed as the number of values from the very bottom to the very top and is given by:

Range = Highest value – Lowest value + 1

These apparently different definitions amount in practice to the same thing. If we regard the highest value as being at the centre of an interval of unit width, then the uppermost interval limit is given by the highest value plus 0.5. Similarly, the lowest interval limit will be given by the lowest value minus 0.5. Consequently, the value of the range is the same whichever method is used.

The following example will illustrate the calculation of the range, and will demonstrate why such a measure may be needed.

Illustration 16 – The range

A recently retired couple are considering investing their pension lump sums in the purchase of a small shop. Two suitable businesses, A and B, are discovered. The average weekly takings of the two shops are quoted as $1,050 and $1,080 for A and B, respectively. Upon further investigation, the investors discover that the averages quoted come from the following recent weekly takings figures:

| **Shop A:** | $1,120 | $990 | $1,040 | $1,030 | $1,105 | $1,015 |
| **Shop B:** | $1,090 | $505 | $915 | $1,005 | $2,115 | $850 |

Advise the couple.

Solution:

You can easily check that the 'averages' quoted are, in fact, the means of the two samples. Based on these two figures alone, it might seem sensible for the couple to prefer shop B to shop A, but a glance at the actual data casts doubt on this conclusion. It is clear that the values for shop B are far more spread out than those for shop A, thereby making the mean for shop B arguably less representative. This difference is illustrated well by the ranges of the two sets:

Range of A = Highest – Lowest + 1 = 1,120 – 990 + 1 = $131

Range of B = 2,115 – 505 + 1 = $1,611

It can be seen that the much larger range in the latter case is almost entirely due to the single value '$2,115'. The retired couple would therefore be well advised to look at larger samples of weekly takings figures to see if this value is a one-off unusual result that won't be repeated and whether shop B does indeed generate higher weekly takings on average.

13 Measures of spread – The standard deviation and variance

The standard deviation is a way of measuring how far away on average the data points are from the mean. In other words, they measure average variability about the mean. As such standard deviation is often used with the mean when describing a data set.

For example, suppose a data set has just two observations: 10 and 30. The mean here is 20 and the standard deviation will be 10 as both observations are 10 units away from the mean.

For more complex examples, calculating the standard deviation involves the following steps:

(1) Look at the difference between each data value and the mean

(2) To get rid of the problem of negative differences cancelling out positive ones, square the results

(3) Work out the average squared difference (this gives the **variance**)

(4) Square root to get the standard deviation

The basic formula for calculating standard deviation is thus

$$S = \sqrt{\frac{\sum(x - \bar{x})^2}{n}}$$

(**Note:** The variance is simply the standard deviation squared. For most calculations and discussions the standard deviation is perfectly adequate but the variance is used in more advanced statistics and probability theory.)

In practice, this formula can turn out to be very tedious to apply. It can be shown that the following, more easily applicable, formula is the same:

$$S = \sqrt{\frac{\sum fx^2}{\sum f} - \left(\frac{\sum fx}{\sum f}\right)^2}$$

Note: The mathematical symbol used to denote standard deviation is σ.

Illustration 17 – The standard deviation

An analyst is considering two categories of company, A1 and A2, for possible investment. One of her assistants has compiled the following information on the price-earnings ratios of the shares of companies in the two categories over the past year.

Price-earnings ratios	Number of category A1 companies	Number of category A2 companies
4.95 – under 8.95	3	4
8.95 – under 12.95	5	8
12.95 – under 16.95	7	8
16.95 – under 20.95	6	3
20.95 – under 24.95	3	3
24.95 – under 28.95	1	4

Compute the standard deviations of these two distributions and comment. (You are given the means of the two distributions as 15.59 and 15.62, respectively.)

Solution:

Concentrating first of all on category A1, we see that we face the same problem as when we calculated the mean of such a distribution, namely that we have classified data, instead of individual values of x. Adopting a similar approach as before, we take the mid-point of each class:

x (mid-point)	x^2	f	fx	fx^2
6.95	48.3025	3	20.85	144.9075
10.95	119.9025	5	54.75	599.5125
14.95	223.5025	7	104.65	1,564.5175
18.95	359.1025	6	113.70	2,154.6150
22.95	526.7025	3	68.85	1,580.1075
26.95	726.3025	1	26.95	726.3025
		25	389.75	6,769.9625

Thus the standard deviation is:

$$S = \sqrt{\frac{\sum fx^2}{\sum f} - \left(\frac{\sum fx}{\sum f}\right)^2}$$

$$S = \sqrt{\frac{6{,}769.9625}{25} - \left(\frac{389.75}{25}\right)^2}$$

$$= \sqrt{270.7985 - 243.0481} = \sqrt{27.7504} = 5.27$$

The standard deviation of the price-earnings ratios for category A1 is therefore 5.27.

Adopting a similar approach for A2:

x (mid-point)	x^2	f	fx	fx^2
6.95	48.3025	4	27.80	193.21
10.95	119.9025	8	87.60	959.22
14.95	223.5025	8	119.60	1,788.02
18.95	359.1025	3	56.85	1,077.3075
22.95	526.7025	3	68.85	1,580.1075
26.95	726.3025	4	107.80	2,905.21
		30	468.50	8,503.075

Thus the standard deviation is:

$$S = \sqrt{(283.4358 - 243.8803)} = \mathbf{6.289}$$

The standard deviation in the case of category A2 is 6.29.

These statistics again emphasise the wider spread in the category A2 data than in the category A1 data. Note how a full degree of accuracy (four decimal places) is retained throughout the calculation in order to ensure an accurate final result.

Test your understanding 13

Using the following data relating to absences from work in a company over a period of 22 working days, calculate the standard deviation (to 2 dp).

No. of employees absent (x)	No. of days (frequency) (f)
2	2
3	4
4	3
5	4
6	3
7	3
8	3

Tip: It is probably easiest to calculate fx^2 by multiplying fx by x, for example:

$(2 × 2) × 2$

$(3 × 4) × 3$

$(4 × 3) × 4$ etc.

Test your understanding 14

Using the data relating to output of product Q, find the standard deviation.

Output of Q (kg)	No. of days (frequency)
350 – under 360	4
360 – under 370	6
370 – under 380	5
380 – under 390	4
390 – under 400	3

14 Measures of spread – The coefficient of variation

The coefficient of variation is a statistical measure of the dispersion of data points in a data series around the mean. It is calculated as follows:

$$\text{Coefficient of variation} = \frac{\text{Standard deviation}}{\text{Mean}}$$

The coefficient of variation is the ratio of the standard deviation to the mean, and is useful when comparing the degree of variation from one data series to another, even if the means are quite different from each other. Dividing by the mean gives a sense of scale to the standard deviation, so the coefficient of variation is often given as a percentage to aid comparison.

In a financial setting, the coefficient of variation allows you to determine how much risk you are assuming in comparison to the amount of return you can expect from an investment. The lower the ratio of standard deviation to mean return, the better the risk-return trade-off will be.

Note that if the mean in the denominator of the calculation is negative or zero, the ratio will not make sense.

If the means of two sets of data are similar, then it is relatively easy to compare the spreads by looking at the standard deviation figures alone. Another example will show that it is not always so straightforward.

Illustration 18 – The coefficient of variation

Government statistics on the basic weekly wages of workers in two countries show the following. (All figures are shown in $)

Country V: mean = 120   standard deviation = 55

Country W: mean = 90   standard deviation = 50

Can we conclude that country V has a wider spread of basic weekly wages?

By simply looking at the two standard deviation figures, we might be tempted to answer 'yes'. In doing so, however, we would be ignoring the fact that the two mean values indicate that wages in country V are inherently higher, and so the deviations from the mean and thus the standard deviation will tend to be higher. To make a comparison of like with like we must use the coefficient of variation:

$$\text{Coefficient of variation} = \frac{\text{Standard deviation}}{\text{Mean}}$$

Thus

$$\text{Coefficient of variation of wages in country V} = \frac{55}{120} = 45.8\%$$

$$\text{Coefficient of variation of wages in country W} = \frac{50}{90} = 55.6\%$$

Hence we see that, in fact, it is country W that has the higher variability in basic weekly wages.

Test your understanding 15

In country P, the coefficient of variation for the salaries of trainee accountants is 40%, while in country Q it is 60%.

Which of the following statements can be made on the basis of this information? Select all that apply.

A   In P, 40% of trainee accountants have a below-average salary.

B   In Q, the lowest salary of trainee accountants is 60% of the average.

C   Salaries of trainee accountants are more variable in Q than in P.

D   Salaries of trainee accountants are higher on average in Q than in P.

15   Chapter summary

In this chapter we have looked at how data can be summarised and presented using elements such as tables, charts and diagrams. We have also looked at how this data might be interpreted and used to determine factors such as the mean, the probability and the standard deviation.

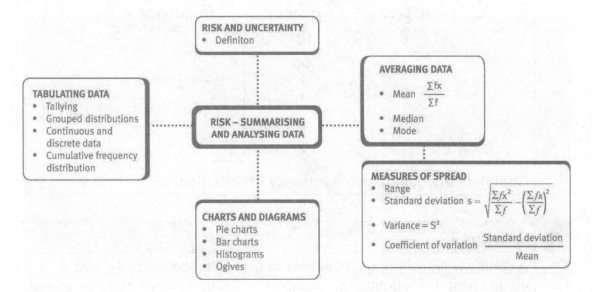

These factors can then be used in assessing uncertainty and quantifying risk to, in turn, aid in business decision making. This idea will be explored in the next chapter.

16 End of chapter questions

Question 1

The following distribution of the number of employees absent per day over a period is given

Number absent	Frequency	Cumulative frequency
0	10	
1	15	
2	7	
3	4	
4	2	

Complete the cumulative frequency distribution.

Question 2

A company is reviewing the number of orders it receives daily over a 40 day period. The frequency distribution and cumulative frequencies are as follows:

Sales	Frequency	Cumulative frequency
10 and under 15	7	7
15 and under 20	16	23
20 and under 25	13	36
25 and under 30	4	40

Based on this the following ogive has been drawn.

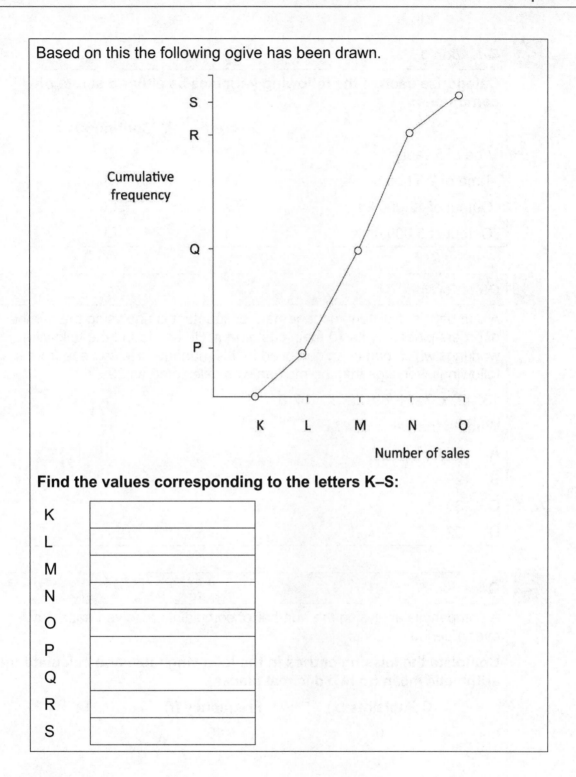

Find the values corresponding to the letters K–S:

K	
L	
M	
N	
O	
P	
Q	
R	
S	

Question 3

Categorise each of the following variables as either discrete or continuous:

	Discrete	Continuous
Age of 5 years	☐	☐
Time of 2.5 hours	☐	☐
Output of 12,000 kg	☐	☐
Output of 5,000 units	☐	☐

Question 4

A company's assistant management accountant is analysing the number of orders placed by its 10 main customers. He has found the following workings which had been compiled by his manager. He can see from the followings workings that the median was calculated as 29.

13, 42, x, 7, 51, 69, 28, 33, 14, 8

What is the value of x?

A   25

B   29

C   30

D   32

Question 5

A company is analysing the number of complaints received each day over a period.

Complete the missing entries in the following table and calculate the arithmetic mean (to two decimal places).

Complaints (x)	Frequency (f)	fx
0	10	?
1	15	?
2	25	?
3	5	?
Totals	?	?

Question 6

Which TWO of the following statements about the mode are true? Select all that apply.

A   It is the most widely used average.

B   It is a measure of dispersion.

C   It gives the most common value.

D   Some distributions have several modes.

E   It is the middle point of a set of values.

Question 7

RST manufactures 5 products (A, B, C, D and E). Using the sales revenue figures for the five products, the following pie chart has been produced. You are told that the sales revenue of product A was $155,000.

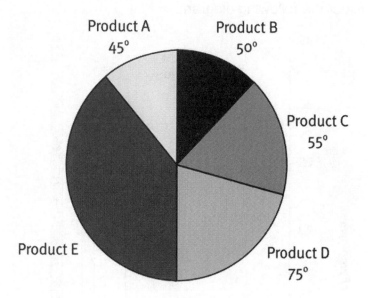

Calculate the sales revenue of Product E. $_____

Question 8

At a factory the daily outputs of product (Q) are measured to the nearest kg and are recorded as:

Daily output, kg

			383	351
362	377	392	369	351
368	382	398	389	360
359	373	381	390	354
369	375	372	376	361

Tally these data into a frequency distribution using the intervals 350 – under 360; 360 – under 370 and so on.

Question 9

Consider the following diagram.

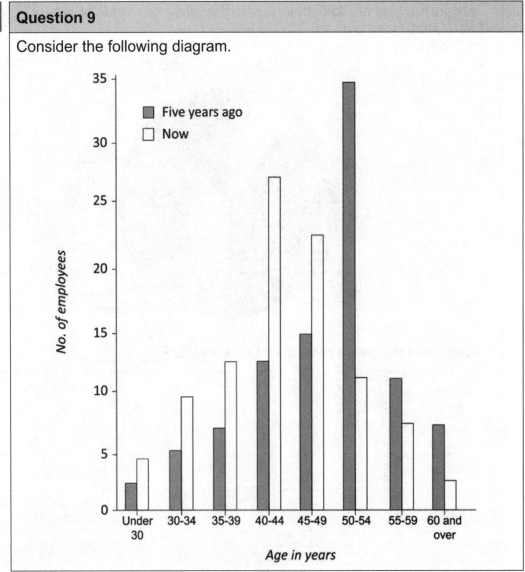

Which TWO of the following statements are true?

A   This diagram is known as a component bar chart.

B   The number of employees aged 60 or over has increased from 5 years ago.

C   The number of employees in the younger age ranges have increased while the number in the older age ranges have reduced in the last 5 years.

D   The most common age range 5 years ago was 50 – 54.

E   The most common age range now is 45 – 49.

Question 10

Match the following terms to the correct definition.

Mean	the value which occurs most often in a data set
Median	the answer derived by dividing the sum of a set of values by the number of values
Mode	the middle of a set of values

Test your understanding and end of chapter answers

Test your understanding 1

Set up the frequency distribution for the possible values. The number of employees absent in the period lies between 2 and 8.

No. of employees absent	Tally	No. of days (frequency)
2	II	2
3	IIII	4
4	III	3
5	IIII	4
6	III	3
7	III	3
8	III	3
		___
		22
		___

Test your understanding 2

Output of A units	No. of days (frequency)
30 – under 35	1
35 – under 40	3
40 – under 45	4
45 – under 50	6
50 – under 55	4
55 – under 60	4

Test your understanding 3

Output of A units	Frequency	Cumulative frequency
under 30	0	0
under 35	1	1
under 40	3	4
under 45	4	8
under 50	6	14
under 55	4	18
under 60	4	22

Test your understanding 4

Category	Sales	Angle,°
Settees	34	95
Armchairs	27	75
Dining sets	38	106
Shelving	18	50
Others	12	34
Total	129	360

The angle is given by 360° × (sales/total sales), for example 360° × 34/129 = 95, rounded to the nearest degree. The resulting pie chart is shown below:

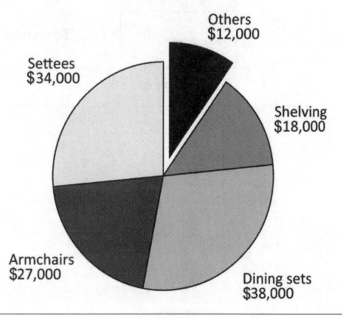

Test your understanding 5

(a)

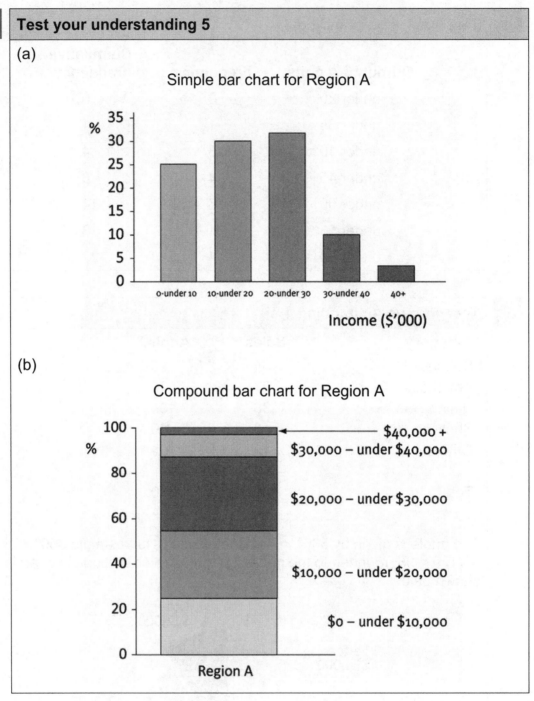

(b)

In drawing this chart it is easiest to first calculate cumulative frequencies:

Income ($000)	Region A	Cumulative
0 – less than 10	25	25
10 – less than 20	30	55
20 – less than 30	32	87
30 – less than 40	10	97
40 or more	3	100
	___	
Total	100	

(c)

Multiple bar chart

Test your understanding 6

Time taken (minutes)	Class width	Frequency	Frequency density
10 – under 20	10	63	63
20 – under 30	10	52	52
30 – under 40	10	46	46
40 – under 60	20	60	60/2 = 30
60 – under 80	20	48	48/2 = 24
80 – under 120	40	40	40/4 = 10

We have taken the standard class width to be ten minutes. For the two classes whose widths are twice the standard, we have divided frequency by two to get the frequency density. We have divided by four for the final class, whose width is four times the standard. The figure below shows the histogram.

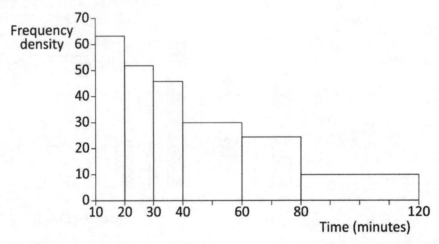

Test your understanding 7

B

The interval is 12.50/10.00 = 1.25 times the standard width, so the score to be plotted is 80/1.25 = 64.

Test your understanding 8

x	f	fx
2	2	4
3	4	12
4	3	12
5	4	20
6	3	18
7	3	21
8	3	24
Σf =	22	Σfx = 111

Mean, $\bar{x} = \dfrac{\Sigma fx}{\Sigma f} = \dfrac{111}{22} = 5{,}045 = 5$ employees, to nearest whole number

Test your understanding 9

Mid-point X	Frequency f	fx
355	4	1,420
365	6	2,190
375	5	1,875
385	4	1,540
395	3	1,185
Σf =	22	Σfx = 8,210

Mean, $\bar{x} = \dfrac{\Sigma fx}{\Sigma f} = \dfrac{8{,}210}{22} = 373.18$ kg (to two d.p.)

Test your understanding 10

(a)   First write the data in order of magnitude:

18	25	27	43	52

The median is calculated as (n + 1) ÷ 2, so in this example the median is (5 + 1) ÷ 2 = 3. The median is in the third position and is therefore 27.

(b)   Find cumulative frequencies:

No. of employees absent	No. of days (f)	Cumulative frequency
2	2	2
3	4	6
4	3	9
5	4	13
6	3	16
7	3	19
8	3	22

There are 22 observations, so the position of the median is given by (22 + 1)/2 = 11.5, that is, the median is midway between the eleventh and twelfth observations. From the cumulative frequencies it is clear that both the eleventh and twelfth observations have value 5, so the median is 5.

Test your understanding 11

Output of Q (kg)	No. of days (frequency)	Cumulative frequency
350 – under 360	4	4
360 – under 370	6	10
370 – under 380	5	15
380 – under 390	4	19
390 – under 400	3	22

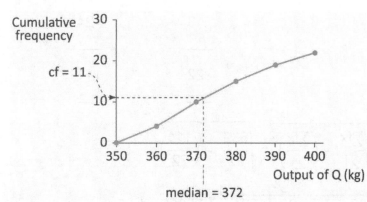

Total frequency is 22, so cumulative frequency (cf) of the median is 22/2 = 11. From the ogive, the median = 372 kg.

Test your understanding 12

From the histogram, the mode is **366.6 kg** (approximately).

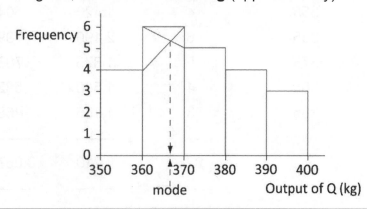

Test your understanding 13

x	f	fx	fx²
2	2	4	8
3	4	12	36
4	3	12	48
5	4	20	100
6	3	18	108
7	3	21	147
8	3	24	192
	22	111	639

$$S = \sqrt{\frac{\sum fx}{\sum f} - \left(\frac{\sum fx}{\sum f}\right)^2} = \sqrt{\frac{639}{22} - \left(\frac{111}{22}\right)^2}$$

$$= \sqrt{(29.0455 - 25.4566)} = \sqrt{3.5889} = 1.89 \text{ (to two d.p.)}$$

Test your understanding 14

Mid-point x	Frequency f	fx	fx²
355	4	1,420	504,100
365	6	2,190	799,350
375	5	1,875	703,125
385	4	1,540	592,900
395	3	1,185	468,075
	22	8,210	3,067,550

$$S = \sqrt{\frac{\sum fx^2}{\sum f} - \left(\frac{\sum fx}{\sum f}\right)^2} = \sqrt{\frac{3,067,550}{22} - \left(\frac{8,210}{22}\right)^2}$$

$$= \sqrt{(139,434.0909 - 139,264.6694}$$

$$= \sqrt{169.4215} = 13.02 \text{ (to two d.p.)}$$

Test your understanding 15

Only **statement C** can be made on the basis of the information given.

Question 1

The cumulative frequency distribution is as follows:

Number absent	Frequency	Cumulative frequency
0	10	10
1	15	25
2	7	32
3	4	36
4	2	38

Question 2

K	10
L	15
M	20
N	25
O	30
P	7
Q	23
R	36
S	40

In an ogive, cumulative frequencies are plotted (vertically) on the upper limits of the corresponding intervals (horizontally). The cumulative frequency of the very bottom limit (of 10 in this case) is always zero.

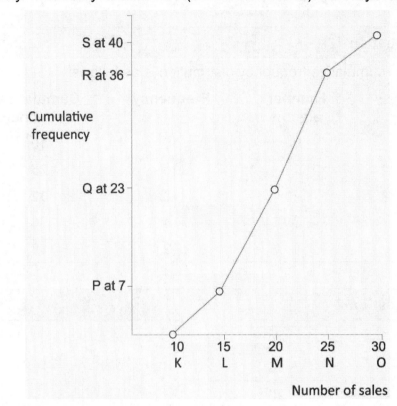

Number of sales

Question 3

Age of 5 years	**Continuous**
Time of 2.5 hours	**Continuous**
Output of 12,000 kg	**Continuous**
Output of 5,000 units	**Discrete**

Question 4

C

In order of magnitude, without x, the values are

7, 8, 13, 14, 28, 33, 42, 51, 69

Including x, there are ten values so the median of 29 is the average of the fifth and sixth. The only possible solution is that x lies between 28 and 33 and has a value such that $(28 + x)/2 = 29$. Hence, $x = 30$.

Question 5

The arithmetic mean is **1.45**

The complete table is:

x	f	fx
0	10	0
1	15	15
2	25	50
3	5	15
Totals	55	80

Arithmetic mean = 80/55 = 1.45

Question 6

C and D are true.

It is the most widely used average. This is false as the most widely used average is the mean.

It is a measure of dispersion. This is false as mode is an averaging measure. Measures of dispersion are range, variance and standard deviation.

It is the middle point of a set of values. This is false as it describes the median.

Question 7

The sales revenue of Product E is **$465,000**

If product A's revenue is $155,000, then the total revenue must be:

$155,000 ÷ 45° × 360° = $1,240,000

The angle of Product E is not given, but can be calculated as: 360° − 45° − 50° − 55° − 75° = 135°.

Therefore the sales revenue of Product E must be: 135° ÷ 360° × $1,240,000 = $465,000

Question 8

Output of Q kg	No. of days (frequency)
350 – under 360	4
360 – under 370	6
370 – under 380	5
380 – under 390	4
390 – under 400	3

Question 9

C and D

This diagram is known as a multiple bar chart.

The number of employees aged 60 or over has reduced from 5 years ago.

The most common age range now is 40 – 44.

Question 10

The correct match is:

Mean	the answer derived by dividing the sum of a set of values by the number of values
Median	the middle of a set of values
Mode	the value which occurs most often in a data set

Risk 2 – Probability

Chapter learning objectives

After completing this chapter, you should be able to

- demonstrate the use of expected values and joint probabilities in decision making

- demonstrate the use of the normal distribution.

1   Session content diagram

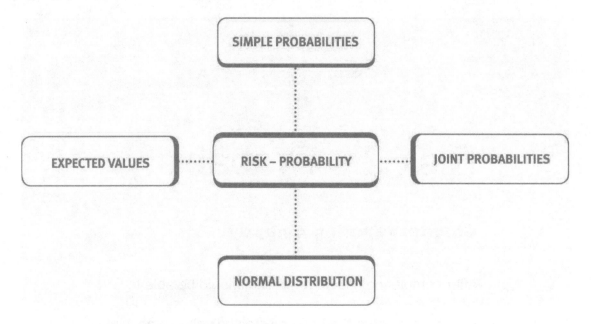

2   Introduction

In the previous chapter we introduced risk and uncertainty and touched on the concept of probability. We will now look at probability in more detail.

We learned that risk is quantifiable; that possible outcomes can be assigned probabilities but that with uncertainty we cannot assign probabilities. Most people have an intuitive, common-sense understanding of probabilities.

For example, consider the following statements:

- "If I flick a coin, then there is a 50:50 chance of getting heads or tails."

- "If I am playing a board game and need to roll a die, then there is a one in six probability of rolling a four."

- "Experience suggests we have a one in ten chance of winning a tender for a new contract."

All of these statements relate to the idea of probability.

3 Definitions of probability

A probability expresses the **likelihood of an event occurring**.

Note the terminology here. The 'event' referred to is simply what we want to calculate the probability for, such as 'winning the tender' or 'rolling a six'.

Basic ideas

- If an event is certain to occur, then it has a probability of one.

- If an event is impossible, then it has a probability of zero.

- For any event, the probability of it occurring must lie between zero and one. If you calculate a probability bigger than one, then you have made a mistake!

- The higher the probability is, then the more likely it is that the event will happen.

- In any given scenario, the probabilities associated with all possible outcomes must add up to one.

For example, if trying to win a particular tender for new work, then there are only two possible outcomes. You either win or you don't. If the probability of winning the tender is 0.4 (40%), then the probability of not winning must be 0.6 (60%) as the two probabilities must add up to one.

Notation

The probability of event 'A' occurring is written as P(A).

This allows us to write down some of the above rules more concisely, for example:

P(NOT A) = 1 – P(A), where P(NOT A) means the probability of event A not occurring.

This is known as the 'complementary rule'.

4 Simple probabilities

In situations where it is possible to compile a complete list of all the equally likely outcomes, we can define the probability of an event, denoted P(event):

$$P(event) = \frac{\text{Total number of outcomes which constitute the event}}{\text{Total number of possible outcomes}}$$

Illustration 1 – Simple probabilities

An ordinary six-sided die is rolled.

What is the probability that it will show a number less than three?

Solution:

Here it is possible to list all the possible equally likely outcomes, namely the whole numbers from one to six inclusive:

1, 2, 3, 4, 5, 6

The outcomes that constitute the 'event' under consideration, that is, 'a number less than three' are:

1, 2

Hence the proportion of outcomes that constitute the event is 2/6 or 1/3, which is therefore the desired probability.

We could write this as P(Getting a number < 3) = 1/3

Note: Most people would have arrived at this answer using intuition.

Test your understanding 1

Four people are asked to select a card at random from a standard pack of playing cards *. The card is replaced before the following selection so each selection is from the full pack. You are told that

(a) A picked a king

(b) B picked a red card

(c) C picked a club

(d) D picked the Ace of Spades

Determine the probability for each selection.

(a) The probability that A picked a king is _____.

(b) The probability that B picked a red card is _____.

(c) The probability that C picked a club is _____.

(d) The probability that D picked the Ace of spades is _____.

* A standard pack of playing cards has 52 cards.

These are split into four 'suits':

- 'hearts'
- 'clubs'
- 'diamonds'
- 'spades'

Each 'suit' has 13 cards – the Ace, 2, 3, 4, 5, 6, 7, 8, 9, 10, Jack, Queen and King.

Hearts and diamonds are red cards whereas clubs and spades are black.

Test your understanding 2

A tennis club organises the draw for its annual men's singles tournament by picking names from a hat. There are 32 men in the draw this year.

In the last two years J has had to play S, his brother in the first round.

What is the probability that J will have to play S in the first round this year?

Types of probabilities

There are different types of probabilities. Probabilities can be:

Exact. These can be applied to the population of outcomes, e.g. the probability of a certain card being drawn from a pack of cards.

Empirical. These can be calculated from samples of observations from the past, e.g. the probability of a certain level of sales occurring in a day.

Subjective. These are based on judgement, e.g. the probability of winning a new order, or finding oil in a new drilling area.

Constructing a discrete probability distribution

We use the word discrete here to describe a variable that can assume only certain values, regardless of the level of precision to which it is measured.

For example, the number of errors made on an invoice is a discrete variable as it can be only 0 or 1 or 2 or . . .and never 2.3, for example.

A discrete probability distribution consists of a list of all the values the variable can have (in the case of exact probabilities) or has had (in the case of empirical probabilities), together with the appropriate corresponding probabilities.

Probabilities can be used in an **exact** sense when applied to the population of outcomes, or in an **empirical**, approximate sense when applied to a sample. **Subjective** probabilities arise from individuals' or a group's judgement.

There are therefore three ways of constructing the probability distribution:

(1) **Using theory to determine exact probabilities**

Suppose we are looking at throwing two dice and adding their scores.

What are the probabilities of the different outcomes?

Firstly we need to assume that both die are fair and that each of the numbers 1 to 6 has an equal chance of being rolled for each dice.

We can then use our approach to simple probabilities described above. For example out of the 36 possible outcomes for the two dice (1 and 1, 1 and 2, 1 and 3,..., 6 and 6) only one outcome (6 and 6) sums to 12.

Thus the probability of getting 12 is 1/36.

(2) **Using past data to determine empirical probabilities**

The key assumption here is that the past is a good indicator of the future.

A simple example will illustrate.

The records of a shop show that, during the previous 50 weeks' trading, the number of sales of a certain item have been

Number of sales/week	Number of weeks
0	4
1	16
2	22
3	6
4 or more	2

Construct the corresponding probability distribution.

Probabilities can be based on the empirical data given.

$$P(0 \text{ sales in a week}) = \frac{4}{50} = 0.08$$

Proceeding in this way, we can build up the distribution:

Number of sales/week	P(number of sales/week)
0	0.08
1	0.32
2	0.44
3	0.12
4 or more	0.04
	1.00

Note that the total probability sums to 1.

(3) **Estimation of subjective probabilities**

Based on a mixture of past experience, judgement and pure guess work, a sales manager may believe that the company has a 1 in 3 chance of winning a forthcoming sales pitch to a potential new client. Even though the basis of this probability may be suspect, it still allows the company to plan accordingly.

Estimating empirical probabilities

One reason organisations carry out market research is to obtain data to allow empirical probabilities to be estimated. For example, a supermarket may be planning to release a new food product. Before attempting a national launch, they may run some focus groups. Suppose in the focus groups 10% of customers said they would buy the new product. The supermarket could then estimate that 10% of its national customers would buy it if launched in all stores, **assuming the focus group was representative**.

Market research may involve either:

- **Primary research**, which generates new, primary data, such as through the trial above. This also known as field research.

- **Secondary research**, where existing research findings are reviewed. This is also known as desk research and the data referred to as secondary data.

Test your understanding 3

A quality controller wishes to estimate the probability of a component failing within 1 year of installation.

How might she proceed?

Using tables with simple probabilities

In some assessment questions you have to do some analytical work on the information given before you can start to calculate probabilities. This is often easier if you use a table to set out the different possibilities.

Illustration 2 – Using tables

A sample of 100 companies has been analysed by size and whether they pay invoices promptly.

The sample has been broken down as follows:

- Large and small companies

- Fast and slow payers.

Suppose that

- sixty of the companies analysed are classified as large, of which forty are slow payers.

- in total, thirty of all the companies are fast payers.

The probability that a company chosen at random is a fast paying, small company is?

A   0.10

B   0.20

C   0.30

D   0.40

Solution:

If we try to set up a table covering all possibilities, then we know the following:

	Fast	Slow	Total
Large	?	40	60
Small	?	?	?
	30	?	100

We now need to deduce the missing figures. For example:

- Looking at the final column, there must be 40 small companies as we have 100 in total and 60 are large

- Looking at the top row, out of the 60 large companies, 20 must be fast payers.

Once we have filled in the easier figures, we can deduce others until we end up with:

	Fast	Slow	Total
Large	20	40	60
Small	10	30	40
	30	70	100

Now we can answer the question: P(fast and small) = 10/100 = 0.1

Answer: A

Test your understanding 4

In a group of 100 CIMA students, thirty are male, fifty-five are studying Certificate level, and six of the male students are not studying Certificate level. A student chosen at random is female.

What is the probability that she is NOT studying Certificate level?

A   0.80

B   0.56

C   0.44

D   0.20

5   Expected values

Many business situations require a choice between numerous courses of action. Given that these choices relate to future outcomes, the results will be uncertain. Clearly, the decision-maker's experience and judgement are important in making 'good' choices in such instances. It is important to make these choices as good as possible as they can affect the future of the organisation, so decision makers will use various techniques to help in making these choices. No technique can totally replace human judgement in business decisions but some can help make the choices clearer and therefore make it easier to decide between them.

One technique which can help judge the financial outcomes of various options is **expected value** (EV). An expected value is a long run average. It is the weighted average of a probability distribution.

While techniques such as EV can help assess the financial aspect of a decision, there are many other non-financial considerations which must be taken account of in any business decision.

Expected value is calculated as follows:

$$EV = \sum PX$$

Where X is the outcome and P is the probability of the outcome.

Illustration 3 – Expected values

A company has recorded the following daily sales over the last 200 days:

Daily sales (units)	Number of days
100	40
200	60
300	80
400	20

What will be the expected sales level in the future?

Solution:

Firstly we will assume that the past is a good indicator of the future.

Next we can convert the above results into a probability distribution (i.e. show the range of possible outcomes and their associated probabilities):

Daily sales (units) (X)		Probability (P)
100	40/200 =	0.2
200	60/200 =	0.3
300	80/200 =	0.4
400	20/200 =	0.1
		___
		1.0
		___

Note: Always check that the probabilities add up to one.

The expected value (EV) of the future sales is then given by:

$EV = \sum PX$

$EV = (0.2 \times 100) + (0.3 \times 200) + (0.4 \times 300) + (0.1 \times 400) = 240$ units

So what does this mean?

- On average we will sell 240 units a day.

- On a particular day we will sell 100 or 200 or 300 or 400, so the average cannot actually happen.

- While this worries some, most managers are happy to make decisions based on expected values.

Test your understanding 5

An entity must make a decision between three options, A, B and C. The possible profits and losses are:

- Option A: a profit of $2,000 with probability 0.5 or otherwise a loss of $500

- Option B: a profit of $800 with probability 0.3 or otherwise a profit of $500

- Option C: a profit of $1,000 with probability 0.7, or $500 with probability 0.1 or otherwise a loss of $400

Using EV, which option should be chosen?

Test your understanding 6

A decision-maker is faced with the following options, which can result in the profits shown:

	High sales P = 0.5	**Medium sales** P = 0.4	**Low sales** P = 0.1
Option 1	$50,000	$10,000	($60,000)
Option 2	$40,000	$10,000	($20,000)
Option 3	$30,000	$15,000	$0

Required:

(a)   If the intention is to maximise expected profit, which option should be taken?

(b)   Comment on the riskiness of the choice facing the decision-maker.

Payoff tables

Payoff tables (also known as expected value tables) can be useful in more complex scenarios.

Illustration 4 – Payoff tables

A storeholder has to decide how many units of the perishable commodity X to buy each day. Past demand has followed the distribution:

Demand (units)	Probability
0	0.1
1	0.2
2	0.4
3	0.3

Each unit is bought for $8 and sold for $20, giving a profit of $12. At the end of each day, any unsold units must be disposed of with no financial return.

The decision here involves risk. If too many units are purchased, the unsold units would be disposed of with no financial return resulting in a loss. If too few units are purchased, potential sales will be lost.

Using EV, how many units should be bought daily?

Solution:

If we assume that the past demand pattern will continue in the future, we see that, logically, the store-holder has only three initial choices: buy one, two or three units per day. There are also only four possible outcomes each day, a demand of zero, one, two or three units. We can therefore construct a payoff table showing the financial effects of the twelve possible combinations (three choices by four outcomes).

		Order		
Demand	Prob	1	2	3
0	0.1	$(8)	$(16)	$(24)
1	0.2	$12	$4	$(4)
2	0.4	$12	$24	$16
3	0.3	$12	$24	$36
	EV =	$10	$16	$14

The monetary values in each case show the daily profit/(loss). We have given the calculations here for the outcomes of ordering 2 units. All the other entries are calculated in the same way.

- order 2, demand 0: cost = $16, revenue = $0; so loss = $16

- order 2, demand 1: cost = $16, revenue = $20; so profit = $4

- order 2, demand 2: cost = $16, revenue = $40; so profit = $24

- order 2, demand 3: cost = $16, revenue = $40; so profit = $24 (in this case, the demand for the third unit would be unsatisfied).

Using the probabilities for the various levels of demand, we can now calculate the expected daily profit for each order number:

EV (order 1) = (0.1 × (8)) + (0.2 × 12) + (0.4 × 12) + (0.3 × 12) = **$10**

EV (order 2) = (0.1 × (16)) + (0.2 × 4) + (0.4 × 24) + (0.3 × 24) = **$16**

EV (order 3) = (0.1 × (24)) + (0.2 × (4)) + (0.4 × 16) + (0.3 × 36) = **$14**

Thus, in order to maximise daily profit, the storeholder should **order two units per day**.

It should be noted that the feature that makes the construction of the table possible is that the outcomes (demand) are independent of the decision taken (number of units ordered).

Test your understanding 7

A shopkeeper buys an item at $10 and sells it at $50 but if it is not sold by the end of the day it will be thrown away. The probability of each level of demand is shown below.

Demand (units)	Probability
0	0.3
1	0.4
2	0.3

Use EV to advise the shopkeeper on how many units he should order per day.

6 Probability trees

A way of showing the probability of all of the different options is by using a probability tree (or decision tree). This uses the expected value technique but shows the information in a more graphical way. All possible outcomes are shown along with their associated probabilities. Expected values can then be calculated.

Probability trees should be used where a problem involves a series of decisions being made and several outcomes arise during the decision-making process. Probability trees force the decision maker to consider the logical sequence of events. A complex problem can be broken down into smaller, easier to handle sections.

The trees are easy to draw:

- they use lines called branches

- squares depict decision points

- circles depict chance outcome points.

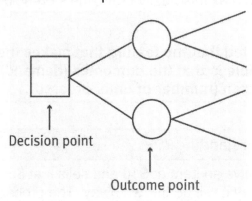

- the probabilities of the outcomes are shown on the branches. (remember, probabilities should add up to 1)

- the financial outcomes are shown at the end of the branches, and the expected values are calculated by working back, right to left, along the branches.

Three step method

Step 1: Draw the tree from left to right, showing appropriate decisions, events/outcomes and probabilities.

Step 2: Evaluate the tree from right to left carrying out these two actions:

(a) Calculate an EV at each outcome point.

(b) Choose the best option at each decision point.

Step 3: Recommend a course of action to management.

Illustration 5 – Probability trees

A university is looking at one of its post-graduate programmes.

The number of students starting the programme is dependent on economic conditions:

- If conditions are poor it is expected that the programme will attract 40 students without advertising. There is a 60% chance that economic conditions will be poor.

- If economic conditions are good it is expected that the programme will attract only 20 students without advertising. There is a 40% chance that economic conditions will be good.

- If 20 students are attracted, a profit of $15,000 is estimated while if 40 students are attracted a profit of $115,000 is estimated.

This can be shown in the following probability tree:

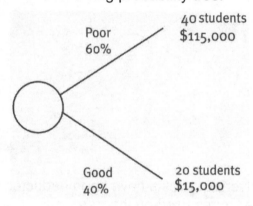

From the probability tree, the expected values can be calculated by working right to left along each branch.

Where conditions are expected to be poor, expected value is (0.6 × $115,000) = $69,000

Where conditions are expected to be good, expected value is (0.4 × $15,000) = $6,000

The university is now considering advertising the programme and have estimated the following.

If the programme is advertised and economic conditions are poor, there is a 65% chance that the advertising will stimulate further demand and student numbers will increase to 50. If economic conditions are good there is a 25% chance the advertising will stimulate further demand and numbers will increase to 25 students.

If 25 students are attracted, a profit of $40,000 is estimated while if 50 students are attracted a profit of $165,000 is estimated. These figures do not include the advertising cost which would be $15,000.

We can now draw a probability tree to show the whole situation and to assess whether it is worth undertaking the advertising or not:

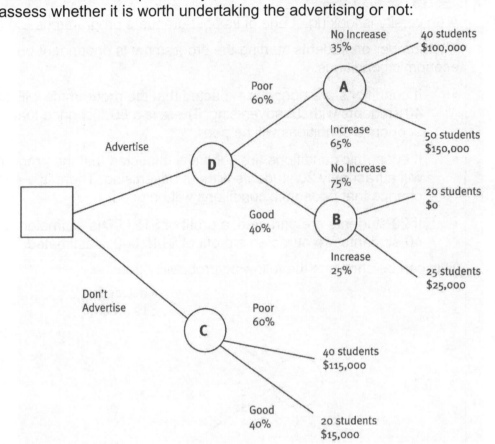

Note: The advertising costs have been deducted where relevant in arriving at the figures used on the tree.

For example, the gain for the top right outcome for 40 students = $115,000 – $15,000 = $100,000

We can now evaluate the tree from right to left carrying out these two actions:

Calculate an Expected Value at each outcome point. Working from top to bottom, we can calculate the EVs as follows:

EV (Outcome Point A)

= (35% × $100,000) + (65% × $150,000) = **$132,500**

EV (Outcome Point B)

= (75% × $0) + (25% × $25,000) = **$6,250**

EV (Outcome Point C)

= (60% × $115,000) + (40% × $15,000) = **$75,000**

EV (Outcome Point D)

= (60% × $132,500) + (40% × $6,250) = **$82,000**

Recommend a course of action:

Choose the best option at each decision point. Here we only have one decision point (advertise or do not advertise). At the decision point in our tree, we should **choose the option to advertise** as the expected value at outcome D (advertise) is $82,000 while the expected value at outcome C (do not advertise) is only $75,000.

Test your understanding 8

A company produces one product, X. The current annual profit of X is budgeted at $500,000.

The company is considering an investment in a new type of technology, which they estimate has a 40% change of enhancing the profit to $650,000. However the technology is untested and there is a 60% chance that it could reduce the profit to $450,000. The new technology would cost $20,000.

Use a probability tree to advise management whether they should invest in the new technology.

7 Joint probabilities

So far only a very small number of alternatives have been considered in the examples. In practice a greater number of alternative courses of action may exist, uncertainty may be associated with more than one variable and the values of variables may be interdependent, giving rise to many different outcomes.

Where we are considering the joint probability of two independent variables, we multiply their probabilities together.

For example in a factory it was found that there was a 2% chance of a fault in the product and a 4% chance of a fault in the packaging of the product. These faults are independent of each other.

The chance that a final, packaged product there will be a fault in both the product and the packaging would be 0.02 × 0.04 = 0.0008, or 0.08%.

Illustration 6 – Joint probabilities

Suppose a company is considering a new project and has estimated the following:

In the first year there is a 60% probability that sales will be 10,000 units and a 40% probability that sales will be 6,000 units.

If sales are high in the first year, then in the second year there is a 70% chance of sales of 12,000 units and a 30% chance of sales of 8,000 units.

If sales are low in the first year, then in the second year there is a 50% chance of sales of 7,000 units and a 50% chance of sales of 5,000 units.

Construct the probability distribution for the sales in each year.

Solution:

Year 1

Sales	Probability
10,000	0.6
6,000	0.4
	___
	1.0
	___

Year 2

Sales	Working	Probability
12,000	0.6 × 0.7	0.42
8,000	0.6 × 0.3	0.18
7,000	0.4 × 0.5	0.20
5,000	0.4 × 0.5	0.20
		___
		1.00
		___

Working:

P(12,000 in year 2) = P(10,000 in year 1) × P(12,000 in year 2) = 0.6 × 0.7 = 0.42

Further joint probabilities example

A company has estimated that, depending on market conditions, contribution from sales will be $100,000, $75,000 or $60,000. They have estimated the following probabilities:

Contribution from sales	Probability
$100,000	30%
$75,000	60%
$60,000	10%

In addition they have estimated their fixed costs, including rent. There is uncertainty surrounding the rent figure as they are currently renegotiating their rent for the next few years. The fixed cost figure could therefore be $80,000 or $50,000. There is a 30% chance that it will be the higher figure.

In this case, we have two independent variables. To work out the joint probabilities, we will have to multiply the probabilities together.

It can be useful in a problem like this to show all the possible outcomes in a table.

Contribution	Fixed costs	Profit (loss)	Joint probability	Expected value
$000	$000	$000		$000
100	80	20	0.3 × 0.3 = 0.09	1.8
100	50	50	0.3 × 0.7 = 0.21	10.5
75	80	(5)	0.6 × 0.3 = 0.18	(0.9)
75	50	25	0.6 × 0.7 = 0.42	10.5
60	80	(20)	0.1 × 0.3 = 0.03	(0.6)
60	50	10	0.1 × 0.7 = 0.07	0.7
			———	———
			1.00	22.0
			———	———

Always check that the total of the probabilities sums to 1.

As the number of variables grows, these tables can become large. With more complex problems, it can be useful to show the options on a probability tree.

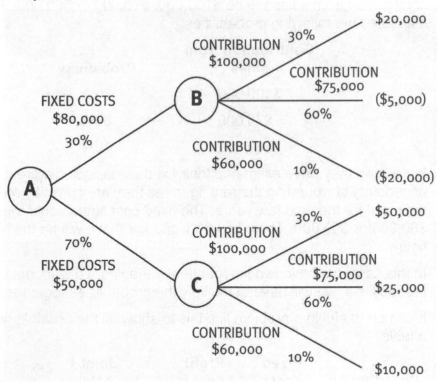

Working back through the branches from right to left, we can work out the expected value at B:

(0.3 × 20,000) + (0.6 × (5,000)) + (0.1 × (20,000)) = 1,000

The expected value at C:

(0.3 × 50,000) + (0.6 × 25,000) + (0.1 × 10,000) = 31,000

Therefore the expected value at A:

(0.3 ×1,000) + (0.7 × 31,000) = **$22,000**

 ## Limitations of expected values

We are not advocating that the expected value approach is ideal. It is merely an aid to decision-making. At the end of the day, decisions are made by managers using their knowledge, experience and judgement.

Techniques such as expected value can provide information to aid that decision but can never replace the human decision-maker.

A limitation of expected value, which is shared with most other attempts to model reality, is that the outcomes and probabilities need to be estimated. The subsequent analysis can never be more reliable than the estimations upon which it is based.

There is also often a considerable degree of simplification with very limited discrete probability distributions being used when more complex ones or perhaps continuous distributions might be more appropriate.

When the probabilities are empirical, arising from past experience, then they have some degree of reliability unless demand patterns change dramatically. In other cases only subjective estimates of probabilities may be available, and their reliability may be open to question. There is therefore a doubt over this approach when subjective probabilities are used.

If the scenario is a repeated decision, made every day, then the expected values can have a commercial meaning: they are long-term averages. In many cases, however, individuals or companies use this technique in one-off decisions. The result in these cases is of little or no use as the activity will only be carried out once and not repeated many times.

Finally, expected values take no account of the decision-makers' attitude to risk. Avoiding significant downside exposure may be more important than possible gains, although expected values consider each equally. Particularly with one-off decisions, it can only give a guide to decision-makers.

Even with objective testing it is still important to be aware of the limitations of methods. The failure to take account of risk is a key criticism of this approach.

8 Normal distribution

We will now combine what we have learned about probability with what we learned in the previous chapter about mean and standard deviation and look at normal distributions. Distribution refers to the way data is spread out.

Remember in the previous chapter we looked at calculating mean and standard deviation. In the following section we will be using the notation μ for mean and σ for standard deviation.

Consider the following histograms:

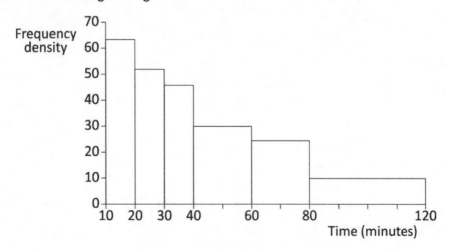

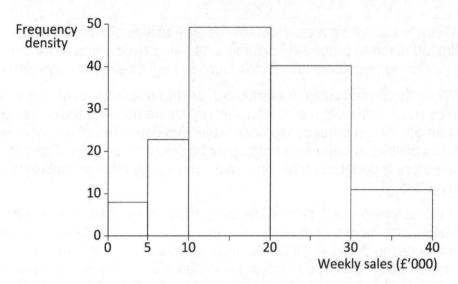

We can see that the 'distribution' or spreading out of the data is different in each of these examples.

Now consider the following histogram:

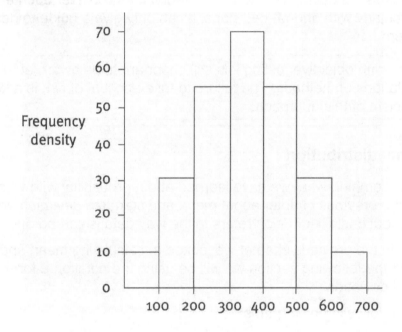

In this case the data is symmetrical and peaks in the centre. This is called a **normal distribution**. We can draw a line around this distribution to show the shape more clearly. This is called a bell curve.

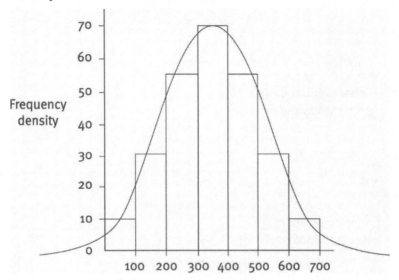

We will use this bell curve throughout this section to show a normal distribution.

Normal distributions can be found when we measure things such as:

- Exam results
- Staff performance gradings
- The heights of a group of people etc.

A normal distribution has the following characteristics:

The mean is shown in the centre of the diagram and the curve is symmetrical about the mean. This means that 50% of the values will be below the mean and 50% of the values will be above the mean.

Note: The mean, median and mode will all be the same for a normal distribution.

How far the values spread out from the mean is the standard deviation. This can be seen in the following diagram:

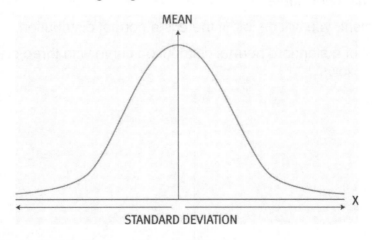

The total area under the curve is equal to 1.

Consider the following three diagrams.

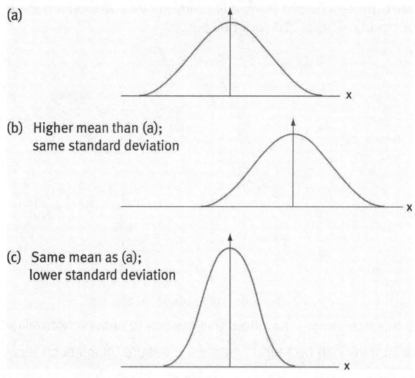

(a)

(b) Higher mean than (a); same standard deviation

(c) Same mean as (a); lower standard deviation

You can see that in diagram (b), the mean is further to the right, so (b) has a higher mean than (a). If you look at the spread of (a) and (b), you can see that they are the same, so (a) and (b) have the same standard deviation.

Diagram (c) has the same mean as (a), but you can see that it is taller and narrower than (a). The standard deviation in (c) is lower than in (a).

Now that we have looked at what normal distribution is, we now have to consider what use this will be to us in our decision making.

Note: To be able to use the normal distribution the distribution must be:

* Continuous

* Symmetrical

* Shaped as a bell curve.

In an assessment, you will be told if there is a normal distribution.

If we can think of a standard normal distribution curve with three standard deviations as follows:

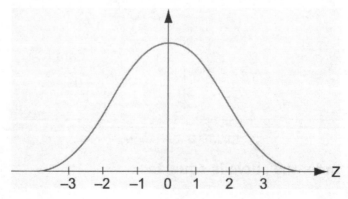

In general 68% of values are within one standard deviation (between –1 and 1), 95% of values are within two standard deviations (between –2 and 2) and 99.7% of values are within three standard deviations (between –3 and 3). We will look at where these figures come from in the next section.

From this we can see that if we look at a set of data which fits a normal distribution the majority of values will occur closer to the mean, with fewer and fewer occurring the further from the mean we move.

So how can we use this in decision making?

If we know the mean and the standard deviation for a distribution we can work out the percentage chance (probability) of a certain value occurring. For example a light bulb manufacturer may want to know how many bulbs will fail after a certain amount of time, or a chocolate bar manufacturer may want to know how many chocolate bars will weigh less than the minimum weight shown on the packaging.

As the curve is symmetrical, the values on the positive side will be exactly the same as the values on the negative side. In this way we can calculate either and assume it will be the same for the other side, for example if the chocolate bar manufacturer found that 0.05% of bars were lower that the acceptable weight, then 0.05% bars will also be higher than the acceptable weight.

The percentage figures can be obtained using normal distribution tables, which are given in your exam. **Note:** The tables only show the positive values.

To use the tables we must first convert our normal distribution to a **standard normal distribution**.

A standard normal distribution has:

> a mean of 0

> a standard deviation of 1.

This special distribution is denoted by z and can be calculated as:

$$z = \frac{x - \mu}{\sigma}$$

Where:

z is the z score

x is the value being considered

μ is the mean

σ is the standard deviation

This calculation is used to convert any value to a standard normal distribution.

Note: When we look at normal distribution, we will be using the notation μ for mean and σ for standard deviation.

Looking up the normal distribution tables

Once we have calculated our 'z score' we can look this up on the normal distribution table to find the area under the curve, which equates to the percentage chance (probability) of that value occurring.

So if we have calculated a z score of 1.00. From the table the value is 0.3413.

This means that $(0.3413 \div 1.0)$ or 34.13% is the area shown from $0 - 1$ on the diagram.

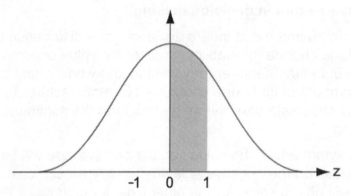

From this we can deduce that 34.13% would be the area shown from 0 to -1 on the diagram. So we can say that 68.26% values will fall within one standard deviation (-1 to 1).

Look up a few more z values to get used to using the table:

Example

What is the table value for $z = 2.63$?

With this value you look down the first column to find 2.6, then along the top row till you find 0.03. Where they intersect gives the value for 2.63. The value is 0.4957, or 49.57%.

To use the normal distribution tables, there are a few rules which will be helpful.

We shall use the abbreviation TE to mean 'table entry' so that, for example, TE(1) gives the area under the graph from the middle ($z = 0$) to the value $z = 1$ as shown in the above graph. (**Please note that TE is not an abbreviation in standard usage**.)

If a and b are positive values then you find probabilities from the table as follows:

$P(a < z < b) = \text{TE}\,(b) - \text{TE}\,(a)$

$P(z < b) = 0.5 + \text{TE}\,(b)$

$P(z > b) = 0.5 - \text{TE}\,(b)$

$P(z < -b) = P(z > b) = 0.5 - \text{TE}\,(b)$

$P(z > -b) = P(z < b) = 0.5 + \text{TE}\,(b)$

$P(-a < z < 0) = P(z < a) = 0.5 + \text{TE}\,(a)$

$P(-a < z < b) = \text{TE}\,(a) + \text{TE}\,(b)$

$P(-a < z < -b) = P(b < z < a) = \text{TE}\,(a) - \text{TE}\,(b)$

Illustration 7 – Looking up normal distribution tables

Consider the areas shown under the following graphs and using the above rules, look up the normal distribution tables to find the probability of the shaded areas.

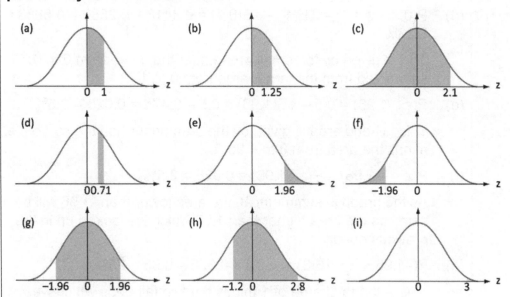

These areas are shown using the following:

(a)   P(0 < z < 1); the probability that our z score falls between 0 and 1

(b)   P(0< z < 1.25); the probability that our z score falls between 0 and 1.25

(c)   P(z < 2.1); the probability that our z score is negative or is under 2.1

(d)   P(0.7 < z < 1); the probability that our z score falls between 0.7 and 1

(e)   P(z > 1.96); the probability that our z score is higher than 1.96

(f)   P(z < –1.96); the probability that our z score is lower than –1.96

(g)   P(–1.96 < z < 1.96); the probability that our z score falls between – 1.96 and 1.96

(h)   P(–1.2 < z < 2.8); the probability that our z score falls between –1.2 and 2.8

(i)   P(z > 3); the probability that our z score is higher than 3

Solution:

(a)   P(0 < z < 1) = TE(1.00) = 0.3413 = **34.13%**.

   In the table this is the entry in row 1.0 and column 0.00.

(b)   P(0 < z < 1.25) = TE(1.25) = 0.3944 = **39.44%**.

   In the table this is the entry in row 1.2 and column 0.05.

(c) P(z < 2.1) = 0.5 + TE(2.1) = 0.5 + 0.4821 = 0.9821 = **98.21%**.

This probability includes all the negative values of z, which have a probability of 0.5, as well as those between 0 and 2.1 which can be found on the table in row 2.1.

(d) P(0.7 < z < 1) = TE(1) – TE(0.7) = 0.3413 – 0.2580 = 0.0833 = **8.33%**.

This is given by the small area under the curve from 0 to 0.7 subtracted from the larger area from 0 to 1.

(e) P(z > 1.96) = 0.5 – TE(1.96) = 0.5 – 0.475 = 0.025 = **2.5%**.

This tail-end area is given by the area under half the curve (i.e. 0.5) minus the area from 0 to 1.96.

(f) P(z < – 1.96) = P(z >1.96) = 0.025 = **2.5%**.

As the graph is symmetrical, the area lower than -1.96 will be the same as the area higher than 1.96 which we looked up in the previous question.

(g) P(–1.96 < z < 1.96) = 1 – 2 × 0.025 = 0.95 = **95%**.

This is the total area of 1 minus the two tail-ends which we calculated in the previous two questions. Look at the area on graph (g). 95% of entries will fall within the shaded area.

(h) P(–1.2 < z < 2.8) = TE(1.2) + TE(2.8) = 0.3849 + 0.4974 = 0.8823 = **88.23%**.

We have split this area into two. That from 0 to 2.8 is simply the table entry and that from –1.2 to 0 equals the area from 0 to +1.2 by symmetry, so it can be looked up in the table.

(i) P(z > 3) = 0.5 – 0.49865 = 0.00135 = **0.135%**.

The method here is the standard one for tail-end areas but we wanted to make two points. The first is that virtually all normal frequencies lie between three standard deviations either side of the mean. The second is that, for symmetrical data, the standard deviation will be approximately one-sixth of the range.

Test your understanding 9

Evaluate the following probabilities from the standard normal distribution (mean = 0; standard deviation = 1):

A   P(0 < z < 2.03)

B   P(–1.27 < z < 0)

C   P(z > 0.55)

D   P(z < –1.55)

E   P(z > –1.23)

F   P(z < 0.88)

G   P(–0.91 < z < 1.08)

H   P(0.23 < z < 0.34).

The normal distribution can be used to answer many types of questions. For example a food producer could be concerned about ensuring that the weight of each product unit is within a small tolerance of the stated weight on the packaging.

Illustration 8 – Normal distribution example

RST is a food producer, specialising in dried fruit and nuts. The dried fruit and nuts are prepared within the factory and packed into small bags which are sold as snacks in supermarkets.

The weights of the snack bags are normally distributed with a mean weight of 70g and a standard deviation of 5g.

RST can use normal distribution to calculate the probabilities that a bag selected at random would be of an acceptable weight.

Required:

(a)   **Calculate the probability that a bag selected at random weighs less than 60g**

First calculate the z score.

$$z = \frac{x - \mu}{\sigma}$$

Z = (60 – 70) ÷ 5 = –2

We want P(Z < –2).

We know that the area less than –2 is equal to the area above 2. Look up the table figure for 2. It is 0.4772.

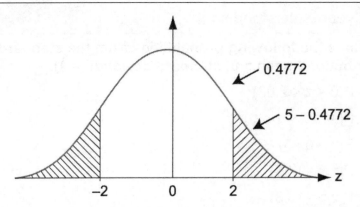

Therefore the probability that a bag selected at random weighs less than 60g = (0.5 – 0.4772) = 0.0228 or **2.3%**.

(b) **Calculate the probability that a bag selected at random weighs more than 85g**

Z = (85 – 70) ÷ 5 = 3

We want P(Z > 3). Look up the table figure for 3. It is 0.49865.

Therefore the probability that a bag selected at random weighs more than 85g = (0.5 – 0.49865) = 0.00135 or **0.13%**.

(c) **Calculate the maximum weight that has no more than a 1% chance of being exceeded**

In this question we have been given the probability of 1 %. We want to work out what weight that relates to.

Working back, to get a probability of 1 %, the table entry must have been:

0.5 – 0.01 = 0.49

Look up the tables for the entry of 0.49. This equates to a Z value of between 2.32 and 2.33. Because we want a probability of no more than 1 % we shall use the 2.33.

Converting this back to pack weights gives a figure of 70 + (5 × 2.33) = **81.65g**.

Test your understanding 10

A machine produces components with diameter of mean 5 cm and standard deviation 0.1 cm. The production of this component follows a normal distribution.

What proportion of the components produced will have diameters of the following dimensions?

A   between 5 and 5.2 cm

B   between 4.9 and 5 cm

C   over 5.15 cm

D   between 4.8 and 5.1 cm

E   between 5.1 and 5.2 cm

9   Chapter summary

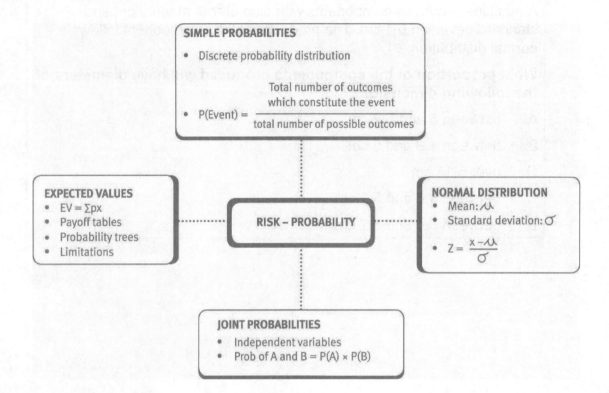

SIMPLE PROBABILITIES
- Discrete probability distribution

- $P(Event) = \dfrac{\text{Total number of outcomes which constitute the event}}{\text{total number of possible outcomes}}$

EXPECTED VALUES
- $EV = \Sigma px$
- Payoff tables
- Probability trees
- Limitations

RISK – PROBABILITY

NORMAL DISTRIBUTION
- Mean: μ
- Standard deviation: σ

- $Z = \dfrac{x - \mu}{\sigma}$

JOINT PROBABILITIES
- Independent variables
- Prob of A and B = $P(A) \times P(B)$

10 End of chapter questions

Question 1

A company has estimated that, depending on market conditions, contribution from sales will be $50,000 or $20,000. They have estimated the following probabilities:

Contribution from sales	Probability
$50,000	60%
$20,000	40%

In addition they have estimated that their fixed costs could be $10,000 or $8,000. They have estimated the following probabilities:

Fixed costs	Probability
$10,000	70%
$8,000	30%

Complete the table below showing the joint probabilities.

Contribution	Fixed costs	Joint probability
$000	$000	
50	10	
20	10	
50	8	
20	8	

Question 2

A project may result in profits of $20,000 or $12,000, or in a loss of $5,000, with probabilities 0.3, 0.5 and 0.2, respectively.

What is the expected profit of the project?

A $11,000

B $27,000

C $9,000

D $12,000

Question 3

FGH stocks a weekly magazine which advertises local second-hand goods. The owner can buy the magazines for 15c each and sell them at the retail price of 25c. At the end of each week unsold magazines are obsolete and have no value.

The owner has estimated a probability distribution for weekly demand as follows:

Weekly demand in units	Probability
10	0.20
15	0.55
20	0.25
___	___
	1.00
	___

Required:

(a) Calculate the expected value of demand.

(b) The owner should order 10 / 15 / 20 units per week. Delete as appropriate.

Question 4

A company has three production departments. From a sample of 361 items, It has compiled the following data about the production of faulty or acceptable items.

	P	**Q**	**R**	**Total**
		Department		
Faulty	6	13	3	22
Acceptable	94	195	50	339
	___	___	___	___
Total	100	208	53	361
	___	___	___	___

Use the data to answer the following questions. Give all answers to four decimal places.

A   What is the probability that an item is faulty?

B   What is the probability that an item is from either department P or Q?

C   What is the probability that two items are both faulty?

Question 5

An entity produces 62% of items in department A and the rest in department B. In A, 4% of production is faulty whereas in B the proportion is 5%.

Complete the following table, giving answers correct to two decimal places.

	Department A	Department B	Total
Faulty			
Acceptable			
Total			100

Question 6

Match the definitions and the examples to the type of probability being described.

Type	Definition	Example
Exact	These are based on judgement	The probability of winning a new contract
Empirical	These can be calculated from samples of observations from the past	Selecting a card from a pack of cards
Subjective	These can be applied to the population of outcomes	The likely level of sales in a week

Question 7

A company has a normally distributed sales pattern for one of its products, with a mean of $110. The probability of a sale worth more than $120 is 0.0119.

Using normal tables, the standard deviation, to two decimal places, associated with sales is:

A $4.41

B $4.42

C $4.43

D $4.44

Question 8

The weights of a certain mass-produced item are known, over a long period of time, to be normally distributed with a mean of 8 kg and a standard deviation of 0.02 kg.

Required:

(a) If items whose weight lie outside the range 7.985 – 8.035 kg are deemed to be faulty, what percentage of products will be faulty?

(b) If it is required to reduce the percentage of items that are too heavy (with weight over 8.035 kg) to 2%, to what value must the mean weight be decreased, leaving all other factors unchanged?

(c) If it is required to reduce the percentage of items that are too light (with weight below 7.985 kg) to 2%, to what value must the standard deviation be decreased, leaving other factors unchanged?

Question 9

A pharmaceutical company has developed a new headache treatment that is being field-tested on 1,000 volunteers. In a test, some volunteers have received the treatment and some a placebo (a harmless neutral substance). The results of the test are as follows:

	Treatment received	Placebo received
Some improvement	600	125
No improvement	150	125

Calculate the following:

(a) The probability that a volunteer has shown some improvement.

(b) On the basis of this survey, does the treatment appear to be effective?

Question 10

A company provides catering for outdoor venues. It has operated at a weekend music festival for the last three years, with mixed success. Its profit at the festival is linked to the weather. If the weather is dry, it expects to make profits of $200,000, while if the weather is wet its profits would only be $10,000.

This year it is considering building a tented shelter at the festival. The shelter would cost $120,000 to build but it has estimated that if the weather is wet, profits would rise to $300,000. It does not anticipate any change in profit if the weather is dry.

Recent forecasts have suggested that during the weekend of the festival, there is 45% of it being dry.

Using a probability tree, advise the company as to whether or not they should build the shelter.

Test your understanding and end of chapter answers

Test your understanding 1

(a)   The probability that A picked a king is **1/13**.

(b)   The probability that B picked a red card is **1/2**.

(c)   The probability that C picked a club is **1/4.**

(d)   The probability that D picked the Ace of spades is **1/52**.

Workings:

There are 4 kings in a pack of 52 cards, so the probability = 4/52 = **1/13**

There are 26 red cards (hearts + diamonds) in a pack of 52 cards, so the probability = 26/52 = **1/2**

There are 13 clubs in a pack of 52 cards, so the probability = 13/52 = **1/4**

There is only one Ace of Spades in a pack of 52 cards, so the probability = **1/52**

Test your understanding 2

The probability that J will have to play S in the first round this year is 1/31.

Assuming that the draw is fair, then J has an equal likelihood of playing any of the 31 other players in the draw in the first round.

Thus P(playing S) = 1/31

Note: The results of previous draws is irrelevant, unless it indicates that in some way the method of picking names is biased or unfair.

Test your understanding 3

To find this probability from an exact approach would necessitate obtaining a list of the lifetimes of all the components, and counting those of less than 1 year. It is clearly impossible to keep such a detailed record of every component, after sale.

An alternative, feasible approach is to take a sample of components, rather than the whole population, and test them under working conditions, to see what proportion fail within one year. Probabilities produced in this way are known as empirical and are essentially approximations to the true, but unobtainable, exact probabilities. In this case, the quality controller may choose to sample 1,000 components. If she then finds that 16 fail within 1 year:

P (Component failing within 1 year) = $\dfrac{16}{1,000}$ or 0.016

For this approximation to be valid, it is essential that the sample is representative. Further, for a more accurate approximation, a larger sample could be taken, provided that the time and money are available.

Test your understanding 4

B

The classifications we need in the table are

- certificate/not certificate

- male/female.

Table (note figures in bold are those given in the question)

	Male	Female	Total
Certificate level	24	31	**55**
Not Certificate level	**6**	39	45
Total	**30**	70	**100**

P(female but not studying Certificate) = 39/70 = 0.56

Test your understanding 5

Option A should be chosen.

The expected value of each option is:

EV(A) = **$750**

EV(B) = **$590**

EV(C) = **$670**

Workings:

Option A	Profit/(loss) (X) $	Probability (P)	PX
	2,000	0.5	1,000
	(500)	0.5	(250)
		1.0	750

Option B	Profit/(loss) (X) $	Probability (P)	PX
	800	0.3	240
	500	0.7	350
		1.0	590

Option C	Profit/(loss) (X) $	Probability (P)	PX
	1,000	0.7	700
	500	0.1	50
	(400)	0.2	(80)
		1.0	670

However, when we look at the workings above, we can see that while A gives the highest expected value, there is a 50% chance that there will be a loss of $500. It may be the case that the organisation could not afford this loss, or would maybe not be prepared to take that risk. Option B gives the lowest expected value but it is a 'safer' option in that both potential outcomes result in a profit. So while expected value can aid decision making, other factors must be considered, such as the decision maker's attitude to risk.

Test your understanding 6

(a) **Option 1 should be taken.**

Working:

Option 1		Probability	Profit $000	EV
	High	0.5	50	25
	Medium	0.4	10	4
	Low	0.1	(60)	(6)
		1.0		**23**

Option 2		Probability	Profit $000	EV
	High	0.5	40	20
	Medium	0.4	10	4
	Low	0.1	(20)	(2)
		1.0		**22**

Option 3		Probability	Profit $000	EV
	High	0.5	30	15
	Medium	0.4	15	6
	Low	0.1	0	0
		1.0		**21**

(b) Notice that option 1 is very risky, with a 10% chance of making a loss greater than the maximum possible profit. Many decision-makers would choose option 2 as having a very similar expected profit with considerably lower risk.

Test your understanding 7

The shopkeeper should order two units per day.

Payoff table (in $ per day)

		Order		
Demand	Probability	0	1	2
0	0.3	0	−10	−20
1	0.4	0	40	30
2	0.3	0	40	80
	Expected value =	**0**	**25**	**30**

Expected values:

　EV of order of 0 = $0

　EV of order of 1 = (−10 × 0.3) + (40 × 0.40) + (40 × 0.3) = $25

　EV of order of 2 = (−20 × 0.3) + (30 × 0.4) + (80 × 0.30) = $30

The shopkeeper risks a loss of $20 a day compared with $10 a day on an order of one, but in the long term this strategy gives an improved expected profit of $5 per day.

Test your understanding 8

Financially, it is worthwhile to invest in the new technology as it will increase expected profit by $10,000.

The probability tree should be drawn as follows:

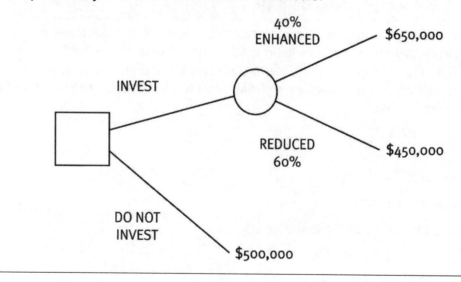

If the company does not invest then the profit will be **$500,000**

The expected value if it does invest will be (0.4 × $650,000) + (0.6 × $450,000) = **$530,000**

After deducting the cost of the new technology the expected value will be $530,000 – $20,000 = $510,000. Comparing this to the expected profit without the investment of $500,000, it is worthwhile to invest in the new technology as it should increase profit by $10,000.

Test your understanding 9

A   P(0 < z < 2.03) = TE(2.03) = 0.4788 = **47.88%**

B   P(–1.27 < z < 0) = TE(1.27) = 0.3980 = **39.8%** (by symmetry)

C   P(z > 0.55) = 0.5 – TE(0.55) = 0.5 – 0.2088 = 0.2912 = **29.12%**

D   P(z < –1.55) = P(z > 1.55) = 0.5 – TE(1.55) = 0.5 – 0.4394 = 0.0606 = **6.06%**

E   P(z > –1.23) = P(z < 1.23) = 0.5 + TE(1.23) = 0.5 + 0.3907 = 0.8907 = **89.07%**

F   P(z < 0.88) = 0.5 + TE(0.88) = 0.5 + 0.3106 = 0.8106 = **81.06%**

G   P(–0.91 < z < 1.08) = TE(0.91) + TE(1.08) = 0.3186 + 0.3599 = 0.6785 = **67.85%**

H   P(0.23 < z < 0.34) = TE(0.34) – TE(0.23) = 0.1331 – 0.0910 = 0.0421 = **4.21%**

Test your understanding 10

Although this question concerns proportions, it is essentially a problem on probabilities. We are dealing with a normal distribution with $\mu = 5$ and $\sigma = 0.1$. The values in the tables are for a normal distribution with $\mu = 0$ and standard deviation = 1 so we will need to standardise the values in this question using:

$$z = \frac{x - \mu}{\sigma}$$

Where:

z is the z score

x is the value being considered

μ is the mean

σ is the standard deviation

This calculation is used to convert any value to standard normal distribution.

Working for A:

If x = 5: $z = \dfrac{5-5}{0.1} = 0$

If x = 5.2: $z = \dfrac{5.2-5}{0.1} = 2$

Then we get the equivalent probability involving z: **P(0 < z < 2)**

All of the other parts are calculated in the same way, so we end up with:

	Question	Standardised
A	P(5 < x < 5.2)	P(0 < z < 2)
B	P(4.9 < x < 5)	P(–1 < z < 0)
C	P(x > 5.15)	P(z > 1.5)
D	P(4.8 < x < 5.1)	P(–2 < z < 1)
E	P(5.1 < x < 5.2)	P(1 < z < 2)

We can now look up these Z values on the normal distribution tables.

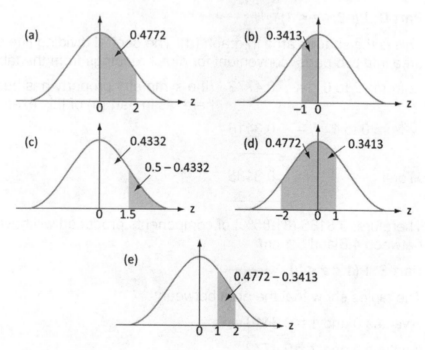

Part A: P(0 < z < 2)

This probability (area) is depicted as the shaded area in graph (a). From the tables we get 0.4772. T

Therefore 0.4772 (47.72%) of components produced will have diameters between 5 and 5.2 cm

Part B: P(–1 < z < 0)

This probability (area) is depicted as the shaded area in graph (b). This is the area shown in graph (b). However, we recall that the normal curve is symmetric about its mean; hence the shaded area is the same as the corresponding area to the right of the central dividing line, between the z-values 0 and 1. Tables give this area to be 0.3413.

Therefore, 0.3413 (34.13%) of components produced will have diameters between 4.9 and 5 cm

Part C: P(z > 1.5)

This area, shown in graph (c), cannot be read directly from the table of probabilities. However, the area immediately to its left (between z-values 0 and 1.5) can: it is 0.4332. Now, as the total area under the curve is 1, and the central dividing line splits the area into two symmetrical halves, the area to the right of the dividing line is 0.5. Hence the area required is 0.5 – 0.4332 = 0.0668.

Therefore, 0.0668 (6.68%) of components produced will have diameters over 5.15 cm

Part D: P(–2 < z < 1)

This is the shaded area in graph (d). The central dividing line splits this area into two parts, convenient for direct readings from the table:

z from –2 to 0	=	0.4772 (the symmetry property has been used here, as in part (b) of this example
z from 0 to 1	=	0.3415
		_____
Total	=	0.8185
		_____

Therefore, 0.8185 (81.85%) of components produced will have diameters between 4.8 and 5.1 cm

Part E: P(1 < z < 2)

The tables show that the area between:

z-values 0 and 1 = 0.3413

z-values 0 and 2 = 0.4772

Now, the shaded area in graph (e) can be seen to be the difference between these:

0.4772 – 0.3413 = 0.1359

Therefore 0.1359 (13.59%) of components produced will have diameters between 5.1 and 5.2 cm.

Note: The crucial role of the diagrams above should be noted. Such graphs need not be drawn very accurately, but their use is strongly advised in order to make correct use of the probabilities taken from the table.

Question 1

The completed table is:

Contribution $000	Fixed costs $000	Joint probability
50	10	0.6 × 0.7 = **0.42**
20	10	0.4 × 0.7 = **0.28**
50	8	0.6 × 0.3 = **0.18**
20	8	0.4 × 0.3 = **0.12**

Question 2

A

Expected profit = ($20,000 × 0.3) + ($12,000 × 0.5) − ($5,000 × 0.2) = $11,000

Question 3

(a)   EV of demand = (10 × 0.20) + (15 × 0.55) + (20 × 0.25) = **15.25 units per week**.

(b)   The owner should order **15** units per week.

Workings:

The first step is to set up a decision matrix of possible strategies (numbers bought) and possible demand, as follows:

Outcome (number demanded)	Strategy (number bought)		
	10	15	20
10			
15			
20			

The 'pay-off' from each combination of action and outcome is then computed:

No sale: cost of 15c per magazine.

Sale: profit of 25c – 15c = 10c per magazine

Pay-offs are shown for each combination of strategy and outcome.

Probability	Outcome (number demanded)	Decision (number bought)		
		10	**15**	**20**
0.20	**10**	100	25	(50)
0.55	**15**	100	150	75
0.25	**20**	100	150	200
1.00	EV	100c	125c	81.25c

Conclusion: The strategy which gives the highest expected value is to stock 15 magazines each week.

Calculations:

If 10 magazines are bought, then 10 are sold no matter how many are demanded and the payoff is always 10 × 10c = 100c.

If 15 magazines are bought and 10 are demanded, then 10 are sold at a profit of 10 × 10c = 100c, and 5 are scrapped at a loss of 5 × 15c = 75c, making a net profit of 25c.

The other contributions are calculated in the same way.

Question 4

A   P(faulty) = 22/361 = 0.0609 = **6.09%**

B   P(P or Q) = (100 + 208)/361 = 0.8532 = **85.32%**

C   P(two items both faulty) = P(1st faulty) × P(2nd faulty) = (22/361) × (21/360) = 0.0036 = **0.36%**

Question 5

The table should look as follows:

	Department A	Department B	Total
Faulty	2.48	1.90	4.38
Acceptable	59.52	36.10	95.62
	———	———	———
Total	62.00	38.00	100.00
	———	———	———

Just fill in what you know on the table. This is only the total of 100 and that 62 come from Department A. You can work out from this that 38 must come from Department B.

You are told that 4% of production in A is faulty, so that is 0.04 × 62 = 2.48. You can then work out that 62 – 2.48 = 59.52 is acceptable. In B, 5% is faulty = 0.05 × 38 = 1.9, so 38 – 1.9 = 36.1 is acceptable.

Question 6

The correct matching is:

Type	Definition	Example
Exact	These can be applied to the population of outcomes	Selecting a card from a pack of cards
Empirical	These can be calculated from samples of observations from the past	The likely level of sales in a week
Subjective	These are based on judgement	The probability of winning a new contract

Question 7

B

P(sale > 120)	=	0.0119
P(110 < sale < 120)	=	0.5 – 0.0119
	=	0.4881

which corresponds to z = 2.26 from normal tables.

$$z = \frac{x - \mu}{\sigma}$$

2.26 = (120 – 110) ÷ σ

σ = (120 – 110) ÷ 2.226 = **$4.42**

Question 8

(a) **26.67% of products will be faulty**

If weight is 7.985 kg:

$$z = \frac{x - \mu}{\sigma}$$

$Z = (7.985 - 8) \div 0.02 = -0.75$

If weight is 8.035 kg:

$Z = (8.035 - 8) \div 0.02 = 1.75$

So we want $P(-0.75 < z < 1.75) = TE(0.75) + TE(1.75) = 0.2734 + 0.4599 = 0.7333$

Faulty items are outside this range so the probability that an item is faulty is $1 - 0.7333 = 0.2667$.

(b) **The mean weight must be decreased to 7.994 kg.**

The tail-end probability of 2% corresponds to the table entry 48% = 0.48, and so to the z-value 2.05.

Use the formula to work back to calculate the mean:

$2.05 = (8.035 - \mu)/0.02$

$\mu = 8.035 - (2.05 \times 0.02) = 7.994$.

(c) **The standard deviation must fall to 0.0073 kg.**

From the logic above, the z-value must now be -2.05

Use the formula to work back to calculate the standard deviation:

$-2.05 = (7.985 - 8)/\sigma$

$\sigma = -0.015 \div -2.05 = 0.0073$

Question 9

(a) Probability (some improvement) = 725/1,000 = **0.725**

(b) **Yes, the treatment does seem to be effective.**

Initial workings:

	Treatment received	Placebo received	Total
Some improvement	600	125	725
No improvement	150	125	275
Total	750	250	1,000

Question 10

The company should build the shelter as it would increase its expected value from $95,500 to $135,000.

The probability tree is shown below:

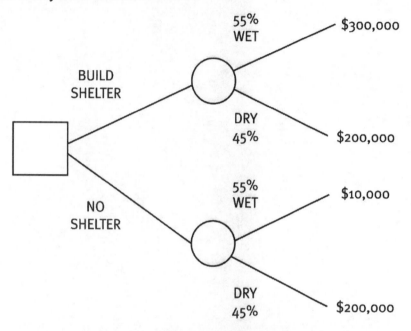

If the company builds the shelter, the expected profit will be:

(0.55 × $300,000) + (0.45 × $200,000) − $120,000 = **$135,000**

If the company does not build the shelter, the expected profit will be:

(0.55 × $10,000) + (0.45 × $200,000) = **$95,500**

Short-term decision making

Chapter learning objectives

After completing this chapter, you should be able to

- apply breakeven analysis

- demonstrate make or buy decisions

- calculate the profit maximising sales mix after using limiting factor analysis.

1 Session content diagram

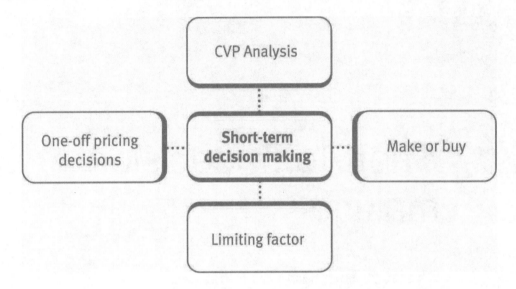

2 Introduction

In the next two chapters we will consider some decision making techniques in more detail. Short-term decision making will be considered in this chapter and long-term decision making will be considered in the next chapter.

Some common short-term decisions which organisations make are:

- Pricing decisions for a one-off product or job.

- How many units to produce and sell – this is known as breakeven analysis.

- Limiting factor decision – where the company tries to operate at the maximum profitability despite being constrained in some way.

- Make or buy decisions – where a company decides whether to make components in house, or buy them from an external supplier.

Decision making will involve many of the techniques that we have already looked at in earlier chapters. In particular it may be worth recapping on relevant costs from the cost identification and classification chapter, and the calculation of contribution from the marginal and absorption costing chapter. We also saw in the previous two chapters that risk and uncertainty will have an impact on decision making.

3 Pricing decisions for a one-off product or job

Remember that in all decision making the rules of relevant cost apply.

When making a one-off pricing decision only **relevant cash flows** should be used. We looked at relevant cost earlier in the cost identification and classification chapter.

To recap the main relevant cost rules:

- Only future, incremental cash flows should be included (i.e. those which will change as a result of the decision).

- Sunk costs and committed costs should be excluded.

- Non-cash flows are excluded (for example depreciation, provisions or allocated fixed costs).

- Notional costs are excluded.

- Opportunity costs should always be included. Remember opportunity costs are the value of the benefit sacrificed when one course of action is chosen in preference to an alternative.

Relevant cost of materials

Many relevant cost questions will involve the use of materials. For example if the company is asked to price a one-off job.

There are a number of alternative costs which could be relevant for materials: purchase price, replacement cost, net realisable value or opportunity cost. The relevant cost will depend on the given situation.

The following decision tree can help to determine the relevant cost of materials.

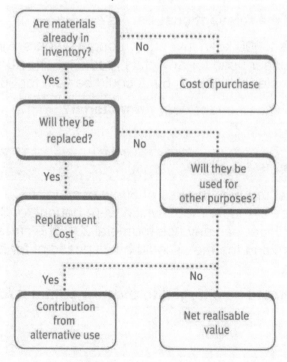

Note: The contribution from alternative use is the **opportunity cost**.

Illustration 1 – Relevant cost of material

XYZ has 50 kg of material P in inventory which was bought five years ago for $70. It is no longer used but after incurring additional packing cost of $1/kg it could be sold for $4/kg

XYZ is currently pricing a job that requires 40 kg of material P.

Required:

The relevant cost of material P that should be included in the contract is $ _____ .

Solution:

Using the decision tree:

Are materials already in inventory? Yes

Will they be replaced? No, (no longer used)

Will they be used for other purposes? No

Relevant cost = Net realisable value: 40 kg × ($4/kg – $1/kg) = **$120**

Test your understanding 1

EFG is currently considering a job that requires 1,000 kg of raw material. There are two possible situations.

(a) The material is used regularly within the company. The present inventory is 10,000 kg which was purchased at $1.80 per kg. The current purchase price is $2.00 per kg.

What is the relevant cost per kg?

(b) EFG has 2,000 kg in inventory, bought 2 years ago for $1.50 per kg, but no longer used for any of its products. The current market price for the material is $2.00, but it could be sold for $0.80 per kg.

What is the relevant cost for material?

Test your understanding 2

A new contract requires the use of 50 kg of metal ZX. There are 25 kg of ZX in inventory at the moment, which were bought for $200 per kg. The company no longer has any use for metal ZX. The current purchase price is $210 per kg, and the metal could be disposed of for net scrap proceeds of $150 per kg.

What cost should be charged to the new contract for metal ZX?

Relevant cost of labour

As with material, it can be difficult to determine the relevant cost of labour. With questions involving labour costs, the key question is whether spare capacity exists. The following decision tree can help to determine the relevant cost of labour.

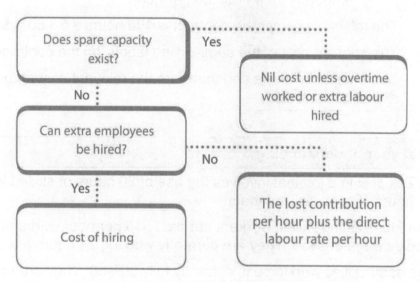

Note: When there is no spare capacity and no alternative labour can be hired, labour must be taken from existing projects. The contribution from alternative products which must be abandoned to create spare capacity is the **opportunity cost**. To work out the relevant cost, take the lost contribution per hour and add on the direct labour rate per hour:

Relevant cost = Contribution forgone from alternative product per hour **PLUS** direct labour cost per hour.

Illustration 2 – Relevant cost of labour

(a) 100 hours of unskilled labour are needed for a contract. The company has no surplus capacity at the moment, but additional temporary staff could be hired at $6.50 per hour.

What is the relevant cost of the unskilled labour on the contract?

(b) 100 hours of semi-skilled labour are needed for a contract. The company currently has 300 hours' worth of spare capacity. There is a union agreement that there are no lay-offs. The workers are paid $8.50 per hour.

What is the relevant cost of the semi-skilled labour on the contract?

Solution:

(a) The relevant cost of the unskilled labour on the contract is $650.

Using the decision tree, spare capacity does not exist, but extra employees can be hired, therefore the relevant cost is the cost of hiring temporary staff at $6.50 per hour.

The relevant cost for the contract is 100 hours × $6.50 = **$650**.

(b) The relevant cost of the semi-skilled labour on the contract is NIL.

Spare capacity exists and therefore the relevant cost of the semi-skilled labour is **$0**.

Test your understanding 3

XYZ is pricing a job that involves the use of 20 hours of skilled labour and 50 hours of semi-skilled labour.

The four existing skilled workers are paid $15 per hour with a minimum weekly wage of $450. They are currently working 24 hours a week.

The semi-skilled workforce is currently fully utilised. They are each paid $10 per hour, with overtime payable at time and a half. Additional workers may be hired for $12 per hour.

Calculate the relevant labour cost for XYZ's job.

Test your understanding 4

A mining operation uses skilled labour costing $14 per hour, which generates a contribution (after deducting the labour costs) of $3 per hour.

A new project is now being considered which requires 5,000 hours of skilled labour. There is a shortage of the required labour and no additional labour can be hired.

What is the relevant cost of using the skilled labour on the project?

The relevant cost of overheads

In addition to calculating the relevant cost of materials and labour, you may also be required to calculate the relevant cost of overheads.

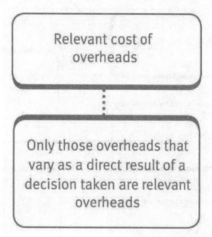

Example

JKL absorbs overheads on a machine hour rate, currently $20/hour, of which $7 is for variable overheads and $13 for fixed overheads. The company is deciding whether to undertake a contract in the coming year. If the contract is undertaken, it is estimated that fixed costs will increase for the duration of the contract by $3,200.

Identify the relevant fixed and variable overhead costs for the contract.

Solution:

*   The variable cost per hour of overheads is relevant since this cost would be avoidable if the contract were not undertaken. The relevant cost of variable overheads is therefore **$7 per machine hour**.

*   Actual fixed costs would not increase by $13 per hour, but by $3,200 in total, so the relevant cost of fixed overheads is therefore **$3,200**.

Relevant cost of non-current assets

The relevant costs associated with non-current assets, such as plant and machinery, are determined in a similar way to the relevant costs of materials.

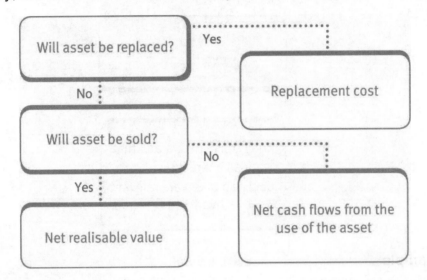

Where there is a choice between selling an asset, or using the asset, the higher of the net realisable value and the cash flows from the use of the asset (the economic value) should be selected as the relevant cost.

 Illustration 3 – Relevant cost of non-current assets

A machine which cost $10,000 four years ago has a written-down value of $6,000 and the depreciation to be charged this year is $1,000. It has no alternative use, but it could be sold now for $3,000. In one year's time it will have no resale value.

Relevant cost of the machine = $ _____

Solution:

- The $10,000 (the cost of the machine four years ago) is a sunk cost and is not relevant to the decision.

- The $6,000 (written-down value of the machine) is not relevant because it is determined by accounting conventions and not by future cash flows.

- The $1,000 (depreciation charge this year) is not relevant because this is a non-cash flow cost.

- The $3,000 (sale proceeds if the machine were sold now) is a relevant cost (future cash flow).

The cost of keeping the machine and selling it in a year's time is $3,000 because this is the amount that you will miss out on if you don't sell it now.

Test your understanding 5

Equipment owned by a company has a net book value of $1,800 and has been idle for some months. It could now be used on a six month contract that is being considered. If not used on this contract, the equipment would be sold now for a net amount of $2,000. After use on the contract, the equipment would have no resale value and would be dismantled.

What is the total relevant cost of the equipment to the contract?

Relevant cost forms the foundation for much of the decision making organisations undertake. Remember to always use COMMON SENSE in decision making questions.

4 Breakeven analysis

With breakeven analysis we start to consider the effects on future profit caused by changes in elements such as fixed and variable costs, sales price and volume. This type of analysis is also referred to as cost-volume-profit analysis (CVP).

Breakeven analysis and CVP analysis

In practice, the terms 'breakeven analysis' and 'CVP analysis' tend to be used interchangeably. The term breakeven analysis is misleading, since it implies that the focus of the analysis is the **breakeven point** (the level of activity which produces neither profit nor loss). You will see in this chapter that the scope of CVP analysis is much wider than this.

Cost–volume–profit (CVP) analysis is defined in CIMA's Terminology as the 'study of the effects on future profit of changes in fixed cost, variable cost, sales price, quantity and mix'.

Breakeven analysis (or CVP analysis) involves a number of useful calculations:

* Breakeven point
* Margin of safety
* C/S ratio.

As well as an understanding of two charts:

* Breakeven chart
* PV chart.

Students will require a good knowledge of all of these calculations and charts.

The contribution calculation is used extensively in CVP analysis. This concept was covered in the marginal and absorption costing chapter. To recap:

CONTRIBUTION = SALES VALUE – VARIABLE COSTS

5   Breakeven point

An important concept for decision-makers is breakeven. At a level of zero sales, the company's total contribution will be zero, therefore they will make a total loss equal to the level of their fixed costs. As sales revenues grow, the contribution will grow and will start to cover the fixed costs. Eventually a point will be reached where neither profit nor loss is made, this is the **breakeven point**. At this point the total contribution must exactly match the fixed costs. Any additional contribution made above this level will constitute profit.

If we know how much contribution is earned from each unit sold, then we can calculate the number of units required to break even as follows:

$$\text{Breakeven point in units} = \frac{\text{Fixed costs}}{\text{Contribution per unit}}$$

For example, suppose that an organisation manufactures a single product, incurring variable costs of $30 per unit and fixed costs of $20,000 per month. If the product sells for $50 per unit, then the breakeven point can be calculated as follows:

$$\text{Breakeven point in units} = \frac{\$20,000}{(\$50 - \$30)} = \textbf{1,000 units per month}$$

Test your understanding 6

ABC manufactures a single product. The unit costs of the product are as follows:

	$
Direct materials	36
Direct labour	12
Direct expenses	9
Variable overheads	13

The product sells for $95. The fixed costs for the period were $55,000.

Required:

The breakeven number of units is _____.

6   The margin of safety

 The margin of safety is the difference between the expected level of sales and the breakeven point. The larger the margin of safety, the more likely it is that a profit will be made.

Margin of safety can be expressed in units or as a % of projected sales:

> **Margin of safety in units = projected sales – breakeven sales**

or

> **Margin of safety % = $\dfrac{\text{projected sales – breakeven sales}}{\text{projected sales}}$**

Example: If a company has a breakeven level of sales of 1,000 and is forecasting sales of 1,700, the margin of safety can be calculated as follows:

Margin of safety = 1,700 – 1,000 = 700 units

or

Margin of safety % = (1,700 – 1,000)/1,700 = 0.41 = 41%

Using the margin of safety % puts it in perspective. To quote a margin of safety of 700 units without relating it to the projected sales figure is not giving the full picture.

Note: The margin of safety % is also referred to as the margin of safety ratio.

Illustration 4 – Margin of safety calculations

RST manufactures one product. The product sells for $250, and has variable costs per unit of $120. Fixed costs for the month were $780,000. The monthly projected sales for the product were 8,000 units.

First calculate the breakeven sales:

Breakeven point in units = $\dfrac{\text{Fixed costs}}{\text{Contribution per unit}}$

$$= \frac{\$780,000}{(\$250 - \$120)} = \textbf{6,000 units}$$

Margin of safety in units	=	projected sales – breakeven sales
	=	8,000 – 6,000 = **2,000 units**
Margin of safety %	=	(projected sales – breakeven sales)/projected sales
	=	(8,000 – 6,000)/8,000 = **25%**

Using margin of safety to calculate profit

The margin of safety can also be used as one route to a profit calculation. We have seen that the contribution goes towards fixed costs and profit. Once breakeven point is reached the fixed costs have been covered.

After the breakeven point there are no more fixed costs to be covered and all of the contribution goes towards making profits.

From the above example, the monthly profit from sales of 8,000 units would be $260,000. This can be calculated in the normal way:

Contribution per unit	$130
	$
Total contribution ($130 × 8,000)	1,040,000
Fixed costs	780,000
Profit	**$260,000**

Or using margin of safety:

Margin of safety	= 2,000 units per month
Monthly profit	= 2,000 × contribution per unit
	= 2,000 × $130
	= **$260,000**

Test your understanding 7

LMN plans to produce and sell 4,000 units of product C each month, at a selling price of $18 per unit. The unit cost of product C is as follows:

	$ per unit
Variable cost	8
Fixed cost	4
	12

Required:

To the nearest whole number, the margin of safety, as a percentage of planned sales is _____ %.

---

7   The contribution to sales (C/S) ratio

The contribution to sales ratio is a useful calculation in CVP analysis. It is usually expressed as a percentage. It can be calculated as follows.

$$\text{C/S ratio} = \frac{\text{Contribution}}{\text{Sales}}$$

The C/S ratio can be calculated using contribution and sales at either a unit level, or at a total level.

A higher contribution to sales ratio means that contribution grows more quickly as sales levels increase. Once the breakeven has been passed, profits will accumulate more quickly than for a product with a lower contribution to sales ratio.

You might sometimes see this ratio referred to as the **profit-volume (P/V) ratio**.

Using the RST example from Illustration 4, the C/S ratio can be calculated as:

$$\text{C/S ratio} = \frac{\text{Contribution}}{\text{Sales}}$$

C/S ratio = 130/250 = 0.52 = **52%**

If we assume that a unit's variable cost and selling price remain constant then the C/S ratio will also remain constant.

The C/S ratio can be used in the calculation of the breakeven point. When we use the C/S ratio on the bottom of the breakeven formula, we get the answer in $ of sales revenue, rather than in units:

$$\text{Breakeven point in \$ of sales revenue} = \frac{\text{Fixed costs}}{\text{C/S ratio}}$$

Using the data from Illustration 4:

$$\text{Breakeven point in \$ of sales revenue} = \frac{\text{Fixed costs}}{\text{C/S ratio}} = \frac{\$780,000}{0.52} = \textbf{\$1,500,000}$$

Note: This could have been calculated as: breakeven point × selling price

$$= 6,000 \times \$250 = \textbf{\$1,500,000}$$

8 Sales required for a target profit

A further calculation which is used as part of CVP analysis is the calculation of the level of sales required to achieve a certain level of profit. As with the breakeven point, this can be calculated in sales units or in $ of sales revenue.

The calculations are as follows:

$$\text{Sales units required to achieve a profit of X} = \frac{\text{(Fixed costs + X)}}{\text{Contribution per unit}}$$

or

$$\text{Sales revenue required to achieve a profit of X} = \frac{\text{(Fixed costs + X)}}{\text{C/S ratio}}$$

Test your understanding 8

A company manufactures and sells a single product which has the following cost and selling price structure

	$/unit	$/unit
Selling price		120
Direct material	22	
Direct labour	36	
Variable overhead	14	
Fixed overhead	12	
		84
Profit per unit		36

The fixed overhead absorption rate is based on the normal capacity of 2,000 units per month. Assume that the same amount is spent each month on fixed overheads.

Budgeted sales for next month are 2,200 units.

Calculate the following:

(i)   the breakeven point, in sales units per month

(ii)   the margin of safety for next month

(iii) the budgeted profit for next month

(iv) the sales units required to achieve a profit of $96,000 in a month.

9 Breakeven charts

Conventional breakeven chart

A conventional, or basic, breakeven chart records costs and revenues on the vertical axis (y) and the level of activity on the horizontal axis (x). Lines are drawn on the chart to represent costs and sales revenue. The breakeven point can be found where the sales revenue line cuts the total cost line.

We will use a basic example to demonstrate how to draw a breakeven chart. Data from JKL's budget are given below:

Selling price	$50 per unit
Variable cost	$30 per unit
Fixed costs	$20,000 per month
Forecast sales	1,700 units per month

> While you will not be required to draw a graph to scale in the assessment, learning to draw a chart to scale will provide a firm foundation for your understanding of breakeven charts. To give yourself some practice, it would be a good idea to follow the step-by-step guide which follows to produce your own chart on a piece of graph paper.

Step 1: Select appropriate scales for the axes and draw and label them.
Your graph should fill as much of the page as possible. This will make it clearer and easier to read.

The highest point on the vertical axis will be the monthly sales revenue, that is:

1,700 units × $50 = $85,000

The highest point on the horizontal axis will be monthly sales volume of 1,700 units. Make sure that you do not need to read data for volumes higher than 1,700 units before you set these extremes for your scales.

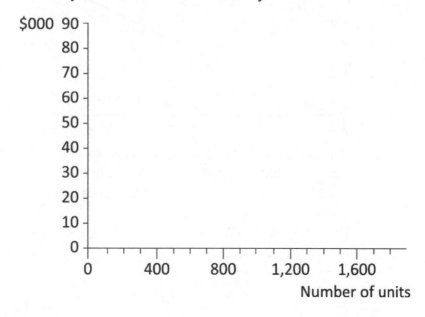

Step 2: Draw the fixed cost line and label it. This will be a straight line parallel to the horizontal axis at the $20,000 level.

The $20,000 fixed costs are incurred in the short term even with zero activity.

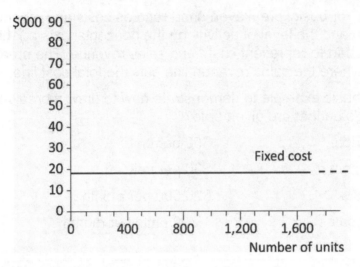

Step 3: Draw the total cost line and label it. The best way to do this is to calculate the total costs for the maximum sales level, which is 1,700 units in our example. Mark this point on the graph and join it to the cost incurred at zero activity, that is, $20,000.

	$
Variable costs for 1,700 units (1,700 × $30)	51,000
Fixed costs	20,000
Total cost for 1,700 units	71,000

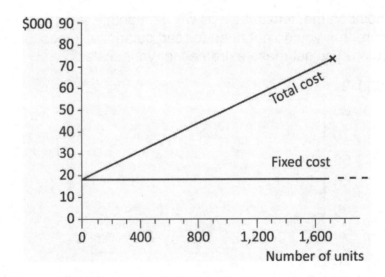

Step 4: Draw the revenue line and label it. Once again, the best way is to plot the extreme points. The revenue at maximum activity in our example is 1,700 × $50 = $85,000. This point can be joined to the origin, since at zero activity there will be no sales revenue.

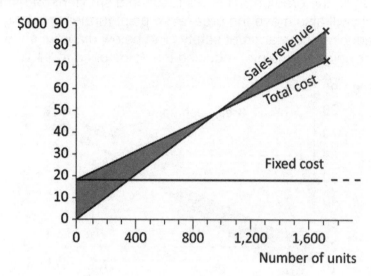

Step 5: Mark any required information on the chart and read off solutions as required. You can check that your chart is accurate by reading off the breakeven point and then checking this against the calculation for breakeven:

$$\text{Breakeven point in units} = \frac{\text{Fixed costs}}{\text{Contribution per unit}}$$

$$= \frac{\$20,000}{(\$50 - \$30)} = 1,000 \text{ units}$$

The margin of safety can be seen as the area to the right of the breakeven point up to the forecast sales level of 1,700.

The completed graph is shown below:

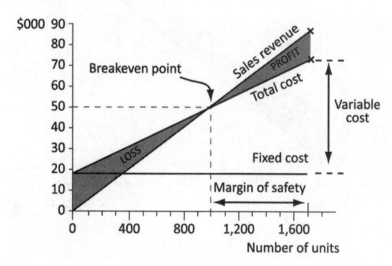

Changes in any of the variables will impact on the breakeven point and resulting margin of safety. For example:

- A reduction in the selling price will lower the end point of the sales revenue line, reducing the gradient. This will result in a smaller shaded area for profit. This will also move the breakeven point further to the right along the x axis, reducing the margin of safety. The below diagram shows the effect on our previous example of reducing the sales price to $45:

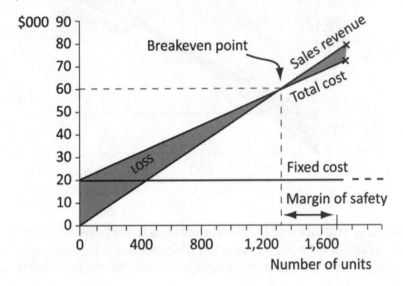

- An increase in the variable cost will increase the gradient of the total cost line. Again, this will shift the breakeven point to the right on the graph, reducing the margin of safety. The below diagram shows the effect of variable costs being increased to $35:

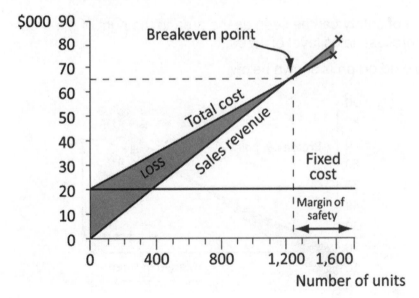

- Finally, an increase in the fixed costs will shift the total cost line upwards. The gradient of the total cost line will remain the same. The breakeven point will therefore move further along the x axis and the margin of safety reduce. The below diagram shows the effect of increasing fixed costs to $30,000 per month:

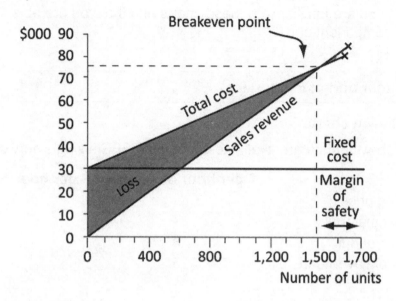

The contribution breakeven chart

One of the problems with the conventional or basic breakeven chart is that it is not possible to read contribution directly from the chart. A contribution breakeven chart is based on the same principles but it shows the variable cost line instead of the fixed cost line. The same lines for total cost and sales revenue are shown so the breakeven point and profit can be read off in the same way as with a basic breakeven chart. However, with this chart it is also possible to read the contribution for any level of activity.

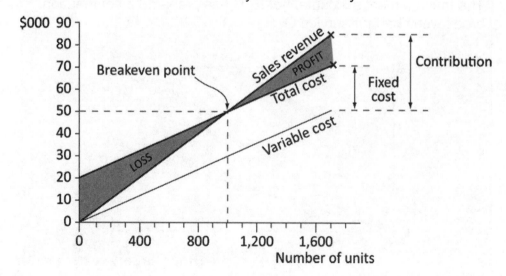

Using the same basic example as for the conventional chart, the total variable cost for an output of 1,700 units is 1,700 × $30 = $51,000. This point can be joined to the origin since the variable cost is nil at zero activity.

The contribution can be read as the difference between the sales revenue line and the variable cost line.

This form of presentation might be used when it is desirable to highlight the importance of contribution and to focus attention on the variable costs.

 Ensure you are familiar with these charts and that you are able to identify all the component parts.

 Test your understanding 9

Breakeven charts

The following data are available concerning EFG's single service Q.

	$ per hour of service	$ per hour of service
Selling price		50
Direct material	7	
Direct labour	8	
Variable overhead	5	
	___	20
		___
Contribution		30
Fixed overhead		15
		___
Profit		15
		___

1,000 hours of service Q are provided to customers each month.

The management accountant of EFG has prepared a contribution breakeven chart for service Q.

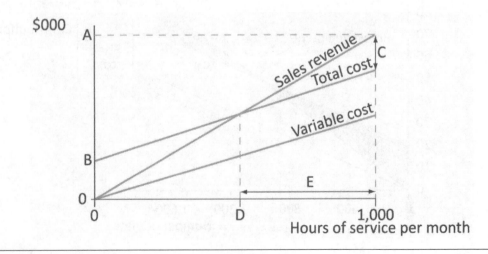

The values or quantities indicated by A to E on the chart are:

A $		
B $		
C $		
D		hours
E		hours

Profit–volume chart (PV chart)

Another form of breakeven chart is the profit–volume chart. This chart plots a single line depicting the profit or loss at each level of activity. The breakeven point is where this line cuts the horizontal axis.

Earlier in the chapter we drew a breakeven chart for JKL. Using the same data:

Selling price	$50 per unit
Variable cost	$30 per unit
Fixed costs	$20,000 per month
Forecast sales	1,700 units per month

A profit–volume chart can also be drawn:

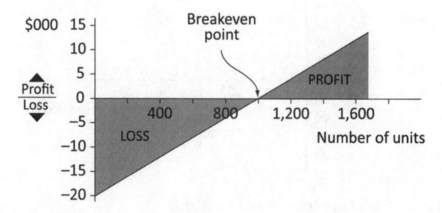

The vertical axis shows profits and losses and the horizontal axis, showing units, is drawn at zero profit or loss.

At zero activity the loss is equal to $20,000, that is, the amount of fixed costs. The second point used to draw the line could be the calculated breakeven point or the calculated profit for sales of 1,700 units.

The profit–volume graph is also called a profit graph or a contribution– volume graph.

The main advantage of the profit–volume chart is that it is capable of depicting clearly the effect on profit and breakeven point of any changes in the variables.

PV chart illustration

A company manufactures a single product which incurs fixed costs of $30,000 per annum. Annual sales are budgeted to be 70,000 units at a sales price of $30 per unit. Variable costs are $28.50 per unit.

(a)   **Draw a profit–volume graph, and use it to determine the breakeven point.**

The company is now considering improving the quality of the product and increasing the selling price to $35 per unit. Sales volume will be unaffected, but fixed costs will increase to $45,000 per annum and variable costs to $33 per unit.

(b)   **On the same graph as for part (a), draw a second profit–volume graph and comment on the results.**

Solution:

The profit–volume charts are shown below:

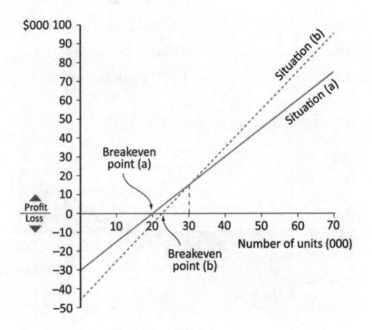

The two lines have been drawn as follows:

(a)   The profit for sales of 70,000 units is $75,000.

	$000
Contribution 70,000 × $(30 – 28.50)	105
Fixed costs	30
Profit	75

This point is joined to the loss at zero activity which will be the amount of the fixed costs, that is $30,000.

(b) The profit for sales of 70,000 units is $95,000.

	$000
Contribution 70,000 × $(35 – 33)	140
Fixed costs	45

Profit	95

This point is joined to the loss at zero activity which will be the amount of the fixed costs, that is $45,000. **Comment on the results.** The chart clearly shows the potentially larger profits available from option (b). It also shows that the breakeven point increases from 20,000 units to 22,500 units but that this is not a large increase when viewed in the context of the projected sales volume. It is also possible to see that for sales volumes above 30,000 units the profit achieved will be higher with option (b). For sales volumes below 30,000 units option (a) will yield higher profits (or lower losses).

The profit–volume graph is the clearest way of presenting information like this. If we attempted to draw two conventional breakeven charts on one set of axes the result would be difficult to interpret.

Test your understanding 10

LMN manufactures one product only, and for the last accounting period has produced the simplified statement of profit or loss below:

	$	$
Sales		300,000
Costs:		
Direct materials	60,000	
Direct wages	40,000	

Prime cost	100,000	
Variable production overhead	10,000	
Fixed production overhead	40,000	
Fixed administration overhead	60,000	
Variable selling overhead	40,000	
Fixed selling overhead	20,000	

		270,000

Net profit		30,000

Required:

(a) Draw a profit–volume graph for LMN's product.

    (i) The profit line drawn on the graph would cut the vertical axis (y-axis) at the point where y is equal to $ _____

    (ii) The profit line drawn on the graph would cut the horizontal axis (x-axis) at the point where x is equal to $ _____

    (iii) The margin of safety indicated by the graph would be $ _____.

(b) For each of the following changes, indicate whether the gradient of the profit line and the breakeven point will increase, decrease or remain unchanged.

The gradient of the profit line will:

Variable changed	Increase	Decrease	Remain unchanged
(i) Increase in selling price	❑	❑	❑
(ii) Increase in fixed cost	❑	❑	❑
(iii) Decrease in variable cost per unit	❑	❑	❑

The breakeven point will:

Variable changed	Increase	Decrease	Remain unchanged
(i) Increase in selling price	❑	❑	❑
(ii) Increase in fixed cost	❑	❑	❑
(iii) Decrease in variable cost per unit	❑	❑	❑

The economist's breakeven chart

The creation of the charts so far has relied on certain assumptions made by accountants to simplify their calculations (such as that the selling price per unit will remain constant). An economist would make no such assumptions and would take a view over a wider range of activity level. Typically, an economist would depict a breakeven chart as shown below:

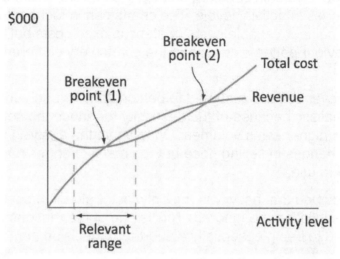

The total cost line is not a straight line which climbs steadily as in the accountant's chart. Instead it begins to reduce initially as output increases because of the effect of economies of scale. Later it begins to climb upwards according to the law of diminishing returns.

The revenue line is not a straight line as in the accountant's chart. The line becomes less steep to depict the need to give discounts to achieve higher sales volumes.

However, you will see that within the middle range the economist's chart does look very similar to the accountant's breakeven chart. This area is marked as the relevant range on the chart.

For this reason, it is unreliable to assume that the cost–volume–profit relationships depicted in breakeven analysis are relevant across a wide range of activity. In particular, the economist's chart shows that the constant cost and price assumptions are likely to be unreliable at very high or very low levels of activity. Managers should therefore ensure that they work within the relevant range, that is, within the range over which the depicted cost and revenue relationships are more reliable.

> The relevant range in the context of cost behaviour patterns was discussed in the cost identification and classification chapter.

10 The limitations of breakeven (or CVP) analysis

The limitations of the practical applicability of breakeven analysis and breakeven charts stem mostly from the assumptions which underlie the analysis:

- Costs are assumed to behave in a linear fashion. Unit variable costs are assumed to remain constant and fixed costs are assumed to be unaffected by changes in activity levels. The charts can in fact be adjusted to cope with non-linear variable costs or steps in fixed costs but too many changes in behaviour patterns can make the charts very cluttered and difficult to use.

- Sales revenues are assumed to be constant for each unit sold. This may be unrealistic because of the necessity to reduce the selling price to achieve higher sales volumes. Once again the analysis can be adapted for some changes in selling price but too many changes can make the charts difficult to use.

- It is assumed that activity is the only factor affecting costs, and factors such as inflation are ignored. This is one of the reasons why the analysis is limited to being essentially a short-term decision aid.

- Apart from the unrealistic situation of a constant product mix, the charts can only be applied to a single product or service. Not many organisations have a single product or service and if there is more than one, then the apportionment of fixed costs between them becomes arbitrary.

- The analysis seems to suggest that as long as the activity level is above the breakeven point, then a profit will be achieved. In reality certain changes in the cost and revenue patterns may result in a second breakeven point after which losses are made.

11 Limiting factor analysis

In most business situations only a limited number of business opportunities may be undertaken. Some factor will limit the ability to undertake all the alternatives. This factor is referred to as the **limiting factor**.

 A limiting factor is any factor which is in scarce supply and which limits the organisation's activities.

The limiting factor for many trading organisations is sales volume because they cannot sell as much as they would like. However, other factors may also be limited, especially in the short term. For example, machine capacity or the supply of skilled labour may be limited for one or two periods until some action can be taken to alleviate the shortage.

Illustration 5 – Identifying the limiting factor

VWX makes a single product (Z) that requires $5 of materials and two hours of labour. There are only 80 hours of labour available each week and the maximum amount of material available each week is $500.

Assuming unlimited demand for product Z, which of these two factors is a limiting factor on production?

Solution:

It can be said that the supply of both labour hours and materials is limited and that therefore they are both scarce resources. The maximum production within these constraints can be shown to be:

Materials: $500/$5 = 100 units

Labour hours: 80 hours/2 hours = 40 units

Thus the shortage of labour hours is the limiting factor.

Test your understanding 11

A company makes and sells three products. Information for the three products is as follows:

	Product E $ per unit	Product F $ per unit	Product G $ per unit
Direct labour ($15 per hour)	7.50	22.50	15.00
Direct material ($8 per kg)	12.00	10.00	16.00
Maximum demand per period (units)	380	520	240

Labour hours are limited to 1,300 hours each period and the supply of material is limited to 1,450 kg each period.

What is the company's limiting factor(s)?

A   Direct labour

B   Direct material

C   Both direct material and direct labour

D   Neither direct material nor direct labour

Note: In *Fundamentals of Management Accounting*, questions will only examine single limiting factors. Therefore always establish which factor is the limiting factor and base all calculations on this. Later CIMA subjects will examine situations with more than one limiting factor.

Decisions involving a single limiting factor

The concept of **contribution** can be used to make decisions about the best use of a limited resource.

If an organisation is faced with a single limiting factor, for example machine capacity, then it must ensure that a production plan is established which maximises the profit from the use of the available capacity. Assuming that fixed costs remain constant, this is the same as saying that the contribution must be maximised from the use of the available capacity. The machine capacity must be allocated to those products which earn the most contribution per machine hour.

> This decision rule can be stated as:
>
> **'maximising the contribution per unit of limiting factor'.**

To calculate the contribution per unit of limiting factor:

> **Contribution per unit**
> ──────────────────────────
> **Amount of limiting factor required per unit**

When limiting factors are present, contribution (and therefore profits) are maximised when products earning the highest amount of contribution per unit of limiting factor are manufactured first. The profit-maximising production mix is known as the **optimal production plan**.

The optimal production plan is established as follows.

- **Step 1:** If not clearly given in the question, establish the single limiting factor.

- **Step 2:** Calculate the contribution per unit for each product.

- **Step 3:** Calculate the contribution per unit of limiting factor for each product.

- **Step 4:** Rank the products according to their contribution per unit of limiting factor.

- **Step 5:** Allocate the limiting factor to the highest-ranking product.

- **Step 6:** Once the demand for the highest-ranking product is satisfied, move on to the next highest-ranking product and so on until the (limiting factor) scarce resource is used up.

Illustration 6 – The optimal production plan

LMN manufactures three products L, M and N. The company which supplies the two raw materials which are used in all three products has informed LMN that their employees are refusing to work overtime. This means that supply of the materials is limited to the following quantities for the next period:

Material A   1,030 kg

Material B   1,220 kg

No other source of supply for materials A and B can be found for the next period.

Information relating to the three products manufactured by LMN is as follows:

Quantity of material used per unit manufactured:	L	M	N
Material A (kg)	2	1	4
Material B (kg)	5	3	7
Maximum sales demand (units)	120	160	110
Contribution per unit sold	$15	$12	$17.50

Recommend a production mix which will maximise the profits of LMN for the forthcoming period.

Solution:

- **Step 1:** Check whether the supply of each material is adequate or whether either or both of them represent a limiting factor.

   Material A required to produce the total sales demand of products L, M and N:

   (120 × 2) + (160 × 1) + (110 × 4) = **840 kg** (available: 1,030 kg)

   Therefore material A is not a limiting factor.

   Material B required to produce the total sales demand of products L, M and N:

   (120 × 5) + (160 × 3) + (110 × 7) = **1,850 kg** (available: 1,220 kg)

   Therefore material B is the liming factor.

- **Step 2:** Calculate the contribution per unit of product. This is given in the question:

	L	M	N
Contribution per unit sold	$15	$12	$17.50

- **Step 3:** Calculate the **contribution per unit of limiting factor**.

	L	M	N
Contribution per unit sold	$15	$12	$17.50
Material B (kg)	5	3	7
Contribution per kg of material B	$3	$4	$2.50

- **Step 4:** Rank the products

	L	M	N
Contribution per kg of material B	$3	$4	$2.50
Ranking	**2**	**1**	**3**

- **Step 5/6:** Allocate material B to the products according to this ranking. Once the demand for the highest ranking product is satisfied, move to the next highest ranking product, and so on, until all of material B is used up.

Product	Production (units)	Material B utilised (kg)	
M	160 (max)	480	(160 × 3)
L	120 (max)	600	(120 × 5)
N	20	140	(balance)
		1,220	

The available material B is able to satisfy the maximum market demand for products M and L. The balance of available material is allocated to the last product in the ranking, product N.

The optimum production mix is to produce:

160 units of M

120 units of L

20 units of N

If required by the question, calculate the maximum profit (or contribution if the question has no fixed costs). It is best to use total contribution for this calculation:

Product M	Product L	Product N	Total
(160 × 12) +	(120 × 15) +	(20 × 17.50) =	**$4,070**

Note: This is the maximum profit which can be made given the limiting factor. No other combination can achieve a higher profit.

Test your understanding 12

ABC makes three products, all of which use the same machine, which is available for 50,000 hours per period.

The unit costs of the product are:

	Product A	Product B	Product C
	$	$	$
Direct materials	70	40	80
Direct labour:			
Machinists ($8/hour)	48	32	56
Assemblers ($6/hour)	36	40	42
Total variable cost	154	112	178
Selling price per unit	200	158	224
Maximum demand (units)	3,000	2,500	5,000

Fixed costs are $300,000 per period.

Required:

(a) The deficiency in machine hours for the next period is _____ hours.

(b) The optimum production plan that will maximise ABC's profit for the next period is:

Product A [   ] units

Product B [   ] units

Product C [   ] units

12 Make or buy decisions

Businesses may be faced with the decision about whether to make components or products themselves (in-house) or to obtain these from outside suppliers.

If the items are bought in from external suppliers, their purchase cost is wholly marginal (i.e. direct). However, if it is decided to manufacture the items internally, the comparative costs of doing so will be the **variable production cost** (direct materials and direct labour costs, plus the variable factory overhead). Allocated fixed costs will not be relevant to the decision as they will not change, but any **specific** or **avoidable** fixed costs incurred in the production of the item under consideration would be included as part of the internal manufacturing cost.

Note: Relevant costing principles are behind all decisions, remember to look out for opportunity costs.

If the total internally manufactured cost is greater than the cost of obtaining similar items elsewhere, it is obviously uneconomic to produce these items internally and they would be purchased externally. An item should be made in-house only if the relevant cost of making the product in-house is less than the cost of buying the product externally.

If spare capacity exists:

The relevant cost of making the product in-house = the variable cost of internal manufacture plus any fixed costs directly related to that product.

If no spare capacity exists:

The relevant cost of making the product in-house = the variable cost of internal manufacture plus any fixed costs directly related to that product **plus** the opportunity cost of internal manufacture (e.g. lost contribution from another product).

Illustration 7 – Make or buy decision

XYZ manufactures three components (A, B and C) All the components are manufactured using the same general purpose machinery. The following production cost data are available, together with the purchase prices from an outside supplier.

	A	B	C
Production cost:	$	$	$
Direct material	14	20	10
Direct labour	24	13	12
Variable overhead	8	7	8
Allocated fixed overhead	9	6	4
Total	55	46	34
Purchase price from outside supplier	54	50	28

Which, if any, components should be purchased from the outside supplier?

Solution:

When comparing internal production costs and external buy in costs, the relevant cost to use for the internal production cost is the **variable cost of production**.

	A	B	C
	$	$	$
Internal production cost (variable production costs only)	46	40	30
Purchase price from outside supplier	54	50	28
Incremental (cost)/saving	(8)	(10)	2

In this case, XYZ should purchase component C externally. Components A and B should be manufactured internally.

Test your understanding 13

Following on from Illustration 7, further details of A, B and C are now available:

	A	B	C
Machine hours per unit	2	5	4

The external price of C has risen to $42.

Manufacturing requirements show a need for 1,500 units of each component per week. The maximum number of general purpose machinery hours available per week is 15,000.

What should be purchased from the outside supplier?

13   Chapter summary

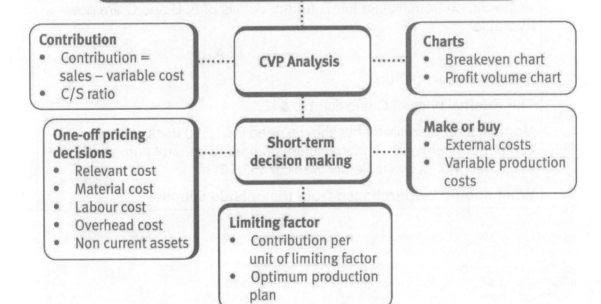

Breakeven analysis

- Breakeven sales units = $\dfrac{\text{Total fixed costs}}{\text{Contribution per unit}}$

- Breakeven sales revenue = $\dfrac{\text{Total fixed costs}}{\text{C/S ratio}}$

- Margin of safety (units) = Projected sales – Breakeven sales

- Margin of safety (%) = $\dfrac{\text{Projected sales – Breakeven sales}}{\text{Projected sales}}$

- Sales revenue for $X of profit = $\dfrac{\text{Total fixed costs} + \$X}{\text{C/S ratio}}$

Contribution
- Contribution = sales – variable cost
- C/S ratio

CVP Analysis

Charts
- Breakeven chart
- Profit volume chart

One-off pricing decisions
- Relevant cost
- Material cost
- Labour cost
- Overhead cost
- Non current assets

Short-term decision making

Make or buy
- External costs
- Variable production costs

Limiting factor
- Contribution per unit of limiting factor
- Optimum production plan

14   End of chapter questions

Question 1

A summary of a manufacturing company's budgeted statement of profit or loss for the next financial year is given below:

	$	$
Sales 9,000 units at $32		288,000
Production costs		
Direct materials	54,000	
Direct wages	72,000	
Fixed production overhead	42,000	
Variable production overhead	18,000	
		186,000
Gross profit		102,000
Non-production costs		
Fixed	36,000	
Variable	27,000	
		63,000
Operating profit		39,000

Calculate:

(a)   The breakeven point in units. _____ units

(b)   The number of units which must be sold to achieve a profit of $45,500. _____ units

Question 2

A contract is under consideration that requires 800 labour hours. There are 450 hours of spare labour capacity for which the workers are still being paid the normal rate of pay. The remaining hours required for the contract can be found either by overtime working paid at 50% above the normal rate of pay or by diverting labour from the manufacture of product OT.

If the contract is undertaken and labour is diverted, then sales of product OT will be lost. Product OT takes seven labour hours per unit to manufacture and makes a contribution of $14 per unit. The normal rate of pay for labour is $8 per hour.

What is the total relevant labour cost for the contract?

A $3,500

B $4,200

C $4,500

D $4,900

Question 3

A manufacturer of mobile phones is considering the following actions.

Tick whether the action will increase or decrease their C/S ratio.

	Increase in C/S ratio	Decrease in C/S ratio
Taking advantage of quantity discounts for bulk purchases of material		
Introducing training programmes designed to improve labour efficiency		
Following the actions of a competitor who has cut prices substantially		
Reducing exports to countries where there is intense price competition		
Offering retailers a lower price if they display the product more prominently		

Question 4

Match the following terms with the labels **a** to **d** on the graph. Write a, b, c or d in the relevant boxes.

	Margin of safety
	Fixed cost
	Contribution
	Profit

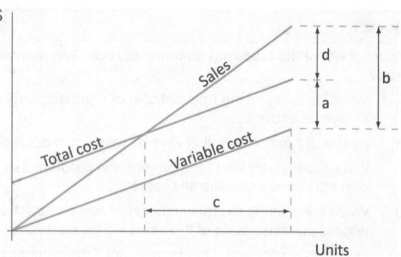

Question 5

Select **true** or **false** for each of the following statements about a profit–volume chart.

(a)   The profit line passes through the origin.

    True   ❑

    False   ❑

(b)   Other things being equal, the gradient of the profit line becomes steeper when the selling price increases.

    True   ❑

    False   ❑

(c)   Contribution cannot be read directly from the chart.

    True   ❑

    False   ❑

(d)   The point where the profit line crosses the vertical axis is the breakeven point.

    True   ❑

    False   ❑

(e) Fixed costs are shown as a line parallel to the horizontal axis.

True ☐

False ☐

(f) The gradient of the profit line is directly affected by the P/V ratio.

True ☐

False ☐

Question 6

Which TWO of the following statements regarding relevant costs are true?

A When considering the relevant cost of a project, sunk costs should always be excluded.

B Allocated fixed costs will always be relevant in decision making.

C If the material required for a project is in constant use, the relevant cost will be the net realisable value.

D When considering the relevant cost of non-current assets, the original purchase price of the asset will be irrelevant.

E Opportunity cost would not be relevant if the company had spare capacity.

Question 7

XYZ manufactures three products, the selling price and cost details of which are given below:

	Product X	Product Y	Product Z
	$	$	$
Selling price per unit	75	95	95
Costs per unit:			
Direct materials	10	5	15
Direct labour	16	24	20
Variable overhead	8	12	10
Fixed overhead	24	36	30

In a period when direct materials are restricted in supply, the most and the least profitable uses of direct materials are:

	Most profitable	Least profitable
A	X	Z
B	Y	Z
C	Z	Y
D	Y	X

Question 8

PQR manufactures a number of products including the XZ. Currently PQR has spare capacity in its factory. A supermarket chain has offered to buy a number of units of product XZ each month, and this would utilise the spare capacity. The supermarket is offering to purchase XZ at a price of $8 per unit. The cost structure of XZ is as follows:

	$ per unit
Direct material	3
Direct labour	2
Variable overhead	1
Fixed overhead	3
	9

Fixed costs would not be affected by the supermarket contract.

On a purely financial basis, the supermarket's offer should be accepted/rejected. Delete as appropriate.

Question 9

OPQ manufactures three products. Production cost details per unit are given:

	R	S	T
Direct material (kg)	10	12	6
Direct labour ($)	20	16	12
Specific fixed costs ($)	4	2	–
Allocated fixed overhead ($)	13	16	21

The direct material cost per kg is $2.50 and variable production overheads are 150% of direct labour.

An external company has offered to provide the 3 products for:

R: $75

S: $75

T: $50

State which products should be purchased externally:

	Yes	No
R	❑	❑
S	❑	❑
T	❑	❑

Question 10

The following information is available for a product:

Margin of safety	5,000
C/S ratio	60%
Selling price per unit	$10

Budgeted fixed costs are $120,000 for the year.

Required:

Calculate the budgeted sales volume for the year. _____ units

Test your understanding and end of chapter answers

Test your understanding 1

(a) **The relevant cost per kg is $2.00**

The material is in inventory and is used regularly. It will therefore be replaced. The relevant cost per kg is therefore the current purchase cost of $2.00.

(b) **The relevant cost is $800**

The materials are in inventory, but are no longer in use therefore will not be replaced. There is no alternative use for the material, therefore the relevant cost will be the net realisable value of $0.80 per kg. The relevant cost of material = 1,000 kg × $0.80 = $800.

Test your understanding 2

$9,000 should be charged to the contract

The only alternative use for the material held in inventory is to sell it for scrap. To use 25 kg on the contract is to give up the opportunity of selling it for:

25 × $150 = $3,750

The organisation must then purchase a further 25 kg, and assuming this is in the near future, it will cost $210 per kg.

The contract must be charged with:

	$
25 kg × $150	3,750
25 kg × $210	5,250
	9,000

Test your understanding 3

The relevant labour cost for XYZ's job = **$600**.

Skilled workers – 20 hours required.

Minimum weekly wage covers $450/$15 = 30 hours work.

Each worker is currently working 24 hours, therefore has 6 hours per week spare capacity which is already paid for.

In total, the four workers will have 6 × 4 = 24 hours available, which is sufficient for the job. Relevant cost is therefore = **$0**.

Semi-skilled workers – 50 hours required.

There is no spare capacity, therefore either additional staff must be hired, or overtime must be worked.

Hiring additional staff will cost $12 per hour.

Working overtime will cost: $10 × 1.5 = $15 per hour.

It is therefore cheaper to hire additional workers. Relevant cost is therefore = 50 hours × $12 = **$600**.

Test your understanding 4

The relevant cost of using the skilled labour on the project is $85,000

Using the decision tree, spare capacity does not exist, and no additional labour can be hired so the labour must be taken from the existing activity.

How much contribution is lost if the labour is transferred from the existing activity?

	$
Contribution per hour lost	3
PLUS: labour cost per hour	14
Relevant cost per labour hour	17
The relevant cost of using the skilled labour on the project is 5,000 hours × $17	$85,000

Test your understanding 5

The relevant cost of the equipment is $2,000.

The asset will not be replaced, but it could be sold now for $2,000. If not sold now, it would have no other value. Therefore the relevant cost is the opportunity cost = **$2,000**.

Test your understanding 6

The breakeven number of units is **2,200**.

Contribution = $95 − ($36 + $12 + $9 + $13) = $25

$$\text{Breakeven point in units} = \frac{\text{Fixed costs}}{\text{Contribution per unit}}$$

$$= \frac{\$55,000}{\$25} = \textbf{2,200 units}$$

Test your understanding 7

To the nearest whole number, the margin of safety, as a percentage of planned sales is **60%**.

First calculate the monthly fixed costs: 4,000 units × $4 = $16,000.

Then calculate the contribution per unit: sales − variable costs = (18 − 8) = $10.

Then calculate the breakeven point in units:

$$\text{Breakeven point in units} = \frac{\text{Fixed costs}}{\text{Contribution per unit}}$$

$$= \frac{\$16,000}{\$10} = 1,600 \text{ units}$$

$$\text{Margin of safety \%} = \frac{\text{Projected sales − breakeven sales}}{\text{Projected sales}}$$

$$= \frac{4,000 − 1,600}{4,000} = \textbf{60\%}$$

Test your understanding 8

(i) the breakeven point, in sales units per month is **500 units**

(ii) the margin of safety for next month is **1,700 units**

(iii) the budgeted profit for next month is **$81,600**

(iv) the sales units required to achieve a profit of $96,000 in a month is **2,500 units**

Workings:

(i) To calculate the breakeven point, first determine the contribution per unit.

Contribution = $120 – ($22 + $36 + $14) = $48

$$\text{Breakeven point} = \frac{\textbf{Fixed costs}}{\textbf{Contribution per unit}}$$

$$= \frac{\$12 \times 2,000}{\$48} = \textbf{500 units}$$

Note: The fixed costs are based on the budgeted level of output.

(ii) Margin of safety = Projected sales – Breakeven sales

= 2,200 – 500

= **1,700 units**

(iii) Once the breakeven point has been reached, all of the contribution goes towards profits because all of the fixed costs have been covered.

Budgeted profit = 1,700 units margin of safety

× $48 contribution per unit

= **$81,600**

(iv) To achieve the desired level of profit, sufficient units must be sold to earn a contribution which covers the fixed costs and leaves the desired profit for the month.

$$\textbf{Sales units required for a profit of X} = \frac{\textbf{(Fixed costs + X)}}{\textbf{Contribution per unit}}$$

$$= \frac{(\$12 \times 2,000) + \$96,000}{\$48}$$

$$= \textbf{2,500 units}$$

Test your understanding 9

A   Total sales revenue for 1,000 hours of service = **$50,000** (1,000 hours × $50 selling price)

B   Fixed cost at zero activity = **$15,000** (1,000 hours × $15 fixed overhead absorption rate)

C   Profit for 1,000 hours = **$15,000** (1,000 hours × $15 profit per hour)

D   Breakeven point = **500 hours** (see workings below)

E   Margin of safety = **500 hours** (1,000 hours – 500 hours)

Workings:

$$\text{Breakeven point} = \frac{\text{Fixed costs}}{\text{Contribution per hour}} = \frac{\$15,000}{\$30} = \textbf{500 hours}$$

Test your understanding 10

(a) (i)   **–$120,000** (The profit line cuts the vertical axis at the point equal to the fixed costs, that is, the loss when no sales are made)

(ii)   **$240,000** (The profit line cuts the horizontal axis at the breakeven point)

(iii)   **$60,000** (The margin of safety is the difference between the projected sales and the breakeven level of sales)

Workings:

Total fixed costs = $40,000 + $60,000 + $20,000 = **$120,000**

C/S ratio = (300,000 – 100,000 – 10,000 – 40,000)/300,000 = 50%

$$\textbf{Breakeven point} = \frac{\text{Fixed costs}}{\text{C/S ratio}} = \frac{\$40,000 + 60,000 + 20,000}{0.5} = \textbf{\$240,000}$$

Margin of safety = Projected sales – Breakeven sales

= $300,000 – $240,000 = **$60,000**

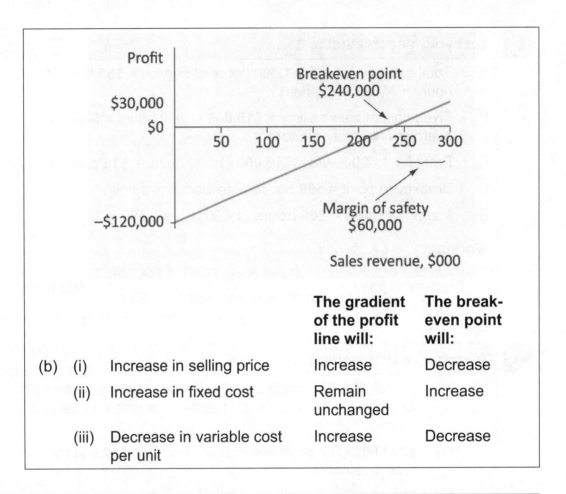

			The gradient of the profit line will:	The break-even point will:
(b)	(i)	Increase in selling price	Increase	Decrease
	(ii)	Increase in fixed cost	Remain unchanged	Increase
	(iii)	Decrease in variable cost per unit	Increase	Decrease

Test your understanding 11

B

Labour hours required for maximum demand = (380 units × 0.5 hours) + (520 units × 1.5 hours) + (240 units × 1 hour) = 1,210 hours

Since 1,300 hours are available, labour is not a limiting factor.

Material required for maximum demand = (380 units × 1.5 kg) + (520 units × 1.25 kg) + (240 units × 2 kg) = 1,700 kg

Since only 1,450 kg is available, **material is the limiting factor**.

Test your understanding 12

(a)   Deficiency in machine hours for next period is **13,000 hours**

	Product A	Product B	Product C	Total
Machine hours per unit	48/8 = 6	32/8 = 4	56/8 = 7	
Maximum demand (units)	3,000	2,500	5,000	
Total machine hours to meet maximum demand	18,000	10,000	35,000	63,000
Machine hours available				50,000
				———
Deficiency of machine hours				13,000
				———

(b)   To maximise profits, the company should make:

Product A – **3,000 units**

Product B – **2,500 units**

Product C – **3,142 units**

	Product A $	Product B $	Product C $
Selling price per unit	200	158	224
Variable cost per unit	(154)	(112)	(178)
	———	———	———
Contribution per unit	46	46	46
	———	———	———
Machine hours per unit	6	4	7
Contribution per machine hour	$7.67	$11.50	$6.57
Ranking	**2**	**1**	**3**

Therefore, make

	Machine hours
2,500 units of product B (4 × 2,500)	10,000
3,000 units of product A (6 × 3,000)	18,000
	———
	28,000
3,142 units of product C (balance = 22,000/7)	22,000
	———
	50,000
	———

Test your understanding 13

300 units of B should be purchased externally

	A	B	C
Variable production cost	$46	$40	$30
External cost	$54	$50	$42
Incremental cost	($8)	($10)	($12)
Hours per unit	2	5	4
Incremental cost per hour	($4)	($2)	($3)
Ranking – lowest cost	**3rd**	**1st**	**2nd**

It is now cheaper to make ALL the components within the factory, however there is a limit on the number of machinery hours available.

First check if all components can be made in house:

Hours required to make 1,500 units of each component:

(1,500 × 2) + (1,500 × 5) + (1,500 × 4) = 16,500 hours

The company only has 15,000 hours available. So, 1,500 hours of work must be sub-contracted. The CHEAPEST component per hour should be bought externally. This is component B.

1,500 hours of time on B equates to 1,500 ÷ 5 = 300 units of B to be purchased externally.

Question 1

(a) The breakeven point in units is **6,000 units**.

(b) The number of units which must be sold to achieve a profit of $45,500 is **9,500 units**.

Workings:

(a) First calculate the contribution per unit.

Contribution = Sales – Variable costs

Total contribution = 288,000 – (54,000 + 72,000 + 18,000 + 27,000) = $117,000

Contribution per unit = $117,000/9,000 units = $13

Now you can use the formula to calculate the breakeven point:

$$\text{Breakeven point} = \frac{\text{Fixed costs}}{\text{Contribution per unit}}$$

$$= \frac{\$42,000 + \$36,000}{\$13} = \textbf{6,000 units}$$

(b) In this case the contribution must be sufficient to cover both the fixed costs and the required profit. If we divide this amount by the contribution earned from each unit, we can determine the required sales volume.

$$\text{Required sales} = \frac{\text{Fixed costs} + \text{Required profit}}{\text{Contribution per unit}}$$

$$= \frac{(\$42,000 + \$36,000 + \$45,500)}{\$13} = \textbf{9,500 units}$$

Question 2

A

800 labour hours are required. The relevant cost must be considered in two parts:

Spare capacity: 450 hours of spare capacity exists. The relevant cost for these 450 hours would be **$0** as the workers are being paid whether they work these hours or not.

No spare capacity: a further 350 hours are required for the contract. Either workers need to be diverted from the production of product OT, or overtime must be worked.

The relevant cost of diverting workers from the manufacture of product OT will be the contribution lost per hour plus the direct labour rate:

Contribution lost per hour ($14 ÷ 7 hours) $2 + Direct labour rate $8 = $10 per hour

Working overtime will cost: $8 + 50% = $12 per hour

It is therefore cheaper to divert workers from the manufacture of product OT. The relevant cost is therefore 350 hours × $10 = **$3,500**.

Question 3

	Increase in C/S ratio	Decrease in C/S ratio
Taking advantage of quantity discounts for bulk purchases of material	✓	
Introducing training programmes designed to improve labour efficiency	✓	
Following the actions of a competitor who has cut prices substantially		✓
Reducing exports to countries where there is intense price competition	✓	
Offering retailers a lower price if they display the product more prominently		✓

Taking advantage of quantity discounts for bulk purchases of material will result in lower variable costs per unit and a higher contribution per unit.

Introducing training programmes designed to improve labour efficiency will result in lower variable costs per unit and higher contribution per unit.

Following the actions of a competitor who has cut prices substantially will result in lower selling price per unit and lower contribution per unit.

Reducing exports to countries where there is intense price competition will result in higher average contribution per unit.

Offering retailers a lower price if they display the product more prominently will result in lower selling price per unit and lower contribution per unit.

Question 4

c	Margin of safety
a	Fixed cost
b	Contribution
d	Profit

Question 5

(a) **False.** The profit line passes through the breakeven point on the horizontal axis, and cuts the vertical axis at the point where the loss is equal to the fixed costs.

(b) **True.** Profits increase at a faster rate if the selling price is higher.

(c) **True.** A contribution breakeven chart is needed for this.

(d) **False.** The point where the profit line crosses the vertical axis is the total loss, which is equal to the level of fixed costs. The breakeven point is where the profit line cuts the horizontal axis.

(e) **False.** No fixed cost line is shown on a profit–volume chart.

(f) **True.** The higher the P/V ratio or contribution to sales ratio, the higher will be the contribution earned per $ of sales and the steeper will be the gradient of the profit line.

Question 6

A and D.

When considering the relevant cost of a project, sunk costs should always be excluded. This is true as costs which have already been incurred will not change as a result of the decision being made.

Allocated fixed costs will always be relevant in decision making. This is false as fixed costs will only be relevant if the total fixed cost changes as a result of the decision being made.

If the material required for a project is in constant use, the relevant cost will be the net realisable value. This is false because if material is in constant use, the material used in the project will have to be replaced, so the relevant cost will be the replacement cost.

When considering the relevant cost of non-current assets, the original purchase price of the asset will be irrelevant. This is true as the original purchase price will be a sunk cost.

Opportunity costs should always be included. Remember opportunity costs are the value of the benefit sacrificed when one course of action is chosen in preference to an alternative.

Question 7

B

	X	Y	Z
Contribution/unit (W1)	$41.00	$54.00	$50.00
$ of materials	$10	$5	$15
Contribution/$ material	$4.10	$10.80	$3.33
Ranking	2	1	3

(W1) Contribution/unit

X = $75 – ($10 + $16 + $8) = $41

Y = $95 – ($5 + $24 + $12) = $54

Z = $95 – ($15 + $20 + $10) = $50

Question 8

On a purely financial basis, the supermarket's offer should be accepted.

On a purely financial basis, the price of $8 per unit exceeds the variable cost of $6 per unit. Since the fixed cost would not be affected, the units sold to the supermarket will each earn a contribution of $2.

Question 9

Only R should be purchased externally. S and T are cheaper to produce in-house.

	R	S	T
Direct material	25	30	5
Direct labour	20	16	12
Variable overheads	30	24	18
Specific fixed costs	4	2	–
Total internal production cost	79	72	45
External purchase price	75	75	50

Question 10

The budgeted sales volume for the year is **25,000 units**

Budgeted sales volume = breakeven sales volume + margin of safety.

$$\text{Breakeven sales revenue} = \frac{\text{Fixed costs}}{\text{C/S ratio}}$$

$$= \frac{\$120,000}{0.6} = \$200,000$$

As selling price is $10 per units, breakeven sales units = $200,000/$10 = 20,000 units

So budgeted sales volume = 20,000 + 5,000 = **25,000 units**

Long-term decision making

Chapter learning objectives

Upon completion of this chapter you will be able to:

- explain the time value of money
- apply financial mathematics
- calculate the net present value, internal rate of return and payback for an investment or project.

1 Session content diagram

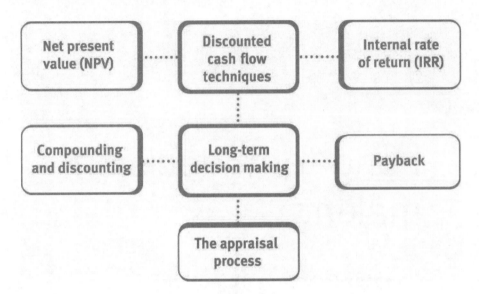

2 The capital investment process

In this chapter we will look at long term decision making, specifically capital investment decisions.

Capital investment decisions normally represent the most important decisions that an organisation makes, since they normally commit a substantial proportion of the organisation's resources to actions that are likely to be long-term or irreversible. Many different capital investment projects exist including: replacement of assets, cost reduction schemes, new product/service developments and product/service expansions. Some may be statutory; others may be carried out for growth or environmental reasons.

To appraise a potential capital project:

- Estimate the costs and benefits from the investment

- Select an appraisal method and use it to assess if the investment is financially worthwhile

- Decide whether or not to go ahead with the project.

It is important to note that the costs and benefits from the investment are estimates. Many take place in the future and many assumptions are made in calculating these figures. The costs and benefits for the investment are called **cash flows**. Remember that all the rules of relevant cost also apply to investment decisions; only **relevant cash flows** should be used.

Appraisal methods

There are a number of appraisal methods which are used to assess how financially worthwhile investments are. The three techniques covered in the *Fundamentals of Management Accounting* are:

- Payback.

- Net present value (NPV).

- Internal rate of return (IRR).

Each method uses a different calculation. It is important to know how to do each of the calculations, and the decision rule used in each. The different methods can give different answers. In practice, most organisations use more than one appraisal method.

Based on the decision rule of the method used, a decision can be made as to whether the investment is financially worthwhile, although there will be other, non-financial considerations which must also be taken into account.

3 Payback

The payback technique considers the time a project will take to pay back the money invested in it. It is based on expected cash flows and provides a measure of liquidity. Cash and profit are very different. When appraising a possible capital investment it is necessary to use the actual cash flows in and out of the business rather than profits as profits are subjective and cannot be spent. If provided with profit figures you would therefore be expected to make adjustments to get back to the actual cash flows, before calculating the payback period. Such adjustments might include:

- Adding back non-cash flow costs, such as depreciation
- Adding back notional costs, such as apportioned head-office costs

To use the payback technique a company must set a **target payback period**.

Decision criteria

- Compare the payback period to the company's target return time and if the payback for the project is quicker the project should be accepted.

- Faced with mutually exclusive projects choose the project with the quickest payback.

Illustration 1 – Payback example

JKL is considering purchasing a new machine. The machine will cost $550,000. The management accountant of JKL has estimated the following additional cash flows will be received over the next 6 years if the new machine is purchased:

Year 1: $40,000

Year 2: $65,000

Year 3: $140,000

Year 4: $175,000

Year 5: $160,000

Year 6: $70,000

JKL has a target payback period of 4 years.

Calculate the payback period for the new machine and advise JKL whether or not to proceed with the investment.

Solution:

Note: The investment is shown in year 0.

We treat year 0 as today and assume that the investment is made today. We show the initial investment as a negative cash flow for year 0.

Work out the **cumulative cash flow** for each year until the cash flow becomes positive. This will highlight when payback has been achieved.

Year	Cash flow	Cumulative cash flow
	$000	$000
0	(550)	(550)
1	40	(510)
2	65	(445)
3	140	(305)
4	175	(130)
5	160	30
6	70	100

You can see that payback is achieved between years 4 and 5.

The payback period is usually given in years and months. To calculate the payback in years and months you should go to the year where the cumulative cash flow becomes positive. In this case year 5, so payback is 4 years plus a number of months. To calculate the months, take the cumulative cash flow from the previous year (year 4) divided by the cash flow in the year (year 5), then multiply the decimal fraction of a year by 12 to calculate the number of months.

Note: The number of months calculated should be rounded up.

Here the cumulative cash flow becomes positive in year 5, so payback is 4 years plus (130/160 × 12) months = 4 years 10 months.

JKL have a target payback period of 4 years. The payback is after this target, so the advice to JKL would be to not undertake the investment.

Test your understanding 1

LMN are considering two projects. Both cost $450,000 and only one may be undertaken. LMN use the payback method for appraising investments and require payback within three years.

The details of the cash flows for the two projects are given:

Year	Project A	Project B
	$000	$000
1	200	50
2	150	120
3	100	190
4	50	310
5	20	260

Advise LMN which project they should undertake.

Test your understanding 2

BCD is considering a project which requires an initial investment of $500,000. The following profits have been forecast for the life of the project.

These profit figures have taken account of annual depreciation which has been calculated as $15,000 per annum.

Year	Profit
1	$90,000
2	$120,000
3	$150,000
4	$130,000

The company uses payback to appraise investments and requires a payback within 3 years.

Calculate the payback for the investment in years and months and advise if BCD should accept the project.

The payback for the investment is _____ years _____ months.

The investment should be accepted/rejected.

Constant annual cash flows

In some cases, the cash flows estimated for the project are the same each year. We call these **constant annual cash flows**. In these cases, the payback calculation can be simplified by using the following formula:

$$\text{Payback period} = \frac{\text{Initial investment}}{\text{Annual cash flow}}$$

Example

A project will cost $300,000. The annual cash flows are estimated at $90,000 per annum. Calculate the payback period.

$$\text{Payback period} = \frac{\text{Initial investment}}{\text{Annual cash flow}}$$

$$= \frac{\$300,000}{\$90,000} = \textbf{3.33 years}$$

In years and months: 3 years plus (0.33 × 12) = **3 years 4 months.**

Test your understanding 3

An investment of $1 million is expected to generate net cash inflows of $200,000 each year for the next 7 years.

Calculate the payback period for the project.

Advantages and disadvantages of payback

Advantages	Disadvantages
• Simple to understand. • Payback is a simple measure of risk. A project with a long payback period tends to be riskier than one with a short payback period. • Uses cash flows, not subjective accounting profits. • If payback is used in selecting projects, companies may avoid liquidity problems. • Attaches greater importance to cash flows in earlier years.	• It is not a measure of absolute profitability. • Ignores the time value of money. It assumes that $100 received in year 5 would be worth the same as $100 received in year 1. We will look at this in more detail later in the chapter. • Does not take account of cash flows beyond the payback period.

4 The time value of money

One characteristic of all capital expenditure projects is that the cash flows arise over the long term (a period usually greater than 12 months). This makes it necessary to carefully consider **the time value of money**.

 Money received today is worth more than the same sum received in the future, i.e. it has a time value – the sooner it is received the better (the more it is worth)

If you were offered $1,000 today or $1,000 in 2 years, you would select to receive the money now as you believe it is worth more. For example you could earn interest on $1,000 for the two years if you received and invested it now.

When we looked at the payback method, we recognised that one of its disadvantages was that it did not take account of the time value of money. The other two appraisal methods covered in this chapter (Net present value and Internal rate of return) take account of the time value of money. These methods achieve this by using **discounted cash flows** in their calculations.

Before looking at discounting, we have to firstly understand **compounding**.

Compounding

Compounding calculates the future value of a given sum invested today for a number of years. To compound a sum, the figure is increased by the amount of interest it would earn over the period. Interest is then also earned on interest gained in earlier periods.

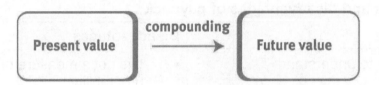

Illustration 2 – Compounding

$100 is invested in an account for five years. The interest rate is 10% per annum. Find the value of the account after five years.

For this calculation we are going to use **compound interest**. With compound interest we add interest to the initial figure in the first year. In the second year the interest is calculated on the initial figure plus the interest earned in the first year, and so on.

This can be compared to simple interest. With simple interest the interest is only ever calculated on the initial sum.

Using compound interest in our example:

If $100 is invested, by the end of the first year this will be worth:

Year 1: $100 + 10% = **$110**

If the $110 is now invested for a further year, by the end of the 2nd year it will be worth:

Year 2: $110 + 10% = **$121**

If this is continued for 5 years, at the end of 5 years it will be worth:

Year 3: $121 + 10% = **$133.10**

Year 4: $133.10 + 10% = **$146.41**

Year 5: $146.41 + 10% = **$161.05**

There is a formula to speed up this calculation:

Formula for compounding

$$V = X(1 + r)^n$$

Where: V = Future value

X = Initial investment (present value)

r = Interest rate (expressed as a decimal)

n = Number of time periods

Using the example from Illustration 2:

$$V = X(1 + r)^n$$
$$= 100(1 + 0.1)^5$$
$$= \$161.05$$

Test your understanding 4

$5,000 is invested in an account earning 2.75% interest p.a.

Calculate the account value after 12 years.

Test your understanding 5

$5,000 is invested for 10 years in an account earning 5% interest p.a.

Calculate how much this will be worth at the end of the 10 years.

Discounting

Discounting performs the opposite function to compounding. Compounding finds the future value of a sum invested now, whereas discounting considers a sum receivable in the future and establishes its equivalent value today. This value in today's terms is known as the **Present Value**.

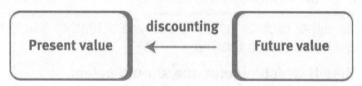

In investment projects, cash flows will arise at many different points in time. Calculating the present value of future cash flows will be a key technique in investment appraisal decisions.

Formula for discounting

The formula is simply a rearrangement of the compounding formula:

$$\text{Present value (X)} = \frac{\text{Future value (V)}}{(1 + r)^n}$$

This can be presented as:

$$\text{Present value} = \text{Future value} \times \frac{1}{(1 + r)^n}$$

or Present value = Future value $\times (1 + r)^{-n}$

Where $\dfrac{1}{(1 + r)^n}$ or $(1 + r)^{-n}$

is known as the **discount factor**

> We can therefore simplify the formula as:
>
> **Present value = Future value × Discount factor**

Illustration 3 – Discounting

How much should be invested now in order to have $250 in 8 years' time if the account pays 12% interest per annum?

Solution:

Present value = Future value × Discount factor

$= \$250 \times (1 + 0.12)^{-8}$

$= \$250 \times 0.404$

$= \mathbf{\$101}$

Test your understanding 6

Calculate the present value of $2,000 receivable in 6 years' time, if the interest rate is 10% p.a.

Test your understanding 7

Miss K can either receive $12,000 in 2 years' time or $14,000 in 4 years' time. The interest rate is 6% p.a.

Advise Miss K which receipt she should select.

Present value table

The discount factor, $(1 + r)^{-n}$ can be looked up in tables which are given in the assessment.

On the **present value table**, look along the top row for the interest rate and down the columns for the number of years, where the two intersect you can read off the discount factor.

Example

Consider a cash flow of $10,000 receivable 3 years from now. Using an interest rate of 7% we can calculate the present value as follows:

Present value $= 10,000 \times (1 + 0.07)^{-3}$

$= 10,000 \times 0.8163$

$= \mathbf{\$8,163}$

On the present value table, find the column for 7%, then look down to where this intersects with the row for 3 years. The discount factor given is **0.816**.

Note: There can be small differences due to rounding.

The present value table covers whole interest rates from 1% to 20% for years 1 to 20. If a question requires an interest rate which is not a whole number or is higher than 20%, or if the investment is for longer than 20 years, then the formula must be used to calculate the discount factor.

Note: At the top of the present value table, you are given the formula for calculating the discount factor.

Test your understanding 8

Now go back to Test your understandings 6 and 7 and check the calculations using the present value tables.

Interest rate

In the above calculations we have referred to the rate of interest (r). There are a number of alternative terms used to refer to the rate an organisation should use to take account of the time value of money:

- Cost of capital

- Discount rate

- Required return.

Whatever term is used, the rate of interest used for discounting reflects the cost of the finance that will be tied up in the investment.

The level of interest is affected by a number of factors such as risk and inflation and for how long you will not have access to your cash.

It is effectively a reward and we have assumed that you would rather have $1,000 today than $1,000 in one year's time. Having the $1,000 now gives certainty. If you cannot get the money for one year, there is a risk that you may not receive it. In addition if inflation is present then $1,000 in a year's time will buy less than $1,000 today. Interest is a way of compensating you for these factors. The higher the risk, the higher the inflation and the longer you are denied access to your money, the higher the interest rate you would require in compensation.

Non-annual time periods

In all of our calculations so far (and it most of the questions that you will see in the examination) we have been dealing with cash flows that occur once per year. But there are many instances where cash flows may occur more than once per year. For example, loan repayments may be made monthly or cash receipts from an investment may come in on a quarterly basis. We therefore need to be able to deal with scenarios where the cash flows are non-annual.

The basic techniques will be the same (whether discounting, compounding etc.). But to cope with non-annual periods we need to use a non-annual interest rate.

This converts the annual rate into, say, a monthly or quarterly rate by applying the following formula:

$$\text{Non-annual rate} = (1 + r)^{n/12} - 1$$

Where: r = Annual interest rate (expressed as a decimal)

              n = How often the cash flow occurs

For example, if the annual interest rate is 10% and cash flows are paid monthly, the monthly cost of capital would be calculated as

Non-annual rate = $(1 + 0.1)^{1/12} - 1 = 0.008 = 0.8\%$

Or if the cash flows were received every 3 months the 3 monthly rate would be

Non-annual rate = $(1 + 0.1)^{3/12} - 1 = 0.024 = 2.4\%$

The technique for discounting and compounding would then be applied using these non-annual rates.

Example

An investor will deposit $4,000 today. The annual interest rate is 18% p.a. but interest will be paid on a monthly basis and the interest rate will be time apportioned. What will be the value of the deposit after 6 months?

Firstly, we need to calculate the monthly interest rate:

Monthly rate = $(1 + 0.18)^{1/12} - 1 = 1.4\%$

Then we apply the normal compounding technique to grow the value of the deposit up by 6 months/periods:

$$
\begin{aligned}
V &= X(1 + r)^n \\
&= 4,000 \times (1 + 0.014)^6 \\
&= \$4,348
\end{aligned}
$$

Test your understanding 9

A project will return $60,000 every 6 months for two years. The annual cost of capital is 14%.

What is the present value of these returns

Investment appraisal using discounted cash flow

We can now move on to the investment appraisal methods which use discounting. The two methods which use discounted cash flow (DCF) techniques are:

- **Net Present Value (NPV)**
- **Internal Rate of Return (IRR).**

5 Net Present Value (NPV)

Typically an investment opportunity will involve a significant capital outlay initially with cash benefits being received in the future for several years. To compare all these cash flows on a like for like basis it is usual practice to convert all future cash flows into present values. Hence a net present value can be established.

The NPV represents the surplus funds (after funding the investment) earned on the project. This tells us the impact the project has on shareholder wealth.

Decision criteria

- Any project with a positive NPV is viable. It will increase shareholder wealth

- Faced with mutually-exclusive projects, choose the project with the highest NPV.

Initial assumptions in NPV calculations:

- All cash inflows and outflows are known with certainty.

- All cash flows are assumed to occur at the end of the year.

- Sufficient funds are available to undertake all profitable investments.

- There will be no inflating of cash flows within the calculations and no tax. These elements will be considered in higher level subjects.

 Illustration 4 – NPV example

Consider the following cash flows for a project with an initial investment of $30,000.

Year	Cash flow
1	$5,000
2	$8,000
3	$10,000
4	$7,000
5	$5,000

If we added up all of the cash flows, the total is $35,000. Given the initial investment of $30,000, it looks like the project has generated an additional $5,000 (total cash inflows less initial investment), but this assumes that the $5,000 received in year 5 is worth exactly the same as the $5,000 received in year 1. We know that this is not the case due to the time value of money. The technique used here (total cash inflows less initial investment) is a sound one, but first we must discount all the cash flows back to the present value.

Assume an interest rate of 10%.

When you have a number of cash flows to discount, it is easier to use a table to lay out your workings:

Year	Cash flow ($)	Discount factor (10%)	Present value (future value × discount factor)
0	(30,000)	1	(30,000)
1	5,000	0.909	4,545
2	8,000	0.826	6,608
3	10,000	0.751	7,510
4	7,000	0.683	4,781
5	5,000	0.621	3,105
		NPV =	(3,451)

$5000 \times (1.1)^{-1}$

Note: The initial investment is shown as a negative in year zero. Year zero is today, so this figure is already in present day terms, therefore **the discount factor in year zero is always 1**.

We can now add the discounted cash flows in the present value column together as they are all in present value terms.

The present value of the total cash inflows less initial investment is called the **Net Present Value (NPV)**.

In this example the NPV is negative $3,451. The decision rule is that projects with a positive NPV should be accepted and those with a negative NPV should be rejected, therefore in this case **the project should be rejected**.

Test your understanding 10

MNO is considering two mutually exclusive projects with the following details:

	Project A ($000)	Project B ($000)
Initial investment	45	10
Scrap value in year 5	2	1
Cash flow year 1	20	5
Cash flow year 2	15	4
Cash flow year 3	10	3
Cash flow year 4	10	2
Cash flow year 5	10	2

Assume that the initial investment is made at the start of the project and the annual cash flows are at the end of each year. The scrap values should be treated as cash inflows in year 5.

Calculate the Net Present Value for Projects A and B if the cost of capital is 10%.

Year	Discount factor 10%	Project A		Project B	
		Cash flow $000	PV $000	Cash flow $000	PV $000
0					
1					
2					
3					
4					
5					

Using the NPV technique, recommend which project MNO should undertake.

Test your understanding 11

A project requires an initial investment of $500,000. The following cash flows have been estimated for the life of the project:

Year	Cash flow
1	$120,000
2	$150,000
3	$180,000
4	$160,000

Using a discount rate of 7%, calculate the NPV of the project and recommend whether the project should be undertaken.

Advantages and disadvantages of NPV

Advantages	Disadvantages
• Considers the time value of money.	• Fairly complex.
• It is a measure of absolute profitability.	• Not well understood by non-financial managers.
• Uses cash flows and not subjective accounting profits.	• It may be difficult to determine the cost of capital.
• Considers the whole life of the project.	
• Should maximise shareholder wealth.	

Advantages and disadvantages of NPV

When appraising projects or investments, NPV is considered to be superior (in theory) to most other methods. This is because it:

- Discounting cash flows back to present value takes account of the impact of interest. This is ignored by the payback method.

- The NPV of an investment provides an absolute number that represents the actual surplus raised by the project. This allows a business to plan more effectively.

- The subjectivity of profits makes them less reliable than cash flows used in NPV and therefore less appropriate for decision making.

- Methods such as payback only consider the earlier cash flows associated with the project. NPV takes account of all relevant flows. Discounting the flows takes account of the fact that later flows are less reliable.

- Accepting projects with positive NPVs should lead to the maximisation of shareholder wealth. If the cost of capital reflects the shareholders' required return then the NPV reflects the theoretical increase in their wealth. For a commercial company, this is considered to be the primary objective of business.

However there are several potential drawbacks:

- It is difficult to explain to managers. To understand the meaning of the NPV calculation requires an understanding of discounting. The method is not as intuitive as methods such as payback.

- It requires knowledge of the cost of capital. The calculation of the cost of capital is, in practice, a complex calculation.

- It is relatively complex. For the reasons explained above NPV may be rejected in favour of simpler techniques.

6 Annuities and perpetuities

In the special case where a project has equal annual cash flows, the discounted cash flow can be calculated in a quicker way. There are two types of equal annual cash flows:

Annuity – a constant annual cash flow for a number of years

Perpetuity – a constant annual cash flow that continues indefinitely.

Here we are presuming that the investment occurs today (T_0) and the cash flows will be starting in one year's time (T_1).

Annuities

When a project has equal annual cash flows for a number of years the **annuity factor** may be used to discount the cash flows.

The annuity factor (AF) is the name given to the sum of the individual discount factors.

The PV of an annuity can therefore be quickly found using the formula:

PV = Annual cash flow × AF

As when calculating a discount factor, the annuity factors (AF) can be found using an annuity formula:

The formula is:

$$AF = \frac{1 - (1 + r)^{-n}}{r}$$

Where

r = cost of capital

n = the number of periods

Annuity factors, like discount factors, can also be found on a table. The annuity (cumulative present value) table is given in the assessment. In this table the annuity factor assumes that cash flows start in year 1. Remember our earlier assumption that all cash flows occur at the end of the year. This is not always the case and will be looked at in more detail later in the chapter.

Example: What would be the annuity factor for a six-year annuity at 10%?

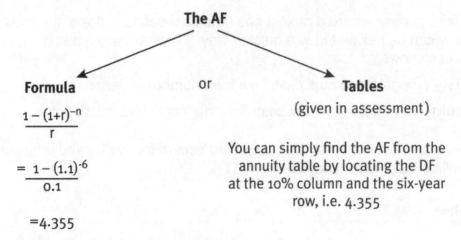

The AF

Formula	or	Tables
$\dfrac{1-(1+r)^{-n}}{r}$		(given in assessment)

Formula:

$$\dfrac{1-(1+r)^{-n}}{r}$$

$$= \dfrac{1-(1.1)^{-6}}{0.1}$$

$$=4.355$$

Tables (given in assessment):

You can simply find the AF from the annuity table by locating the DF at the 10% column and the six-year row, i.e. 4.355

Note: There can be small differences due to rounding.

Note: Annuity tables are titled cumulative present value tables in the assessment. The annuity formula is shown at the top of the cumulative present value table.

NPV example using annuities

P has been offered a project costing $30,000. The returns are expected to be $10,000 each year for 5 years. The cost of capital is 7%. Calculate the NPV of the project and recommend if it should be accepted.

Solution, using the normal discounting method:

Year	Cash flow ($)	Discount factor (7%)	Present value ($)
0	(30,000)	1	(30,000)
1	10,000	0.935	9,350
2	10,000	0.873	8,730
3	10,000	0.816	8,160
4	10,000	0.763	7,630
5	10,000	0.713	7,130
		NPV =	**11,000**

There is a lot of repetition as we multiply each of the discount factors by the same amount. If we add up all of the discount factors from years 1 to 5 we get 4.100. This is known as the 5 year **annuity factor**.

The annuity factor can be looked up on the cumulative present value table. Look along the top row for the interest rate (7%) and down the column for the number of years (5), where the two intersect you can read off the annuity factor (4.100). (there can be small differences due to roundings)

It would have been quicker to calculate the NPV as follows, using the annuity method.

Solution, using the annuity method:

Year	Cash flow ($)	Annuity factor (7%)	Present value ($)
0	(30,000)	1	(30,000)
1 – 5	10,000	4.100	41,000
		NPV =	**11,000**

In this case, the NPV is positive therefore **the project should be accepted**.

Illustration 5 – Comparing investments using annuities

A company is considering two annuities, both of which will involve the same purchase price.

- Annuity A pays $5,000 each year for 20 years, while
- Annuity B pays $5,500 each year for 15 years.

Receipts from both start in year 1.

Assuming an interest rate of 8%, which annuity would be preferred?

Solution:

Using tables, the cumulative PV factors are 9.818 for A and 8.559 for B. This gives:

- PV of annuity A = $5,000 × 9.818 = $49,090
- PV of annuity B = $5,500 × 8.559 = $47,075

Therefore annuity A is the better choice.

Note: You will only be able to use the tables given in your assessment if the period of the annuity is 20 years or less and if the rate of interest is a whole number between 1% and 20%. It is, therefore, essential that you practise using the formula as well. The formula is shown at the top of the cumulative PV table. You may notice some rounding, when tables are used.

Test your understanding 12

A payment of $3,600 is to be made every year for seven years, the first payment occurring in one year's time. The interest rate is 8%.

Calculate the present value of the annuity.

Test your understanding 13

A company is considering three options, only one of which can be undertaken. All three have the same initial outlay, but there are different revenue patterns available from each.

- Investment A pays $2,000 each year for the next 5 years.

- Investment B pays $1,000 in the first year, increasing by $500 each year until the final payment of $3,000 in the fifth year.

- Investment C pays $4,000 in the first year, $3,000 in the second year, and $2,000 in the third year.

Using an interest rate of 10%, which investment should the company select?

Perpetuities

While an annuity is a constant annual cash flow for a set number of years, a **perpetuity** is a constant annual cash flow which continues indefinitely.

It is often described as a cash flow continuing 'for the foreseeable future'.

The PV of a perpetuity is found using the formula:

$$PV = \frac{\text{cash flow}}{r}$$

'r' in the formula is the company's required rate of return (or cost of capital)

or

$$PV = \text{cash flow} \times \frac{1}{r}$$

$\frac{1}{r}$ is known as the perpetuity factor

Illustration 6 – Perpetuities

The present value of a perpetuity can be found using the formula:

$$PV = \text{cash flow} \times \frac{1}{r}$$

Where r = interest rate.

In order to earn a perpetuity of $2,000 per annum how much would need to be invested today? Assume an interest rate of 10%.

Solution:

Initial investment required = $2,000 ÷ 0.10 = **$20,000**

Test your understanding 14

An investment of $50,000 is expected to yield $5,670 per annum in perpetuity.

Calculate the net present value of the investment opportunity if the cost of capital is 9%.

Advanced annuities and perpetuities

In all of the examples we have considered so far the outlay, or initial investment occurs immediately (today). In our calculations we have shown this as Year 0 (or T0). Cash inflows start in Year 1 (T1). The use of annuity factors and perpetuity factors both assume that the first cash flow will be occurring in one year's time (T1).

It is possible that cash flows start **immediately (in year 0).** In this case we have to adjust our calculations.

Illustration – Advanced annuity

A 5-year $600 annuity is starting today. Interest rates are 10%. Find the present value of the annuity.

Solution:

If we consider the five receipts, this is essentially a standard 4-year annuity with an additional payment at T0. The present value could be calculated as follows:

	T_0	T_1	T_2	T_3	T_4
CF	600	600	600	600	600
PV	600	+		600 × 4-year 10% AF	

PV = 600 + (600 × 3.17) = 600 + 1,902 = $2,502

Remember from your NPV calculations, the discount factor for T0 = 1. Using this, the same answer can be found more quickly by adding 1 to the AF:

PV = 600 × (1 + 3.17) = 600 × 4.17 = $2,502.

Illustration – Advanced perpetuity

A perpetuity of $2,000 is due to commence immediately. The interest rate is 9%. What is the PV?

Solution:

This is essentially a standard perpetuity with an additional payment at T0. The PV could be calculated as follows:

T_0	T_1	T_2	T_3	T_4 ....
2,000	$2,000 \to \infty$			

PV (2,000) + (2,000 × 9% perpetuity factor)

2,000 + (2,000 × (1 ÷ 0.09)) = $24,222.

$$2,000 \times \left(1 + \frac{1}{0.09}\right) = 2,000 \times 12.11 = \$24,222$$

Delayed annuities and perpetuities

In the last example the cash flows started at T0. It is also possible that the cash flows are delayed and start later than T1.

Illustration – Delayed annuity

What is the PV of $200 received each year for four years, starting in three years' time, if the discount rate is 5%?

Solution:

Consider the cash flows:

T0	T1	T2	T3	T4	T5	T6
			200	200	200	200

Here, we cannot use the normal 4 year annuity factor as that includes years 1, 2, 3 and 4. In this case the receipts are for years 3, 4, 5 and 6.

Using the cumulative present value table, the annuity factor can be calculated as follows:

		years included
Annuity factor (6 years)	5.076	1, 2, 3, 4, 5, 6
less Annuity factor (2 years)	1.859	1, 2
	3.217	3, 4, 5, 6

The PV = $200 × 3.217 = **$643.40**

Illustration – Delayed perpetuity

What is the PV of a $300 perpetuity due to commence in year 2? Assume an interest rate of 6%.

Solution:

This would have the following cash flows:

T0	T1	T2	T3	T4......
		300→ ∞		

The PV of the perpetuity can be found by

$300 × (1 ÷ 0.06) = $5,000

But this assumes that the first receipt in year 1. We will therefore have to deduct the PV of the perpetuity for Year 1 which is ($300 × 0.943 = $282.90)

Therefore the PV of the perpetuity is $5,000 – $282.90 = **$4,717.10**.

Test your understanding 15

An entity has arranged a 10-year lease, at an annual rent of $8,000. The first rental payment has to be paid immediately, and the others are to be paid at the end of each subsequent year.

What is the present value of the lease at 12%?

A $50,624

B $53,200

C $45,200

D $65,288

Always read the questions carefully to make sure you base your calculations on the correct years.

7 Internal Rate of Return (IRR)

The next investment appraisal technique, which is linked to NPV, is Internal Rate of Return (IRR).

IRR calculates the rate of return at which the project has an NPV of zero. The IRR is compared to the company's cost of capital (this is the target rate).

Decision criteria

- If the IRR is greater than the cost of capital the project should be accepted.

- Faced with mutually exclusive projects choose the project with the higher IRR.

Graphs showing IRR

If we draw a graph showing the NPVs for a project at different discount rates we would typically get something like the following:

Note: Projects with unusual cash flow patterns can give different looking graphs, but we will focus on this more typical graph.

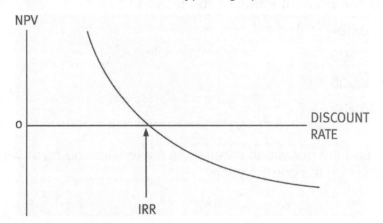

You can see that the IRR is found at the point where the curve intersects with the x axis.

Drawing an accurate graph to find IRR in this way is difficult so we can approximate IRR by assuming a linear relationship between NPV and the discount rate and using interpolation.

We can calculate the NPV at two discount rates, and plot these on a graph. We can then draw a straight line between the points and interpolate to find the IRR (the discount rate at which NPV is zero).

On the following graph:

L = lower discount rate

H = higher discount rate

N_L = NPV at the lower discount rate

N_H = NPV at the higher discount rate.

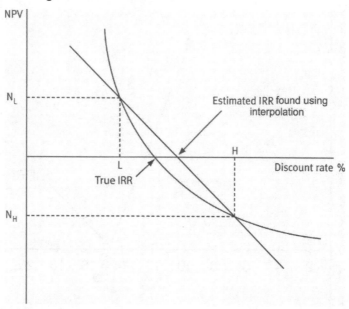

You can see that the IRR using the straight line is not the same as the 'true' IRR from the curve but we can use it as an approximation.

Calculating the two NPVs

When we calculate the NPV at the two different discount rates, ideally one should yield a small positive NPV and one should yield a small negative NPV. The closer the NPVs are to zero, the better our approximation of the IRR will be.

Remember the higher the discount rate, the lower the NPV so if your first NPV is positive, select a higher discount rate for the second one and vice versa.

Illustration 7 – Calculating IRR

Consider a project where the NPV at 10% has been calculated as $8.45m and the NPV at 16% has been calculated as –$1.71 m. Plotting these on a graph gives:

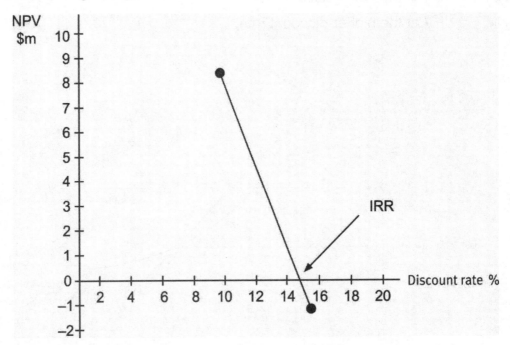

From this we can estimate the IRR in different ways:

Reading from the graph

Reading from the graph, we can estimate the IRR to be 15%.

Interpolating using proportions

When the discount rate dropped 6 percentage points (from 16% to 10%), the NPV dropped from $8.45m to –$1.71 m which is a drop of $10.16m. If we assume a linear relationship, then we can interpolate between the points. How far from 10% do we have to move along till NPV becomes zero?

From 10% we will have to move along the x axis by the proportion of (8.45 ÷ 10.16), that is (8.45 ÷ 10.16 × 6%) = 5%. So 10% + 5% means that we will have an NPV of zero at a rate of approximately 15%.

Formula method

You can also calculate the IRR using the following formula:

$$IRR \approx L + \frac{N_L}{N_L - N_H} (H - L)$$

where: L = lower discount rate

H = higher discount rate

N_L = NPV at the lower discount rate

N_H = NPV at the higher discount rate.

$$IRR \approx 10 + \frac{8.45}{8.45 - (-1.71)} (16 - 10)$$

IRR = **15%**

Note: This formula works whether or not one of the NPVs is positive and one negative. It can still be used if both are positive or both are negative.

Test your understanding 16

The NPV of a project has been calculated at two different discount rates:

At 10% the NPV is $13,725

At 15% the NPV is – $40,520

Calculate the IRR.

Calculating IRR with constant annual cash flows

In the same way that we can speed up the NPV calculation when we have constant annual cash flows, we can also speed up the IRR calculation in the same situation.

Illustration 8 – IRR with annuities

A company is considering investing in a project costing $100,000. It is expected that the project will generate cash flows of $45,000 in each of the next three years.

Calculate the IRR for the project.

Solution, using the annuity factor method:

When we have an annuity, there is a quicker method for calculating the IRR. This method involves using the cumulative present values tables and 'working backwards' to work out the discount rate.

We know that IRR is the discount rate when NPV = zero.

If we set up the NPV calculation with what we know:

Year	Cash flow $	DF	Present value $
0	(100,000)		
1–3	45,000		
		NPV =	

We are trying to work out the discount rate when NPV is zero. We know that the discount factor for year 0 is 1, so the present value of the investment is $(100,000). If we set the NPV to be zero, then the present value of the cash flows in years 1 – 3 must be $100,000.

Year	Cash flow $	DF	Present value $
0	(100,000)	1	(100,000)
1–3	45,000	?	100,000
		NPV =	0

From here we can work out what annuity factor we have used for years 1 to 3.

100,000 ÷ 45,000 = **2.222**

We can now use the cumulative present values tables to work out the interest rate this relates to. This will give us an approximate value for IRR.

On the cumulative present value table, go along the year 3 row until you find the annuity factor closest to 2.222. You will see that it lies **between 16% and 17%**.

This is a useful method as it can speed up IRR calculations where you have constant annual cash flows for a set period. It could also be used to calculate the interest rate of a bank loan if we know the equal instalments being repaid.

Example: A loan of $15,000 is being repaid over 4 years at a constant repayment amount of $360 per month.

Calculate the interest rate being charged on the loan.

The interest rate is approximately 6%.

Year	Cash flow $	DF	Present value $
0	(15,000)	1	(15,000)
1–4	360 × 12 = 4,320	?	15,000
		NPV =	0

The annuity factor used for years 1 to 4 = 15,000 ÷ 4,320 = 3.472.

We can now use the cumulative present values tables to estimate the interest rate this relates to.

From the cumulative present value table, go along the year 4 row until you find the annuity factor closest to 3.472. You will see that it lies close to 6%.

Illustration 9 – IRR with perpetuities

If the constant cash flow continues indefinitely, the following formula can be used to calculate the IRR:

$$IRR = \frac{\text{Annual cash inflow}}{\text{Initial investment}} \times 100$$

Example: Find the IRR of an investment costing $20,000 which is expected to generate a cash inflow of $1,600 for the foreseeable future.

$$IRR = \frac{1,600}{20,000} \times 100 = \textbf{8\%}$$

Test your understanding 17

A company is considering investing in a project costing $500,000.

Estimate the IRR for the project if the estimated cash flows are:

(a) $150,000 in each of the next five years.

(b) $90,000 in perpetuity.

Advantages and disadvantages of IRR

Advantages	Disadvantages
• Considers the time value of money.	• It is not a measure of absolute profitability.
• % measure therefore easy to compare projects of different sizes.	• Fairly complicated to calculate.
• Uses cash flows, not subjective accounting profits.	• Calculation only provides an estimate.
• Considers the whole life of the project.	
• Should maximise shareholder wealth.	

Advantages and disadvantages of IRR

IRR is closely linked to the NPV method and shares most of the advantages of NPV:

- Considers the time value of money. Discounting cash flows to present value takes account of the impact of interest. This is ignored by the payback method.

- Is based on cash flows not profits. The subjectivity of profits makes them less reliable than cash flows and therefore less appropriate for decision making.

- Considers the whole life of the project. Methods such as payback only considers the earlier cash flows associated with the project. As IRR is based on NPV, it takes account of all relevant flows. Discounting the flows takes account of the fact that later flows are less reliable.

- Should lead to the maximisation of shareholder wealth. If all projects which generate a rate of return higher than the cost of capital are accepted, this should increase shareholder's wealth. For a commercial company, this is considered to be the primary objective of business.

Where IRR differs from NPV is that it is a relative (%) measure rather than an absolute measure. This makes IRR easy to understand and aids comparisons between projects of different sizes.

However there are several potential drawbacks:

- It is difficult to explain to managers. To understand the meaning of IRR, users must first understand the NPV calculation and this requires an understanding of discounting. The method is not as intuitive as methods such as payback.

- The IRR calculation does not yield an exact answer, but is an approximation.

- Unlike NPV it is not an absolute measure. It does not give an indication of absolute profitability as NPV does.

- In some cases, IRR can be impossible to calculate.

Given the choice of methods, NPV is seen as the superior method.

N

8   Chapter summary

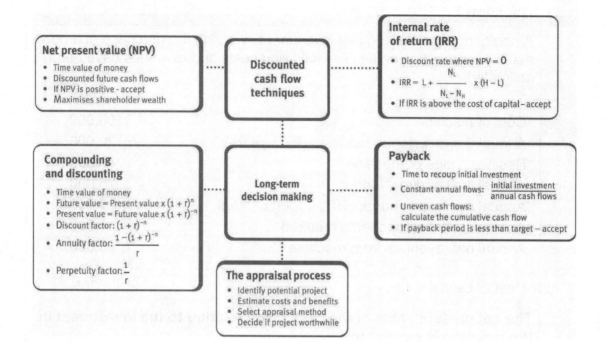

9 End of chapter questions

Question 1

A company is considering an investment involving the purchase of a new machine with a 3 year life. The following costs and revenues have been estimated:

	$
Cost of machine	100,000
Annual depreciation of machine (for 3 years)	20,000
Residual value of machine	40,000
Annual cost of direct labour	25,000
Annual overhead charge (10% apportionment)	7,000
Annual cost of components required	13,000
Annual net revenues from machine	80,000
Cost of capital	20%

The net present value of the cash flows relating to the investment in the machine is closest to:

A   ($13,000)

B   ($11,380)

C $11,620

D $22,370

Question 2

Which of the following statements regarding the internal rate of return are true? Select all that apply.

A   The internal rate of return is the interest rate that equates the present value of expected future net cash flows to the initial cost of the investment outlay.

B   If the internal rate of return for a project is greater than the company's cost of capital, the project should be accepted.

C   With mutually exclusive projects, the project with the lowest internal rate of return should be selected.

D   An advantage of internal rate of return is that it is an absolute measure.

E   If all projects with an internal rate of return higher than the company's cost of capital are accepted, this should lead to the maximisation of shareholder wealth.

Question 3

ABC receives a constant cash inflow of $12,000 per annum.

Using an interest rate of 6%, calculate the present value of the income, assuming the cash flow is received in perpetuity.

Question 4

A company is considering two projects. Both cost $900,000 and only one may be undertaken. The payback method for appraising investments is used and the company requires payback within 4 years.

The details of the cash flows for the two projects are given:

Year	Project A	Project B
	$000	$000
1	200	100
2	200	200
3	200	300
4	200	400
5	200	100

Using the payback method of investment appraisal, the company would select Project A/Project B. Delete as appropriate.

Question 5

Details of two projects are given.

Project A

Initial investment	$450,000				
Year:	1	2	3	4	5
Annual cash flows ($000)	250	150	100	100	100

Project B

Initial investment	$100,000					
Year:		1	2	3	4	5
Annual cash flows ($000)		50	40	30	20	20

The company has a cost of capital of 10%.

Required:

The NPV of project A is $ _____. The project should be accepted/ rejected. Delete as appropriate.

The NPV of project B is $ _____. The project should be accepted/ rejected. Delete as appropriate.

Question 6

A small company has a maximum of $15,000 to invest and two potential investments.

	Project A $000	Project B $000
Initial outlay	14	12
Inflow at end of:		
Year 1	7	10
Year 2	7	8
Year 3	7	5
Year 4	7	5
Year 5	7	5
Year 6	7	5

The prevailing rate of interest is 11%.

Compare the two potential investments and advise the company of which one to select.

The NPV of project A is $ _____.

The NPV of project B is $ _____.

The company should select project _____.

Question 7

What is the present value of $2,000 received every month for 6 months if the annual cost of capital is 79.6%?

Question 8

A project costing $1,000,000 has expected annual cash flows for the next 7 years of $240,000.

Using the annuity factor method, the IRR is closest to

A   13%

B   14%

C   15%

D   16%

Question 9

Consider the following characteristics of investment appraisal methods:

- Considers the whole project

- Uses the time value of money

- Uses cash flows

- It is a measure of absolute profitability.

Drag the characteristics under the appraisal method to which they relate.

Note: Characteristics can relate to more than one method.

Payback	NPV	IRR

Question 10

XYZ, a manufacturing company, is considering investing in a new machine costing $200,000. The machine will last for five years, after which time it will be able to be sold for scrap for $10,000.

Cash flows generated from the machine are estimated at $50,000 per year.

XYZ uses a cost of capital of 13%.

Complete the boxes A – E in the NPV calculation.

Year	Cash flow $	DF	Present value $
0	(200,000)	1	(200,000)
1–4	50,000	B	C
5	A	0.543	D
		NPV =	E

Question 11

Use both graphical and calculation methods to estimate the IRR for the following project.

Year	Cash flow ($000)
0	(100)
1	50
2	50
3	20

Test your understanding and end of chapter answers

LMN should undertake Project A.

Project A:

Year	0	1	2	3	4	5
Annual cash flow ($000)	(450)	200	150	100	50	20
Cumulative cash flow	(450)	(250)	(100)	0	50	70

Project B:

Year	0	1	2	3	4	5
Annual cash flow ($000)	(450)	50	120	190	310	260
Cumulative cash flow	(450)	(400)	(280)	(90)	220	480

LMN require a payback of 3 years.

Project A pays back in exactly 3 years

Project B pays back in 3 years plus (90/310 × 12) months = 3 years 4 months

Note: This question demonstrates a problem with using payback as an investment appraisal method. You can see from the above tables that Project B is in fact more financially worthwhile than Project A. Over the 5 years Project A has net cash flows of $70,000, while Project B has $480,000.

Using payback method, LMN would select Project A as it pays back the initial investment sooner. One of the problems with payback is that it does not take account of the cash flows over the whole project, but only looks at the cash flows up to the target payback period.

Test your understanding 2

The payback for the investment is **3 years 8 months**.

The investment should be **rejected**.

Year	Cash flow ($)	Cumulative cash flow ($)
0	(500,000)	(500,000)
1	90,000 + 15,000 = 105,000	(395,000)
2	120,000 + 15,000 = 135,000	(260,000)
3	150,000 + 15,000 = 165,000	(95,000)
4	130,000 + 15,000 = 145,000	50,000

To calculate cash flow from accounting profit, depreciation must be added back on.

Payback = 3 years + (95,000 ÷ 145,000 ×12) months = **3 years and 8 months**.

This is longer than the 3 year target so the investment should be **rejected**.

Test your understanding 3

The payback period is **5 years**.

$$\text{Payback period} = \frac{\text{Initial investment}}{\text{Annual cash flow}}$$

= 1,000,000/200,000 = **5 years**

Test your understanding 4

Future Value (V) = $5,000 $(1.0275)^{12}$ = **$6,923.92**

Test your understanding 5

Future Value (V) = $5,000 $(1.05)^{10}$ = **$8,144.47**

Test your understanding 6

Present value = **$1,129**

Present value = Future value × Discount factor

$= \$2{,}000 \times (1 + 0.10)^{-6}$

$= \$2{,}000 \times 0.5645 = $ **$1,129**

Test your understanding 7

It would be better to receive $14,000 in 4 years' time.

Receive $12,000 in 2 years' time:

Present value = Future value × Discount factor

$= \$12{,}000 \times (1 + 0.06)^{-2}$

$= \$12{,}000 \times 0.89 = $ **$10,680**

Receive $14,000 in 4 years' time:

Present value = Future value × Discount factor

$= \$14{,}000 \times (1 + 0.06)^{-4}$

$= \$12{,}000 \times 0.792 = $ **$11,088**

Test your understanding 8

Test your understanding 5:

The discount factor for 10%/6 years is 0.564.

Present value = Future value × Discount factor

$= \$2{,}000 \times 0.564 = $ **$1,128**

Test your understanding 6:

Receive $12,000 in 2 years' time:

The discount factor for 6%/2 years is 0.89.

Present value = Future value × Discount factor

$= \$12{,}000 \times 0.89 = $ **$10,680**

Receive $14,000 in 4 years' time:

The discount factor for 6%/4 years is 0.792.

Present value = Future value × Discount factor

$= \$14{,}000 \times 0.792 = $ **$11,088**

Test your understanding 9

The present value would be $204,154.

6 monthly rate = $(1 + 0.14)^{6/12} - 1 = 6.8\%$

Present value of future cash flows:

Timing	PV calculation	$
Period 1: 6 months	$60,000 \times (1 + 0.068)^{-1}$	56,180
Period 2: 12 months	$60,000 \times (1 + 0.068)^{-2}$	52,603
Period 3: 18 months	$60,000 \times (1 + 0.068)^{-3}$	49,253
Period 4: 24 months	$60,000 \times (1 + 0.068)^{-4}$	46,118
Total present value		204, 154

Test your understanding 10

Project A should be selected.

Both projects have positive NPVs, so both are worth doing but Project A has an NPV of $7,360 and Project B has an NPV of $3,330.

Year	Discount factor	Project A Cash flow $000	Project A Present value $000	Project B Cash flow $000	Project B Present value $000
0		(45)	(45)	(10)	(10)
1	0.909	20	18.18	5	4.55
2	0.826	15	12.39	4	3.30
3	0.751	10	7.51	3	2.25
4	0.683	10	6.83	2	1.37
5	0.621	10+2 = 12	7.45	2+1 = 3	1.86
		NPV =	**7.36**	**NPV =**	**3.33**

Test your understanding 11

The project has a positive NPV of $12,110, therefore **the project should be undertaken**.

Year	Cash flow ($)	Discount factor (7%)	Present value ($) (future value × discount factor)
0	(500,000)	1	500,000)
1	120,000	0.935	112,200
2	150,000	0.873	130,950
3	180,000	0.816	146,880
4	160,000	0.763	122,080
		NPV =	**12,110**

Test your understanding 12

$$\frac{1-(1+r)^{-n}}{r} = \frac{1-(1.08)^{-7}}{0.08} = 5.206$$

$3,600 × 5.206 = **$18,741.60**

Note that the annuity factor of 5.206 could have been taken straight from the cumulative present value tables.

Test your understanding 13

The investor should choose C as it has the highest NPV.

From tables, the cumulative present value factor for a constant inflow at 10% for 5 years is 3.791; therefore the NPV of investment A is:

$2,000 × 3.791 = **$7,582**

The other two investments do not involve constant inflows, and so the PVs for individual years have to be summed.

Year	PV factor	Investment B Cash flow ($)	PV ($)	Investment C Cash flow ($)	PV ($)
1	0.909	1,000	909.00	4,000	3,636.00
2	0.826	1,500	1,239.00	3,000	2,478.00
3	0.751	2,000	1,502.00	2,000	1,502.00
4	0.683	2,500	1,707.50	–	–
5	0.621	3,000	1,863.00	–	–
			7,220.50		7,616.00

In summary, the NPVs of investments are:

A: $7,582.00

B: $7,220.50

C: $7,616.00

Test your understanding 14

NPV = ($5,670 ÷ 0.09) − $50,000 = **$13,000**

Test your understanding 15

A

The payment starts in T0, therefore:

Present value = $8,000 + (present value of an annuity of $8,000 for 9 years at 12%)

= 8,000 + (8,000 × 5.328)

Present value = **$50,626**

Test your understanding 16

IRR ≈ 11.3%.

H = 15%

L = 10%

N_H = ($40,520)

N_L = $13,725

$$IRR \approx L + \frac{N_L}{N_L - N_H}(H - L)$$

$$IRR \approx 10 + \frac{13,725}{13,725 - (-40,520)} \times (15 - 10)$$

IRR ≈ 11.3%

The formula method has been used here, but it could also have been calculated using proportions.

Test your understanding 17

(a) **The IRR lies between 15% and 16%.**

Year	Cash flow $	DF	Present value $
0	(500,000)	1	(500,000)
1–5	150,000	?	500,000
		NPV =	**0**

The annuity factor used for years 1 to 5 = 500,000 ÷ 150,000 = 3.333

We can now use the cumulative present values tables to estimate the interest rate this relates to.

From the cumulative present value table, go along the year 5 row until you find the annuity factor closest to 3.333. You will see that it lies between 15% and 16%.

(b) IRR = **18%**

$$IRR = \frac{\text{Annual cash inflow}}{\text{Initial investment}} \times 100$$

$$= \frac{90,000}{500,000} \times 100 = \textbf{18\%}$$

Question 1

C

Remember only to use the relevant cash flows:

Revenue – Components – Labour = $80,000 – $13,000 – $25,000 = $42,000

Depreciation is excluded as it a non-cash item.

The apportionment of the overhead is also excluded as it is not an incremental cost.

The residual value is included as a cash flow in year 3.

Year	Cash flow $000	Discount factor (20%)	Present value ($000)
0	(100)	1	(100)
1	42	0.833	34.99
2	42	0.694	29.15
3	42 + 40 = 82	0.579	47.48
		NPV =	11.62

Net present value = **$11,620**

Question 2

A, B and E are true.

With mutually exclusive projects, the project with the lowest internal rate of return should be selected. This is false. With mutually exclusive projects, the project with the highest internal rate of return should be selected.

An advantage of internal rate of return is that it is an absolute measure. This is false. Internal rate of return is a relative measure.

Question 3

For a perpetuity of $12,000 per annum, discounted at 6%, the present value is 12,000 ÷ 0.06 = **$200,000**.

Question 4

Using the payback method of investment appraisal, the company would select **Project B**.

Project A:

As this project has constant cash flows, the payback can be calculated as follows:

$$\text{Payback period} = \frac{\text{Initial investment}}{\text{Annual cash flow}}$$

$$= \frac{\$900,000}{\$200,000} = \textbf{4.5 years}$$

$$= \textbf{4 years 6 months}$$

Project B:

Year	0	1	2	3	4	5
Annual cash flow ($000)	(900)	100	200	300	400	100
Cumulative cash flow	(900)	(800)	(600)	(300)	100	200

Project B pays back in 3 years plus (300/400 × 12) months = **3 years 9 months**

Question 5

The NPV of Project A is **$106,650**. The project should be **accepted**.

The NPV of Project B is **$27,100**. The project should be **accepted**.

Year	Discount factor (10%)	Project A		Project B	
		Cash flow $000	Present value $000	Cash flow $000	Present value $000
0		(450)	(450)	(100)	(100)
1	0.909	250	227.25	50	45.45
2	0.826	150	123.9	40	33.04
3	0.751	100	75.1	30	22.53
4	0.683	100	68.3	20	13.66
5	0.621	100	62.1	20	12.42
		NPV =	106.65	NPV =	27.10

Question 6

The NPV of Project A is **$15,617**.

The NPV of Project B is **$16,096**.

The company should select **Project B**.

Project A

Year	Cash flow $	DF	Present value $
0	(14,000)	1	(14,000)
1–6	7,000	4.231	29,617
		NPV =	15,617

Project B

Year	Cash flow $	DF	Present value $
0	(12,000)	1	(12,000)
1	10,000	0.901	9,010
2	8,000	0.812	6,496
3–6	5,000	2.518	12,590
		NPV =	16,096

Note: For project B, years 3 to 6 are constant so we have used the annuity factor for years 3 to 6. This is found by taking the 6-year annuity factor and subtracting the 2-year annuity factor. (4.231 – 1.713 = 2.518)

Question 7

The present value is **$10,152**.

Monthly rate = $(1 + 0.796)^{1/12} - 1 = 5\%$

From the tables, the 5% annuity factor for 6 periods is 5.076

The present value = 5.076 × $2,000 = $10,152

Question 8

C

Year	Cash flow $	DF	Present value $
0	(1,000,000)	1	(1,000,000)
1–7	240,000	4.167	1,000,000
		NPV =	0

The annuity factor we have used for years 1 to 7 = 1,000,000 ÷ 240,000 = **4.167**

We can now use the cumulative present values tables to work out the interest rate this relates to. This will give us an approximate value for IRR.

On the cumulative present value table, go along the year 7 row until you find the annuity factor closest to 4.167. You will see that it is very close to 15%.

Question 9

Payback	NPV	IRR
• Uses cash flows	• Considers the whole project • Uses the time value of money • Uses cash flows • It is a measure of absolute profitability	• Considers the whole project • Uses the time value of money • Uses cash flows

Question 10

The complete NPV calculation is shown below:

Year	Cash flow $	DF	Present value $
0	(200,000)	1	(200,000)
1–4	50,000	2.974	148,700
5	60,000	0.543	32,580
		NPV =	(18,720)

Question 11

Firstly calculate the NPV at two different discount rates.

Year	Cash flow ($000)	Discount factor 5%	Present value $000	Discount factor 15%	Present value $000
0	(100)	1	(100)	1	(100)
1	50	0.952	47.6	0.87	43.5
2	50	0.907	45.4	0.756	37.8
3	20	0.864	17.3	0.658	13.2
		NPV =	10.3	NPV =	(5.5)

Using the graph:

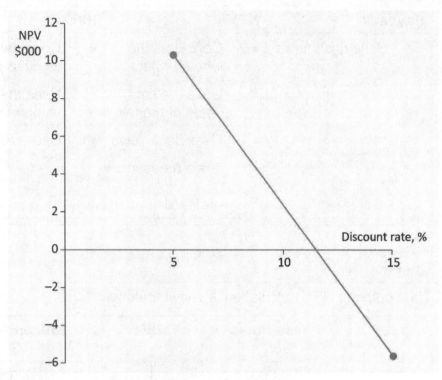

From the graph the estimate of IRR is **11.5%**

Using proportions:

When the discount rate dropped 10 percentage points (from 15% to 5%), the NPV dropped from $10,300 to -$5,500 which is a drop of $15,800.

From 5% we will have to move along the x axis by the proportion of ($10,300 ÷ $15,800), that is ($10,300 ÷ $15,800 × 10%) = 6.5%. So 5% + 6.5% means that we will have an NPV of zero at a rate of approximately **11.5%**.

Using the formula:

$$IRR \approx L + \frac{N_L}{N_L - N_H}\,(H - L)$$

$$IRR \approx 5 + \frac{10,300}{10,300 - (-5,500)} \times (15 - 5)$$

IRR = **11.5%**

Mock Assessment

Chapter learning objectives

This section is intended for use when you have completed your study and initial revision. It contains a complete mock assessment.

This should be attempted as an exam conditions, timed mock. This will give you valuable experience that will assist you with your time management and examination strategy.

CIMA Certificate in Business Accounting

Fundamentals of Management Accounting – BA2

You are allowed two hours to complete this assessment.

The assessment contains 60 questions.

All questions are compulsory.

Do not turn the page until you are ready to attempt the assessment under timed conditions.

Question 1

RST absorbs overheads based on units produced. In one period, 110,000 units were produced and the actual overheads were $500,000. Overheads were $50,000 over-absorbed in the period.

Calculate the overhead absorption rate (to the nearest cent).

$ _____ per unit.

Question 2

XYZ operates an integrated accounting system. The Work-in-Progress account at the end of the period showed the following information:

Work-in-Progress account

	$		$
Stores control a/c	100,000	X	200,000
Wages control a/c	75,000		
Production overhead a/c	50,000	Balance c/d	Y
	———		———
	225,000		Z
	———		———

Select the correct term to complete each sentence.

Entry X for $200,000 represents the value of the transfer to the Cost of sales account/ Sales account/ Finished goods account.

Entry Y for the value of the balance carried down is $0/ $25,000/ $50,000.

Entry Z for the total of the credit side of the ledger is $200,000/ $225,000/ $250,000.

Question 3

ABC has completed the initial allocation and apportionment of its overhead costs to cost centres as follows.

Cost centre:	Initial allocation $000
Machining	190
Finishing	175
Stores	30
Maintenance	25
	420

The Stores and Maintenance costs must now be reapportioned taking account of the service they provide to each other as follows.

	Machining	Finishing	Stores	Maintenance
Stores	60%	30%	–	10%
Maintenance	75%	20%	5%	

Using the equation method, calculate the total overhead cost of the Machining department after the reapportionment of the service department costs.

$ _____ (to the nearest $000)

Question 4

A project requires an initial investment of $2.4 million. The following cash flows have been estimated for the life of the project:

Year	Cash flow
1	$ 500,000
2	$ 700,000
3	$ 900,000
4	$ 450,000
5	$ 200,000

Using a discount rate of 10%, calculate the NPV of the project.

$ _____ (to the nearest $000).

Question 5

The budgeted contribution for PQR last month was $32,000. The following variances were reported.

Variance	$
Sales volume contribution	800 A
Material price	880 A
Material usage	822 F
Labour efficiency	129 F
Variable overhead efficiency	89 F

No other variances were reported for the month.

Calculate the actual contribution earned by PQR last month.

$ _____. (to the nearest $)

Question 6

The following scatter graph has been prepared for the costs incurred by an organisation that delivers hot meals to the elderly in their homes.

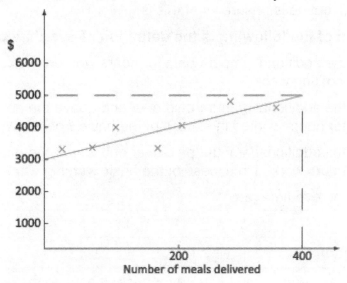

Based on the scatter graph:

(a)   the period fixed cost is $ _____.

(b)   the variable cost per meal delivered is $ _____.

Question 7

Entities use both financial and non-financial information to measure performance.

Select the correct word to complete the sentences regarding financial and non-financial performance measures.

A   An advantage of financial/ non-financial performance measures is that they are not distorted by inflation and are therefore easier to compare year on year.

B   Using only financial/ non-financial performance measures may encourage managers to focus only on short-term objectives.

C   Financial/ non-financial performance measures are open to manipulation such as changing accounting policies to improve the result.

Question 8

A junior management accountant of a company is analysing wage costs. His manager has asked him for the value of overtime premium for the last period, but he is unsure what this is.

Which of the following is the definition of overtime premium?

A   the additional amount paid for hours worked in excess of the basic working week

B   the additional amount paid over and above the normal hourly rate for hours worked in excess of the basic working week

C   the additional amount paid over and above the overtime rate for hours worked in excess of the basic working week

D   the overtime rate

Question 9

FGH has been asked to quote for a job. It aims to make a profit margin of 20%. The estimated total variable production cost for the job is $125.

Fixed production overheads for FGH are budgeted to be $250,000 and are recovered on the basis of labour hours. There are 12,500 budgeted labour hours and this job is expected to take 3 labour hours.

Other costs in relation to selling, distribution and administration are recovered at the rate of $15 per job.

FGH's quote for the job should be:

A $200

B $240

C $250

D $300

Question 10

Which TWO of the following relate to the use of Business Process Outsourcing (BPO)?

❑   It can lead to the adoption of best practice within the organisation

❑   It can result in duplication of effort across the organisation

❑   It provides increased knowledge of business areas

❑   It can lead to the release of capacity within the organisation

❑   It can result in a confidentiality risk

Question 11

The following extract is taken from the overhead budget of RST:

Budgeted activity	50%	75%
Budgeted overhead	$100,000	$112,500

Calculate the overhead budget for an activity level of 80%.

$ _____ .

Question 12

A company's management accountant has produced the following graph.

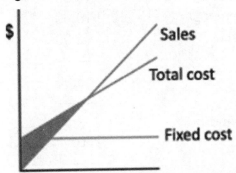

Select the correct term to complete each sentence.

This graph is known as a conventional breakeven chart/ contribution breakeven chart/ profit volume chart.

The shaded area on the graph represents loss/ fixed cost/ variable cost/ profit.

Question 13

A company is considering investing in a new project which will cost $50,000.

If the expected cash inflows from the project are $8,060 for the next 8 years, estimate the IRR of the project.

_____ %. (to the nearest whole number)

Question 14

CDE manufactures three products E, F and G. The products are all finished on the same machine. This is the only mechanised part of the process. The production manager is planning an essential major maintenance overhaul of the machine. This will restrict the available machine hours to 1,400 hours for the next period and mean that full demand for each product cannot be met.

Data for the three products are:

	Product E $ per unit	Product F $ per unit	Product G $ per unit
Selling price	30.00	17.00	21.00
Variable cost	13.00	6.00	9.00
Fixed production cost	10.00	8.00	6.00
Other fixed cost	2.00	1.00	3.50
Profit	5.00	2.00	2.50
Maximum demand (units/period)	250	140	130

No inventories are held.

Fixed production costs are absorbed using a machine hour rate of $2 per machine hour.

The production plan that will maximise profit for the forthcoming period, would be to produce:

E _____ units

F _____ units

G _____ units

Question 15

LMN uses a standard cost integrated accounting system. In a period the actual material usage was greater than the standard material usage.

Tick the entries to record this is in the accounts.

	Debit	Credit	No entry in this account
Material usage variance account	❑	❑	❑
Raw material control account	❑	❑	❑
Work in progress account	❑	❑	❑

The next two questions are based on the following data.

EFG makes a single product T and budgets to produce and sell 7,200 units each period. Cost and revenue data for the product at this level of activity are as follows.

	$ per unit
Selling price	53
Direct material cost	24
Direct labour cost	8
Other variable cost	3
Fixed cost	7
Profit	11

Question 16

Calculate the contribution to sales ratio (P/V ratio) of product T (to the nearest whole number).

_____%.

Question 17

Calculate the margin of safety % for product T (to the nearest whole number).

_____ %

Question 18

LMN is a manufacturing company. Production passes through three departments (P, Q and R). The following analysis of 250 items has been produced showing the production of faulty or acceptable items in the three departments.

| | **Department** | | | |
	P	**Q**	**R**	**Total**
Faulty	7	10	15	32
Acceptable	46	78	94	218
Total	53	88	109	250

If one item, selected at random, is faulty, what is the probability that it came from department P?

A   0.604

B   0.219

C   0.152

D   0.028

Question 19

DEF sells specialist coffees to customers to drink on the premises or to take away.

The manager has established that the cost of ingredients is a wholly variable cost in relation to the number of cups of coffee sold whereas staff costs are semi-variable and rent costs are fixed.

Tick the correct box to show what will happen to the following costs as the number of cups of coffee sold increases.

		increase	**decrease**	**stay the same**
(a)	The ingredients cost per cup sold will	❑	❑	❑
(b)	The staff cost per cup sold will	❑	❑	❑
(c)	The rent cost per cup sold will	❑	❑	❑

Question 20

WXY is about to tender for a one-off contract. The contract will require 100 hours of skilled labour and 200 hours of semi-skilled labour.

The skilled workers will be diverted from production of product P with resulting loss of sales. Each unit of P generates a contribution of $7 and takes two skilled labour hours to make. Semi-skilled workers will be hired as required.

Skilled workers are paid at a rate of $12/hour, while semi-skilled workers are paid $8/hour.

Calculate the relevant cost of labour for the contract.

$ _____.

Question 21

PQR is considering whether to continue making a component or buy it from an outside supplier. It uses 12,000 of the components each year.

The internal manufacturing cost comprises:	$/unit
Direct materials	3.00
Direct labour	4.00
Variable overhead	1.00
Specific fixed cost	2.50
Other fixed costs	2.00
	12.50

Which TWO of the following statements are true?

❑ The variable manufacturing cost for the component is $8.00.

❑ The variable manufacturing cost for the component is $10.50.

❑ The maximum price at which buying is preferable to internal manufacture is $10.50.

❑ The maximum price at which buying is preferable to internal manufacture is $8.00.

Question 22

BCD uses standard costing and has calculated cost and sales variances for the last period. Its sales price variance was $3,600 favourable.

Which TWO of the following could have contributed towards the favourable sales price variance?

☐ The standard sales price per unit was set too high

☐ Price competition in the market was not as fierce as expected

☐ Sales volume was higher than budgeted and therefore sales revenue was higher than budgeted

☐ The product could have been a higher quality than originally planned

---

The next two questions are based on the following data.

JKL operates a standard costing system. The following budgeted and standard cost information is available:

Budgeted production and sales units	10,000

	$ per unit
Selling price	250
Direct material cost – 3 kg × $10	30
Direct labour cost – 5 hours × $8	40
Variable production overheads – 5 hours × $4	20

Actual results for the period were as follows:

Production and sales units	11,500

	$
Sales value	2,817,500
Direct material – 36,000 kg	342,000
Direct labour – 52,000 hours	468,000
Variable production overheads	195,000

Question 23

The sales variances are:

	Sales price	Sales volume contribution
A	$57,500 F	$240,000 F
B	$57,500 A	$240,000 F
C	$317,500 A	$375,000 F
D	$57,500 A	$240,000 A

Question 24

The direct labour variances are:

	Labour rate	Labour efficiency
A	$52,000 A	$16,000 A
B	$8,000 A	$44,000 F
C	$12,000 F	$16,000 F
D	$52,000 A	$44,000 F

Question 25

A company uses the repeated distribution method to reapportion service department costs.

The use of this method suggests which of the following?

A   the company's overhead rates are based on estimates of cost and activity levels, rather than actual amounts

B   there are more service departments than production cost centres

C   the company wishes to avoid under- or over-absorption of overheads in its production cost centres

D   the service departments carry out work for each other

Question 26

GHI is a food processing company. The management accountant of GHI is undertaking a cost analysis.

Which of the following costs would NOT be classified as a production overhead cost for GHI?

A   The cost of renting the factory building

B   The salary of the factory manager

C   The depreciation of equipment located in the materials store

D   The cost of ingredients

Question 27

Which of the following is NOT a role of management accounting as defined by CIMA?

A   Plan long, medium and short-run operations

B   Design reward strategies for executives and shareholders

C   Prepare statutory accounts consisting of statements of profit or loss, statements of financial position and cash flow statements

D   Control operations and ensure the efficient use of resources

Question 28

A company is analysing the relationship between marketing spend (X) and sales (Y) and has calculated the correlation coefficient as 0.85.

Which TWO of the following comments are correct?

❑   Values of Y increase as values of X increase

❑   Y decreases by 0.15 for every increase of 1 in X

❑   The link between X and Y values is very strong

❑   Values of X increase as values of Y increase

❑   Increases in X cause corresponding increases in Y

Question 29

The diagram represents the behaviour of a cost item as the level of output changes:

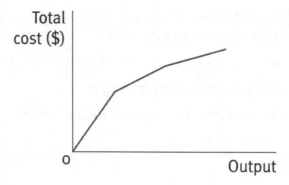

Which of the following situations is depicted by the graph?

A   Discounts are received on additional purchases of material when certain quantities are purchased

B   Employees are paid a guaranteed weekly wage, together with bonuses for higher levels of production

C   A licence is purchased from the government which allows unlimited production

D   Additional space is rented to cope with the need to increase production

Question 30

Extracts from the budget of ABC, a retailer of office furniture, for the six months to 31 December show the following information:

	$
Sales	55,800
Purchases	38,000
Closing inventory finished goods	7,500
Opening inventory finished goods	5,500
Opening receivables	8,500
Opening payables	6,500

Receivables and payables are expected to rise by 10% and 5%, respectively, by the end of the budget period.

Calculate the estimated cash receipts from customers during the budget period.

$ _____ .

Question 31

Having prepared its cash budget for the next accounting period, LMN anticipates that it will experience a temporary cash shortage for two months of the period.

Which TWO of the following actions could be appropriate actions to deal with a temporary cash shortage?

❑   issue additional shares

❑   request additional bank overdraft facilities

❑   sell machinery currently working at half capacity

❑   postpone the purchase of plant and machinery

Question 32

RST absorbs production overheads on the basis of machine hours. The following budgeted and actual information applied in its last accounting period:

	Budget	Actual
Production overhead	$180,000	$178,080
Machine hours	40,000	38,760

Select the correct terms to complete the sentences.

(a) At the end of the period, production overhead will be reported as under-absorbed/over-absorbed.

(b) If actual machine hours were exactly as budgeted, the overhead would be under-absorbed/over-absorbed.

Question 33

Sales of product G are budgeted as follows.

	Month 1	Month 2	Month 3	Month 4	Month 5
Budgeted sales units	340	420	290	230	210

The policy is to hold in inventory at the end of each month sufficient units of product G to satisfy budgeted sales demand for the forthcoming 2 months.

Calculate the budgeted production of product G in month 2.

_____ units.

Question 34

EFG repairs electronic calculators. The wages budget for the last period was based on a standard repair time of 24 minutes per calculator and a standard wage rate of $10.60 per hour.

Following the end of the budget period, it was reported that:

Number of repairs	31,000
Labour rate variance	$3,100 (A)
Labour efficiency variance	Nil

Based on the above information, calculate the actual wage rate per hour during the period.

$ _____ . _____ (to the nearest cent)

Question 35

A company is investigating the cost of absenteeism within its production department. Computer records have created a frequency distribution as follows:

Average days absent last year (mid-point)	Number of people
0	94
3	203
8	105
15	68
25	15
35	10
45	5

Calculate the mean number of days absent last year.

_____ days (to one decimal place).

Question 36

A project requires an initial investment of $2.4 million. The following cash flows have been estimated for the life of the project:

Year	Cash flow
1	$500,000
2	$700,000
3	$900,000
4	$450,000
5	$200,000

Calculate the payback period in years.

_____ years (to one decimal place).

Question 37

Place each of the comments on the left in the correct box, depending on whether it relates to management or financial accounting.

	Management accounting	Financial accounting
Forward looking		
Statutory requirement		
Uses both financial and non-financial information		
Links closely with taxation and auditing		
Used in performance measurement		
Used in internal decision making		

Question 38

Which of the following could be used as a cost object in an entity's costing system? Select all that apply.

- ❑   Customer number 879
- ❑   Department A
- ❑   The finishing process in department A
- ❑   Product H
- ❑   Employee number 776
- ❑   Order processing activity

Question 39

A company produces potato crisps. The weights of the bags of crisps produced follow a normal distribution and have a mean weight of 50g and a standard deviation of 10g.

Calculate the probability that a packet chosen at random will weigh more than 60g.

Question 40

A company manufactures and sells a single product. For this month the budgeted fixed production overheads are $48,000, budgeted production is 12,000 units and budgeted sales are 11,720 units. The entity currently uses absorption costing.

If marginal costing principles were used instead of absorption costing for this month, what would be the effect on the budgeted profit?

A $1,120 higher

B $1,120 lower

C $3,920 higher

D $3,920 lower

Question 41

An entity is about to undertake an investment appraisal for a new project and is considering using the payback method.

Which THREE of the following are advantages of the payback appraisal method?

☐ Easy to understand

☐ Takes account of the time value of money

☐ Provides a simple measure of risk

☐ Uses cash flows

☐ Ensures maximisation of shareholder wealth

Question 42

A perpetuity of $15,000 is due to commence immediately. The interest rate is 6%.

What is the present value of the perpetuity?

A $90,000

B $105,000

C $250,000

D $265,000

Question 43

Which of the following statements about CIMA is FALSE?

A   Confidentiality and accuracy are two of the fundamental principles of the CIMA code of ethics

B   Members of CIMA are known as Chartered Global Management Accountants

C   CIMA is a worldwide organisation

D   CIMA may discipline students or members who bring the profession into disrepute

Question 44

A company is analysing staff salaries over the last 5 years. They have produced the following table which shows the mean and standard deviation salaries now and 5 years ago.

	5 years ago	Now
Mean	$18,950	$25,000
Standard deviation	$10,600	$15,000

From the above data, which of the following statements is correct?

A   The standard deviations show that salaries are now more variable than 5 years ago.

B   The standard deviations show that the average salary has increased.

C   The means show that the average salary has reduced.

D   The means show that variability in salaries has increased.

Question 45

ABC is a manufacturing company which produces a number of products. All products pass through ABC's three production departments.

Details for one unit of product MM are as follows:

	MM
Direct labour	$75
Direct material	$24
Machine hours (all in department 2)	2.5

Direct labour is paid $12.50 per hour. Product MM spends an equal amount of time in each of the three production departments.

The following overhead absorption rates have been calculated for ABC's three production departments:

Department 1: $3.56 per labour hour

Department 2: $2.96 per machine hour

Department 3: $1.37 per labour hour

Calculate the total production cost of one unit of product MM.

$ _____

Question 46

FGH uses a flexible budgeting system to control the costs incurred in its staff canteen. The budget cost allowance for consumable materials is flexed according to the average number of employees during the period.

Complete the following equation by inserting '+', '−' or '×' as appropriate in the gaps:

Flexible budget cost allowance for consumable materials = budgeted fixed cost _____ (budgeted variable cost per employee _____ average number of employees)

Question 47

A company is calculating the total cost of a job it has been asked to quote for. The following costs have been identified:

Direct material: 350 kg @ $121 per kg

Direct labour: 2,500 hours @ $10.50 per hour

Fixed production overheads are budgeted to be $100,000 and are recovered on the basis of labour hours. Budgeted labour hours are 10,000.

The company wishes to make a profit margin of 20%.

The profit on the job will be $ _____, which relates to a _____% mark-up on total production costs.

Question 48

A company is considering investing in one of the following projects.

Project	Expected value $000	Standard deviation $000
A	850	500
B	1,200	480
C	150	200
D	660	640

It wishes to select the project with the lowest risk factor (coefficient of variation).

Select the correct term to complete the sentence.

The project which should be selected is Project A/ Project B/ Project C/ Project D.

Question 49

A company has collected the following data regarding the ages of the staff in one department. The staff members have the following ages in years: 21, 32, 19, 24, 31, 27, 17, 21, 26, 42.

Which TWO of the following are correct?

☐ The median age of the group is 25 years

☐ The median age of the group is 26 years

☐ The mean age of the group is 25 years

☐ The mean age of the group is 26 years

Question 50

Management accountants provide information to different levels of management within a company. The information required at different levels has different characteristics.

Place each of the characteristics of information shown on the left in the correct box on the right, depending on whether it relates to strategic or operational levels.

	Strategic level	Operational level
Detailed		
Historical		
Accurate		
Subjective		
Summarised		

Question 51

TUV has three production departments (Assembly, Machining and Finishing) and a service department (Production services).

The following data have been budgeted for the next period:

	Assembly	Machining	Finishing	Production Services	Total
Direct labour hours	7,250	9,000	15,000		31,250
Machine hours	15,500	20,000	2,500	2,000	40,000
Floor area (m^2)	800	1,200	1,000	1,400	4,400
Equipment value	$160,000	$140,000	$30,000	$70,000	$400,000
Employees	40	56	94	50	240

The template being used by the management accountant to analyse the overheads for the period is shown below:

Cost allocated	Basis	Assembly $	Machining $	Finishing $	Production Services $	Total $
Indirect wages	Allocated					102,000
Apportioned						
Depreciation	Equipment value		A			84,000
Rates	Floor area	B				22,000
Power	Machine hours			C		180,000
Personnel	Employees				D	60,000
Other						48,000
		___	___	___	___	___
						496,000
		___	___	___	___	___

The values that would be entered on the overhead analysis sheet at A to D are:

A	
B	
C	
D	

Question 52

A company is considering an investment. The investment will provide an annuity of $10,000 per annum, payable at the end of each year for 20 years at a discount rate of 5%.

Calculate the present value the annuity (to the nearest $).

$ _____ .

Question 53

The four Global Management Accounting Principles are:

A   Influence, Relevance, Confidentiality and Trust

B   Relevance, Integrity, Value and Accountability

C   Trust, Relevance, Value and Influence

D   Value, Influence, Integrity and Relevance

Question 54

Select the correct words to complete the following sentence regarding risk and uncertainty.

The difference between risk and uncertainty is that risk/ uncertainty is quantifiable while risk/ uncertainty is unquantifiable.

Question 55

The output from service organisations have four main features: intangibility, variability, inseparability and perishability.

Select the correct feature to complete the following sentences.

Intangibility	Variability	Inseparability	Perishability

A _____ means that services cannot be stored for use at a later date.

B _____ means that services cannot be packaged and taken home by the customer.

C _____ means that each service is unique and cannot usually be repeated in exactly the same way.

D _____ means that the service is created at the same time as it is consumed by the customer.

Question 56

ABC is a local council. The council's refuse collection service is currently analysing its costs.

Drag each of the following costs under the correct heading depending on whether they are a direct or an indirect cost for the refuse collection service.

	Direct cost	Indirect cost
Depreciation of the refuse collection vehicle		
Wages paid to refuse collectors		
Cost of leaflets sent to customers to advertise refuse collection times and dates		
Employer's liability insurance premium to cover all council employees		

Question 57

RST operates mobile food vans at outdoor events. It has two types of vans, one selling ice cream and cold drinks and one selling burgers and hot drinks.

It is deciding which van to take to a fun day at a local park in two days' time.

From the weather forecast, there is a 60% chance of rain and a 40% chance of fair weather.

From past experience RST have predicted the following potential daily profits from each van depending on the weather.

	Rain	Fair
Ice cream van	–$50	$150
Burger van	$200	–$10

Advise RST which van to take to the fun day.

Question 58

Which of the following is a method of accounting for overheads which involves attributing overheads to cost units using predetermined rates?

A   overhead allocation

B   overhead apportionment

C   overhead absorption

D   overhead analysis

Question 59

Consider the following profit-volume chart.

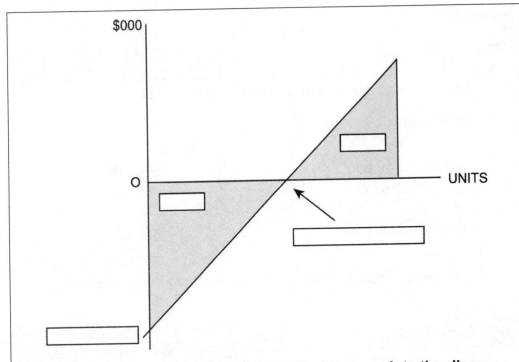

Drag the correct words from the list below to complete the diagram. Not all words will be required.

| BREAKEVEN POINT |
| LOSS |
| MARGIN OF SAFETY |
| PROFIT |
| CONTRIBUTION |
| FIXED COST |

Question 60

XYZ is a charity which uses the 3Es approach to assessing performance.

Select the correct words to complete the sentences below.

A   The 3E measure which deals with inputs is economy/efficiency/effectiveness.

B   The 3E measure which deals with outputs is economy/efficiency/effectiveness.

C   The 3E measure which deals with linking inputs with outputs is economy/efficiency/effectiveness.

Answers

Question 1

The overhead absorption rate was **$5.00** per unit.

Workings:

	$
Actual overheads	500,000
Over-absorption	50,000
Overhead absorbed	550,000

Overhead absorption rate = $550,000/110,000 units = **$5.00**.

Question 2

Entry X for $200,000 represents the value of the transfer to the **Finished goods account**.

Entry Y for the value of the balance carried down is **$25,000**.

Entry Z for the total of the credit side of the ledger is **$225,000**.

The complete ledger account would be:

Work-in-Progress account

	$		$
Stores control a/c	100,000	**Finished goods a/c**	200,000
Wages control a/c	75,000		
Production overhead a/c	50,000	Balance c/d	**25,000**
	225,000		**225,000**

Question 3

After the apportionment of the service department costs, the total overhead cost of the Machining department will be **$230,000**.

Let Stores = S and Maintenance = M

S = 30 + 0.05 M

M = 25 + 0.1 S

M = 25 + 0.1(30 + 0.05M)

M = 25 + 3 + 0.005M

0.995M = 28

M = 28.14

So, S = 30 + (0.05 × 28.14)

S = 31.41

Machining = 190 + (0.6 × 31.41) + (0.75 × 28.14) = 229.95

To the nearest $000, the total overhead cost for Machining will be **$230,000**.

Question 4

NPV = **($260,000)**

Year	Cash flow ($)	Discount factor (10%)	Present value (future value × discount factor)
0	(2,400,000)	1	(2,400,000)
1	500,000	0.909	454,500
2	700,000	0.826	578,200
3	900,000	0.751	675,900
4	450,000	0.683	307,350
5	200,000	0.621	124,200
		NPV =	**(259,850)**

Question 5

The actual contribution earned by PQR last month was **$31,360**.

$(32,000 – 800 – 880 + 822 + 129 + 89) = **$31,360**.

Question 6

(a)   The period fixed cost is **$3,000**

(b)   The variable cost per meal delivered is **$5**

Workings:

The period fixed cost is where the line crosses the y axis = **$3,000**

Variable cost per meal = $\dfrac{\$5{,}000 - \$3{,}000}{400 - 0}$ = **$5**

Question 7

A   An advantage of **non-financial** performance measures is that they are not distorted by inflation and are therefore easier to compare year on year.

B   Using only **financial** performance measures may encourage managers to focus only on short-term objectives.

C   **Financial** performance measures are open to manipulation such as changing accounting policies to improve the result.

Question 8

B

Overtime premium is the additional amount paid over and above the normal hourly rate for hours worked in excess of the basic working week.

Question 9

C

	$
Variable production costs	125
Fixed production overheads (W1)	60
Selling, distribution and administration	15
Total cost	200
Profit margin (W2)	50
Quote	**250**

(W1) Fixed production overhead absorption rate = (250,000 ÷ 12,500) = $20

Fixed production overheads = 20 × 3 = $60

(W2) Profit margin = $200 × (0.2 ÷ 0.8) = $50

Question 10

☐   It can lead to the adoption of best practice within the organisation

☐   It can result in duplication of effort across the organisation

☐   It provides increased knowledge of business areas

☑   It can lead to the release of capacity within the organisation

☑   It can result in a confidentiality risk

BPO can lead to the release of capacity within the organisation. The more routine tasks are carried out externally leaving the retained function more capacity to concentrate on value adding activities. It can however result in a confidentiality risk as information is in the hands of a third party.

BPO will not generally provide increased knowledge of business areas. This is usually seen as an advantage of business partnering.

BPO will not generally result in duplication of effort across the organisation. This is usually seen as a disadvantage of business partnering.

BPO will not generally lead to the adoption of best practice within the organisation as the function is being carried out externally. This is usually seen as an advantage of a shared services centre.

Question 11

The overhead budget for an activity level of 80% would be **$115,000**.

Workings:

Using the high/low method

		$
High	75%	112,500
Low	50%	100,000
Change	25%	12,500	– variable cost of 25%
	1%	500	– variable cost of 1%

Substitute into 75% activity	$
Total overhead	112,500
Variable cost element 75 × $500	37,500
Fixed cost element	75,000

Total overhead for 80% activity	
Variable cost element 80 × $500	40,000
Fixed cost element	75,000
Total overhead	**115,000**

Question 12

The graph is known as a **conventional breakeven chart**.

The shaded area on the graph represents **loss**.

Question 13

The IRR of the project will be approximately **6%**.

Using the annuity method:

Time		Cash flow ($)	DF %	PV ($)
0	Investment	(50,000)	1	(50,000)
1–8	Inflow	8,060	?	50,000
				———
				0
				———

The aim is to find the discount rate that produces an NPV of nil.

Therefore the PV of inflows must equal the PV of outflows, $50,000.

If the PV of inflows is to be $50,000 and the size of each inflow is $8,060, the Discount Factor (DF) required must be 50,000 ÷ 8,060 = 6.20.

The discount rate for which this is the 8-year factor can be found by looking along the 8-year row of the cumulative present value tables.

The figure of 6.210 appears under the 6% column suggesting that IRR is approximately **6%**.

Question 14

The optimum production plan is to produce:

E: 202 units

F: zero units

G: 130 units

The first step is to calculate the contribution per machine hour from each of the products. The products can then be ranked on that basis.

	Product E $	Product F $	Product G $
Selling price per unit	30	17	21
Variable cost per unit	13	6	9
	—	—	—
Contribution per unit	17	11	12
	—	—	—
Machine hours per unit (W1)	5	4	3
Contribution per hour	$3.40	$2.75	$4.00
Ranking	**2**	**3**	**1**

The available hours can be allocated according to this ranking.

	Units to be produced	Machine hours required
Product G (maximum demand)	130	390
Product E (balance of hours)	202	1,010
		1,400

(W1) Fixed production costs are absorbed at a rate of $2 per machine hour, so we can use the fixed production cost to work out the number of machine hours:

E: ($10 ÷ $2) = 5 machine hours

F: ($8 ÷ $2) = 4 machine hours

G: ($6 ÷ $2) = 3 machine hours

Question 15

	Debit	Credit	No entry in this account
Material usage variance account	☑	❑	❑
Raw material control account	❑	❑	☑
Work in progress account	❑	☑	❑

Question 16

The contribution to sales ratio (P/V ratio) of product T is **34%**.

Contribution per unit of product T = $(53 – 24 – 8 – 3) = $18

Contribution to sales ratio = 18/53 = **34%**

Question 17

The margin of safety % of product T is **61%**.

Period fixed costs = 7,200 × $7 = $50,400

$$\text{Breakeven point} = \frac{\text{Fixed costs}}{\text{Contribution per unit}}$$

$$\text{Breakeven point} = \frac{\$50,400}{\$18} = 2,800 \text{ units}$$

Margin of safety % = (Budgeted sales – Breakeven sales) ÷ Budgeted sales

Margin of safety as percentage of budgeted sales = (7,200 – 2,800)/7,200 = **61%**

Question 18

B

7 out of the 32 faulty items come from P, therefore the probability is 7/32 = **0.219**

Question 19

As the number of cups of coffee sold increases:

(a) the ingredients cost per cup sold will **stay the same**.

(b) the staff cost per cup sold will **decrease**.

(c) the rent cost per cup sold will **decrease**.

Question 20

The relevant cost of labour is **$3,150**

Working:	$
Skilled workers:	
Basic pay (100 hours × $12)	1,200
Opportunity cost of lost contribution (100 × $7/2 per hour)	350
Semi-skilled: basic pay (200 hours × $8)	1,600
Total relevant cost of labour	**3,150**

Question 21

☑ The variable manufacturing cost for the component is $8.00.

☐ The variable manufacturing cost for the component is $10.50.

☑ The maximum price at which buying is preferable to internal manufacture is $10.50.

☐ The maximum price at which buying is preferable to internal manufacture is $8.00.

The relevant internal manufacturing cost in this make versus buy decision comprises:

	$
Variable manufacturing cost	8.00
Specific fixed cost	2.50
	10.50

The specific fixed cost is included because it is specific to the component. It would not be incurred if the component was not made.

Question 22

☐ The standard sales price per unit was set too high

☑ Price competition in the market was not as fierce as expected

☐ Sales volume was higher than budgeted and therefore sales revenue was higher than budgeted

☑ The product could have been a higher quality than originally planned

The first option would result in an adverse variance. The third option would not necessarily result in any sales price variance because all the units could have been sold at standard price.

Question 23

B

Sales price variance:

	$	
11,500 units should sell for (× $250)	2,875,000	
But did sell for	2,817,500	
Sales price variance	**57,500**	**A**

Sales volume contribution variance:

Actual sales volume	11,500	units
Budget sales volume	10,000	units
Variance in units	1,500	F
× standard contribution per unit*	× $160	
Sales volume contribution variance	**$240,000**	**F**

* Standard contribution per unit = $(250 − 30 − 40 − 20) = $160

Question 24

D

Direct labour rate variance:

	$	
52,000 hours should cost (× $8)	416,000	
but did cost	468,000	
Direct labour rate variance	**52,000**	**A**

Direct labour efficiency variance:

11,500 units should take (× 5 hours)	57,500	hours
but did take	52,000	hours
Difference	5,500	hours
× std rate per hour	× $8	
Direct labour efficiency variance	**$44,000**	**F**

Question 25

D

The use of this method suggests the service departments carry out work for each other.

Question 26

D

The cost of ingredients is a direct cost. The others are all production overheads.

Question 27

C

Prepare statutory accounts consisting of statements of profit or loss, statements of financial position and cash flow statements is a financial accounting role.

Question 28

☑   Values of Y increase as values of X increase

☐   Y decreases by 0.15 for every increase of 1 in X

☑   The link between X and Y values is very strong

☐   Values of X increase as values of Y increase

☐   Increases in X cause corresponding increases in Y

The correlation coefficient is positive, therefore values of sales (Y – the dependent variable) increase as values of marketing spend (X – the independent variable) increase. Numerically its value is close to 1 and hence the link between marketing spend and sales is very strong.

We cannot deduce cause and effect from any correlation coefficient, however large, so the second and final options are incorrect. The fourth option is incorrect as it treats sales as the independent variable and marketing as the dependent variable.

Question 29

A

Discounts are received on additional purchases of material when certain quantities are purchased. The graph depicts a variable cost where unit costs decease at certain levels of production.

Question 30

The estimated cash receipts from customers during the budget period are **$54,950**.

Cash received = Sales + opening receivables – closing receivables (W1)

= $(55,800 + 8,500 – 9,350)

= **$54,950**.

(W1) Closing receivables = $8,500 + 10% = $9,350

Question 31

☐ issue additional shares

☑ request additional bank overdraft facilities

☐ sell machinery currently working at half capacity

☑ postpone the purchase of plant and machinery

These are short term actions to cover a temporary cash shortage. The other options would be more appropriate for a longer term cash shortage.

Question 32

(a) At the end of the period, production overhead will be reported as **under-absorbed**.

(b) If actual machine hours were exactly as budgeted, the overhead would be **over-absorbed**.

Production overhead will be reported as $3,660 under absorbed.

Machine hour rate = $180,000/40,000 = $4.50 per machine hour

	$
Overheads incurred	178,080
Overheads absorbed (38,760 × $4.50)	174,420
Under-absorbed	**3,660**

(b) If actual machine hours were exactly as budgeted, the overhead would be over-absorbed by $1,920.

	$
Overheads incurred	178,080
Overheads absorbed (40,000 × $4.50)	180,000
Over-absorbed	**1,920**

Question 33

The budgeted production of product G in month 2 is **230 units**.

	Units	
Closing inventory month 2 (290 + 230)	520	
Month 2 sales requirements	420	
	940	
Less opening inventory month 2 (420 + 290)	(710)	
Budgeted production month 2	**230**	(month 4 sales volume)

Question 34

Actual wage rate per hour = **$10.85**

Labour efficiency variance = zero, therefore hours worked = standard hours for 31,000 repairs.

Hours worked = 31,000 × 24/60 = 12,400 hours

Adverse rate variance per hour = 3,100/12,400 = $0.25

Therefore, actual wage rate per hour = $10.60 + $0.25 = **$10.85**

Question 35

The mean number of days absent last year is **6.8 days**.

Average days absent last year (x)	Frequency (f)	fx
0	94	0
3	203	609
8	105	840
15	68	1,020
25	15	375
35	10	350
45	5	225
Total	500	3,419

Mean = $\Sigma fx \div \Sigma f$ = 3,419 ÷ 500 = 6.838 days

Question 36

Payback period = **3.7 years**

Year	Cash flow ($000)	Cumulative cash flow
0	(2,400)	(2,400)
1	500	(1,900)
2	700	(1,200)
3	900	(300)
4	450	150
5	200	350

Payback period = 3 years + (300/450) = 3.7 years

Question 37

Management accounting	Financial accounting
Forward looking	
	Statutory requirement
Uses both financial and non-financial information	
	Links closely with taxation and auditing
Used in performance measurement	
Used in internal decision making	

Question 38

☑ Customer number 879

☑ Department A

☑ The finishing process in department A

☑ Product H

☑ Employee number 776

☑ Order processing activity

The *CIMA Terminology* provides the following description of a cost object: 'for example a product, service, centre, activity, customer or distribution channel in relation to which costs are ascertained'.

Question 39

The probability that a packet chosen at random will weigh more than 60g is **15.87%**.

First calculate the Z score.

$$Z = \frac{x - \mu}{\sigma}$$

$$Z = \frac{60 - 50}{10} = 1$$

We want to find P(Z > 1)

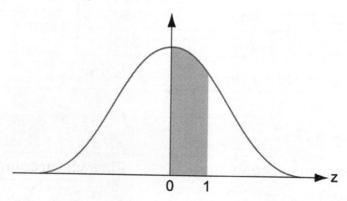

The shaded area represents a z score of between 0 and 1. From the normal distribution tables, this value 0.3413.

Therefore P(Z > 1) = 0.5 – 0.3413 = 0.1587 or **15.87%**.

Question 40

B

Fixed production overhead per unit = $48,000/12,000 units = $4.

Sales volume is less than production volume by 280 units.

In absorption costing, this means that some fixed overheads will be carried forward in the closing inventory value. Fixed overheads in this addition to inventory = 280 units × $4 = $1,120.

As inventory is increasing , marginal costing profit would be **lower than the absorption costing profit by $1,120**.

Question 41

☑ Easy to understand

☐ Takes account of the time value of money

☑ Provides a simple measure of risk

☑ Uses cash flows

☐ Ensures maximisation of shareholder wealth

Payback does not take account of the time value of money and decisions based on payback will not necessarily result in the maximisation of shareholder wealth. These are advantages of the NPV method.

Question 42

D

This is essentially a standard perpetuity with an additional payment at T_0. The PV could be calculated as follows:

T_0	T_1	T_2	T_3	T_4 ....
15,000	15,000 $\rightarrow \infty$			

The present value of the perpetuity from year 1 = ($15,000 ÷ 0.06) = $250,000

As the perpetuity starts immediately, you need to add on the $15,000 in year 0

$250,000 + $15,000 = **$265,000**

Question 43

A

Accuracy is not one of the fundamental principles of the CIMA code of ethics. The five fundamental principles are confidentiality, objectivity, integrity, professional competence and due care and professional behaviour.

Question 44

A

Both the mean and the standard deviation have increased. The mean measures the average salary level whilst the standard deviation measures the variability.

Question 45

The total production cost per unit of product MM is **$116.26**

	$
Prime cost ($75 + $24)	99.00
Production overhead:	
Department 1 ($3.56 × 2)	7.12
Department 2 ($2.96 × 2.5)	7.40
Department 3 ($1.37 × 2)	2.74
	———
Total production cost	116.26
	———

Product MM requires $75 ÷ $12.50 = 6 labour hours per unit in total. One unit of MM will therefore spend (6 ÷ 3) = 2 labour hours in each production department.

Question 46

Flexible budget cost allowance for consumable materials = budgeted fixed cost ____ + ____ (budgeted variable cost per employee ____ × ____ average number of employees).

Question 47

The profit on the job will be **$23,400**, which relates to a **25%** mark-up on total production costs.

Calculate the total production costs and profit using the profit margin of 20%:

	$
Direct material: 350 kg × $121 per kg	42,350
Direct labour: 2,500 hours × $10.50 per hour	26,250
Fixed production overheads (100,000 ÷ 10,000) × 2,500	25,000
	———
Total production cost	93,600
	———

So, profit = 93,600 × (0.2 ÷ 0.8)   **23,400**

If the profit is $23,400 and the total production costs is $93,600. The % mark-up on total production costs is 23,400 ÷ 93,600 = **25%**

Remember, profit margin is based on sales and mark-up is based on cost.

Question 48

The project which should be selected is **Project B**.

Project	Expected value $000	Standard deviation $000	Coefficient of variation
A	850	500	0.59
B	1,200	480	0.40
C	150	200	1.33
D	660	640	0.97

Question 49

☑   The median age of the group is 25 years

☐   The median age of the group is 26 years

☐   The mean age of the group is 25 years

☑   The mean age of the group is 26 years

Putting the ages in order gives 17, 19, 21, 21, 24, 26, 27, 31, 32, 42

Given we have an even number of observations, the median is 25.

The mean is (21+32+19+24+31+27+17+21+26+42) ÷ 10 = 26.

Question 50

Strategic level	Operational level
	Detailed
	Historical
	Accurate
Subjective	
Summarised	

Question 51

A: ($140,000/$400,000) × $84,000 = **$29,400**

B: (800/4,400) × $22,000 = **$4,000**

C: (2,500/40,000) × $180,000 = **$11,250**

D: (50/240) × $60,000 = **$12,500**

Question 52

The present value of the annuity is **$124,620**

Present value = Future value × annuity factor

= 10,000 × 12.462 = $124,620

Question 53

C

The four Global Management Accounting Principles are:

- Influence

- Relevance

- Trust

- Value

Question 54

The difference between risk and uncertainty is that **risk** is quantifiable **uncertainty** is unquantifiable.

Question 55

A   **Perishability** means that services cannot be stored for use at a later date.

B   **Intangibility** means that services cannot be packaged and taken home by the customer.

C   **Variability** refers to the fact that each service is unique and cannot usually be repeated in exactly the same way.

D   **Inseparability** means that the service is created at the same time as it is consumed by the customer.

Question 56

Direct cost	Indirect cost
Depreciation of the refuse collection vehicle	
Wages paid to refuse collectors	
Cost of leaflets sent to customers to advertise refuse collection times and dates	
	Employer's liability insurance premium to cover all council employees

The direct costs of the service can be specifically attributed to the refuse service provided.

The indirect cost applies to all council employees, not only to those who are providing the refuse collection service.

Question 57

RST should take the burger van.

Compare the expected value of the outcome from taking each van:

Ice cream van: EV = (0.6 × −$50) + (0.4 × $150) = $30

Burger van: EV =(0.6 × $200) + (0.4 × −$10) = $116

so RST should take the burger van.

Question 58

C

Overhead allocation is the allotment of whole items of cost to cost units or cost centres. Overhead apportionment is the sharing out of costs over a number of cost centres according to the benefit used. Overhead analysis refers to the whole process of recording and accounting for overheads.

Mock Assessment

Question 59

The completed diagram is shown below.

Question 60

A   The 3E measure which deals with inputs is **economy**.

B   The 3E measure which deals with outputs is **effectiveness**.

C   The 3E measure which deals with linking inputs with outputs is **efficiency**.

676

Index